CW00455547

INTELLIGENCE ELSEWHERE

INTELLIGENCE ELSEWHERE
Spies and Espionage outside the Anglosphere

PHILIP H. J. DAVIES
and
KRISTIAN C. GUSTAFSON
Editors

Georgetown University Press
Washington, DC

© 2013 Georgetown University Press. All rights reserved. No part of this book may be reproduced or utilized in any form or by any means, electronic or mechanical, including photocopying and recording, or by any information storage and retrieval system, without permission in writing from the publisher.

LIBRARY OF CONGRESS CATALOGING-IN-PUBLICATION DATA

Davies, Philip H. J.
  Intelligence elsewhere : spies and espionage outside the anglosphere / Philip H. J. Davies and Kristian C. Gustafson, Editors.
    p.   cm.
  Includes bibliographical references and index.
  ISBN 978-1-58901-956-0 (pbk. : alk. paper)
  1. Intelligence service—Cross-cultural studies.   2. Spies.   3. Espionage.   I. Gustafson, Kristian, 1974–   II. Title.
JF1525.I6.D39   2013
327.12—dc23
                                                                                    2012021672

⊗ This book is printed on acid-free paper meeting the requirements of the American National Standard for Permanence in Paper for Printed Library Materials.

15   14   13   9 8 7 6 5 4 3 2   First printing

CONTENTS

Part I: Introduction and Theory

1 An Agenda for the Comparative Study of Intelligence:
Yet Another Missing Dimension 3
Philip H. J. Davies and Kristian C. Gustafson

2 Political Culture: Approaches and Prospects 13
Stephen Welch

Part II: Intelligence Culture outside the Anglosphere

3 Subversive Information: The Historical Thrust of Chinese
Intelligence 29
Ralph D. Sawyer

4 The Original Surveillance State: Kautilya's *Arthashastra* and
Government by Espionage in Classical India 49
Philip H. J. Davies

5 Protecting the New Rome: Byzantine Influences on Russian
Intelligence 67
Kristian C. Gustafson

6 Origins of an Arab and Islamic Intelligence Culture 89
Abdulaziz A. Al-Asmari

Part III: Current Practice and Theory

7 Pakistan's Inter-Services Intelligence 115
Robert Johnson

8 Iranian Intelligence Organizations 141
Carl Anthony Wege

9   Intelligence and Security-Sector Reform in Indonesia   157
Peter Gill and Lee Wilson

10   A Reconstruction of Japanese Intelligence: Issues and Prospects   181
Ken Kotani

11   The Processes and Mechanisms of Developing a Democratic
Intelligence Culture in Ghana   199
*Emmanuel Kwesi Aning, Emma Birikorang, and Ernest
Ansah Lartey*

12   Intelligence Community Reforms: The Case of Argentina   219
Eduardo E. Estévez

13   Sweden: Intelligence the Middle Way   239
Wilhelm Agrell

14   Intelligence Culture, Economic Espionage, and the Finnish
Security Intelligence Service   265
Lauri Holmström

Part IV: Conclusion

15   Legacies, Identities, Improvisation, and Innovations of
Intelligence   287
Philip H. J. Davies and Kristian C. Gustafson

Contributors   299

Index   303

PART I

Introduction and Theory

An Agenda for the Comparative Study of Intelligence

Yet Another Missing Dimension

Philip H. J. Davies and Kristian C. Gustafson

In the decades since Christopher Andrew and David Dilks resurrected Sir Alexander Cadogan's description of intelligence as the "missing dimension of diplomatic history," scholars of intelligence have themselves been uncovering assorted additional absent axes within the study of intelligence.[1] Indeed, there are moments when intelligence scholars begin to feel a little like quantum physicists who find themselves wrestling with the idea of large numbers of different dimensions curled up, or "compactified," in normal, three-dimensional space.[2] Among the compactified dimensions that have begun to unravel under scrutiny are questions of organizational structure and behavior, cultural analysis,[3] and even foreign language competency.[4] All these approaches have been found wanting in a field dominated by historical study on one side of the Atlantic and normative political and policy analysis on the other. This should come as no surprise in a comparatively newborn field of study. Before the 1960s intelligence and related activities such as covert action and protective security policy were so shrouded by strong formal and informally constituted rules of secrecy that the necessary evidence base for intelligence studies simply did not exist.[5] There was also a sense that the underhanded nature of espionage meant that intelligence was not quite a respectable sphere of study for academics. However, there has since been a sea change both in the availability of information and in perceptions of the need to have a scholarly understanding of intelligence—accelerated in recent years by events such as the September 11, 2001, terrorist attacks on the United States and the furors over the role of intelligence in the US decision to invade Iraq in 2003.

One of the compactified dimensions of the study of intelligence that still needs to be properly examined (and that actually entails many different axes of inquiry in its own right) is the comparative analysis of intelligence institutions and processes in government. Comparative politics is, of course, a well-established field. And the tools and conventions of overall comparative analysis have been clearly articulated. But they have yet to be applied really vigorously and systematically to the cross-national study of intelligence. Comparative investigation has been widely advocated since the 1980s, but very little actual in-depth, systematic comparative work has been undertaken.[6] And yet comparative analysis is one of the most powerful methodological tools available in the contemporary social science arsenal.

Comparison as Protection

There is, to be sure, a tendency to view comparative methods as being mainly a protection against the limitations of stand-alone cases. Scholars are fond of invoking comparative analysis as a protection against "ethnocentrism."[7] But the idea of ethnocentrism is not particularly transparent, and it can all too easily carry with it the pejorative suggestion of chauvinism rather than a merely limitedly parochial perspective. In practical terms the main problem with examining cases in isolation rather than comparatively is that it can induce two alternative but complementary optical illusions regarding the case at hand. It is, for example, all too easy to approach a case with the conviction that it is somehow unique and then develop a characterization of that case that supposedly identifies distinctive features that are actually not unique at all. By the same token, it is all too easy for one to assume that the way things are done in one's own community or context represents inherent criteria for the task that must be echoed in every instance. This is perhaps the classic sense of ethnocentrism, but it might more usefully be thought of as the illusion of universality. Thus one finds accounts of the US machinery of government built on organizational politics, and neoinstitutional paradigms of internecine organizational relations,[8] that take that internecine nature as not merely universal but also as intrinsic to institutional processes.[9] The problem here is that these approaches work very well for poorly coordinated systems but fail entirely to account for more orderly and integrated governmental machineries such as the UK central government.[10]

At the same time, one can find attempts to articulate phenomena that are putatively particular or unique, such as Michael Turner's 2002 effort to articulate a distinctive US intelligence identity or culture. Among the distinctive features of the American approach to intelligence are an emphasis on secrecy, "intelligence exceptionalism" (the idea that intelligence is a different order of information from other sources), the separation of intelligence and law enforcement, a multiagency "confederal structure," the separation of intelligence from policy, its role in policy support, debates over the merits of in-depth analysis as against the demands of current intelligence, and the provision of "accurately, timely and relevant intelligence" as among the distinguishing features of US intelligence. Although other elements of Turner's model—such as the "primacy" of analysis (i.e., the broad as opposed to narrow view of intelligence that will feature throughout this volume), competitive intelligence, and the so-called can-do attitude—might be more pronounced in America than elsewhere, the rest are pretty uniform to the intelligence communities of all the Anglo-American liberal democracies. Certainly they are just as true of the United Kingdom as they are of the United States. Though they may indeed be characteristics of the US system, they are hardly particular to it; they are not actually distinctive.[11] Consequently, some sort of comparative effort is required to test whether an issue is common or purely localized.

Comparison as Diagnostic

However, comparative analysis can do more. It can help articulate judgments of degree in qualitative matters where articulating quantitative metrics may be intractable for various reasons. In the absence of an absolute cardinal measure of, say, more or less effective interagency coordination, one can make an ordinal judgment that this case is more well ordered than that one and then set about identifying variations between them and the relevance and consequences of these variations. Indeed, this is the strength of the fundamental logic of the comparative method that was originally articulated by John Stuart Mill in the nineteenth century, in particular his notion of arguments from difference and from similarity—in other words, taking two outwardly similar cases with a different outcome and then asking what drives them apart, or taking two different cases with similar outcomes and seeking to understand what drives them together.

It can be very useful to visualize comparative analysis in this role as being loosely analogous to resolving multiple parallel equations in algebra. In algebra one arranges the assorted equations with their shared variables in a common order and then performs some elementary arithmetic manipulations to one by one eliminate variables from expressions on the left hand side of the system until one is left with one value for the remaining variable. In principle the methods of similarity and difference are likewise also about eliminating variables. Where one has similar cases with different outcomes, one is in the business of knocking out features that the cases have in common in order to be left with those points of difference, some or all of which may drive the cases to different outcomes. Conversely, one may eliminate differences between a number of cases to identify those properties that they share, some or all of which drive them to a common outcome. Unfortunately, like most social science, such logical strategies are not much more than heuristic in practice and are virtually impossible to apply with the same rigor as in mathematics. Part of the problem is that parallel equations are only resolvable when one has at least the same number of equations as variables; otherwise, one is left with an ineradicable residual uncertainty in the need to express at least some variables in terms of other variables. And the real-world, comparative study of humanity is actually always a situation where the number of potential variables in society and historical events exceeds the number of possible cases for which one could even realistically hope.

To make matters worse, the "variables" in social sciences—such as political, economic, physical, and personal impact—are not what mathematicians call countable. That is, they cannot be treated as wholly separate, individually discrete items. Instead they all have overlapping, fuzzy edges (and often fuzzy centers), where economic matters are also inherently political ones, the conduct of individual personalities is inextricable from their institutionalized background expectations and worldviews, and so on. As a result, even cataloguing the variables or factors one is trying to eliminate or include is a pretty rough-and-ready affair and could entirely be reasonably articulated very differently from an alternative analytical point of view. In principle, however, like alternative mathematical solutions to a common problem (e.g., using algebra, matrices, or integral calculus to solve a rectangular volume), those alternative articulations should be at least homomorphic; the terminology may differ, and the workings on paper vary, but the essential shape of the answer one reaches is logically equivalent even if rhetorically seemingly far removed. Like Marxist concepts of "ideology" and "material forces" or "superstructure" and "base" placed alongside functionalist notions like Talcott Parsons's duality of "norms" and "conditions" (in his earlier formulations[12]) or "information" and "energy" in later expressions, there is actually a common underlying and basic idea of how the world works, despite variations in normative perspective (consequently, much theoretical debate involves thinkers actually and regrettably talking past one another).[13] And so, at some level, articulating a consistent framework for analysis is almost more important than which framework one employs. And in a field like comparative analysis, where trying to step outside the bounds of parochial viewpoints is one of the principal goals, this is a natural point of departure.

Intelligence and Commensurability

In its way, intelligence is a subject especially well suited to comparative analysis. Unlike many areas of government, which may depend on profoundly different basic forms of social organization, the various functions and principal logical components or steps of the intelligence field tend to provide a relatively common set of activities that can be identified and differing implementations that can be examined methodically. In its way intelligence bears a closer resemblance to the study of very concrete public policy tasks like road building and national accounts than to conceptually subtler issues such as constitutions or judiciaries. As with transportation policy, there are common basic problems that different governments need to resolve. In building roads one must lay something down that gets from A to B and manages the flow of traffic as safely and efficiently as available resources permit. In intelligence one must acquire information, figure out what it means, and make sure that it gets to the places and people who need it because that is why the information is required in the first place. It makes relatively little difference if the information is about drug cartels for the police, foreign trade negotiations for a foreign or economic ministry, or uncovering putative counterrevolutionary conspiracies to reinforce the stability of some nouvelle regime. Like the iron ingot that can be forged as plough or sword, or even heated, beaten, and reshaped from one to the other, intelligence is not intrinsically good or bad; it may serve democracy or tyranny, and it may be conducted in many walks of life, both within and outside government.

The kind of built-in commensurability that makes intelligence a good medium for comparative analysis is illustrated by what might be most usefully termed the "core functions" of intelligence. In whatever form, or whatever social locus, certain basic tasks—requirements, collection, analysis, and dissemination—constitute common problems for doing intelligence. These are often arranged sequentially as an intelligence cycle, but their relationship is more fluid than the sort of procedural clockwork that the idea of a cycle suggests. To be sure, one might subdivide the steps in analysis between the interpretation of information and identifying its implications, as does the American approach, which distinguishes between "processing" and "analysis," or one might distinguish between "analysis" and "assessment," as is done in the United Kingdom; but one must interpret and understand that which has been collected.[14] There might be differences over whether the collectors decide for themselves what to collect or should be given shopping lists by the people who use that information to make decisions. But no one has the resources to scrutinize everything, everywhere at once, so some decisions must be made about requirements and priorities. Dissemination might be an integral part of the analytical process or might be passed on to briefing officers elsewhere, but the information also must get to the user. If used in this fashion, the core functions paradigm should constitute a case of the optical illusion of universality discussed above, because it is not about uprooting one particular parochial institutional practice and finding parallels elsewhere; it is about basic functional tasks that can be chopped, changed, and redistributed, but without which intelligence, however organized and institutionalized, cannot happen.

There may be cross-connections and feedback loops between the functions of intelligence, with raw reports being presented hurriedly to national leaders or analysts telling the collectors what they need to know and what needs to be collected to make their appreciations sound. But the essential logical steps do not simply evaporate; like dividing oncoming traffic into separate lanes or even ensuring that the road surface is reasonably flat and smooth, they are basic requirements of the task at hand. And of course the core functions of intelligence may be performed more or less efficiently or competently, and sometimes (like maintaining proper road surfaces or actually obeying the highway code) may not happen at all. The presence, absence, or adequacy will have palpable consequences—the policy and operational equivalents of road mortality rates.

Within these core logical functions there are likewise similar tasks: Information must be acquired from sources, exfiltrated, evaluated for both truthfulness and content if true; fragmentary reporting must be collated, and its net meaning and implications must be identified. Any nation operating surveillance satellites must cope with common technological and procedural processes; and any nation trying to break codes must grapple with similar technical and managerial challenges. All these activities must be managed institutionally, paid for one way or another, and somehow fit into wider machineries of government or governance—whether as subordinate gofers providing information support to the decisions of others in Anglo-American liberal democracies or as Soviet-style underpinning architectures of social control and political order in what John Dziak has called "counterintelligence states."[15] In the last analysis, therefore, one of the virtues of the study of intelligence is that it often provides common axes of comparison between outwardly diverse individual cases.

The Aim and Structure of This Book

In the intelligence field there has, of course, been a substantial amount of area studies work, with a sizable literature evolving on the Soviet and post-Soviet systems, and a lesser body of work on France and China. There has even been some work done looking at Latin American intelligence structures. But unfortunately there has been little real comparative scholarship across nations. This volume provides a first step toward remedying this shortfall.

This book deals with the comparative study of matters of national intelligence and security outside the Anglo-Saxon and great-power Western European mainstream. Much of the existing literature on intelligence is heavily focused on the traditional intelligence powers of the ABCA (America–Britain–Canada–Australia) countries, with sidelines for the major European players: France, Germany, and, of course, Russia. This edited volume takes a different approach. First, it starts with the deep historical and cultural origins of the intelligence services of India, China, the Arab world, and indeed Russia, the last via a route not normally followed in describing this former Cold War adversary of the West. In all these chapters the point of origin is not, as with most volumes, the beginning of the last century, but the last millennium, and even still further back in history. This section of each chapter is underlined by a foray into the comparative cultural approach to intelligence and its relevance for understanding intelligence practice today. Next, we produce a range of authors writing on intelligence practice in places not normally discussed, but that show organizations that have been significantly different from those in the mainstream: Pakistan, Iran, Indonesia, Japan, Ghana, Argentina, Sweden, and Finland. Various chapters deal with matters of intelligence history, current practice, and security-sector reform.

In short, this book has two simple themes: First, in the deep cultural origins of nation-states and peoples, we find the roots of particular state behaviors, and particularly in intelligence, "the second-oldest profession." And the second theme is that intelligence practice is not isomorphic. Simply, this means that just because an intelligence agency in country B has the same duties and aims as those in Western countries, this does not mean that they will look or behave alike. These two themes mark the two main parts of this book. Part II thus deals with intelligence culture, and part III deals with current practice. Prefacing both is part I, which, along with chapter 1, the agenda for the study, includes a methodological examination, chapter 2, by Stephen Welch. This chapter explains not only the difficulties but also the great payouts of an approach to comparative political studies that places an emphasis on cultural issues. It shows what is meant by "intelligence culture" and how this culture meaningfully alters how we understand intelligence practice elsewhere—that is, outside the North Atlantic axis with which we are overly familiar.

To begin the analysis in part II, the historical section of the volume, in chapter 3, the noted Chinese analyst Ralph Sawyer places the work of Sun Tze in the context of intelligence and likewise shows that, as the aphorism goes, "still waters run deep." Then, in chapter 4, we learn from Philip Davies the origins of Indian practice in Kautilya, the often-forgotten "Indian Sun Tze." In chapter 5 Kristian Gustafson explains the error of many in assuming that Russia's security practices would be democratized after the fall of the Soviet Union. He shows that Russian behavior has deeper roots in Russia's Byzantine political inheritance, rather than from its (historically) brief diversion into Marxist-Leninist rule. And in chapter 6 the Saudi Arabian diplomat Abdulaziz Al-Asmari outlines for the first time how deeply the ancient practice of the

Prophet Muhammad, and the early caliphs, has impressed the current practice of intelligence in the Arab and Muslim world. Assumptions have always been that Arab countries' practice reflected that of their Soviet or American advisers, but Al-Asmari makes a compelling case for indigenous origins.

To open part III, in chapter 7 Robert Johnson undertakes a fascinating examination of Inter-Services Intelligence's enigmatic role within the Pakistani state. In chapter 8 Carl Anthony Wege, an experienced analyst on Iran and on terrorist issues, shows us how Tehran's intelligence bureaucracies and various clerical factions have become pillars of the Islamic Republic of Iran, which ties back to Al-Asmari's discussion of the Islamic practice of intelligence. In chapter 9 the volume continues its tour around the world, as Peter Gill and Lee Wilson tackle security-sector reform in postauthoritarian Indonesia. Then, in chapter 10, Ken Kotani of the Japanese Defense Ministry discusses the place of intelligence within Japan's self-defense forces and their problems adapting to new challenges. In chapter 11 Emmanuel Kwesi Aning, Emma Birikorang, and Ernest Ansah Lartey of the Kofi Annan Peacekeeping Centre in Accra cover the development of intelligence culture in Ghana, one of Africa's most stable states, in a postcolonial context. In chapter 12 Eduardo Estévez discusses the increasingly stable intelligence culture in postdictatorship Argentina. In chapter 13 the Swedish scholar Wilhelm Agrell shows how, despite his nation's strong bureaucratic tradition and socialist tendencies, its intelligence structure has remained remarkably independent and powerful in comparison with those of other modern states. And in chapter 14, the Finnish researcher Lauri Holmström shows that though still European, Finland's intelligence practices differ greatly from those of other Western countries; he does so by looking at the Finnish Security Service, and at how protection from economic espionage has become a matter of national security concern. The book concludes with part IV, consisting of chapter 15, which discusses the legacies, identities, improvisation, and innovations of intelligence.

As a final point, the editors note that this volume would not have been possible without the support of a seminar series grant (RES-451–26–0480) from the United Kingdom's Economic and Social Sciences Research Council, which funded the original workshop at which a number of the papers that now make up this book were originally presented.

Notes

1. Christopher Andrew and David Dilks, *The Missing Dimension: Government and Intelligence in the 20th Century* (London: Macmillan, 1984), 1.

2. See, e.g., Philip H. J. Davies, "The Missing Dimension's Missing Dimension," *Public Policy and Administration* 25, no. 1 (January 2010). However, the "organization piece" can be traced back much further, to the beginnings of contemporary intelligence studies in the mid-1960s and to Harold Wilensky, *Organizational Intelligence* (New York: Basic Books, 1967).

3. The culture issue became an active area of discussion in early 2000s with three scholars articulating broadly similar approaches and ideas entirely independently of one another. See Philip Murphy, "Creating a Commonwealth Intelligence Culture: The View from Central Africa 1945–1960," *Intelligence and National Security* 17, no. 3 (Summer 2002); Philip H. J. Davies, "Ideas of Intelligence: Divergent National Concepts and Institutions," *Harvard International Review* 24, no. 3 (Fall 2002); and Michael Turner, "A Distinctive US Intelligence Identity," *International Journal of Intelligence and Counterintelligence* 17, no. 1 (January 2004). Also, however, a substantial earlier contribution was made by H. Bradford Westerfield, "American Exceptionalism and American Intelligence," *Freedom Review* 28, no. 2 (Summer 1997).

4. Hilary Footitt, "Another Missing Dimension? Foreign Languages in World War II Intelligence," *Intelligence and National Security* 25, no. 3 (June 2010).

5. The secrecy surrounding intelligence was often as much a function of consensual taboos as official secrets legislation. The 1976 Church Committee final report noted that the emerging pressure for openness on intelligence resulted in the first instance from the breakdown of just such a consensus (chiefly because of Vietnam and Watergate); see, e.g., Loch K. Johnson, *A Season of Inquiry: The Senate Intelligence Investigation* (Lexington: University Press of Kentucky, 1985), 11. A somewhat paradoxical comparison is the United Kingdom, where the *Official Secrets Act 1911* covered the *entirety* of Civil Service activity and the particular concerns about intelligence were little more than a somewhat tenuous special case; see K. G. Robertson, *Public Secrets* (London: Macmillan, 1984); and K. G. Robertson, "The Politics of Secret Intelligence: British and American Practice" in *British and American Approaches to Intelligence*, edited by K. G. Robertson (London: Macmillan, 1987).

6. See, variously, Angelo Codevilla, "Comparative Historical Experience of Doctrine and Organization" in *Intelligence Requirements for the 1980s: Analysis and Estimates*, edited by Roy Godson (Washington, DC: National Strategy Information Center, 1986; orig. pub. 1980); Adda Bozeman, "Political Intelligence in Non-Western Societies," in *Comparing Foreign Intelligence*, edited by Roy Godson (Washington, DC: National Strategy Information Center, 1985); Angelo Codevilla, "Comparative Historical Experience of Doctrine and Organization," in *Intelligence Requirements*, ed. Godson; K. G. Robertson, "Preface," in *British and American Approaches to Intelligence*, by K. G. (Ken) Robertson (London: Macmillan, 1987), xii; Kevin M. O'Connell, "Thinking about Intelligence Comparatively," *Brown Journal of World Affairs* 11, no. 1 (Summer–Fall 2004); and Peter Gill, "Knowing the Self, Knowing the Other: The Comparative Analysis of Security Intelligence," in *Handbook of Intelligence Studies*, edited by Loch Johnson (London: Routledge, 2009).

7. See, e.g., Mattei Dogan and Dominique Pelassy, *How to Compare Nations: Strategies in Comparative Politics* (Chatham, NJ: Chatham House, 1984), 6, 8.

8. In wider defense, the classic illustration of this approach is taken by Graham T. Allison, *Essence of Decision: Explaining the Cuban Missile Crisis* (New York: HarperCollins, 1971). In the 1990s Amy Zegart applied the neoinstitutional approach to the Joint Chiefs of Staff, National Security Council, and Central Intelligence Agency; Amy Zegart, *Flawed by Design* (Stanford, CA: Stanford University Press, 1999).

9. That sense of intrinsic conflict is a fundamental approach to the later, neoinstitutional derivatives of the original organizational politics paradigm, such as the "garbage can theory" articulated by James G. March (a founder of the original organizational politics model) and Johan P. Olsen; see, e.g., James G. March and Johan P. Olsen, "The New Institutionalism: Organizational Facts in Political Life," *American Political Science Review* 78 (1984):

734–49. Also see M. D. Cohen, "A Garbage Can Model of Organizational Choice," *Administrative Science Quarterly* 17 (1972).

10. Philip H. J. Davies, "Intelligence and the Machinery of Government: Conceptualizing the Intelligence Community," *Public Policy and Administration* 25, no. 1 (January 2010): 39–40.

11. Turner, "Distinctive US Intelligence Identity." It is important to stress that the issue here is not the *accuracy* of Turner's account but the suggested *particularity* of the specific characterization.

12. Talcott Parsons, *The Structure of Social Action* (New York: Free Press, 1937).

13. Talcott Parsons and Jackson Toby, eds., *The Evolution of Societies* (Englewood Cliffs, NJ: Prentice Hall, 1979).

14. Although the American direction–collection–processing–analysis–dissemination version of the intelligence cycle is commonly seen, the distinction between analysis and assessment within a common superclass of "processing" in the NATO version of the cycle is articulated most explicitly by Lord Butler, *Review of Intelligence on Weapons of Mass Destruction* (London: TSO, 2004), 10.

15. John J. Dziak, *Chekisty: A History of the KGB* (Lexington, MA: Lexington Books, 1985).

CHAPTER 2

Political Culture

Approaches and Prospects

Stephen Welch

The idea of "intelligence culture" is not a free-standing invention of intelligence studies but rather is a projection into it of numerous applications of the concept of culture in the social sciences, most obviously the concept of "political culture" that has developed primarily (though not exclusively) within political science. Neither, however, is "political culture" a free-standing invention of political science; rather, it is the projection into it of wider currents of thought that have eddied around the concept of culture since it first began to be used by historians and social philosophers around the time of, and largely in reaction to, the Enlightenment. In the idea of intelligence culture, therefore, we find an application of an already applied concept.

It does not, however, follow that one can find out all one needs to know about the concept of intelligence culture by looking at the concept of political culture; nor, by the same token, that the history of the uses of the concept of culture would be a complete guide to the issues surrounding the concept of political culture in political science. When concepts are transplanted, they embark on a new phase of growth within their new environment of discipline or field. At the same time, if the borrowing is anything more than the most superficial deployment of a portentous phrase, various genetic legacies from the donor fields will continue to make their presence felt.

All this is by way of situating the task of this chapter, which is to outline the concept of political culture for the purpose of elucidating that of intelligence culture. It is also by way of acknowledging how presumptuous it would be to dictate to intelligence studies from the perspective of political science how it should conduct its business with the new concept, not least because political science has struggled to define its own applied "culture" concept, political culture, in a manner that frees it from its genetic inheritance. It is by no means a complete guide to the usage of "intelligence culture" to lay out how political culture has been understood. But nor is it irrelevant; and it is the premise of this chapter that it may be helpful. And, incidentally, the possibility that the development of the derivative concept within intelligence studies may in turn, reciprocally, offer useful cues for thinking about political culture should not be overlooked.

In this chapter, then, I outline the development and current condition of political culture research and offer a few words about its prospects. In noting how the disciplinary setting of political science both inherits and modifies disputes over culture more generally, I imply the same possibilities for the field of intelligence studies as it works with the new concept of intelligence culture, possibilities that are further considered in the remaining chapters of this collection.

The Positivist Mainstream of Political Culture Research: The Almondian Paradigm

It has become conventional, despite one or two earlier uses of the phrase "political culture," to situate the beginning of political culture research in modern political science with the proposal by Gabriel Almond in 1956 that political culture be seen as "a particular pattern of orientations to political action," in which "every political system is embedded." Of particular importance, he also said: "Because political orientation involves cognition, intellection, and adaptation to external situations, as well as the standards and values of the general culture, it is a *differentiated part of the culture* and has a certain autonomy" (emphasis added).[1] Almond did two things with this coinage: He invoked the connotations of "culture," and he simultaneously tried to contain them.

Almond's standing as the founder of political culture research is further supported by his coauthorship with Sidney Verba in 1963 of *The Civic Culture*, the first major empirical study using the new concept.[2] Here, indeed, was the real founding moment of political culture research in the variant that became its mainstream. We need not look closely at the book's argument, but its aim and method are of interest. Its aim was to contribute to the empirical theory of democracy by discovering what cultural orientations were necessary in order for a stable democratic political system to be successfully embedded. Political culture research is thereby implicitly established as a part of the study of comparative politics; its units of analysis are countries. Its method was to discover these orientations by administering attitude questionnaires, and to infer from the correlation of orientations with political systems the set of orientations, or the political culture, appropriate for stable democracy.

With the survey extending to only five countries, one might not be entirely persuaded by the discovered "correlation" between one particular type of political culture, dubbed the "civic culture," and the democratic outcome. Questions have also been raised about the construction of the model of the civic culture itself. Nevertheless, Almond and Verba's book remains important, because it established a template for future use of the political culture concept. According to this template, political culture could be seen as a variable, in part at least as an independent variable—that is, a quantifiable cause of democratic stability. It was made quantifiable by virtue of a particular "operationalization" (mode of measurement) of the concept: the attitude survey. Needless to say, much has happened by way of methodological refinement, and expansion of empirical coverage, of the concept of political culture since 1963, not to mention some ups and downs in its scholarly reputation. But the basic idea of the measurement of mostly national political cultures using surveys and the correlation of the results with general political outcomes has persisted.

The idea of measuring political culture using attitude surveys might seem rather obvious and unproblematic. But looked at more closely, it is a little odd. Political culture is not supposed to be the same as public opinion. Whereas public opinion accounts for the rise and fall of particular political leaders and governments (in democracies, typically), political culture is supposed to account for broader phenomena, such as the persistence of democracy itself. It is also often said to be psychologically "deeper"—for instance, to be "taken for granted," to consist of "values" as opposed to fleeting opinions, and in general, as Almond put it, to "tend to persist in some form and degree and for a significant period of time."[3] Yet it is measured by the same method as highly volatile public opinion. The operationalization is nevertheless a crucial step, because it is by means of the attitude survey method that political science seeks to establish the "certain autonomy" of its concept of political culture from "the general culture."

Among the research programs that have descended from the Almondian paradigm (using this word in Thomas Kuhn's sense of an exemplary scientific achievement),[4] one might mention international survey projects such as the Eurobarometer and the World Values Survey, and studies that have used the resulting data such as Inglehart's theory of the replacement of "materialist" by "postmaterialist" values (values emphasizing "belonging, self-expression and quality of life" rather than distributive economic issues).[5] Transitions to democracy, such as in Southern Europe in the 1970s and Eastern Europe in the 1990s, have produced not only an incentive to study political cultures in terms of their suitability to democracy but also the opportunity to do so by administering surveys, contributing to one of the periodic revivals of political culture research.[6] The most recent of these revivals is in the form of a multicollaborator and multivolume research project called, along with its key book, *Culture Matters*, which has looked at the contribution of political culture to economic development.[7]

Political culture research in the Almondian paradigm therefore represents a major element of present-day political science. But its development has not gone unchallenged. Doubts about it have stemmed from two opposite quarters. From the perspective of rational choice theory, a perspective derived from economics that has become prominent across the social sciences during the last two decades or so, political culture research still betrays some of the unscientific wooliness of the more general concept of culture, a term described by Raymond Williams as "one of the two or three most complicated words in the English language."[8] Rational choice theory (and its derivatives game theory and public choice theory) denies the significance of cultural difference and instead seeks to explain political outcomes in terms of the interaction of preferences under different starting conditions but universally similar capacities for rational calculation.[9] For critics of this persuasion, when political scientists invoke culture, they line up alongside various nationalist and often undemocratic thinkers and leaders who try to resist democratization by suggesting the immutability of culture—as, for example, in the "Asian values" debate.[10]

However, such politically motivated exaggerations notwithstanding, it is difficult to dispense altogether with the idea of cultural difference, so numerous are the cases in which similar arrangements or interventions seem to produce quite distinct outcomes in different settings. The idea of intelligence culture, for example, responds to the fact that functionally very similar governmental purposes are put into effect quite differently, even in closely related and partly integrated settings such as the intelligence apparatuses of Britain and the United States. Almondian political culture research responds in general by seeking to define and operationalize political culture in a way that makes it respectable from a scientific point of view and particularly in line with the positivistic aspiration to validate causal theories by correlating quantitative variables. Indeed, political culture can be seen as the expression of the maximum reach of the "behavioralist" movement in political science, which sought to extend its coverage from formal to informal aspects of politics, to extend the geographical scope of the discipline, and to do all this while retaining the claim to scientific validity by using objective and replicable measurement techniques.[11] More pointedly, the use of the survey method allows this expansion of the scope of political science to take place without threatening its distinctiveness vis-à-vis other disciplines; the survey data become the discipline's proprietary materials, and it thereby wards off the threat of becoming a branch of any of the other disciplines, such as anthropology, that claim expertise in the analysis of culture. Thus the concept of political culture was an important resource in the disciplinary consolidation of political science in the postwar period.

The opposite quarter from which critique of the Almondian paradigm has been launched finds not a failure to live up to the highest standards of scientific (particularly quantitative) rigor, but rather an error in aspiring to them in the first place.

The Interpretive Alternative in Political Culture Research: The Geertzian Paradigm

An interpretive alternative within political culture research arose at an early stage; indeed, it could already be glimpsed nascently in the second major piece of empirical political culture research, Pye and Verba's *Political Culture and Political Development*. In this book's conclusion, Verba advocated a "broad and rather loose definition" of political culture, intended to "direct attention to a general area of concern," recognizing that "if political culture is so generally defined, it is of little use to say that the political culture of nation X explains why it has political structures of form Y."[12] In this usage, political culture already ceases to be identified as a variable, though it remains unclear what its use will be. One explanation of the difference in approach from the Almondian one (which was a noteworthy difference, coming from Verba, Almond's *Civic Culture* coauthor) was no doubt the task faced by the Pye and Verba volume, which focused on developing countries, of characterizing political culture without the benefit of surveys. The same difficulty faced a group of authors who applied the concept of political culture to communist states during the 1970s, and in this setting a more explicit defense of an alternative way of looking at political culture was advanced. Robert Tucker is the chief contributor in this vein, asking in 1973, "Might not the central importance of a concept like that of political culture be that it assists us to take our bearings in the study of the political life of a society, to focus on what is happening or not happening, to describe and analyze and order many significant data, and to raise fruitful questions for thought and research—*without explaining anything?*" (emphasis in the original).[13]

Tucker is important as an early promoter in political science of the work of the anthropologist Clifford Geertz, particularly his collection of essays *The Interpretation of Cultures*.[14] In the methodological debate that arose in communist studies between those who favored following the Almondian paradigm and those who advocated an interpretive approach, Geertz was the authority most often cited by the latter.[15] He has also been an important source for the cultural historians who began their rise to prominence in this discipline at about the same time.[16] And his arguments have recently been restated forcefully, though somewhat forgetfully of their earlier deployment, in a critique of political culture research by Chabal and Daloz titled *Culture Troubles*, whose specific critical target is the *Culture Matters* book and project mentioned earlier.[17] Geertz therefore merits closer scrutiny.

In the political culture literature, Geertz's most often cited essay is "Thick Description: Toward an Interpretive Theory of Culture." Probably its most quoted passages are these: "Believing, with Max Weber, that man is an animal suspended in webs of significance he himself has spun, I take culture to be those webs, and the analysis of it to be therefore not an experimental science in search of law but an interpretive one in search of meaning." Also: "Culture is not a power, something to which social events, behaviors, institutions or processes can be causally attributed; it is a context, something within which they can be intelligibly—that is, thickly—described."[18]

From these passages and similar ones in Geertz's later essays (though not his earlier ones), one can get a clear idea of to what Geertz objects.[19] The Almondian search for the political-cultural variable that can be correlated with outcomes such as stable democracy—a "science in search of law" that construes culture as a "power" impeding certain outcomes and promoting others—is firmly rejected. Indeed, Geertz goes further in a later essay, when he announces: "Calls for 'a general theory' of just about anything social sound increasingly hollow, and claims to have one megalomanic."[20] He instead embraces a "semiotic" or "hermeneutic" conception of culture. Its implications are stated more explicitly in his "Deep Play" essay, where he says that his approach "shifts the analysis of cultural forms from an endeavor in general parallel to dissecting an organism, diagnosing a symptom, deciphering a code, or ordering a system . . . to one in general parallel with penetrating a literary text."[21]

Geertz's skeptical pronouncements tap into long-standing doubts about the possibility of a scientific and particularly quantitative grasp of human social life. These doubts first surfaced when aspirations to create such a science became prominent around the time of the Enlightenment, when hopes were high that the progress in natural science exemplified by Isaac Newton could be replicated in the study of society. Indeed, it was the concept of culture that was a principal vehicle for the expression of these doubts among anti-Enlightenment, "romantic," and "historicist" writers. One of these, Johann Gottfried von Herder, was indeed the first to coin the term "political culture," which ironically therefore first appeared as a reaction against the current of thought that was to lead to Almond's political culture paradigm.[22]

Needless to say, this reactive current of thought has gone through many twists and turns between its emergence in the late eighteenth century and its expression by Geertz.[23] Indeed, the twists have continued; Geertz's work itself has been criticized by subsequent anthropological critics who find the concept of culture to represent all too confident an assertion of the "readability" of the alien social setting, as if it were a text.[24] Little of this complex story seems to be known to the promoters of Geertz's position in political science, who despite their extradisciplinary reach, are perhaps as keen as Almond was to confine that reach to a narrow range—like his, it is really more of an extradisciplinary border raid.

This tends to leave Geertz as an unchallenged authority for his followers in the study of politics. An "endeavour . . . in general parallel with penetrating a literary text" is, however, in need of considerable further specification when it is adopted as a method in political science. In Chabal and Daloz's recent and forceful restatement of the Geertzian paradigm, the emphasis is recurrently on "context," understood as semiotic or interpretive context; on discovering what politics means, how it is understood, in the alien locality, and taking care not to import alien understandings such as those of Western political science. There is something salutary in the warning against "dogmatic theory" that these authors issue, but like Geertz they take an antitheoretical posture too far. As was noted above, Geertz's supposition that the anthropologist can achieve a grasp of the context by immersion in a narrow locality for a prolonged period has itself been challenged by later anthropological critics; but the difficulty of achieving such a grasp must be considerably greater when one's field of study, as for Chabal and Daloz (and something similar can be said for students of politics generally), extends to a context as large as that of Sub-Saharan Africa.

In such a case the method must be quite different from ethnographic fieldwork. One cannot experience a context as large as a global region or even a nation-state directly (if indeed one can experience any social context directly), and it is therefore necessary for the interpreter of culture or political culture on such a scale to work indirectly.[25] What this typically means is drawing on existing general descriptions such as those of historians, journalists, diplomats, and so forth. One gets to a Geertzian understanding of social life as a text by literally reading texts. This is the set of methods previously known by the name of "area studies"—the source, indeed, of the contributions made to political culture and political development, among other examples of political culture research.[26] To be sure, the practitioner of area studies would, like an ethnographer, need to be well versed in the area, ideally to have lived there for a time, and to be able to speak the local language. Opposing universal generalizations would be his or her stock in trade. But quite wide local generalizations would nevertheless be made, as expressions of the synoptic grasp that area studies would claim of the cross-disciplinary range of materials (from history to theology and philology) upon which it necessarily drew.

In the use of such a method, a large and visible role is played by the interpretive contribution of the analyst. When one speaks of the "interpretive context" therefore, as the Geertzian paradigm bids us do, a deep equivocation arises as to who is doing the interpreting. And the contribution of the observer ultimately stands in need of some kind of warrant. In the Geertzian paradigm this can never be anything other than the sheer authority of the writer, or of some other writer who is his or her source. Hence the tendency for Geertz's somewhat oracular sayings to be taken as a kind of interpretive holy writ.

Beyond the Dialectic of Paradigms?

There are, then, two antithetical modes of political culture research, deriving from the different ways in which culture has been imported into political science, and ultimately from a larger and longer-standing dialectic in the way culture itself has been understood. One must at once acknowledge that this dialectic is not always as open to view as it is, for example, in Chabal and Daloz's explicit critique of the Almondian mainstream of political culture research. Somewhat more common, in fact, is the attempt, usually implicit, to combine these approaches. This tactic relies on the deployment of explanatory vagueness at crucial moments. Lucian Pye, for instance, writes (under the heading "In Defense of Political Culture," in case the presence or absence of the adjective is thought to make a difference) that "culture is . . . a remarkably durable and persistent factor in human affairs. . . . [It] resides in the personality of everyone who has been socialized to it."[27] But if from the use of the word "factor" one were to imagine the possibility of comparatively testing explanatory potency, Pye warns us that "probably the greatest weakness of social scientists is their general inability to weigh the relative importance of causal factors."[28] No more help is offered by Pye's invocation of socialization and psychology, for to illustrate what constitutes the personality basis of culture, Pye offers the analogy of a musical tradition, with its "inner 'structure' or 'logic'" and "inherent 'fit.'"[29]

One can indeed sympathize with the desire to get past the seemingly endless dialectic of approaches to culture, but I do not think this simple juxtaposition of interpretive and causal language is the way to do it. It involves an avoidance of the hard questions in cultural explanation. How does culture cause political outcomes? The positivistic answer is that culture equates to psychologically deep values that, in a seemingly contradictory maneuver, we can access using surveys. The interpretive answer is to avoid the question of causation altogether by supposing the connectedness of all the observable activity in an "interpretive context," some kind of semiotic unity, which is "grasped" by the skilled and immersed observer—though in the end causal questions always creep back in if one wants to say that this unity somehow exists in the setting studied and not just in the mind of the analyst.

Political culture, as I said at the outset, is an applied concept of culture in the sense that it seeks to make culture account for a set of outcomes in a specific social field, the field designated "political." The same is true of concepts such as "economic culture," "policy culture," "strategic culture," and of course "intelligence culture."[30] The narrower these get, the easier it seems to be to ignore the kinds of questions I have been airing.[31] One might, for instance, think of intelligence culture as a causal factor or variable, without doing any surveys. Instead, one might draw on existing surveys, or recount in the interpretive style established notions of, for instance, what it means to be British. My claim, however, is that the problem of the dialectic of culture should not be ignored, because ultimately it is a challenge to the theoretical adequacy of the explanations offered.

I do not, however, wish to end here, with a reminder of the contested background in political culture research from which the idea of intelligence culture draws, and of the further background shared by all such applied theories of culture in the dialectical history of this concept itself. Instead, I offer the suggestion that concepts like intelligence culture might offer some resources for getting beyond the dialectic in ways other than by simply ignoring it or unthinkingly juxtaposing its alternatives. Perhaps it is not the case that first the concept of culture must be sorted out, then that of political culture, and finally the narrower applications such as intelligence culture. Perhaps some enlightenment can flow in the other direction.

I can make this case only very briefly in the space available. The first thing to notice is the narrowness of the application of the concept of culture that the idea of intelligence culture represents. This means that when looking at intelligence culture, one is looking at a very highly delimited field of activity, so that pretty much unavoidably, one is looking at human behavior quite closely. To be sure, the special qualities of intelligence as a field of study include the secrecy that surrounds the production of intelligence, so that intelligence organizations are not going to be the easiest organizations to study. Still, the scope of the concept does provide a strong incentive to think of the study in terms of specific organizational locations.

Here one might make a quick jump to the idea of "organizational culture" as a resource for the study of intelligence culture. This is not of immediate benefit, however, given that the study of organizational culture itself is riven by the same disputes that I have been describing in the case of political culture, even if these are not quite so visible and explicitly stated. There is something akin to an Almondian paradigm in the work of the influential writer Geert Hofstede, who employs surveys and points toward the assertion that organizational behavior in organizations such as the large corporation (IBM) that he studied is the expression of one of a small set of value orientations that these surveys reveal.[32] But it has received criticism in somewhat Geertzian vein that "cultures have meanings which depend upon the entire context. No one element in that context dictates meaning to the whole."[33] In turn, this position encounters the problem of characterizing the "entire context," which inevitably moves the emphasis back to the virtuosity of the interpreter.

So organizational culture does not, any more than political culture, provide a finished off-the-peg concept. Nor does it necessarily capture the advantage of close scrutiny to which I have alluded. The advantage of close scrutiny lies in what one can bring into view. Two kinds of things become visible, I suggest, when one looks closely at behavior inside any organization. One of these is standard operating procedures, routines, or habits. The other is how these are represented, justified, or accounted for. It is important not to confuse these two orders of things. In seeking to describe political culture by conducting surveys, for example, research in the Almondian paradigm assumes that what people say, or can say, about their motivations (i.e., their values) sufficiently explains their behavior. When there is a mismatch, it means that the behavior is not genuine—that, for instance, it is coerced, as in communist states where severe penalties were attached to behavioral nonconformity. A Geertzian approach, conversely, might indeed look at the behavior itself, but it seeks to interpret its meaning. If this is not to turn into a variant of the Almondian approach, by doing a survey to find out the meaning, it has the sole recourse of calling on the interpretive skill of the analyst, and in effect substituting his or her intuition of the participants' motives for their own. This happens all the more clearly when the scale of analysis is such that ethnographic fieldwork is out of the question, as in most applications of political culture under the area studies heading. Here, behavior might not be closely observed at all; attention turns to general descriptions in history, literature, or comparative religion.

When looking closely, however, one has the opportunity to observe behavior directly. One can see that it has a continuous and habitual character not because of the values that cause it or the meanings that inform it, but because it is simply self-perpetuating, locked into relatively unthinking routines by the mutual adaptation to them of a number of individuals who rely on each other's capacity for coordinated action within these routines. Of course, they also talk about their behavior, rather incessantly in fact in "clerical" organizational settings. But the talk about behavior, or the rules written down to control it, need not exhaust or fully explain the reality of behavior. As Ludwig Wittgenstein pointed out in one of his most influential arguments, a rule never provides complete instructions for following it.[34] There are always instances lying beyond the ones whereby one learned the rule. Following a rule is therefore not capable of analysis in terms of the content of the rule; "knowing how to go on" in relation to the rule is rather a "technique," a "custom," or a "practice."

The insight that what one does, and what one says about what one does, are two different things does not at first seem to be a very penetrating one. Yet it has powerful implications for how one thinks about cultural continuity and cultural differences. Indeed, it has implications for how one understands the very idea of an attitude, and therefore treats the method of the attitude survey. Social psychologists in recent years have developed some interesting arguments, quite substantially backed up by experimental studies, to suggest that very often behavior is caused by factors of which the actors are not consciously aware; that the causes of one's actions and the motives one can bring to mind as attitudes when asked to do so are two sets of phenomena running in parallel.[35] This means that surveys reveal not motives—that is, the real causes of behavior—but rather the prevailing modes of accounting for behavior in the relevant setting. Such theories of "dual attitudes" or "automaticity" lead one toward a dualistic understanding of culture, an understanding that recognizes the duality of culture itself. And a theoretical understanding of the duality of culture is something very different from a recurrent and unresolved dialectic of *approaches* to culture.

The study of intelligence culture, and of other applied forms of cultural study on this kind of scale, encourages the sort of bottom-up theoretical construction of political culture and culture more generally that I have briefly been recommending. That is, it need not start with an understanding of a broader cultural setting and try to read this in a narrower sense—to read intelligence culture in Britain, for example, as an expression of British cultural values. It might very well note that these are invoked, in one form or another, in the accounts that participants give of their organizational practice, particularly when they are asked to compare their organizational practice with that in agencies elsewhere. It does not follow, however, that these accounts are an adequate explanation of the continuities and differences that can be observed in practice. These may have a simpler explanation in skills and habits, and their mutual coordination, that form the standard operating procedures of the setting. When these encounter friction or disruptions—as they are likely to when, for instance, interagency contacts occur—there will be a natural tendency to account for them in terms of prevailing cultural stereotypes. Depending on what sort of friction is occurring, these may be stereotypes of, for instance, the "American way" of thinking; or in other cases of the military mindset as contrasted with the civilian one. In some cases there will be an incentive for participants to think of intelligence culture as nationally varying; in others, one would tend to think of it as a sui generis type of organizational culture (defined, perhaps, by its vocation of secrecy or its concern with "national security"), to be contrasted with others not so defined. These are differences in accounts; they need not constitute the actual causes of the observed frictions. Both the accounting and the behavior of which it is an accounting constitute the dual reality of the cultural process. Close scrutiny of this process in a narrow, applied context is the particular advantage that the study of intelligence culture might be able to realize.

Concepts of Culture

To conclude, I outline the principal lines of debate within political science as to the definition and use of the concept of political culture. This concept is an application of the broader concept of culture, though the extent to which the connotations of the broader concept should feed into the narrower one is one of the main points of controversy. Intelligence culture is, in turn, an application of the idea of political culture in the specific field of intelligence studies. As in other applied fields of cultural analysis, such as strategic culture, the extent to which serious attention is paid to the debates in the donor discipline is likely to vary. My argument has been, however, that they are indeed relevant, and problematic, for the new field.

Despite this, and more positively, I have argued that the study of intelligence culture need not wait upon the unlikely prospect of a resolution of the long-standing dialectic of cultural analysis. There may be ways, offered by the narrowness of the setting of intelligence culture studies and the close scrutiny it affords, of thinking differently about culture in this setting. The overt organizational design, the mission statements and explicit rules, and the everyday justificatory talk of actors in the intelligence setting are all worthy of study as the discursive aspects of intelligence culture. So, too, are the operating procedures, habits, and routines that will always outrun what the rules can encompass. Whether the participants' own discursive rendering of these behavioral patterns emphasizes their national, intelligence, or specific agency characteristics, or perhaps numerous others, depends on the kind of frictions that arise between different sets of practices, and the availability of ways of accounting for them. Such points of friction therefore become exceptionally interesting sites of study. And in the field of intelligence, with its links to national security, its distinctive reliance on secret information, and its proliferation of agencies—all in the context of a perceived global threat that appears to mandate maximum coordination—such sites are not difficult to find.

Notes

1. Gabriel A. Almond, "Comparative Political Systems," *Journal of Politics* 18, no. 3 (August 1956): 391–409, at 396.

2. Gabriel A. Almond and Sidney Verba, *The Civic Culture: Political Attitudes and Democracy in Five Nations*, abridged ed. (Newbury Park, CA: Sage, 1989; orig. pub. 1963).

3. Gabriel A. Almond, "Communism and Political Culture Theory," *Comparative Politics* 15, no. 2 (January 1983): 127–38, at 127.

4. Thomas S. Kuhn, *The Structure of Scientific Revolutions*, 2nd ed. (Chicago: Chicago University Press, 1970), 10f.

5. Ronald Inglehart, *Modernization and Postmodernization: Cultural, Economic, and Political Change in 43 Societies* (Princeton, NJ: Princeton University Press, 1997).

6. See, e.g., Frederick J. Fleron Jr., "Post-Soviet Political Culture in Russia: An Assessment of Recent Empirical Investigations," *Europe-Asia Studies* 48, no. 2 (March 1996): 225–66.

7. See Lawrence E. Harrison and Samuel P. Huntington, *Culture Matters: How Values Shape Human Progress* (New York: Basic Books, 2000). And for a summary, see Lawrence E. Harrison, *The Central Liberal Truth: How Politics Can Change a Culture and Save It from Itself* (Oxford: Oxford University Press, 2006).

8. Raymond Williams, *Keywords: A Vocabulary of Culture and Society*, rev. ed. (London: Fontana, 1983), 87.

9. For a sample of these critiques, see William H. Reisinger, "The Renaissance of a Rubric: Political Culture as Concept and Theory," *International Journal of Public Opinion Research* 7, no. 4 (Winter 1995): 328–52; and Robert W. Jackman and Ross A. Miller, "A Renaissance of Political Culture?" *American Journal of Political Science* 40, no. 3 (August 1996): 632–59. For a defense of political culture research against rational choice theory, see Harry Eckstein, "A Culturalist Theory of Political Change," *American Political Science Review* 82, no. 3 (September 1988): 789–804; and Harry Eckstein, "Culture as a Foundation Concept for the Social Sciences," *Journal of Theoretical Politics* 8, no. 4 (October 1996): 471–97. For an attempt to combine political-cultural and rational choice approaches, see Ruth Lane, "Political Culture: Residual Category or General Theory?" *Comparative Political Studies* 25, no. 3 (October 1992): 362–87.

10. See Fareed Zakaria and Lee Kuan Yew, "Culture Is Destiny: A Conversation with Lee Kuan Yew," *Foreign Affairs* 73, no. 2 (March–April 1994): 109–26; and Richard Robison, "The Politics of Asian Values," *Pacific Review* 9, no. 3 (1996): 309–27.

11. See Stephen Welch, *The Concept of Political Culture* (London: Macmillan, 1993), 73.

12. Sidney Verba, "Conclusion: Comparative Political Culture," in *Political Culture and Political Development*, edited by Lucian W. Pye and Sidney Verba (Princeton, NJ: Princeton University Press, 1965), 518.

13. Robert C. Tucker, "Culture, Political Culture, and Communist Society," *Political Science Quarterly* 88, no. 2 (June 1973): 173–90, at 179.

14. Clifford Geertz, *The Interpretation of Cultures* (London: Hutchinson, 1975).

15. For discussions of this debate, see Archie Brown, ed., *Political Culture and Communist Studies* (London: Macmillan, 1984); and Stephen Welch, "Issues in the Study of Political Culture: The Example of Communist Party States (review article)," *British Journal of Political Science* 17, no. 4 (October 1987): 479–500.

16. William H. Sewell Jr., "Geertz, Cultural Systems, and History: From Synchrony to Transformation," *Representations* 59 (Special Issue: "The Fate of Culture: Geertz and Beyond"; Summer 1997): 35–55.

17. Patrick Chabal and Jean-Pascal Daloz, *Culture Troubles: Politics and the Interpretation of Meaning* (London: Hurst, 2006).

18. Geertz, *Interpretation of Cultures*, 3–30, at 5, 14.

19. In the earlier essays gathered in *Interpretation of Cultures*, apart from another famous one, "Deep Play: Notes on the Balinese Cockfight," Geertz pays a good deal of homage to Talcott Parsons and Piotr Sorokin, both social theorists who sought to incorporate culture into explanatory theory.

20. Clifford Geertz, *Local Knowledge: Further Essays in Interpretive Anthropology* (London: Fontana Press, 1993), 4.

21. Geertz, *Interpretation of Cultures*, 412–53.

22. F. M. Barnard, ed., *J. G. Herder on Social and Political Culture*, translated by F. M. Barnard (Cambridge: Cambridge University Press, 1969).

23. Isaiah Berlin has been an important documenter of these twists and turns; see, e.g., Isaiah Berlin, *Against the Current: Essays in the History of Ideas*, edited by Henry Hardy (London: Pimlico, 1997).

24. See, e.g., James Clifford and George E. Marcus, eds., *Writing Culture: The Poetics and Politics of Ethnography* (Berkeley: University of California Press, 1986); and Lila Abu-Lughod, "The Interpretation of Culture(s) after Television," *Representations* 59 (Summer 1997): 109–34. And for a response, see Christoph Brumann, "Writing for Culture: Why a Successful Concept Should Not Be Discarded," *Current Anthropology* 40 (Supplement, Special Issue: "Culture: A Second Chance?" 1999): S1–S27.

25. I do not think we can, any more than we can read a literary text without presuppositions, as to, for instance, its genre and its period, and more generally as to the role of literature in our lives.

26. See, e.g., Lucian W. Pye with Mary W. Pye, *Asian Power and Politics: The Cultural Dimension of Authority* (Cambridge, MA: Belknap Press of Harvard University Press, 1985); and Nicolai N. Petro, *The Rebirth of Russian Democracy: An Interpretation of Political Culture* (Cambridge, MA: Harvard University Press, 1995).

27. Pye, *Asian Power and Politics*, 19ff.

28. Ibid., 13.

29. Ibid., 20ff.

30. For examples of the first three, see Paul Egon Rohrlich, "Economic Culture and Foreign Policy: The Cognitive Analysis of Economic Policy Making," *International Organization* 41, no. 1 (Winter 1987): 61–92; Jeremy Richardson, *Policy Styles in Western Europe* (London: George Allen & Unwin, 1982); and Alan Macmillan and Ken Booth, "Appendix: Strategic Culture—A Framework for Analysis," in *Strategic Cultures in the Asia-Pacific Region*, edited by Ken Booth and Russell Trood (London: Macmillan, 1999), 363–72.

31. E.g., in their "framework for analysis" of strategic culture, Alan Macmillan and Ken Booth note briefly both the problem of the relationship of strategic culture and political culture, and problems of definition in the latter—but do not seem to find these an impediment to research on strategic culture. Macmillan and Booth, "Appendix: Strategic Culture," 366.

32. Geert Hofstede, *Culture's Consequences: International Differences in Work-Related Values* (Beverly Hills, CA: Sage, 1980).

33. Charles Hampden-Turner and Fons Trompenaars, "Response to Geert Hofstede," *International Journal of Intercultural Relations* 21, no. 1 (February 1997): 149–59, at 152.

34. Ludwig Wittgenstein, *Philosophical Investigations*, translated by G. E. M. Anscombe (Oxford: Basil Blackwell, 1968), §§ 143–242. In the next sentence in the text, the citations are as follows: "technique," § 150; a "custom," § 198; and a "practice," § 202.

35. See works by John Bargh, Timothy Wilson, and Daniel Wegner, and their respective collaborators, and in particular John A. Bargh and Melissa J. Ferguson, "Beyond Behaviorism: On the Automaticity of Higher Mental Processes," *Psychological Bulletin* 126, no. 6 (November 2000): 925–45; Daniel M. Wegner, *The Illusion of Conscious Will* (Cambridge, MA: MIT Press, 2002); and Timothy D. Wilson, *Strangers to Ourselves: Discovering the Adaptive Unconscious* (Cambridge, MA: Harvard University Press, 2002). For an earlier discussion of some of these arguments in relation to political culture research, see Stephen Welch, "Political Culture, Post-Communism and Disciplinary Normalisation: Towards Theoretical Reconstruction," in *Political Culture and Post-Communism*, edited by Stephen Whitefield (New York: Palgrave, 2005), 105–24.

PART II

Intelligence Culture outside the Anglosphere

CHAPTER 3

Subversive Information

The Historical Thrust of Chinese Intelligence

Ralph D. Sawyer

Spying transcends human affairs. Spies must successfully undertake
actions beyond the capability of other men. How can their achievements be compared with merely assaulting a city, occupying terrain,
capturing an enemy's flag, or killing a general? Their greatness is
incalculable, beyond words.

—SHI ZIMEI

For more than twenty-five-hundred years Chinese intelligence activities
have been marked by vibrant theorizing and dedicated practice—the former encompassed within the essentially continuous military writings; the
latter implemented throughout the virtually interminable warfare that plagued
China, whenever its nominal geopolitical unity was shattered and millenarian
movements ravaged the land.[1] Internally directed security measures also proliferated in both the fragmented states and overarching dynasties as the emperor
and local rulers sought to control not only the populace but also powerful
regional factions, royal family members, court minions, and the bureaucracy at
large. Surprisingly, rather than being dismissed as relics from an antique age,
they continue to be scrutinized by the military institutions of the People's
Republic of China (PRC) for viable methods and applicable techniques that

are in accord with the thrust to formulate and excel at a uniquely Chinese way of warfare.[2]

Spies reportedly assisted the Shang Dynasty in overthrowing the Xia Dynasty; oracular inscriptions indicate that intelligence gathering and reporting date back to the middle Shang (1200 BCE), and historical vestiges confirm that agents were employed in the Spring and Autumn Period (722–481), a time when warfare dramatically escalated. Without accurate information of enemy activities, any of the emergent states then increasingly entangled in the era's multiparty conflict would almost have certainly perished. Battlefield developments and the growing severity of the threat prompted experienced commanders, governmental authorities, and political thinkers to analyze military clashes and ponder collateral diplomatic incidents in a quest to discern replicable patterns and devise essential measures. Unfortunately, the earliest military writings, which were essentially protobooks consisting of often-enigmatic comments written on narrow bamboo strips, now exist only as scattered pronouncements embedded in later works. However, when coupled with fragments preserved in the first historical chronicles, the evolving nature of intelligence activities visible in China's earliest surviving military treatise—the *Art of War*, attributed to the infamous Sunzi (referred to as Sun Tze elsewhere in this volume), perhaps the world's first professional security adviser—becomes apparent.[3]

The Spring and Autumn Period

The dire situation confronting most rulers at the end of the Spring and Autumn Period and the beginning of the aptly named Warring States Period (403–221, during which Qin subjugated the remaining twelve states) prompted Sunzi to commence the *Art of War* by asserting that "warfare is the greatest affair of state, the basis of life and death, the Dao to survival and extinction."[4] He then appropriately concluded that not only "must it be pondered and analyzed," but also that it could not be undertaken without detailed planning and a comprehensive analysis of the relative strengths and weaknesses of both parties. In the world's first known net assessment procedure, detailed calculations were to be undertaken that comparatively weighed seven major factors: "Which ruler has the Dao? Which general has greater ability? Who has gained the advantages of Heaven and Earth? Whose laws and orders are more thoroughly implemented? Whose forces are stronger? Whose officers and troops are better trained? Whose rewards and punishments are clearer?"[5]

Later writers would expand the list of obligatory categories, but even in the *Art of War* some forty mutually defined or otherwise interrelated pairs are already apparent, including Heaven/Earth, hunger/satiety, rested/exhausted, ordered/disordered, fearful/confident, and lax/alert. Deciding whether to undertake an expeditionary campaign or engage an enemy in battle therefore became a question of rationally determining the prospects for victory, all combat being eschewed without certainty that the enemy can be conquered. Furthermore, emotional factors should never become proximate causes for warfare: "If it is not advantageous, do not move. If objectives cannot be attained, do not employ the army. Unless endangered do not engage in warfare. The ruler cannot mobilize the army out of personal anger. The general cannot engage in battle because of personal frustration. When it is advantageous, move; when not advantageous, stop. Anger can revert to happiness, annoyance can revert to joy, but a vanquished state cannot be revived, the dead cannot be brought back to life."[6]

In concert with what might be termed the "ruthless practice of efficient warfare" and the realization that "warfare is the Dao of deception," the *Art of War* stressed manipulating the enemy and shaping, or at least exploiting, the battle space.[7] Enemies must be tricked and maneuvered, lured and enticed, frustrated and enervated until a local tactical imbalance can be created and the army's strategic power can be applied in an overwhelming manner analogous to a whetstone crushing an egg.[8] Effecting these measures requires thorough knowledge of the enemy and oneself:

> If I know our troops can attack but do not know the enemy cannot be attacked, it is only halfway to victory. If I know the enemy can be attacked but do not realize our troops cannot attack, it is only halfway to victory.
>
> Knowing that the enemy can be attacked and knowing that our army can affect the attack, but not knowing the terrain is not suitable for combat, is only halfway to victory. One who truly knows the army will never be deluded when he moves, never be impoverished when initiating an action.
>
> Thus it is said if you know them and know yourself, your victory will not be imperiled. If you know Heaven and know Earth, your victory can be complete.[9]

An often-quoted passage from the *Art of War* reiterating the need for military and political intelligence elucidates some of the essentials: "The prosecution of military affairs lies in according with and learning in detail the enemy's intentions. Anyone who does not know the plans of the feudal lords cannot forge preparatory alliances. Anyone who does not know the topography of mountains and forests, ravines and defiles, wetlands and marshes cannot maneuver the army. Anyone who does not employ local guides will not secure advantages of terrain. Anyone who does not know one of these four or five cannot command the army of a hegemon or a true king."[10]

Although often ignored in actual practice, the *Art of War*'s behest would be reiterated by subsequent military and political thinkers in various forms, including Qi's well-known adviser, Guan Zhong: "Being ignorant about estimations and calculations but yet wanting to undertake military affairs is like wanting to cross over a dangerous river without a boat or oars. Anyone who is not knowledgeable about the enemy's government cannot make plans against them; anyone who is not knowledgeable about the enemy's true situation cannot constrain them with agreements; anyone who is not knowledgeable about the enemy's generals cannot mobilize the army first; and anyone who is not knowledgeable about the enemy's officers cannot deploy an army against them."[11]

An esoteric text known as the *Taibai Yinjing* attributed to Li Quan states, "When the enemy is quiet observe their *yang* aspects (visible behavior), when they move investigate their *yin* (silent, hidden) side. First observe their traces, thereafter know the enemy's mind."[12] The dynasty's most successful early military commander, Li Jing, similarly stressed the importance of deliberately acquiring knowledge of the enemy: "The measures for achieving decisive victory lie in investigating the opposing general's talent and abilities; analyzing the enemy's strengths and weaknesses; determining the configuration and strategic advantages of terrain; observing the advantages of the appropriate moment; and first being victorious, only thereafter engaging in combat and defending positions without losing them. This is termed the Dao for certain victory."[13]

Several later writers, echoing Sunzi's broad condemnation of commanders who failed to undertake the necessary intelligence-gathering efforts, also acerbically condemned rulers. In the late Song Dynasty (960–1279), Shi Zimei conclusively attacked both of them:[14]

> Armies remain locked in a standoff for years to fight for victory on a single day, yet generals begrudge bestowing ranks and emoluments of one hundred pieces of gold and therefore do not know the enemy's situation. This is the ultimate inhumanity. Such a person is not a general for the people, an assistant for a ruler, or the arbiter of victory.
>
> Rulers easily acquire things, but the enemy's true situation is especially difficult to know. If easily acquired things such as money and gold can be employed to gain elusive information, how can anyone be parsimonious and not give them in exchange? Furthermore, victory or defeat may be decided on a single momentous day, so being incapable of employing agents to spy upon the enemy's situation would be the greatest inhumanity!"

In about the mid–sixteenth century an unknown author proclaimed that "any general who, having assumed the mantle of authority over the Three Armies and controlling the fate of ten thousand men, confronts fierce enemies or pursues them into the wilds to engage in a standoff but does not know the enemy's situation, is a blockhead. When two forces struggle to control each other, anyone who does not undertake spycraft techniques is a wild animal."[15]

In ancient China, particularly during the Shang Dynasty, the prospects for victory and thus the advisability of undertaking military actions were determined by consulting the ancestors through divination, a practice that continued to have a major impact in the Western Zhou Dynasty and often thereafter when the *Yi Jing* came to be employed.[16] However Sunzi, who advanced a strong economic argument for deploying agents in the first paragraphs of his "Employing Spies," banished esoteric methods in favor of human agency by boldly asserting that "the means by which enlightened rulers and sagacious generals moved and conquered others, that their achievements surpassed the masses, was advance knowledge. Advance knowledge cannot be gained from ghosts and spirits, inferred from phenomena, or projected from the measures of Heaven, but must be gained from men, for it is the knowledge of the enemy's true situation."[17]

For Sunzi, this knowledge was both broad and highly detailed: "You must first know the names of the defensive commander, his assistants, staff, door guards, and attendants for any armies that you want to strike, cities you want to attack, and men you want to assassinate."[18] Therefore, only human agents operating in the enemy's environment can possibly acquire it. "You must have your spies search out and learn them all." In the middle of the fourth century BCE, the "Military Methods" compiled by Sun Bin, Sunzi's brilliant descendant, thus emphasized the importance of knowledge gained through spy activities: "One who does not use spies will not be victorious."[19]

The late Sung Dynasty *Unorthodox Strategies*, a much-pondered text in recent PRC military science reformulation, similarly asserts: "Whenever planning to conduct a major military expedition you should first employ spies to determine the enemy's troop strength, emptiness or fullness, and movement and rest, and only thereafter mobilize the army. Great achievements can then be attained and you will always be victorious in combat."[20] Continuity through the Ming Dynasty is apparent in this paragraph from the mid-sixteenth-century *Toubi Futan*, which coincidentally indicates the *fundamentally active nature* of Chinese agents:

> Attacking other states through their ruler is more intelligent than attacking them yourself. Plotting against people through their ministers is more intelligent than plotting against them yourself. Dispersing alliances and bringing allies together in conflict is more intelligent than engaging them in combat yourself. In this fashion you can attack others through their ruler, plot against men through their ministers, disperse their alliances and instigate conflict among them. But without agents, how can you investigate their true nature, without spies how can you employ these techniques? Moreover, whenever two armies stand off against each other, it is not just we who plot against the enemy, but also the enemy who plots against us. To fail to gain accurate information about the enemy's situation but recklessly engage in battle is senseless.[21]

Such pronouncements are not just found in the military treatises but also Warring States Period works on statecraft, such as the work attributed to Han Feizi, sometimes contemptuously disparaged in the West as "China's Machiavelli."

Treatise on Spycraft

Whenever the *Art of War* was actually completed, the laconic "Employing Spies" not only remains the world's first theoretical treatise on spycraft but was also the progenitor of all subsequent Chinese thought about covert agents and activities. Later writers would expand the categories, detail the methods, offer countermeasures, and even contradict the basic formulations, but never ignore them.[22] Minus the paragraphs already cited, this brief chapter may be translated as follows:

> When you send an army of a hundred thousand forth on a campaign, marching them out a thousand *li*, the expenditures of the common people and the contributions of the feudal house will be one thousand pieces of gold per day. Those inconvenienced and troubled both within and without the border, who are exhausted on the road or unable to pursue their agricultural work, will be seven hundred thousand families.
>
> Armies remain locked in a standoff for years to fight for victory on a single day, yet generals begrudge bestowing ranks and emoluments of one hundred pieces of gold and therefore do not know the enemy's situation. This is the ultimate inhumanity. Such a person is not a general for the people, an assistant for the ruler, or the arbiter of victory.
>
> Thus there are five types of spies to be employed: local spy, internal spy, turned spy [double agent], dead [expendable] spy, and the living spy. When all five are employed together and no one knows the Tao of their employment, it is termed "spiritual methodology." They are a ruler's treasures.
>
> Local spies employ people from the local district. Internal spies employ their officials. Double agents employ the enemy's spies. Expendable spies employ them to spread disinformation outside the state. Provide our expendable spies with false information and have them leak it to enemy agents.[23] Living spies return with their reports.
>
> Thus, of all the Three Armies' affairs, no relationship is closer than with spies; no rewards are more generous than those given to spies; no affairs are more secret than those pertaining to spies.[24]
>
> Unless someone has the wisdom of a Sage, he cannot use spies; unless he is benevolent and righteous, he cannot employ spies; unless he is subtle and perspicacious, he cannot perceive the substance in intelligence reports. It is subtle, subtle! There are no areas in which one does not employ spies.
>
> If the mission is exposed before it has begun, the spy and all those he informed should be put to death.
>
> You must search for enemy agents who have come to spy on us. Tempt them with profits, instruct and retain them, thereby obtaining and employing double agents. Through knowledge gained from them you can recruit both local and internal spies. Through knowledge gained from them the expendable spy can spread his falsehoods and be used to misinform the enemy. Through knowledge gained from them our living spies can be employed as the moment requires.

The ruler must know these five aspects of espionage work. Because such knowledge invariably depends on turned spies, you must be generous to double agents.

In antiquity, when the Shang arose they had Yi Yin in the Xia and when the Zhou arose they had Lu Ya in the Shang. Thus enlightened rulers and sagacious generals who are able to get intelligent spies invariably attain great achievements. This is the essence of the military, what the Three Armies rely on to move.

Although Sunzi's designations adequately characterize each agent's role, much can be learned from later commentaries and interpretations. First of all, "local agents" are far more encompassing than at first seems apparent, at least in part because of the historical examples that would be cited in subsequent writings and mentioned in the *Art of War* itself, Yi Yin and the Tai Gong (Lu Ya). For example, the *Taibai Yinjing* lists seven examples through which "rulers became emperors": "In antiquity when the Shang arose, Yi Yin was a cook in the Xia; when the Zhou arose, the Tai Gong was a fisherman in the Shang; when the Qin established imperial rule, Li Si was a hunter in Shandong; when Han Gaozu ventured forth, Han Xin was an exiled soldier from Chu; and Cao Cao found Xun Huo, Yuan Shao's cast-off minister. Sima Tan became emperor of Jin because Jia Chong had been entrusted with the government in Wei, while Wei itself arose because Cui Hao had made Jin his home."

Rather than agents recruited in enemy areas who then engage in clandestine spy work within a foreign state, a function normally performed by internal spies, local spies or guides are knowledgeable individuals temporarily resident outside their native habitant. They therefore included emigrants, experienced travelers, and even peripatetic advisers who routinely integrate information about other states into their persuasions. China's first spies were actually exiles, essentially defectors who could provide valuable general information about government officials and local configurations of terrain. Du You commented that "by relying on the enemy's local people, one learns the enemy's internal and external affairs, his vacuities and substantialities."[25]

In contrast, he further noted that "living spies" are "often talented individuals of exceptional perspicacity who can be dispatched to foreign states, sometimes in diplomatic guise, to observe and then report back. They normally comprise the greatest number of agents so as to provide the state with multiple means for acquiring data. Rely on those among the enemy who have lost their government positions, such as the sons and grandsons of those who suffered corporeal punishment and families who have been fined. Rely on fissures in order to successfully recruit them." Zhang Zhao, another famous commentator, advised that "among the enemy's officials, there will be those who resent having been dismissed for some offense, favorites and concubines no longer loved, those who are not employed, and those who lack conviction and love profits. All of them can be secretly lured in and forced to inform us about the enemy's secret affairs."

The two categories of expendable and double or turned agents occasioned the most conceptual difficulty throughout Chinese history and therefore the most extensive discussion. Sunzi's original concept of expendable agents being spies deliberately dispatched on missions likely to result in their deaths became somewhat muddled over the centuries and eventually encompassed any agent who died in the performance of their mission. It was generally assumed that to be effective the agent would never know that they were about to be sacrificed to accomplish some greater goal, and many of the most famous exemplars were in fact unaware that they were doomed.

Enemy agents could also be deliberately deceived, provided with false information and specious plans that they would report back to their masters, causing them to be executed for their incompetence or apparent collusion with the enemy when events unfolded or the truth was unveiled. Thus Du You commented, "Undertake feigned and false affairs outside the state and leak them about. Inform our agents about something and dispatch them into the enemy's midst so that they will divulge it when captured. When the enemy, believing their accounts, follows up but our actions differ, the spy will be executed." Zhang Zhao, who took a somewhat different approach, stated that "expendable agents transmit disinformation outside the state. Have our spies learn of something and transmit it to the enemy's agents. When their spies hear of it they will report back to the enemy." Citing this, Shi Zimei concluded that "this should be understood as creating some sort of secret affair that is leaked to our spies. Our spies in turn see that it is leaked to the enemy's agents so that the enemy will learn of this feigned affair. When it proves to be a ruse, the enemy's spies will be executed!" Even though they hardly fit into the category of "expendable agents," the enemy's spies are thus eliminated.

Sunzi's definition of double or turned agents was premised upon them having been dispatched by the enemy and subsequently and, most important, consciously turned. However, as has already become apparent, the concept came to entail the manipulation of enemy personnel whether they were active agents or not, consciously recruited or not. Sunzi highly esteemed true double agents because they were the most likely to provide extensive, detailed information about the enemy's internal situation. Shi Zimei subsequently observed:

> Zhang Zhao said that "we employ agents to spy on others and other men also employ agents to spy on us. It is vitally necessary to preserve deep secrecy and not leak out the crux of affairs. For this reason when the enemy has agents spy on us, we must strive to learn of their coming and turn them around to our own use." Probably it is normal human emotion that if we satisfy their desires they will do what we want. If we coerce them with their anxieties, they will not know that we are using them. When an agent who comes to spy on us can be

turned around and employed, it is as a double agent. If we are to recruit him to work for us and spy on them, we must have techniques. Accordingly, lure him with profits or lead and release him. In order to entice him through his desires, you cannot begrudge rank, salary, or the hundred gold coins that will satisfy his desires. To lead and release him, let him see our encampment's fortifications and actions in order to coerce him with anxiety. Open and lead him with affairs, and then release him to report back.

Li Quan, writing in the *Taibai Yinjing*, advised that the enemy's spies can be converted into local guides: "We can capitalize upon the men dispatched by the enemy to observe our defects by offering them higher ranks and making their salaries more generous. Thereafter, investigate their words and compare them with actuality. If they prove accurate, you can then employ them; if specious, you can execute them. Employ them as 'local guides.'"[26]

In the late Ming Dynasty, more than two thousand years later, the innovative military thinker Jie Xuan expanded the list of *jian*, a term normally understood as referring to human agents, to encompass several techniques and a few inanimate objects. His explanation, which again shows the aggressive activities envisioned for agents, marks the culmination of the intelligence tradition in China:[27]

Those who enter among the enemy and implement unorthodox measures are termed "agents."[28] Agents strike fear in the enemy's general staff, slay the enemy's beloved generals, and cause chaos in the enemy's estimates and strategies. The methods for employing agents include living, dead [expendable], written, civil, rumors, prophecy, songs, bribes, things, rank, the enemy, villagers [local guides], friends, women, good will, and awe.

Spies [*die*] who are dispatched and then return are living agents. Those who enter enemy territory but do not return are dead agents.[29] Creating forged letters is clandestine written action. Holding discussions that stupefy the enemy is clandestine civil action. Sullying and contaminating the enemy's generals is clandestine action by rumor. Creating prophetic verses that circulate among the people is clandestine action by prophecy. Songs used to disperse the troops is clandestine action through song.

Using ten thousand ounces of gold to make bribes is clandestine action through bribery. Sometimes seizing things, sometimes granting gifts, is clandestine action through things. To promise rank and position is clandestine bribery through rank. Allowing the enemy's agents to return and report is clandestine action though enemy agents. Forming connections with subordinates and partisan cliques with hamlets is clandestine action through local agents. Influencing people through their friends is clandestine action through friends.

Bribes that penetrate the women's quarters constitutes clandestine action through women. Exploiting personal friendship is clandestine action through goodwill. Inflicting bodily harm to implement plans is clandestine action through awesomeness.

At the end of his explication Jie ruefully concluded that "it is not implementing clandestine activities that is difficult, but employing men that is difficult. Therefore employing agents is more difficult than employing the army."[30]

Assassination and Subversive Programs

By the time of the earliest recorded literature, it had become apparent that military measures that relied on mobilizing the populace and fielding masses of chariots and infantry forces constituted expensive solutions to problems of state and that other, less disruptive solutions might prove more efficacious. The great Warring States general Wu Qi—who identified the four vital points of warfare as *qi* (spirit), terrain, affairs, and strength—defined "affairs" in terms of causing dissension within the enemy's ranks as "being good at controlling clandestine operatives, forcing rulers and ministers to feel mutual annoyance, and higher and lower ranks to reproach each other."[31]

Although unrecorded, clandestine activities such as bribery, estrangement, and deception apparently began simply and early. By the end of the Spring and Autumn period, typical objectives for covert operations included sowing dissension, causing misperception, assassinating key personnel, ruining public confidence, bribing officials, estranging key advisers, debauching important people with women and music, and mounting other political measures to subvert enemy governments and undermine their ability to wage war.[32] As theorists began to ponder the nature and implication of these hitherto extemporaneous efforts, they came to envision coordinated programs designed to weaken and even topple their enemies, and thus achieve Sunzi's ideal of balking plans, thwarting alliances, and conquering the enemy completely, without combat.[33]

Murder had long been widely employed in palace strife, court intrigues, and private vendettas, whereas brief references in the *Art of War* suggest that political and military assassination had already become an accepted practice. Five famous assassins were subsequently lionized in a dedicated *Shiji* chapter, including Juan Zhu, who enabled King Holu to seize the throne from his uncle before going on to employ Sunzi as his national security adviser and preside over Wu's political and military ascension at the end of the Spring and Autumn Period.[34]

Although every imaginable object might be employed as a weapon, including specially cast wine ladles,[35] assassination attempts generally relied upon direct stabbing attacks or, in the case of female operatives, poison.[36] Great personal sacrifice was required to achieve the intended goal, and assassins frequently resorted to mutilating themselves or implementing the stratagem known as "suffering flesh," whereby they voluntarily underwent horrendous tribulations to create a credible legend and thereby gain access to their targets.[37] For example, in order to assassinate the ruler of Zhao, Yu Rang blistered his body with lacquer to disguise his appearance and swallowed charcoal to alter the sound of his voice.[38] Even more heinous, Yao Li reportedly had King Holu conspicuously execute his own wife and children, burn their bodies in the marketplace, and chop off his right hand to establish a reason for his hatred and thus be welcomed by the valiant son of Holu's uncle, then in exile.[39]

Although imperial China resorted to assassins to eliminate troublesome external enemies, particularly those out on the steppe, and to silence threats within the country, this readiness to employ covert agents for assassination purposes was particularly manifest during periods of fragmentation when numerous states were contending for power.[40] Nevertheless, the most famous instance remains Jing Ke's botched attempt late in the Warring States Period to stab the king of Qin with a dagger concealed in a map case.

Prince Dan of Yan adopted this desperate measure to forestall an imminent invasion by overwhelming Qin forces. The exploit, which is preserved in the *Shiji*'s "Assassins" and provided the impetus for recent movies, struck such a responsive cord in subsequent Chinese generations that the name of the warrior chosen for the task, Jing Ke, became a common term for "assassin."[41] It happened that a disfavored Qin general had recently sought refuge with the prince, so the subterfuge of offering his head and a map of Yan was employed to gain access to the heavily isolated emperor. To ensure that the extremely sharp dagger would prove lethal, the prince even had it drenched with poison and "tried out on men whereupon it was found that if their clothes were stained by blood they immediately died."

When the crucial moment arrived, rather than stabbing the emperor, the heroic Jing Ke unexpectedly decided to extort an agreement and was eventually struck down by a physician who used his medicine bag as a weapon. Thus, despite the absence of armed guards on the dais and the emperor's inability to draw his own long sword, the effort devolved into an exercise in righteous futility. Moreover, it compelled the king of Yan to execute his own son for having initiated the plot and to present his head to Qin in an attempt to preserve the state—though to little avail, because Yan was executed five years later in 222 BCE.

The *Art of War* initiated consciousness of the importance of disinformation, but it was the authors of the late Warring States work known as the *Six Secret Teachings* (*Liutao*) who compiled two explosive chapters on clandestine programs that were designed to systematically undermine enemy states, and even overthrow or subjugate them without conflict, thereby realizing the *Art of War*'s ideal of victory without combat.[42] As late as the Ming Dynasty, these two chapters, coupled with the *Art of War*'s "Employing Spies," continued to be viewed as the very foundation of spycraft.[43] The first, titled "Civil Offensive," though purportedly a program developed by the Tai Gong to undermine the Shang emperor, preserves material of such historical and contemporary importance that it merits being reproduced almost completely:[44]

There are twelve measures for civil offensives. First, accord with what the ruler likes in order to accommodate his wishes. He will eventually grow arrogant and invariably mount some perverse affair.

Second, become familiar with those he loves in order to fragment his awesomeness. When men have two different inclinations, their loyalty invariably declines.

Third, covertly bribe his assistants and foster a deep relationship with them. While they still bodily stand in his court, their emotions will be directed outside.

Fourth, assist him in his licentiousness and indulgence in music in order to dissipate his will. Make generous gifts of pearls and jade and ply him with beautiful women. Speak deferentially, listen respectfully, follow his commands, and accord with him in everything.

Fifth, treat his loyal officials very generously but reduce the gifts you provide to the ruler. Delay his emissaries; do not listen to their missions. When he eventually dispatches other men, treat them with sincerity, embrace and trust them. The ruler will then again feel you are in harmony with him. If you then manage to treat his formerly loyal officials very generously, his state can be plotted against.

Sixth, make secret alliances with his favored ministers but visibly keep his less favored outside officials at a distance. His talented people will then fall under external influence while enemy states encroach upon his territory.

Seventh, if you want to bind his heart to you, you must offer generous presents. To gather in his assistants, loyal associates, and loved ones, you must secretly show them the gains that they can realize by colluding with you. Have them slight their work, and then his preparations will be futile.

Eighth, gift him with great treasures and make plans with him. When the plans are successful and profitable, he will have faith in you. This is what is termed "being closely embraced."

Ninth, honor him with praise. Do nothing that will cause him personal discomfort. Display the proper respect accruing to a great power and your obedience will certainly be trusted. Magnify his honor, being the first to gloriously praise him, humbly embellishing him as a Sage.

Tenth, be submissive so that he will trust you and thereby learn about his true situation. Accept his ideas and respond to his affairs as if you were twins. Once you have learned everything, subtly gather in his power.

Eleventh, block up his access by means of the Tao. Among subordinates there is no one who does not value rank and wealth nor hate danger and misfortune. Secretly express great respect toward them, and gradually bestow valuable gifts in order to gather the more outstanding talents. Accumulate your own resources until they become substantial while manifesting an appearance of shortage. Covertly bring in wise knights and entrust them with planning great strategy. Attract courageous knights and augment their spirit. Even when they are sufficiently rich and honored, continue to increase them. When your faction has been fully established, you will have attained the objective referred to as "blocking his access."

Twelfth, support his dissolute officials in order to confuse him. Introduce beautiful women and licentious sounds in order to befuddle him. Send him outstanding dogs and horses in order to tire him. From time to time, allow him great power in order to entice him to greater arrogance.

When these twelve measures are fully employed, they will become a military weapon.

The measures expounded for undermining enemy rulers in the considerably shorter "Three Doubts," though consistent, tend to focus upon isolating and debauching the ruler. For example:

> Cause the estrangement of his favored officials by using his favorites, and disperse his people by means of the people. If you want to cause his close supporters to become estranged from him, you must do it by using what they love, making gifts to those he favors, giving them what they want. Tempt them with what they find profitable, thereby making them ambitions. Anyone who covets profits will be extremely happy at the prospects, and their remaining doubts will be ended.
>
> Now without doubt the Tao for attacking is to first obfuscate the king's clarity and then attack his strength. Debauch him with beautiful women; entice him with profit. Nurture him with flavors and provide him with the company of female musicians. Then after you have caused his subordinates to become estranged from him, you must cause the people to grow distant from him.

Several of the later military writings include at least a few passages on techniques that might be employed to adversely affect, if not fatally subvert, enemy rulers, including Li Quan's "Techniques for Secret Plots," in which economic measures are visible:

> Subjugating the enemy's forces without engaging in combat is the pinnacle of excellence. The pinnacle employs plots and plans, the next highest human affairs, while the lowest conducts warfare by attacking. Those who employ plots and plans mystify and confuse the enemy's ruler; secretly influence his slanderous ministers to affect his affairs; muddle him with sorcerers and soothsayers; and cause him to respect ghosts and serve spirits. They cause him to indulge in colors and embroidery while cheapening the value he places on grains and foodstuffs, thereby emptying out his granaries and warehouses. They send him beautiful women to unsettle his mind and dispatch skilled carpenters to inveigle him into constructing palaces, rooms, and high towers in order to exhaust the state's wealth and dissipate their strength in labor, thus changing the ruler's nature and inducing licentious practices.
>
> When you block off the ruler's access to external information and debauch him with licentiousness, attack him with the lure of profits, pleasure him with

music, nurture his tastes, and cause him to regard the deceitful as the trustworthy, the trustworthy as deceitful, the loyal as rebellious, and the rebellious as loyal, then those who offer loyal remonstrance will perish while sycophants will be rewarded.

When he exiles worthy men to the wilds, retains menial men in official positions, issues urgent orders, and imposes brutal punishments, the people will not sustain his mandate to rule. This is termed overthrowing the ruler through secret plots without fighting. When the destruction of his state has been achieved, if you follow up with troops the ruler can be captured, his state subjugated, his cities seized, and his masses scattered.[45]

Other chapters that advocate causing consternation in the enemy include the aptly titled "Putting the Enemy in Difficulty," in the Song Dynasty *Huqian Jing*, and this entry on "focus," in the late Ming Dynasty *Bingfa Baiyan*:

What the enemy invariably relies upon for their movement is termed their focus. You must first observe the location of the enemy's focus and then seize what they rely upon. If the enemy takes their strategists as their focus, concentrate upon expelling them. If they take their enlightened generals as their focus, concentrate upon eliminating them. If they take their intimate, trusted ministers as their focus, you can estrange them. If they take fame and righteousness as their focus, you can destroy them. Extract their roots; strike their strategic points; defeat their secret plans; alienate their reliable allies; strip away their basis; and destroy their customary profits.

The chapter concludes by advising that, at a minimum, capable commanders should be eliminated through rumor, aspersion, and slander, techniques that were employed with great success in antiquity to dramatically reverse inimical strategic circumstances.[46]

These pronouncements were not simply theoretical but rather thoughtful elaborations based at least in part upon numerous individual historical instances and, by the time of the *Six Secret Teachings*, Yue's annihilation of Wu. Initially, after several years of draconian efforts in preparation for avenging his father's death at Yue's hands, King Fuchai of Wu vanquished Yue in battle. However, King Goujian was allowed to retain a small enclave where he conducted sacrifices to Yue's ancestors. While visibly humbling himself and conspicuously serving Wu, he determinedly nurtured the state's remnant strength and embarked upon a systematic program to debauch Fuchai and subvert his state. Although many of the diabolical measures are known only from semi-historical accounts too extensive to recount here, they exerted inestimable influence upon later military thinkers and therefore deserve at least brief summation.[47]

As portrayed in the *WuYue Chunqiu* chapter known as "Goujian's Secret Strategy," Yue commenced by corrupting the sycophantic minister Bo Pi, who then strove to negate the effects of any criticism directed against Yue and prevent the imposition of restrictive measures.[48] Wen Zhong then formulated the following nine-point program intended to strengthen the state and subvert Wu's government:

> First, revere Heaven and serve ghosts in order to seek their blessings. Second, make generous presents and monetary gifts to the ruler and numerous presents and bribes to please his ministers. Third, make the five grains expensive in order to empty their state, take advantage of what the ruler desires in order to weary his people. Fourth, present the ruler with beautiful women in order to befuddle his mind and confuse his plans. Fifth, send the ruler skilled artisans and excellent materials to stimulate him to undertake palaces and mansions and thereby exhaust their wealth. Sixth, dispatch sycophantic ministers, causing the ruler to become easily attacked. Seventh, stiffen those ministers who dare to remonstrate, forcing them to commit suicide. Eighth, enrich your country and prepare the implements of war. Ninth, discipline your soldiers in order to exploit the ruler's perversity.

The effects of these machinations and Fuchai's profligacy were vigorously opposed by the loyal Wu Zixu, but he was marginalized, slandered, and finally cast aside before dying ignominiously just before Wu's vanquishment. Other than depleting the state's energy in the construction of magnificent palaces with materials sent by Yue, one of the key measures was exploiting Fuchai's licentious tendencies. Two surpassingly beautiful women, the subsequently famous Xi Shi and Zheng Dan, who "were adorned with the finest silks, taught manners and bearing, and educated for three years," were eventually presented. Even though there were historical precedents for the state's being destroyed though the deliberate submission of courtesans—the Xia through Mei Xi, the Shang through Da Ji, and the Zhou through Bao Si—they were not only accepted but even seen as proof of Goujian's loyalty.

Other Means of War

Even more imaginative was what appears to have been the first Chinese use of ecological warfare in a plot that would be condemned as heinous and dastardly for two thousand years. It was implemented by first pretending to be suffering from a grain shortage and borrowing a large quantity from Wu, then repaying it with seeds for a supposedly much-improved, higher-yielding variety that had actually been secretly heated to prevent germination. Wu therefore suffered from a famine that severely enervated it, opening the way for an invasion. Ironically, as only three of the nine measures were ever implemented over the course of many years, when Wen Zhong suffered the fate of many overly clever individuals and was about to be executed, Goujian sarcastically ordered him to employ the remaining six on behalf of his forbearers against Wu's ancestors, who were already resident in the netherworld. Although Goujian's measures required many years before Yue could strike and obliterate Wu, this unimaginable reversal of fortunes created an indelible impression upon subsequent generations, convincing them that systematically implemented subversive programs could achieve epochal results.

Covert methods intended to subvert other states—encompassing bribes, rumors, and estrangement techniques, having proven highly successful—rapidly proliferated in the Warring States period. However, the most thorough exploitation of bribes, estrangement, and even assassination was undertaken by the state of Qin out in the western hinterland.[49] Initially an insignificant, semicivilized state on the periphery of Zhou culture, Qin emerged from the ruthless strife of the Spring and Autumn and Warring States periods as the realm's dominant power by manipulating, battling, and subverting the remaining six powerful contenders. Although Qin's military juggernaut still had to wrest final victory on the battlefield, bribery proved to be the most effective covert practice amid the era's lethal circumstances. When employed as an adjunct to false rumors designed to besmirch and disparage, it ensured the exile and execution of many loyal officials and meritorious commanders. It also empowered the highly successful, systematic policy of disinformation and subversion that was implemented by Qin's persuasive double agents, including the infamous Su Qin.

Aggressively employing bribes to facilitate the achievement of world domination was initially proposed after Qin's enemies convened a ministerial meeting for the purpose of forming an obstructive strategic alliance. Believing that "sumptuous entertainments" and an "ostentatious display of gifts" could mollify adversaries and estrange potential allies from each other, the king appropriated five thousand catties of gold for the task. Even before the allotted amount had been expended, the realm's high officials reportedly fell to fighting among themselves.[50] Slightly later Qin again resorted to these measures when the pivotal states of Han and Wei were targeted by "the king of Qin who provided Dun Ruo with ten thousand catties of gold. Dispatched eastward, he traveled among the states, where he brought Han and Wei's generals and ministers under Qin's influence. Then he went north to traverse Yan and Zhao, where he effected the death of General Li Mu. Thus, when the king of Qi paid a diplomatic visit to Qin, the four other states had to follow."[51] This laconic account understates the significance of the achievements. Li Mu and Sima Shang, Zhao's last capable generals, had recently inflicted heavy casualties on Qin's armies when they successfully repelled several Qin onslaughts. They were eliminated by "making generous gifts of gold to Zhao's favored ministers and employing them as turned agents who claimed that Li Mu and Sima Shang wanted to betray Zhao and join Qin in order to receive generous fiefs. Becoming suspicious, the king had them replaced before executing Li Mu and exiling Sima Shang. Three months later, Wang Jian extensively destroyed Zhao's army through a sudden fervent strike, slew Zhao's commanding general, and captured both the king and his generals. Qin then extinguished the state of Zhao."[52]

About 237 BCE the noted strategist Wei Liaozi similarly advised the king to systematically employ bribes to weaken the other feudal states and "confuse their plans."[53] Concurring, the king appointed him as an adviser, whereupon Li Si, who wielded the government's power, added a lethal dimension by "secretly dispatching strategists bearing gold and jewels to offer as presents as they wandered among the feudal lords exercising their persuasions. Famous officials in the courts of the feudal lords who might be tempted by material goods were to be entangled with abundant gifts; those unwilling to collaborate were to be assassinated with sharp swords. Whenever his plan to estrange the feudal lords from their ministers proved successful, the king of Qin would then have his expert generals follow up with attacks."[54]

In conjunction with the successful implementation of these subversive measures, the specter of Qin's awesome military power, augmented by its reputation for ferocity, cowered many states into abandoning "provocative" military preparations and adopting policies of appeasement. Whether they remained ignorant of the threat's extensiveness or simply wished to avoid antagonizing the king of Qin, they not only failed to conclude strategic partnerships but also stupidly inflicted substantial losses on each other by battling among themselves. Sunzi's ideal of "thwarting their alliances" having been realized, the isolated states were then sequentially defeated with comparative ease, which illustrates well the dual emphasis of traditional Chinese intelligence practice: information coupled with active subversion.

Notes

1. In contrast with the West, spycraft was a much-discussed topic in Chinese antiquity. For earlier Western practices, see N. J. E. Austin and N. B. Rankov, *Exploratio: Military and Political Intelligence in the Roman World from the Second Punic War to the Battle of Adrianople* (London: Routledge, 1995).

2. For a discussion of how traditional theory and historical practice are being employed in contemporary China, see Ralph Sawyer, "Chinese Strategic Power: Myths, Intent, and Projections," *Journal of Military and Strategic Studies* 9, no. 2 (2006); and the final chapters of Ralph Sawyer, *The Tao of Deception: Unorthodox Warfare in Historic and Modern China* (New York: Basic Books, 2007).

3. Historians continue to debate whether the *Art of War* (or at least the core of the text) was composed by Sunzi at the end of the sixth century BCE, compiled by his disciples shortly after his death, or created from lessons derived from fifth-century and early-fourth-century warfare in the mid–fourth century. For an overview, see "Historical Introduction," in Ralph Sawyer, *Sun-tzu Art of War* (Boulder, CO: Westview Press, 1994).

4. Ibid., "Initial Estimations."

5. Ibid. According to Michael Handel, Sunzi was "the first to explicitly discuss the role of what is today termed net assessment." See "Intelligence in Historical Perspective," in Michael Handel, *Go Spy the Land* (Westport, CT: Praeger, 1992), 179–80.

6. Sawyer, *Sun-tzu Art of War*, "Incendiary Attacks."

7. Ibid., "Initial Estimations."

8. The crucial concept of what might best be termed the "strategic configuration of power" is elucidated by ibid., chap. 5. The effects are imagined as the cascade of pent-up water in chap. 4 and the whetstone as well as a boulder rolling down a mountain in chap. 5.

9. Ibid., "Configurations of Terrain." The admonition to know the enemy is the chief reason that the *Art of War* serves as a crucial inspiration for cyber warfare practitioners.

10. Ibid., "Nine Terrains."

11. *Guanzi*, "Seven Standards." An eclectic work traditionally attributed to the great Spring and Autumn governmental adviser Guan Zhong, the *Guanzi* was probably composed during the fourth and third centuries BCE.

12. "Temple Victory." The chapter's title refers to undertaking these calculations in the temple, as in Sunzi's time, and the text quotes heavily from *Art of War* passages referring to them.

13. *Li Weigong Bingfa*.

14. In the middle of the Southern Sung Dynasty, Shi Zimei penned a series of commentaries to the *Seven Military Classics* so extensive as to merit the title of lectures. They were extensively studied and reprinted in both Japan and China over the centuries.

15. *Toubi Futan*.

16. For a discussion of the *Yi Jing*'s employment in the Spring and Autumn period, see Kidder Smith, "Zhouyi Interpretation from Accounts in the *Zuozhuan*," *Harvard Journal of Asiatic Studies* 49, no. 2 (1989): 421–63.

17. Sawyer, *Sun-tzu Art of War*, "Employing Spies." Despite Sunzi's efforts and the strong attack made upon otherworldly methods by the Warring States, *Wei Liaozi*, prognostication would continue to flourish within the military tradition. For a brief discussion, see Ralph Sawyer, "Paradoxical Coexistence of Prognostication and Warfare," *Sino-Platonic Papers* 157 (August 2005); for examples, see Sawyer, "Martial Prognostication," in *Military Culture in Imperial China*, edited by Nicola Di Cosmo (Cambridge, MA: Harvard University Press, 2009).

18. Sawyer, *Sun-tzu Art of War*, "Employing Spies."

19. Sawyer, *Sun-tzu Art of War*, "Selecting the Troops." The *Military Methods* was recently rediscovered after being lost for two thousand years. For a complete translation, see Ralph Sawyer, *Sun Pin Military Methods* (Boulder, CO: Westview Press, 1995).

20. Sawyer, *Sun-tzu Art of War*, "Spies in Warfare."

21. Ibid.

22. The five basic categories of agents are essentially replicated in such writings as the *Li Weigong Bingfa* and the military section of the *Changduan Jing*, a composite text that dates to the first quarter of the eighth century CE that heavily quotes the *Art of War*'s five categories before illustrating them with intriguing historical examples. Even Jie Xuan, compiler of the late Ming Dynasty *Bingfa Baiyan*, acknowledged that his twelve agents were essentially congruent with Sunzi's five.

23. This restatement may be commentary that has become intermixed with the text.

24. Space precludes any consideration of the important topics of secrecy, operations and control, and especially counterintelligence for which Ralph Sawyer consulted, *The Tao of Spycraft* (Boulder, CO: Westview Press, 1998).

25. Du You is one of the important commentators in the well-known *Ten Commentaries* edition of the *Art of War*.

26. "Zingren," which might be translated as "Roving Agents."

27. "Agent" (*jian*) in the *Bingfa Baiyan*. Although they entail some translation problems—requiring something like "agency through" or "clandestine action through"—Jie's concept is clear and the sixteen categories of activities are comprehensive.

28. The concept of the "unorthodox," first articulated in the *Art of War's* "Strategic Military Power," is a cornerstone of both traditional and contemporary Chinese military science. For a study of the "unorthodox," see Ralph Sawyer, *The Tao of Deception: Unorthodox Warfare in Historic and Modern China* (New York: Basic Books, 2007).

29. This differs from Sun-tzu's concept because they are not deliberately sacrificed.

30. Jie and other late writers often contemplated the character of men to be employed as spies, and they generally concluded that they should be drawn from all walks of life, not restricted to the intelligent and morally upright.

31. Wuzi, "Tao of the General."

32. For an extensive recounting of these measures as they emerged and were practiced from about the eighth through fourth centuries BCE, see Sawyer, *Tao of Spycraft*, first few chapters.

33. The ongoing nature and implications of these programs, especially their exploitation in peacetime as well as wartime, might well be noted.

34. China's first comprehensive history, the *Shiji*—a work that has exerted inestimable influence over the past two millennia not just in China but also in Korea and Japan—was compiled around the end of the second century BCE by Sima Qian and his father, Sima Tan.

35. An example appears in the Zhanguoce's *Yanyü*.

36. Jujubes were sometimes employed; e.g., see *Shishuo Xinyu*, "You Hui."

37. The stratagem of suffering flesh numbers among those included in the now-infamous *Thirty-Six Stratatgems* rediscovered about a century ago.

38. The incident is described in the *Shiji* chapter on assassins.

39. According to the semihistorical *WuYueh Chunqiu*, Yao managed to fatally wound Qingji in a boat before chopping off his remaining hand and feet, falling on his sword, and dying.

40. E.g., the Former Han employed an assassin to remove the rebellious king of Loulan. See *Han Shu*, "Fu Chang, Zheng Gan, Chen Duan."

41. A complete translation is given by Burton Watson, *Records of the Grand Historian, Qin Dynasty* (New York: Columbia University Press, 1993), 167–78.

42. They were subsequently condemned by Confucian-oriented literati for their supposed inhumanity and perverse approach to warfare, both held to be inconsistent with antiquity's great sages, prompting Ming Dynasty writers to marvel that they had survived.

43. E.g., Wang Mingle, an experienced, high-level Ming Dynasty commander and author of the *Dengtan Bijiu*, in "Ji Jiandie Shuo."

44. For a complete translation of the *Six Secret Teachings* with historical introduction and analysis, see Ralph Sawyer, *Seven Military Classics of Ancient China* (Boulder, CO: Westview Press, 1994); and Ralph Sawyer, *The Six Secret Teachings on the Way of Strategy* (Boston: Shambhala, 1996).

45. *Taibai Yinjing.*

46. E.g., the loyalty of the great general Yue Yi was questioned by double agents, resulting in him being removed from expeditionary command despite having swiftly conquered all but two of Qi's cities during the Warring States period. For a recounting, see Sawyer, *Tao of Spycraft*, 102ff. Similarly, Chen Ping eliminated Chu's chief strategist during the quest to establish the Han Dynasty.

47. The highly melodramatic story of Fuchai and Goujian's conflict quickly became the stuff of legend, streetside tales, and operas, and thus known to everyone, strategists as well as peasants. Core materials may be found in Wu Zixu's biography in the *Shihji*.

48. The *WuYue Chunqiu* is a somewhat fictionalized account probably written in the first century CE of the dramatic conflict between the two states of Wu and Yüeh. Although the reliability of its dialogues is highly questionable, the author may well have had access to oral transmission and records no longer extant, and was thoroughly knowledgeable about the area.

49. Contemporary Chinese strategists have particularly focused on the rise of the Qin as a model for emulation.

50. "Qinyu, 3," *Zhanguoce*.

51. "Qinyu, 4," *Zhanguoce*.

52. "Zhaoyu," *Zhanguoce*.

53. For a discussion of the incident and a complete translation of the book attributed to Wei Liaozi, see Sawyer, *Seven Military Classics*.

54. *Shi Ji*, "Li Si Liezhuan." The king referred to in the passage is the eventual unifier of all China, the first emperor of the Qin Dynasty.

CHAPTER 4

The Original Surveillance State

Kautilya's *Arthashastra* and Government by Espionage in Classical India

Philip H. J. Davies

The arrow shot by an archer may or may not kill a single man; but skilful intrigue devised by wise men can kill even those who are in the womb.

—KAUTILYA

Although research into ever-more-archaic antecedents of contemporary thought in fields like political theory and strategic thought is well established, only recently has a comparable effort been made with regards to intelligence. In such discussions the typical point of departure is China's Sun Tze whose chapter on the "divine skein" of military intelligence and his taxonomy of spies is often taken as the oldest nonscriptural account of espionage.[1] That discourse has been examined and expanded upon most intensively in recent years by Ralph Sawyer (see chapter 3).[2] More fragmentary information has also been examined to try and draw out a picture of intelligence in classical Rome, but close examination of other traditions such as the Arab and Islamic worlds and Byzantium has had to wait very much for the chapters in the present volume to receive at least some of the attention that they warrant.[3] Much the same might also be said of the Sanskrit tradition of intelligence thought as a branch line within ancient Indian writing on strategy and statecraft. Although there are passing references to the Kautilya, probably the leading figure in this lineage, there has been no detailed attempt to bring that tradition into the wider discussion of intelligence theory.[4] This is long overdue: India has been steadily emerging as one of the globe's leading powers, a crucial (and democratic) counterweight to mainland China in the Asian balance of power, and a major intelligence player in the current international arena.

Kautilya's *Arthashastra* represents one of the oldest treatises on strategy and statecraft. From an intelligence studies point of view, it has two main bases for relevance to the study of so-called intelligence theory. In the first place, unlike Sun Tze's work, the *Arthashastra* is a comprehensive textbook on statecraft, domestic governance, diplomacy, and foreign affairs as well as war. Consequently, it provides an intelligence doctrine relevant to peacetime as well as war and deals with domestic intelligence as well as foreign surveillance issues. This provides a breadth of intelligence doctrine that the "divine skein" does not need to articulate: domestic counter-espionage, criminal intelligence plus covert political and psychological operations, and what today we would term "disruptive action" all feature in the work of Kautilya's "institutes" of spies. Second, the work of spies is a theme that runs through the entire document in a way that Sun Tze's doctrine of what amounts to operational and tactical intelligence alone does not. For Kautilya, espionage underpins almost every domain of government activity. His "institutes of espionage" play key roles in everything from trading standards, taxation and revenue and criminal investigation to civil service performance monitoring, let alone national and regime security concerns more familiar to intelligence scholarship. Kautilya's vision is not merely of a counterintelligence state but an untrammeled espionage state where surveillance and provocation are as essential to the work of government as coinage and road building.

With this in mind, it is impossible not to reflect on what aspects of the Kautilyan tradition may have been resuscitated and carried forward in subcontinental politics since independence. For the most part, a detailed examination of the current influence of Kautilya on intelligence theory and practice on the subcontinent lies beyond the purview of the current discussion apart from some preliminary observations and speculations at the end of this chapter. Neither does the present author pretend to be an authority on Sanskrit or Indian culture and politics. Rather, the goal in the present discussion is to lift out a range of key concepts and lines of reasoning from the *Arthashastra* so that they may be placed alongside other traditions and lineages of and general issues within "intelligence theory." The source text used herein is the fourth edition of Rudrapatnam Shamasastry's translation, published in 1951. Even with the limited ambitions of the current work, however, it is apparent that a profound understanding of Kautilya's thinking on intelligence awaits a return to, and mining down into, the original Sanskrit to unpack subtleties and details of the original that may well have escaped the original translator. Shamasastry was an Orientalist and antiquarian and not a military or intelligence scholar or practitioner.[5] In this capacity, the following discussion should be read as a purely preliminary exploration of the question, and as an exhortation to those with the necessary combination of linguistic and intelligence studies competencies to perform the kind of thorough archaeology of Kautilya's theory of intelligence that it so richly deserves and strategic thought in the globalized twenty-first-century world so seriously needs.

Kautilya's Context

Since Shamasastry's rediscovery of the manuscript of the *Arthashastra* at the turn of the last century, the exact identity of its author and provenance of its specific contents has been subject to considerable uncertainty and debate.[6] In some discussions Kautilya's authorship is accepted as a working hypothesis,[7] whereas in others it is simply taken as a given.[8] However, the actual provenance of the *Arthashastra* is virtually irrelevant to its impact and perceived credibility and consequently its authority and influence in shaping contemporary Indian strategic thought. What matters is the intellectual credibility and authority the *Arthashastra* holds in subcontinental military and strategic thought, and that is more than evident.[9] For the present intents and purposes, it is sufficient to say that the conventional account is that Kautilya was the eminence grise behind the founder of the Maurya Empire, Chadragupta Maurya. The Maurya Empire lasted from approximately 321–185 BC, and was the first empire to consolidate the lion's share of the subcontinent under its third ruler, Ashoka the Great. Kautilya, also known in various contexts as Vishnugupta and more commonly Chanakya, supposedly mentored Chandragupta in establishing the empire, then subsequently served as his prime minister. The *Arthashastra*, which means roughly "science [*shastra*] of politics [*artha*]," was one of three texts attributed to Kautilya as manuals for Chandragupta and his successors on the conduct of government and the economy. The other texts dealt primarily with moral philosophy and so fall outside the current discussion.

Despite its antiquity, the *Arthashastra* was by no means the first Indian text to discuss the role of spies in politics and war. Apart from internal evidence in the text in which Kautilya appears to debate the wisdom of prior authors, the use of spies is discussed in the *Rigveda* religious text, which dates to the second millennium BC and in which spies serve the deities Varuna, Agni, and Soma.[10] The *Arthashastra* does, however, appear to predate the *Baghavad Gita*, which also sees spies playing a role in the conflict between the two great houses of the Pandavas and the Kauravas.[11] It also predates another main text on statecraft, the Ordinances of Manu, which were written in response to the political strife that followed the collapse of the Mauryas. This suggests an attitude toward espionage at least paralleling if not deriving directly from that of Kautilya. As Richard Popplewell has noted of the *Arthashastra*, "Though a prescription for ideal government, [it] undoubtedly describes a state of affairs approximating reality," which was emulated not only by Chandragupta but also by his greatest Maurya successor Ashoka the Great and later by the Islamic Mogul emperors (although they were also inheritors of the Arab and Islamic intelligence tradition discussed elsewhere in this volume).[12]

The *Arthashastra* subsequently appears to have been lost in or around the twelfth century until found by Shamasastry circa 1904. The discovery was virtually by accident, as Shamasastry was sorting through palm-leaf manuscripts at the Oriental Research Institute in Mysore. After having discovered and recognized the document for what it was, Shamasastry edited and published the Sanskrit text in 1909, and then followed with an English translation in 1915.[13] Despite its interval of obscurity, however, Kautilya's text can be said to have a pivotal and formative role in the development of Indian political thought in the early and medieval periods.

The Institutes of Espionage

The core of Kautilya's intelligence doctrine—or rather, espionage doctrine—is the role of several different so-called institutes of espionage. The term "institutes" is confusing because what Kautilya actually appears to be talking about is standardized classes or categories of spy rather than institutes in the sense of agencies or organizations. The term appears to be an artifact of Shamasastry's translation of the Sanskrit word *samstha*, which is used in current parlance to refer to an association or group. This usage seems to have confounded Indian authors as much as anyone else, and they have typically passed over the puzzle by simply treating the use of the term in Kautilya as equivalent to "class" or "category."[14] These categories consist of "spies under the guise of a fraudulent disciple (*kapatika-chhatra*), a recluse (*udasthita*), a householder (*grihapatika*), an ascetic practicing austerities (*tapasa*), a classmate or a colleague (*satri*), a firebrand (*tikshna*), a poisoner (*rasada*), a mendicant woman (*bhikshuki*)." The categorization is further complicated by the fact that fraudulent disciples, recluses, ascetics, householders, and mendicant women are clearly forms of cover; the notion of a "classmate" spy refers to a particular recruitment pool, and the "firebrand" or "fiery spy" and poisoner are particular roles in special operations and irregular warfare.

A further distinction is drawn between principal informant networks that operate in particular vicinities and "wandering spies" who are roaming freely throughout the kingdom. Wandering spies were expected to communicate their information to their masters in government through cipher writing and cutouts (often drawn from members of the resident networks).[15] The two systems are intended to act as cross-checks on one another's reporting, and consequently Kautilya is adamant that neither the regular nor wandering spies should have any knowledge of each other.[16] That being said, both the resident and wandering networks are composed of the five basic types of spy. In parallel, agents from the resident networks could be deployed as roaming spies in their own right under various pretexts. Consequently, Kautilya recommends triangulating what amount to three separate field organizations: resident "institute" spies, wandering spies, and select resident "institute" agents dispatched in a roaming role. The goal here is validation and verification of the lines of reporting generated by the different espionage systems. He recommends: "When the information thus received from these three different sources is exactly of the same version, it shall be held reliable." The same strategy was to be used to detect deception or incompetence because "if they (the three sources) frequently differ, the spies concerned shall be either punished in secret or dismissed."[17]

Of the eight "institutes" or classes of spy elaborated in the *Arthashastra*, half of them are essentially forms of religious cover. India, of course, is a pervasively and intensely religious and spiritual culture, with holy figures from a variety of indigenous and imported faiths who have very real degrees of privileged status and mobility. The traditional Hindu caste system of social stratification was intimately interwoven into the Vedic religious tradition and regulated ritual, political, and economic activity at a very fine level of granularity and with far higher degree of rigidity than either the vassalage and manorialism of European feudalism or the Confucianist classes of imperial China. This meant that access and therefore surveillance across multiple professions and communities were often delimited by constraints imposed by the boundaries of the four principal castes, or *varna*, of the system, which consisted of the religious Brahmins, the politico-military Kshatriyas, the trade and artisan Vaishyas, and the agricultural Sudras.[18] The defining principles of the caste system were, however, articulated and legitimated through religious doctrine. Consequently, religious cover would offer a comparatively high degree of legitimacy and freedom of movement to access the various strata of Hindu society, particularly the social, political, and military leaderships that few other status roles would permit.

Kautilya therefore recommends recruiting "recluses," who are "initiated into asceticism" and "possessed of foresight and good character." The monarch should then support the recluse with funds to provide agricultural land and facilities to support not only himself but also "many disciples" who also serve as subagents under the recluse and recruit their own subordinate subagent networks. All the resulting information should then be channeled through the recluse. In much the same fashion, a "man with a shaved head . . . or braided hair" but who is in need of money can be deployed "under the guise of an ascetic practicing austerities." Like the recluse, the ascetic is expected to recruit disciples as subagents, but he is also expected to make a show of living in poverty as a sign of their holiness—although, Kautilya adds, "he may take in secret his favorite foodstuffs." In a similar fashion, agents may join the retinue of a public or religious figure to serve as "fraudulent disciples" and report on their nominal masters.[19] Wandering female spies were also supposed to employ religious cover. For targeting the upper two castes, the Brahmins and Kshatriyas, Kautilya recommends a "poor widow of Brahman cast, very clever and desirous to earn her livelihood." Such an agent would be "honored in the king's harem [and] shall frequent the residences of the king's prime ministers" reporting on the intimate lives of the highest political elites. Equivalent monitoring of lower-caste communities could be secured by recruiting women from the Sudra caste who would shave their heads and affect a spiritual and ascetic lifestyle.[20]

Among the middle-class Vaishya caste of traders and farmers, the *Arthshastra* recommends recruiting "cultivators" who have fallen on hard times as "householder spies." Provided the individuals in question are gifted, like the recluse, with "foresight and pure character," they should be provided with funds and assistance to reestablish themselves in exchange for acting as informants.[21] Merchants should also be recruited, not only for the information they provide but also to reinforce the cover of agents using religious cover by becoming supposed disciples of recluses and ascetics. In this capacity they could widely attribute supernatural powers to their supposed spiritual leader and also collude with the ascetic in choreographing fraudulent public demonstrations of such powers. This, in turn, would strengthen their reputations and improve the access of recluses and ascetics and of their subagents serving as full-time disciples.[22]

The notion of "classmate spies" (*satri*) is a more idiosyncratic concept. Not so much a form of operational cover as a recruitment pool, *satri* are described as "orphans (*asambindhinah*) who are necessarily fed by the state and are put to study science, palmistry, . . . sorcery, . . . the duties of the various orders of religious life, legerdemain, . . . and reading of omens and augury."[23] From within these professions, *satri* could report on what they observed, but they could also serve as agents provocateurs flushing out opponents of the regime by pretending to be "opposing factions shall carry on disputations in places of pilgrimage . . . in assemblies, houses, corporations, . . . and amid congregations of people."[24] Besides providing their own information, *satri* were also designated as the preferred couriers for the various wandering spies.[25]

Kautilya places a heavy emphasis on provocation and special operations. Consequently, a particularly central role is occupied throughout the *Arthashastra* by *tikshna*, so-called firebrands or fiery spies. Firebrands are colorfully described as "brave desperados of the country who, reckless of their own life, confront elephants or tigers [and] fight mainly for the purpose of earning money."[26] Firebrands were to be recruited to serve as saboteurs, assassins, and provocateurs. Another class of spies employed in the special operations field were "poisoners" (*rasasa*). Poisoners were bluntly described by Kautilya as "those who have no trace of filial affection left in them and who are very cruel and indolent."[27] Their task was, for example, to poison opponents of the regime, or to murder others and arrange for suspicion to be cast on nominal subversive elements.

The result was supposed to be a surveillance network covering the entire country. Within that network one would find "merchant spies inside forts; saints and ascetics in the suburbs of forts; the cultivator and the recluse in country parts; herdsmen in the boundaries of the country," while tribal chieftains in the outlying districts and wilderness would be paid to watch the frontiers. At the same time, informant networks within households were to be recruited in the form of "hump-backed dwarf, the eunuch, women of accomplishments, the dumb" along with ethnic Dravidians who did not subscribe to the Vedic faith and were designated the "Mleccha" caste.[28] Once earmarked as agents, Kautilya recommends that

> those who are of good family, loyal, reliable, well trained in the art of putting on disguises appropriate to countries and trades, and possessed of knowledge of many languages and arts, shall be sent by the king to espy in his own country the movements of his ministers, priests, commanders of the army, the heir-apparent, the door-keepers, the officer in charge of the harem, the magistrate, . . . the collector-general [of taxes], the chamberlain, . . . the commissioner, . . . the city constable, . . . the officer in charge of the city, . . . the superintendent of transactions, . . . the assembly of councillors (*mantraparishad*), heads of departments, . . . the commissary-general, . . . and officers in charge of fortification, boundaries and wild tracts.[29]

Hardly any walk of life was to pass unobserved and unreported. Besides watching domestic developments activities, the network would also hold a counterintelligence brief, in which "spies sent by foreign kings shall also be found out by local spies; spies by spies of like profession."[30] In many respects the intelligence machine was actually the foundation of the rest of the government apparatus to ensure effectiveness, efficiency, and—above all—control.

Espionage in Routine Government

An important distinction between Kautilya and Sun Tze is that whereas the "divine skein" of espionage occupies one chapter in *The Art of War*, espionage is a recurrent, even pervasive theme throughout the *Arthashastra*. It is a central concern at every level of government, from the selection of key ministers and protection of the monarch from all threats—including those self-same ministers—through military activities and law enforcement down to the implementation of commercial standards such as weights and measures. It would not be an exaggeration to describe Kautilya's intelligence doctrine as not merely espionage within government but government by espionage.

Indeed, Kautilya even locates espionage as a central element in the king's daily routine, for which he goes so far as to provide a recommended hour-by-hour schedule. According to the *Arthashastra*,

> During the first one-eighth part of the day he [the king] shall post watchmen and attend to the accounts of receipts and expenditure; during the second part, he shall look to the affairs of both citizens and country people; during the third, he shall not only bathe and dine but also study; during the fourth, he shall not only receive gold . . . but also attend to the appointments of superintendents; during the fifth he shall correspond in writs . . . with the assembly of his ministers *and receive the secret information gathered by his spies*; during the sixth, he may engage himself in his favorite amusements or in self-deliberation; during the seventh, he shall superintend elephants, horses, chariots, and infantry; during the eighth part, he shall consider various plans of military operations with his commander in chief. At the close of the day, he shall observe the evening prayer.[31]

Thus not merely did intelligence form a central component of the ruler's daily routine; he was also fully expected by Kautilya to act as his own intelligence officer.

Although the *Arthashastra* covers domestic and foreign policy and security in considerable depth, Kautilya takes the view that domestic threats "should first be got rid of; for . . . internal troubles, like the fear from a lurking snake, are more serious than external troubles." As a result, internal and regime security occupy the opening chapters of the book, whereas the later portions are concerned with foreign relations and war. This also means that to understand Kautilya's view of intelligence, it is also necessary to take internal security and domestic policy as the point of departure for understanding his approach to espionage and intelligence, even when conducted abroad.

Regime and State Security

A major role of spies in Kautilya's approach to government was concerned with testing the reliability and loyalty of court and government officials. Indeed, espionage, provocation, and entrapment provided the foundation for a monarch's appointment of the entire upper echelons of the machinery of government. Assisted by his prime minister and high priest, the monarch is advised to test prospective senior officials with a range of "allurements." Under "religious allurement," a priest might be dismissed ostensibly for refusing to perform a given ritual for an "outcaste person." The dismissed priest would then send "classmate spies" to various candidate ministers, who would suggest that the king was unrighteous and should be overthrown. Likewise, a general in the military notionally dismissed for corruption would offer others "monetary allurement" to assist him in arranging regicide. Under "love allurement," suggests Kautilya, a "woman-spy, under the guise of an ascetic" and "highly esteemed in the harem" of leading ministers would tempt those ministers with the suggestion that "the queen is enamored of thee and has made arrangements for thy entrance into her chamber; besides this, there is also the certainty of large acquisitions of wealth." In another especially ruthless stratagem, the king would arrest an entire cohort of officials on trumped-up charges. Once they were imprisoned, "a spy, under the guise of a fraudulent disciple, pretending to have suffered imprisonment, may incite each of the ministers thus deprived of wealth and rank, saying that 'the king has betaken himself to an unwise course; well, having murdered him let us put another in his stead. We all think like this; what dost thou think?'" Unsurprisingly, this was termed "allurement under fear."[32]

The result was not merely a variety of "sickener" test to identify those who could be most fully trusted by the king. It actually became a scheme for assigning ministerial tasks. Thus those who passed the religious test would supervise "civil and criminal courts." Individuals resistant to financial temptation "shall be employed in the work of a revenue collector and chamberlain," whereas candidates resistant to "love allurement" were to "superintend the pleasure grounds." Potential ministers who did not give way to fear after being falsely arrested were to become what Shamasastry translates as "immediate service," which perhaps refers to direct employment in the service of the court. Above and beyond these individual tests, "those whose character has been tested under all kinds of allurement" would be employed as the monarch's ministers. This did not mean that those failing were simply dismissed or banished, however. Instead, safe positions were found for them overseeing "mines, timber and elephant forests, and manufactories."[33]

Such vetting of the national leadership was to be merely the leading edge of a more general approach to managing the state and society at large. "Assisted by the council of his ministers tried under espionage the king shall proceed to create spies," according to the doctrine outlined in the previous section.[34] Thereupon, "having set up spies over his [cabinet] ministers, the king shall proceed to espy both citizens and country people."[35] The resulting apparatus would monitor the lower echelons of government as well as urban and rural populations and would also ensure that "treacherous opponents of sovereignty shall be silenced."

Revenue, Commerce, and Law Enforcement

The routine tasks of government, which concerned economic and fiscal policy as well as law enforcement, figure centrally in the *Arthashastra*. In this regard

Kautilya's thought is more detailed than equivalent other thinkers, and espionage plays a central role in all three areas. As Kautilya warns his student comparatively early on, a "government officer, not caring to know the information gathered by espionage and neglecting to supervise the dispatch of work in his own department as regulated, may occasion loss of revenue to the government owing to his ignorance, or owing to idleness."[36] The significance of espionage arises because the misappropriation of funds has fewer obvious indicators than other property crimes like theft. Indeed, concludes Kautilya, "cases of embezzlement . . . can be ascertained through spies alone."[37]

As a result, a central figure in Kautilya's doctrine of intelligence is the collector-general of taxes. Besides the usual tasks of collecting taxes and forwarding the revenue to the Treasury, the collector-general was expected to recruit networks of spies targeted at a number of different requirements. The first target for this activity was to verify that households were contributing their allotted taxes and not underreporting revenues and assets. Toward this the collector-general was to recruit householder spies whose task it was to "ascertain the validity of the accounts (of the village and district officers) regarding the fields, houses, and families of each village—the area and output of produce regarding fields, right of ownership and remission of taxes with regard to houses, and the caste and profession regarding families." These spies were also to "ascertain the total number of men and beasts . . . as well as the amount of income and expenditure of each family." Above and beyond this, they were expected to "find out the causes of emigration and immigration of persons of migratory habit, the arrival and departure of men and women of condemnable . . . character," explained by Shamasastry as including "dancers, actors, and the like." Finally, they were also to report on "the movement of (foreign) spies."[38]

The second arm of this organization was to be provided by merchant spies. Their role was to report on "quantity and price" of items "such as minerals, or products of gardens, forest, and fields, or manufactured articles." Additionally, these agents were to monitor incoming foreign merchandise "of superior or inferior quality" and report to the collector-general on costs to foreign traders, such as road tolls, transportation fares, warehousing fees, and the subsistence costs of those traders.[39] A third network was to be established to keep tabs on the criminal underworld. This consisted of "spies under the guise of old and notorious thieves with their student bands" based at locations as diverse as crossroads, religious sites, bathing houses, and areas of the wilderness ("desert tracts, mountains, and thick-grown forests"). From these vantage points they were to report on "the causes of arrival and departure, and halt of thieves, enemies [of the state]" and, slightly oddly, "persons of undue bravery."[40] The resulting trio of networks would, therefore, provide the collector-general with the means to check reported revenues in the peasant agricultural sector, industry and trade in the cities and across frontiers, and finally the black and gray economies.

Another one of the collector-general's main tasks was detecting individuals who made a "wicked living through foul means" or abusing the powers of any office they held. Thus a range of agents under a bewilderingly diverse assortment of recommended covers—ranging from ascetics and travelers through bards and "buffoons" to "deaf, idiots," cooks, and various tradesmen—were to "ascertain the fair or foul dealings of villagers, or of the superintendents of villagers, and report the same."[41]

As always, however, provocation and entrapment figured centrally in Kautilya's methods. The collector-general's spies were to encourage judges to accept bribes to favor a putative associate, incite "a congregation of villagers" to help extort money from a local figure, or bribe individuals to bear false witness against someone. In much the same manner, suspected counterfeiters were to be encouraged to produce false coinage. In all these cases, of course, the agent would report the target's compliance and banishment of the wrongdoer promptly follow.[42] The collector-general was instructed to then "exhibit in public places these and other arrested criminals, and proclaim omniscient power of the king and among the people at large."[43]

Senior urban administrators were also exhorted to maintain their own agent networks at the municipal level. Consequently, a city superintendent was expected to recruit his own spies who carried an ongoing roving brief to "make a search for suspicious persons in the interior of deserted houses, in the workshops or houses of vintners and sellers of cooked rice and flesh, in gambling houses, and in the abode of heretics."[44]

Kleptocracy

Even as Kautilya recommended espionage to ensure the forthrightness of the monarch's underlings, he also offered it as a means for fraud and theft against those self-same underlings *by* the monarch. In a chapter titled "Replenishment of the Treasury," the *Arthashastra* advises that a king "who finds himself in a great financial trouble and needs money may collect" revenue through fraud conducted by the very covert machinery used to ensure commercial integrity. Toward this end he recommends an assortment of ploys to squeeze additional funds from his populace by deception and manipulation. For example, the monarch should arrange for a highly visible group of benefactors who publicly make a show of paying "handsome donations, and with this example, the king may demand of others," whereas "spies posing as citizens shall revile those who pay less." Fraudulent "sorcerers" should stage false infestations of spirits to panic townsfolk and then demand money to "propitiate" those demons. Other spies might arrange for the spectacle of "a serpent with numberless heads in a well connected with a subterranean passage," which is, in fact, a "drugged cobra," and then would "collect fees" from curiosity seekers who wish to view the monstrosity.[45]

More elaborate frauds included setting an agent up as a wealthy businessman who touts for investors from the populace or secures a sizable assortment of loans. Then, once a suitable amount of funds has been accumulated, "he may cause himself to be robbed of that amount" by other agents of the king. The "examiner of coins" and state goldsmith could also conduct a similar fraud.[46]

Another route was to employ provocation and confiscation. Prostitutes "under the garb of chaste women" could be recruited to become "enamored of persons who are seditious." Then the dissenters could be lured to the prostitutes' residences, the latter unmasked and the former imprisoned for immoral conduct and their wealth and possessions seized.[47] In a similar fashion "a spy, under the garb of a servant of a seditious person, may mix counterfeit coins with the wages . . . and pave the way for his [the master's] arrest." Alternatively, an agent "under the garb of a goldsmith, may undertake to do work in the house of a seditious person, and gather in his employer's house such instruments as are necessary to manufacture counterfeit coins."[48] In a similar, obliquely phrased ruse, one spy "attending as a servant of a seditious person" should plant "certain articles necessary for the installation of a king" and letters from the ruler's enemy on their putative master and then openly call upon a second spy in the household to explain their presence.[49] In both cases such planted evidence would provide the basis for imprisonment and appropriation, rather efficiently providing simultaneous remedies to concerns of both fiscal and regime security.

As something of an afterthought, however, Kautilya adds that "measures such as the above shall be taken only against the seditious and the wicked, and never against others."[50] It is far from clear whether this is a concern for propriety and proportionality or simply a caution not to manage the personal goal of framing and incarcerating one's own sources of political support and legitimacy.

Espionage in Diplomacy and War

As the epigraph to this chapter suggests, Kautilya shares Sun Tze's conviction that the highest level of strategic skill is to defeat a foe without ever engaging in a clash of arms. Kautilya is more direct in some respects, and he specifically advocates intrigue and subterfuge as the principal instruments of state policy for which the use of military force is essentially a fallback option. Indeed, his approach to foreign espionage is conditioned by an assumption similar to the Byzantine philosophy explored by Gustafson in chapter 5 that war rather than peace is the natural state of affairs between governments. Consequently, diplomacy and espionage are treated as being part of a continuum of intrigue, the only question being at what level the conflict is being conducted. Paradoxically, though discussion of diplomacy and war might be the point at which one could reasonably expect Kautilya and Sun Tze to most resemble one another, it is, in many respects, one of their most significant points of divergence. For though spying as information collection figures centrally in the *Arthashastra*'s approach to diplomacy, spying in wartime is described primarily in terms of sabotage, assassination, and irregular warfare—as special operations rather than special intelligence.

Kautilya outlines the role of envoys and their use of spies comparatively early in his volume (as compared with warfare, which is relegated to later but substantial chapters), and he places covert collection at the center of the envoy's role. Apart from assessing a potential adversary by direct observation in his accredited role, the running of espionage networks is taken as a basic task of the diplomatic envoy. In part this was to acquire information that was not overtly available, but it was also partly to verify the envoy's impressions from open sources and liaison: "Whatever information [the envoy] thus gathers he shall try to test by intrigues."[51] Toward these ends, the envoy was enjoined to secure the services of "ascetic and merchant spies" and their disciples, "spies under the disguise of physicians, and heretics" and "individuals receiving salaries from two states." These informants would also inform the diplomat of the activities of groups either favorable or hostile to his own monarch. As a result, in the *Arthashastra* the diplomat's tasks are to include not just the usual above-board tasks of conveying top-level messages and negotiating treaties, but also "gaining of friends, intrigue, sowing dissension among friends, fetching secret force" as well as kidnapping the relatives of foreign leaders, "gathering information about the movements of [enemy] spies, treaty violations and subversion by winning over the favor of envoy and government officers of the enemy."[52]

By the same token, Kautilya warns his readers to be on the outlook for attempts to subvert their state by foreign envoys or covert actors. Thus he recommends deploying spies who warn off his own citizens being wooed by the representative of a foreign power. Failing this, spies "in the garb of traitors" should mix with genuine traitors and distinguish domestic from foreign subversives. As a follow-up, "fiery spies" should then intervene and, having "made friendship with traitors," then "kill them with weapons or poison," and then murder and expose the "plotting foreigners."[53]

Although the chapters on war outline the making of encampments, troop configurations, and the choice between set-piece battles and hit-and-run "treacherous" warfare, there is no equivalent to a chapter on the role of spies in war for operational or tactical intelligence support. Perhaps this is because the preexistence of espionage networks set up by embassies, envoys, and expatriate residents before the outbreak of any conflict is taken by Kautilya as a given. Instead, there are various stratagems for using spies to set foreign states against one another, or for dividing groups and factions within an adversary's polity among themselves. Setting groups against one another over marital relationships plays a central role in much of this,[54] culminating in a chapter concerned entirely with what is termed the "battle of intrigue," in which a weaker king uses such disruptions as jealousy, kidnapping, and planting evidence of atrocities by the rival's troops against his own people to undermine a stronger foe.[55] There are proposed schemes for using fiery spies to engineer the assassination of the rival potentate either directly or by prompting members of his court to consider regicide, divide his military and political leaders, and even encourage "wild tribes" to attack and pillage the opponent on a new front.[56]

There is also an extended discussion of the use of spies to conduct a sabotage campaign. Suggested techniques include using agents to poison food and drink supplies, both for human consumption and that of livestock. Some spies disguised as cowherds or hunters should release dangerous animals to cause chaos and confusion. "Secret spies," it is also suggested, "may slay from behind the chiefs of infantry, cavalry, chariots, or elephants or they may set fire to the chief residences of the enemy." At the same time, "traitors" as well as wild tribes could initiate fighting and try to devastate the countryside and vulnerable transportation routes. Psychological ruses included having spies enter the enemy's capital, blow a large number of trumpets, and falsely claim that the city has fallen. In the confusion they might then kill the king or arrange for others to ambush him in the panic.[57] Spies occupy much the same roles when besieging a city.[58]

The Legacy of the *Arthashastra*

What Kautilya's *Arthashastra* constitutes is not merely a doctrine of espionage within wider statecraft but also one of statecraft built upon espionage as its basic means of internal governance as well as instrument of external strategy. At a certain level, this might seem unremarkably consistent with feudal practices in the West. Elizabethan intelligence under Walsingham and Cecil was as much concerned with uncovering domestic conspiracy as warning of foreign aggression. Moreover, a number of scholars writing on early modern England have noted the equally pervasive but oddly anodyne role of domestic intelligence and reporting networks under the Stuarts. Both Peter Fraser,[59] and Alan Marshall four decades later,[60] noted of the Stuart monarchs how domestic surveillance of the political classes had less to do with regime protection than the government of the day simply trying to measure the temperature of public opinion in an age before the mass media and MORI polls. But this is not really comparable to the *Arthashastra*. Kautilya's "institutes" were routinely directed not merely toward detection but also provocation and disruption both at home and abroad. Indeed, much of the time the use of the term "spy" in Shamasastry's translation is somewhat misleading; a more accurate but less wieldy term might be "clandestine operators," for whom espionage is but one of a range of tasks and not necessarily the most central or significant one. As a result, though at some level the surveillance state of the *Arthashastra* might have required its spies to perform the same basic domestic understanding role as the Stuarts, there was definitely an intrusive and ruthless political ethos above and beyond knowing one's national political self. K. J. Shah has argued in some detail that one must see Kautilya's stratagems as being set in the moderating moral context of *dharma*.[61] But even then he is forced to acknowledge that Kautilya's pursuit of an *artha* that meets the standards of *dharma* does so in terms that are "authoritarian and without the institution of rights."[62]

Although the original *Arthashastra* may have been lost for more than seven centuries between the twelfth and early twentieth centuries, it was in circulation and was influencing Indian thought on statecraft and intelligence for something like twice that duration after it was written. As one Indian scholar has noted of Kautilya's immediate intellectual successor: "The King was advised by Manu to constantly ascertain the strength of his enemy as well as his own through spies, through display of energy and through actual conduct of operations."[63] Thus Kautilya's espionage state provides the underlying context for Popplewell's observation that "one of the most notable differences between the two empires was the unwillingness of the British to continue Mogul practice of controlling both civil service and population through the extensive and systematized use of espionage."[64] In many respects, however, the intelligence agencies of the subcontinent appear to have returned to the Sanskrit pattern of espionage. India's agencies, especially the domestic Intelligence Bureau and external Research and Analysis Wing, have reputations for what might be termed an "action orientation,"[65] après Douglas Porch discussing the French agencies.[66] Much the same might also be said of the Pakistani intelligence apparatus and its sponsorship of Jihadist militants in Khashmir and elsewhere over the decades as what Kautilya would label *tikshna* or "firebrand spies."[67] Even though it passed into obscurity for a substantial interval, the *Arthashastra's* legacy and influence have been substantial throughout the evolution of politics, strategy, statecraft, and intelligence on the Indian subcontinent, and they remain so today.

Epigraph and Acknowledgment

Kautilya, *Kautilya's Arthashastra*, edited and translated by R. Shamasastry (Mysore: Sri Raghuveer Printing Press, 1951) (hereafter, *Arthashastra*), 405. I am deeply indebted to Pal "Paul" Dosaj of Trent University's Department of Philosophy for originally bringing Kautilya to my attention as an undergraduate in 1983.

Notes

1. There are a number of renderings of this particular concept; Griffith's choice of this phrase is a usefully evocative one; see Samuel B. Griffith, ed., *Sun Tzu: The Art of War* (Oxford: Oxford University Press, 1971), 145.

2. See, variously, Ralph D. Sawyer, *The Seven Military Classics of Ancient China* (Oxford: Westview Press, 1993), esp. 145–86; and Ralph D. Sawyer, *The Tao of Spycraft: Intelligence Theory and Practice in Traditional China* (Boulder, CO: Westview Press, 2004).

3. See, e.g., Daniel A. Fournie, "Harsh Lessons: Roman Intelligence in the Hannibalic War," *International Journal of Intelligence and Counterintelligence* 17, no. 3 (Fall 2004). Also see various works by Rose Mary Sheldon—e.g., Rose Mary Sheldon, "The Ancient Imperative: Clandestine Operations and Covert Action," *International Journal of Intelligence and Counter-intelligence* 10, no. 3 (Fall 1997); Rose Mary Sheldon, "Caesar, Intelligence, and Ancient Britain," *International Journal of Intelligence and Counterintelligence* 15, no. 1 (Spring 2002); and Rose Mary Sheldon, "The Spartacus Rebellion: A Roman Intelligence Failure?" *International Journal of Intelligence and Counterintelligence* 6, no. 1 (Spring 1993).

4. See, e.g., Richard Popplewell, *Intelligence and Imperial Defence: British Intelligence and the Defence of the Indian Empire 1904–1924* (London: Frank Cass, 1995), 8–9; and David Kahn, "An Historical Theory of Intelligence," *Intelligence and National Security* 16, no. 3 (Autumn 2001): 80.

5. Similar debates ran for decades concerning the relative merits of the various translations of Sun Tze.

6. The debates and uncertainties concurrent with Shamasastry's various editions of the work can be charted in successive prefaces to the *Arthashastra*, vii–xxxiii.

7. See, e.g., Rashed Uz Zaman, "Kautilya: The Indian Strategic Thinker and Indian Strategic Culture," *Comparative Strategy* 25 (2006): 233–35. I am indebted to Kristian Gustafson for this reference.

8. See, e.g., K. J. Shah, "Of Artha and the *Arthashastra*," in *Comparative Political Philosophy: Studies under the Upas Tree*, edited by Anthony J. Parel and Ronald C. Keith (New Delhi: Sage, 1992), 141–62.

9. Kautilya's authority and authorship are likewise taken as a given by Bhakar, Dikshitar, and Sarkar.

10. S. K. Bhakari, *Indian Warfare: An Appraisal of Strategy and Tactics in War in the Early Medieval Period* (Calcutta: Munshiram Manoharlal, n.d.), 87; V. R. Ramachandra Dikshitar, *War in Ancient India* (Madras: Macmillan, 1944), 351–52; Jagadish Narayan Sarkar, *The Art of War in Medieval India* (Calcutta: Munshiram Manoharlal, 1983), 176.

11. Dikshitar, *War*, 352–53. Current estimates date the *Gita* to the first century BC rather than somewhere between the fifth and second centuries, as had previously been believed.

12. Popplewell, *Intelligence*, 9.

13. A. V. Narasimha Murthy, "Centenary of *Arthashastra*'s Publication R Shamasastry: Discoverer of Kautilya's *Arthashastra*," *Organiser*, June 21, 2009; *Arthashastra*, iii–iv.

14. E.g., Bhakari, *Indian Warfare*, 86, refers to "an organisation [*samstha*] consisting of five categories or institutes" of agents, while Dikshitar, *War*, 354, takes a similar view of *samstha*, referring to a central espionage agency with "four important chapters on [*sic*] this institution." However, as will be seen below, Kautilya actually describes several different intelligence collection offices in departments as diverse as the Treasury, the military, and the monarch's private staff. Shamasastry himself gives the Sanskrit in the *Arthashastra* text in a manner that strongly indicates that *samstha* refers to the categories of spy and not their controlling headquarters, e.g., *Arthashastra*, 19. This is a typical point where an effective understanding of Kautilya still awaits a new interpretation of the original Sanskrit and cross-referencing to other manuscripts of the *Arthashastra* that were located after Shamasastry's original discovery.

15. *Arthashastra*, 20, 21.
16. Ibid., 21.
17. Ibid.
18. Significantly, the list excludes the "outcaste" Dalit communities.
19. *Arthashastra*, 17–18.
20. Ibid., 20.
21. Ibid., 18.
22. Ibid., 18–19.
23. Ibid., 19.
24. Ibid., 22.
25. Ibid., 20.
26. Ibid., 19; the original text here incorporates what appears to be a typographical error, reading instead "confront elephants and tigers in fight mainly. . . ."
27. Ibid., 20.
28. Ibid., 21.
29. Ibid., 20.
30. Ibid., 22.
31. Ibid., 37.
32. Ibid., 15–16.
33. Ibid., 16–17. Somewhat confusingly, Shamasastry employs the term "prime minister" to refer both to a singular first minister and to the equivalent of Cabinet ministers in the plural. Judging from his annotations to the translation, the Sanskrit term *mantri*, which generically means "minister," is apparently used in both contexts.
34. Ibid., 17.
35. Ibid., 22.
36. Ibid., 62.
37. Ibid., 69.
38. Ibid., 159.
39. Ibid., 159–60.
40. Ibid., 237–38.
41. Ibid.
42. Ibid., 238.
43. Ibid., 241.
44. Ibid., 162.
45. Ibid., 273.
46. Ibid., 274.
47. Ibid., 274, infra.
48. Ibid., 275.
49. Ibid., 275 infra.
50. Ibid.
51. Ibid., 31.
52. Ibid., 30, 31.
53. Ibid., 380.
54. Ibid., 407–10.
55. Ibid., 413–15.
56. Ibid., 415–17.
57. Ibid., 418–19.

58. Ibid., 429–32.

59. Peter Fraser, *The Intelligence of the Secretaries of State and Their Monopoly of Licensed News 1660–1688* (Cambridge: Cambridge University Press, 1956).

60. Alan Marshall, *Intelligence and Espionage in the Reign of Charles II, 1660–1685* (Cambridge: Cambridge University Press, 1994).

61. Shah, "Of Artha," 148–51.

62. Ibid., 161.

63. Sarkar, *Art of War*, 177.

64. Popplewell, *Intelligence*, 9.

65. Rigorous academic study of contemporary Indian intelligence remains an underdeveloped branch of the field. There has been a succession of would-be exposés of varying degrees of credibility, e.g., D. Raman, *The Kaoboys of the R&AW: Down Memory Lane* (New Delhi: Lancer, 2007); and Ashok Raina, *Inside RAW* (New Delhi: All India Press, 1993), which have not really been addressed by more sober discussions (I am indebted to Alayna Ahmad for bringing these sources to my attention). Rahul Roy-Chaudhury's contribution to Stuart Farson, Peter Gill, Mark Phythian, and Shlomo Shapiro, *PSI Handbook of Global Security and Intelligence: National Approaches, Volume 1: The Americas and Asia* (Westport, CT: Praeger, 2008), 211–29, is, to be sure, informative in fairly bare-bones terms about the management and administration of the Indian community but in many respects amounts to little more than an elaborated organogram and does not address the more fraught questions of Research and Analysis Wing (R&AW) or Intelligence Bureau clandestine activities.

66. Douglas Porch, *The French Secret Services: From the Dreyfus Affair to the Gulf War* (New York: Farrar, Straus & Giroux, 1995).

67. See, e.g., Rahul Bedi, "Infiltration Continues on Line of Control," *Jane's Intelligence Review* 14, no. 7 (July 2002): 30–31.

CHAPTER 5

Protecting the New Rome

Byzantine Influences on Russian Intelligence

Kristian C. Gustafson

> When we mentally picture Byzantinism, we see before us . . . the austere, clear plan of a spacious and capacious structure. We know, for example, that in politics it means autocracy. In religion, it means Christianity with distinct features, which distinguish it from Western churches, from heresies and schisms. In the area of ethics we know that the Byzantine ideal does not have that elevated and in many instances highly exaggerated notion of terrestrial human individual introduced into history by German feudalism.
>
> —KONSTANTIN LEONTIEV, *Byzantism and Slavdom*, 1875

One of the great hopes of the last generation was that Russia, once freed from the bonds of communism, would rejoin the family of nations as an equal, free, and democratic state. Russia's progress since the collapse of the USSR has of course not proceeded as some might have expected. As Dimitri Obolensky has commented, "There is much in contemporary Russia that seems unfamiliar and puzzling to the modern Western observer—ideas, institutions, and methods of government that seem to run counter to the basic trends of his own culture."[1] With economic and demographic collapse followed by boom, and with the progress of democracy questionable at times, the early hopes of 1991 have long since faded, replaced with a realization that Russia would not ever be a mirror image of any Western state. Though Russia is presumably through the worst of its times, on many counts it strikes many in the West as not a reliable partner but still a potential enemy. "A new Cold War" has been detected by some.[2] One matter that causes particular concern in the West is the behavior of Russia's security services and their relationship with the central authority of the state.

It is clear that the security services in Russia today are as critical and central as they were under communism. As an analyst at one American think tank has stated, Russia is "a state defined and dominated by former and active duty security and intelligence officers."[3] One Russian researcher has noted that more than 25 percent of Russia's current governing elites have backgrounds in either the military or security services, including former president and current prime minister Vladimir Putin as a former KGB and FSB officer.[4] The question posed by several thinkers since the collapse of the USSR is if there has been any real change in the management of Russia and its security services.[5] As Amy Knight commented in the mid-1990s, there had been cosmetic change in the security services, but they remained substantially the same structures because "Lubianka still stood and, although there had been changes at the helm inside, the long-awaited reform of the security services had yet to happen. Indeed, by August 1995, the security services had recaptured much of the ground lost in the first days after the August 1991 coup."[6] Part of the answer to the question of "why have the Russians not changed their political behavior significantly since the end of communism?"—really the question that runs throughout the work of Amy Knight and, more recently, that of Edward Lucas—can be answered by saying that Russia's political behavior between 1917 and 1991 did not seem peculiar to the West because it was communist but because it was *Russian.* Accordingly, if we want to understand Russia's political behavior now, we must understand its cultural origins. Russia has political traditions that did not develop out of the Renaissance and Reformation in Western Europe, and before that from the political and religious traditions of Rome. Rather, Russia's traditions originate from a source largely forgotten in the West: the Byzantine Empire.

One can make more sense of Russia's security and intelligence culture—as opposed to specific communist or postcommunist cultures—by tracing their common philosophical and historic roots back to their point of origin, between five hundred and a thousand years ago in Constantinople and its empire, the long-lived eastern successor of the Roman Empire. The Byzantines had a strongly bureaucratized and institutionalized intelligence and security culture, which formed the heart of their overall political system, and which strongly influenced the behavior of Tsarist and Communist Russia—and likely still influences it today. "There can be no doubt," wrote the Russian Byzantinist Dimitry Obolensky, "that the influence of Byzantium on Russian history and culture was far more profound and permanent than that of the Turko-Mongol hordes and more homogenous than that of the modern West."[7] If not the sole driver, Byzantium is a key driver of Russian political, strategic, and intelligence culture. Thus, understanding the Byzantine security culture can help one understand Russian security culture even today. As we note elsewhere in this volume, culture may not suggest *what* a people will do, but it may suggest *how* they might do it.

The Byzantine Mark in Russian Political Culture

The tsars of Russia considered their state the legitimate and direct political successor of the Byzantine Empire. As the great Russian-born historian of Byzantium, George Ostrogorsky, wrote in his seminal *History of the Byzantine State*:

> Ivan III, the great liberator and consolidator of the Russian lands, married the daughter of the Despot Thomas Palaeologus, the niece of the last Emperor of Byzantium. He assumed the imperial Byzantine two-headed eagle in his arms, introduced Byzantine ceremonial into Muscovy and soon made Russia the leader of the Christian East as Byzantium had once been. Russia became the obvious heir of the Byzantine Empire and it took over from Constantinople Roman conceptions in their Byzantine form: if Constantinople was the New Rome, Moscow became the "Third Rome." The great tradition of Byzantium, its faith, its political ideas, its spirituality, lived on through the centuries in the Russian Empire.[8]

Whether one agrees completely with Ostrogorsky's specific point—and many do not—is not entirely relevant, because what we see in Russia through the first Russian Empire is an emulation of Byzantine norms and, especially, Byzantine political thought, through whatever motivation.[9] Key aspects of this thought included the close pairing of the Church to the state to a degree not seen in the Western traditions surrounding Rome, with the tsars of Moscow regarding themselves "as the successors of the Byzantine emperors, and as the representatives of God upon Earth."[10] This dual conception is referred to by modern theorists as *caeseropapism*: the political combination of temporal and spiritual control in the hands of a strongly centralized or despotic head of state.[11] It is a political idea often perceived in the "Byzantine Commonwealth" (roughly the modern Orthodox world), and it is perhaps unsurprising that the Byzantine clergy were keen to spread it as they proselytized in the Slavic world "as the Byzantines must have looked on the doctrine as a particularly advantageous export."[12] Ultimately, it pointed all converts to the Holy City of Constantinople, and thus to the power of their patriarch and their emperor.[13]

Through their overlapping existence the Russians adhered to the religious leadership of Constantinople, the "second Jerusalem," and their patriarchs were appointed by the patriarch of Constantinople until near the end of the empire.

Only when Constantinople fell to the Turks in 1453 did the Russians seize the mantle both as the temporal inheritors of the empire and also the spiritual inheritors, Kiev and then Moscow assuming leadership (in their minds, if not that of the patriarch in Constantinople) of the Orthodox world. The Soviet scholars I. M. Lotman and B. A. Uspensky commented that "it is characteristic that the idea of Moscow, the Third Rome, could quite soon be transformed into the idea of Moscow, the Third Jerusalem," implying in Russia, as in Byzantium, a sense of universal authority and the duty to spread their Right Belief (the meaning of the Greek word "Orthodox") to the rest of the world.[14] The late-nineteenth-century political theorist Konstantin Leontiev positively used the term "Byzantism" to describe the type of society that the Russian Empire needed to counter the "degenerating" influence of the West. Leontiev praised the Byzantine Empire and the tsarist autocracy as societies with a political system that comprised the authoritative power of the monarch and devout following of the Russian Orthodox Church.[15] A number of scholars have pointed out these traits in the communist empire of the Soviets that succeeded the Russian Empire. Obolensky says "it would be difficult to resist the impression that there is at least something in common between the religious messianism of the Second and the Third Rome and the belief of the Russian Communist in the exclusive truth of the Marxist Gospel, immortally enshrined in the collective works of Marx."[16]

John Dziak, scholar of Soviet security systems, observes that in the Soviet Union one saw something resembling the idea of Christian Empire, but with the Christianity replaced by an alternate ideology: "In a sense a secular theocracy was born in which a priesthood (the party), served by a combined holy office and temple guard (the Cheka), sought to exercise its will."[17] Toynbee saw in the inheritance of Byzantine political theory the seeds of totalitarianism in Russia and the USSR.[18]

Modern Russia is certainly not a modernized simulacrum of Byzantium; this would take the comparison too far, ignoring the many other influences—Eastern, Western, and indigenous—on Russia since the collapse of Byzantium and its "commonwealth."[19] This chapter attempts to make the comparison on a much more restricted scale, by looking primarily at the Byzantine culture of intelligence and security. If we are to discern whether there is some noticeable or significant remnant of Byzantine intelligence and security culture left in modern Russia, we first must establish what that Byzantine culture looked like. We can point, however, to a number of incidents that have led many commentators to say that postcommunist Russia is a very similar polity to the USSR before it: Putin's autocracy and near-permanency at the head of government, deeply flawed elections and press censorship, Russia's behavior in Chechnya and Georgia, its often lethal treatment of political critics of the regime domestically and abroad, and even the persecution of non-Orthodox religious groups.[20] One can take the constructivist view that Russia's political *culture* is greater than its particular political *ideology*—whether imperial, communist, or officially federal and democratic—and that it is this culture that most greatly influences how the state handles such matters as security.

The Byzantine Culture of Intelligence and Security

The Byzantine Empire itself was the direct political successor to the Roman Empire ("Byzantine" is, in fact, a modern term, and these people at the time thought of and called themselves Romanoi, Romans). Indeed, there is no clear agreement on when "Roman" ceases and "Byzantine" begins in terms of empire, though one might say either 324 (the founding of Constantinople) or 395 (the death of Theodosius I). The Byzantines lived alongside what most imagine as the classical Roman Empire of its eponymous city for a troubled century, then continued its evolution from that point, eventually becoming a political entity sui generis, with the politically centralized state organs of the Romans overlaid with the religious/ideological mantle of Orthodox Christianity.

The root of this political system, we must recall, clearly comes in the inheritance of the Roman Empire. The role of the government in Rome was to provide for the security of the polity. In Byzantium we have the addition of the Christian God, and his close association with the emperor, allowing the new theory "that the purpose of action of any kind was to foster the smooth operation of the state machine, of the empire *by the grace of God*."[21] Thus the infrastructure of the state was there primarily for purposes of what we would now call security, specifically that of God through the person of the emperor—not directly for the welfare of citizens. One might look for a modern political equivalent in what Dziak calls the "counterintelligence state."[22] He describes this as a political system that displays "an overarching concern with 'enemies' both internal and external. Security and extirpation of real or presumed threats become the premier enterprise of such systems."[23] The fixation on security, as he describes it, demands that "all societal institutions" are constructed for the aim of security. In this structure, he says, the "security service is the principal guardian of the party; the two together constitute a permanent counterintelligence enterprise to which all other major political, economic and social questions are subordinated."[24] Replacing the word "Church" for "party," Dziak's description of the Soviet state holds up remarkably well when compared with the structures of the Byzantine state.

Byzantium's existence was always precarious. It was the single biggest political entity in the Mediterranean for most of the period from the ninth to twelfth centuries, and was certainly the richest as late as the twelfth century.[25] It had no firm allies, and hungry upstart competitors like the Lombards, Normans, Bulgars, and Turks sought to take from its riches. It was almost constantly at war during the 1,100 years of its existence, and its views on intelligence would have been conditioned by the fact that no foreign (i.e., non-Orthodox and, later, non–Greek-speaking) person or state could be trusted. Indeed, one might argue that the Byzantines would have viewed war as the natural state of being, with peace as an aberration, rather the opposite of the current mindset in the West. What is more, the Byzantines knew that war was expensive and danger-ous. As John Haldon has written, the Byzantine self-image "was one of a belea-guered Christian state fighting the forces of darkness, with foes against whom it had constantly to be on its guard."[26] This mindset—of constant, dangerous, expensive conflict—naturally put the Byzantines' thoughts toward how to avoid war despite its prevalence.[27] As Haldon continued, the Byzantines sought to "evolve a whole panoply of defensive techniques, among which warfare was only one element, and by no means necessarily the most useful."[28] Intelligence, covert action, trickery, and gold-lubricated diplomacy were thus the natural recourse of a state that sought to manage the threats to God and emperor that lurked at every single border.

Byzantium was, in short, paranoid—and justifiably so. In Constantinople the whole machinery of state was geared to security: State infrastructure served to facilitate the movements of armies and the intelligence that triggered their deployments; the functionaries of state—both internal and external, and cen-tral and provincial—had as their main duties the detection of enemies or their destruction; and the Orthodox Church, the source of religious legitimacy for the emperor, played a central role in the security of the state through actual intelligence functions as well as offering strong diplomatic entrée abroad. As with Dziak's description of the USSR, in the Byzantine world all the organs of state were designed to ensure the "self-perpetuation" of the state rather than its well-being.[29] Examining this infrastructure in detail helps in understanding its pervasiveness in the medieval state.

One piece of security infrastructure inherited by the Byzantines from its Rome-based antecedent was the postal system. The sixth-century historian Pro-copius notes in his *Secret History* that the "earlier emperors, in order to gain the most speedy information concerning the movements of the enemy in each territory, seditions or unforeseen accidents in individual towns, and the actions of the governors and other officials in all parts of the Empire, and also in order that those who conveyed the yearly tribute might do so without danger or delay, had established a rapid service of public couriers."[30] If a modern Westerner were to be told that their state's postal system was there primarily to spy on external enemies, governors, and citizens alike, they would likely be slightly concerned, but this system was a natural consequence of the strategic and political environ-ment in which the state existed and which was the cause of its elaborate gover-nance. As a system designed for purposes of security and intelligence, it should not be a revelation that those who worked for the post were in turn security functionaries, the *agentes in rebus* (literally "agents for things," perhaps best translated as "general agents"). Their duties included the supervision of the roads and inns of the *cursus publicus* (later the Hellenized δημουσίος δρόμος), the carrying of letters, and verifying that a traveler was carrying the right warrant (*evectio*, δρνθημα) while using the *cursus*. Other tasks of the *agentes* included supervising the provincial bureaucracy and delivering imperial commands, often staying in the area to ensure their implementation. Being outside the control of the provincial governors, some *agentes*, the *curiosi* (Greek: διατρέχοντες), were appointed as inspectors and acted as a sort of secret police reporting to the emperor.[31] They were used, also, to supervise the arrest of senior officials as required, to escort senior Romans into exile, and so even to assist in the enforcement of government regulation of the Church—a requirement of the *caeseropapist* state.[32]

The public post was part of a larger internal security structure. The tenth-century great hetaeriarch (μέγας έταιρειάρχης), or captain of one of the guard units, was the chief officer responsible for protecting the emperor against plots.[33] One might presume that it was these officers who "at once informed" Emperor Alexius I of the senatorial/military plot against him in 1083, the officers' plot of 1091, the nobles' plot of 1094, and half a dozen other plots besides.[34] Byzantine history is infamous and eponymous for its endless cycle of plots—the contemporary chronicler Michael Psellus describes some nineteen serious plots against emperors in the period 976–1081—and in reading the various Byzantine primary texts, one sees how often these were smashed, often based on what the chroniclers describe only as the information "of a peasant," perhaps "a priest," or often just "somebody."[35]

Ultimately, Byzantium resembles to a good degree Dziak's "counterintelligence state," where people were constantly searching for plots that were assumed to always be present—which in the case of Constantinople they likely were. It was a dangerous business being a Byzantine emperor; between the years 395 and 1453 there were 107 Byzantine emperors, with an average of ten years on the throne. Only 34 of these emperors died natural deaths. Psellus recounts the advice given to the great warrior-emperor Basil II (who would convert the Kievan Slavs to Christianity and begin the great relationship between the Byzantines and the Russians) from his would-be overthrower, Sclerus: "Cut-down the governors who become over-proud. . . . Let no generals on campaign have too many resources. Exhaust them with unjust taxations to keep them busied with their own affairs. Admit no women to the imperial councils. Be accessible to no one. Share with few your intimate plans."[36]

One might think these words were those Stalin himself might have uttered. We can surmise that Alexius I, founder of the Comnene Dynasty, ran a large network of agents to protect his reign. With regard to plotting, phrases such as "the Emperor, however, was not unaware of it" or "he had reliable information" from "many informants" dot the *Alexiad*; indeed, they are pointedly made by Anna Comnena in her *The Alexiad* to show her father's shrewdness in beating the enemies of the state through superior information.[37] The eleventh-century provincial official Kekaumenos offers this advice in his *Strategikon*: "If you hear of [an accusation] against your official, that he is plotting against your majesty, do not let the evil lie hidden within your soul and aim to destroy him. Instead, make a thorough investigation, at first keeping things secret. But if you then discover the truth, the charge against him should be made openly." Failing to collect all the evidence with enough skill, the text then seems to say (it has lacunas), "You then make [him] your enemy and many other [enemies] on account of him."[38] Being clever enough to weed out and condemn plotters had a practical and social value in Byzantium. A sound-minded Byzantine ruler, Kekaumenos suggests, always distrusts the motivations of his servants and actively works to protect against their plotting. We should add that this is not a uniquely Byzantine view of Byzantine life; the Crusaders who came into contact with the empire almost uniformly viewed the Byzantines as perfidious, treacherous, and undependable, as well as unmanly for being so.[39]

Let us go back to the official security structures of the state, which may have helped emperors such as Basil II and Alexius I secure their thrones for so long. As the Byzantine Empire moved past the near-fatal crisis of the Arab invasions of the seventh and eighth centuries, the administration of the postal system evolved, with the senior officer becoming the senior minister and principal adviser to the emperor until superseded in the twelfth century by the *logothete of the secreton* (offices or bureaus, μογοθέτης το σεκρέτον), a position not unlike the "principal secretary" post filled by Sir Francis Walsingham in Elizabethan England.[40] Thus effectively, the roads and the post—the intelligence infrastructure—were managed by the closest thing the Byzantines had to a combined foreign minister and prime minister, which shows the importance of security and intelligence gathering in the governance of the state. Perhaps more interestingly, for our purposes here, it was administratively grouped either with or alongside the Scrinium Barbarorum (βάρβαρος), or Bureau of Barbarians.

Mistaking the Bureau of Barbarians as an espionage office, as has been done by some, betrays a Western cast of mind: that such duties are entrusted to a single agency, whereas in Constantinople security intelligence was the job of much of the government.[41] Regardless, the bureau was established in the mid–fifth century, and it is first mentioned in the Constitution of Theodosius II.[42] It was still in existence at the time of Philotheos in the tenth century, and it is presumed by J. M. Bury to have "exercised supervision over all foreigners visiting Constantinople."[43] Although, on the surface, it was a protocol office—its main duty was to ensure that foreign envoys were properly cared for and received sufficient state funds for their maintenance, and it kept all the official translators—it clearly had a security function as well. Though not directly associated with the Bureau of Barbarians, an anonymous work called *On Strategy* from the sixth century offers advice about foreign embassies and envoys that was no doubt shared by the Bureau: "[Envoys] who are sent to us should be received honorably and generously, for everyone holds envoys in high esteem. Their attendants, however, should be kept under surveillance to keep them from obtaining any information by asking questions of our people."[44] This was the job likely fulfilled by the bureau. A twelfth-century Italian ambassador to Byzantium, Bishop Liudprand of Cremono, spits venom about his Greek minders, whom, he perceived accurately, were there as his jailers rather than his protectors.[45] We know such surveillance failed from time to time; the Arab hostage Al Jarmi sent back to the caliphs of Damascus a detailed Byzantine order of battle in the year 845.[46]

The Byzantines knew well that embassies and envoys were as much for intelligence purposes as for diplomatic, that indeed the former was a precondition for the latter.[47] A number of Byzantine texts thus speak of the role of envoys and how they should be selected and trained, with a premium placed on religious orthodoxy and reliability: "The envoys we send out should be men who have the reputation of being religious, who have never been denounced for any crime or publicly condemned."[48] This same work stresses that the envoy must be able to dissemble and lie about Roman intentions, and not to give too much of the empire's intentions away if he happens to find the receiving state unexpectedly unfriendly. Theophanes offers the example of Daniel of Sinope, an envoy sent to Emir Walid of Syria not really to discuss terms, but "to make a precise examination of the Arabs' move against Romania, and their forces."[49] Above all, the envoy was there to protect the security of the emperor (and thus empire) in any way he could. As Bréhier notes: "It was above all in the relations with the established states, whose power could menace Constantinople, that imperial diplomacy had to deploy all its resources, following with attention the evolutions of their internal politics and producing intelligence on their forces, in an era where the idea of permanent embassies did not exist. Thanks to its strong traditions and its ability to discover the weak points of its enemies, [Byzantine diplomats] several times preserved the existence of the Empire, in instances where [information] proved more advantageous than military force."[50]

For the Byzantines diplomacy was the handmaiden of intelligence, and intelligence was the shield of the state. It seems the polities within the Byzantine sphere of interest understood this well. On receiving a Byzantine envoy in the tenth century, the khagan of the Central Asian Turks asked, "Are you not those Romans who have ten tongues and one deceit?"[51]

The Church, as well as diplomats, was always a potential source of intelligence for the Byzantines. Interestingly, it was monks who were involved in the most famous case of Byzantine *industrial* espionage: the theft of silkworms from

China. According to Procopius and Theophanes, two Nestorian monks offered to steal the secret of silk from China so that the Byzantines could cultivate it themselves.[52] Other priests, monks, and religious figures appear in Byzantine intelligence practice, and this is reflected even in the Arabic record, as Al-Asmari notes in chapter 6 of this volume. In 756 and 757, Theodore, the patriarch of Antioch, was exiled by Salim of Damascus for "revealing their affairs to the Emperor Constantine by letters." Theophanes hastens to note that this was a false accusation.[53] In the compilation on governing commissioned by Constantine VII, *Porphyrogenitus*, we read that itinerant monks acted as secret messengers, and perhaps spies, for the empire in the intrigues against the Armenian princes.[54] One should not be terribly surprised by the role of the religious establishment in the intelligence role. In part, one can point to the intense association of Orthodox Christianity with the throne, making sense of the actions of Patriarch Theodore, who would have viewed Constantine as the protector of the faith against the satanic "Agarenes" (i.e., the "Sons of Hagar," as the Byzantines often called Muslims, and a term still used in the Russian Orthodox Church).[55]

This same "symphony" of Church and state made the Byzantine clergy and monastic community inevitably part of the administrative systems of the empire[56]—and, from 1039 to 1448, when Constantinopolitan bishops served in Kiev and Moscow, the main part of the Russian administrative system as well[57]—and thus both intimately part of the security state and at times even attached to various factions of government. They were most intimately involved when the Church felt the security of the state threatened by heretical sects. When the Church detected heresy, the whole weight of the state's force was laid against them. An Orthodox state was one that took spiritual direction from the patriarch of Constantinople, and because the emperor was the protector of the Church, any truly Orthodox state was by definition an ally of the empire— Bulgaria became an enemy in the tenth century by declaring its Church autocephalous, that is, independent from Constantinople. So the work of men such as Constantine ("Cyril") and Methodius in composing Cyrillic, and keeping parts of what is now Moravia and Romania within the imperial fold while excluding the influence of Rome, was key in turning potential foes into loyal subjects of the one true "holy catholic and apostolic Church" of Constantinople.[58] This is very much akin to the Soviet ideal of spreading Communist ideology to ensure allies, both diplomatic and military, throughout the world, and the vitriol spread by Moscow against any divergent ideology was as strong as that of the Patriarchate against heterodox churches, which included its peer-competitor, Rome. The existential role the Church played in the security of the empire cannot possibly be overstated.

The empire, however unitary and centralized it appeared, depended inevitably upon its governors and generals. By the reign of Emperor Constans II (641–

68) the empire was defended by what was called the "thematic" system, themes being provinces ruled by military governors and defended by militias of settled ex-soldiers.[59] The thematic armies were thus largely static and nonprofessional, and were bolstered by the Tagma, the smaller imperial professional field force kept near the capital. Worse, from the mid-seventh to early tenth centuries, the empire was on the defensive on many fronts, surrounded by enemies, and with never enough troops to deal with everyone at once. Accordingly, much of the day-to-day defense of the empire was delegated to the thematic governors, who had to absorb attacks as best they could, conduct guerrilla and small-unit harassment as they could, and hope the tagmatic forces might show up in time to assist in the destruction of the enemy as it retreated loaded with booty.[60] Edward Luttwak argues persuasively that this "elastic" defensive system suited the empire's more limited military means and naturally placed a premium on intelligence.[61]

Moreover, the enemies of the state varied, and field army commanders needed to know *who* they were fighting to know *how* they were going to fight. As the great warrior-emperor Maurice (582–602) says in his *Strategikon*: "We must now treat of the tactics and characteristics of each race which might cause trouble to our state. The purpose of this chapter is to enable those who intend to wage war against these peoples to prepare themselves properly. For all nations do not fight in a single formation or in the same manner, and one cannot deal with them all in the same way."[62]

Following this is a description of the tactics, techniques, and procedures of many of the neighboring peoples, and in this we can perceive the great intelligence structures the Byzantines maintained. Constantine VII's *De Administrando Imperio* is a critical guide to foreign policy and diplomacy written for the emperor's youthful son, and spends much of its substantial length giving detailed descriptions of the empire's neighboring peoples, their internal politics, and thus how the empire could best deal with them. Romilly Jenkins, an editor of the work, notes how some of the material in this "secret and confidential document" is clearly derived from secret sources.[63] We also know that though Constantine authored this work in his long years of enforced idleness, some of the material is drawn from other, preexisting sources.[64] Was there in Byzantium a system whereby information from diplomats, governors, the Church, the Bureau of Barbarians, the *logothetes*, and other sources was compiled and pushed out to consumers in government and in military commands? We have no information to indicate whether this was the case, but it is possible that it existed at points before the early thirteenth century.

To understand the fullness of the Byzantine approach to intelligence, one therefore needs to look to the numerous military manuals published for the edification of both emperors and governors alike. In the defensive centuries of the empire, a premium was placed on knowing the enemy and on trying to predict its aggressive actions, in order to make the thematic-tagmatic system of defense function. The military governors needed to have information superiority over their opponents in order to allow their smaller forces to cope effectively with the larger field armies of their varied enemies. Spying was thus viewed as part and parcel of both governorship and military strategy. In the first instance, these military manuals place great weight on the standard military practice of a "good number of competent and trustworthy scouts."[65] But scouting is not the complete solution for defense, notes another tenth-century work titled *Campaign Organization*, given that "actual spies, however, are the most useful. They go into the enemy's country and can find out exactly what is going on there and report it back to those who sent them." What is interesting is the universality of the responsibility to spy, and among whom: "The Domestic [the Byzantine equivalent of the commander of land forces was titled the "Domestic of the Schools"] and the generals along the border should be sure to have spies not only among the Bulgarians, . . . [but also among all neighboring peoples, even those at peace,] so that none of their plans will not be known to us."[66] Espionage was a job of all field commanders, both central and provincial, and against all neighboring nations. Everyone was a potential enemy or ally.

The texts spend some time discussing the tradecraft of spying. We have seen how the Byzantines conducted espionage under diplomatic cover at the highest level; at the lower level they also made use of business or commercial cover. They understood that they were working in hostile environments and had to pay special attention to security protocols. *On Strategy*'s author notes:

> Before leaving on his assignment each spy should speak in secrecy about his mission to one of his closest associates. Both should agree upon arrangements for communicating safely with one another, setting a definite place and manner of meeting. The place could be the public market in which many of our people, as well as foreigners, gather. The manner could be on the pretext of trading. In this way they should be able to escape notice of the enemy. One offers our goods for sale or barter, and the other gives foreign goods in exchange and informs us of the enemy's plans against us and of the situation in their country.[67]

Because of the nature of communications in the ancient world—high-speed imperial couriers notwithstanding—the thematic governors had to maintain relations with their corresponding magnates in neighboring provinces. These relations should be used, Nikephoros notes, for the purposes of intelligence. Playing on the deceits that earned the Byzantines such disdain from the later Western Crusaders and Victorian historians, the local governor "should pretend to make friends with the emirs who control the castles in the border regions. He should also write to them and send out men with gift baskets. As a result, with all this coming and going, the general might be able to get a clear picture of the plans and intentions of the enemy."[68] Like the author of *On Strategy*, the emperor suggests that the governor ought to attempt redundant coverage of the foe: "He ought also to have the businessmen go out" to spy.[69] Byzantine leaders were not too class conscious, however, and also "sent spies disguised as beggars," as Leo the Deacon says.[70]

The Byzantines, as one can see, had a very highly developed conception of the role and practice of intelligence. Unlike any other organized polity until the modern era, they maintained *bureaucratically organized* security structures (though never intelligence organizations specifically), which century after century ensured a constant flow of information about the external and internal enemies of the state to leader and field commanders. All levels of the state leadership were engaged in spying on the emperor's ubiquitous foes, in what closely matches Dziak's description of the counterintelligence state. The role of the entire structure of governance was "to put it briefly, to make sure that nothing which [the enemy] might be thinking of will escape us."[71] Because everyone who was not Orthodox or Byzantine was almost by definition a foe, intelligence needed to be an ongoing and natural part of governance. Luttwak argues persuasively that two key tenets of Byzantine "operational code" were "gather intelligence on the enemy and his mentality, and monitor his movements constantly" and "subversion is the path to victory."[72] This ongoing and ambient need for intelligence, and the stress on covert action, made the Byzantines distinct from their predecessors in Rome, Greece, and elsewhere—and were part of what links them to modern Russia.

The Reflections of Byzantine Intelligence in Modern Russia

Knowing that there is a strong Byzantine link in general Russian culture, and then coupling that with what we can construct of the Byzantine intelligence tradition, we might thus be able to see if there are noticeable artifacts of Byzantium's security state within recent and current Russian practice. To reiterate the point made in the introduction to this volume about political inheritance, "the people and the rulers of the Kievan State had good opportunities of becoming acquainted with the main principles of Byzantine political philosophy, . . . [and] it can be seen that many Byzantine ideas were incorporated into the political structure of the State of Kiev, and that they became a basis for Russia's further evolution."[73] Establishing direct antecedence is not the purpose of this chapter, and is really not possible anyway. It is also clear that Byzantine writings on things such as espionage and intelligence are actually quite restricted within the overall restricted literary legacy of Byzantium—we should likely never say that political Russia was ever directly influenced by Byzantine military treatises, for instance. What is being argued here is that the way the Byzantines managed their security and intelligence was a function of the political culture of the state, the same political culture that was inherited later by the Kievan and then the Russian state, and that has served the Soviet and subsequent post-Soviet Russian state.

There are links that show the Tsarist and then Soviet security apparatus to have a Byzantine pedigree based on inherited political culture. The secret chancery, or *prikaz tainykh del*, is described by Russian historians as the personal chancery of the tsar in the seventeenth century. Initially, it was led by a secret clerk called a *d'yak*. This word is interesting because it is etymologically derived from the Greek work *diakonos* (deacon), a monastic or Church rank that hints at the strong role of Byzantine Church governance in Kievan and early Muscovite Russia. The main function of the secret *prikaz* was to supervise both other *prikazy* and other officials of the tsar, such as diplomats and military officers. The *d'yak* reported directly to the sovereign.[74] A subsequent organization was the eighteenth-century *Tainaya rozysknykh del kantselyariya*. Under the leadership of A. I. Ushakov, a veteran from the previous secret chancery, this office supervised the investigation of political suspects throughout the empire and took immediate responsibility for the most dangerous delinquents.[75] These offices bear a resemblance, in bureaucratic terms, to the *logothetes* and *secretum* of tenth-century Byzantium, not surprising given the clerical origin of both. It is in these organizations, modeled at least in part on Byzantine methods of government, that we find the predecessors of the modern Russian security apparatus.[76] The Cheka, the NKVD, and eventually the KGB were all the successors of the Ohkrana "in at least equal size and in more merciless temper, if in somewhat different form."[77] The FSB and SVR would emerge from the Soviet structures much more seamlessly.

One can draw no specific indication of Byzantine bureaucratic organization in the organization of the Soviet and subsequent Russian state, but in spirit, the way the Soviets organized their government for security purposes is still quite Russian. Few would argue that in his control of the security organs of the state, Joseph Stalin's Soviet Union behaved in an imperial fashion and forms the model of Dziak's counterintelligence state. Like the Byzantine system, Amy Knight observed that in early post-Soviet Russia "the president 'directs the activity' of the security services, and [the law] diminishes the role of parliamentary oversight entirely."[78] Other observers have noted, as mentioned above, that modern Russia's government and elites come in large part from the security services.[79] Like their Byzantine forebears, the Soviets drew no particular distinction between "overt" and "covert" in the persecution of the enemies of the state. Diplomacy in the Western usage tries to draw a broad line between its proper functioning and the underhanded methods of the state's intelligence agencies, to the point where organizations such as the UK Secret Intelligence Service (a.k.a. MI-6) are entrusted with the specific task of "secret diplomacy" where their Foreign Office colleagues could not tread.[80] The Soviet term "active measures" (*activinyye meropriatia*) took in both overt and covert actions to influence foreign countries, whereas most other terms used in the West focus on the covert.[81] As Richard Shultz and Roy Godson point out, the terms "special activities" and "covert actions" tend to indicate that they are made of separate stuff from the substance of foreign policy, but "in the Soviet view, . . . no such distinctions are apparent."[82] Whereas a Western ambassador might balk at purposefully deceiving an interlocutor for fear of losing credibility, the Byzantine, Russian, or Soviet diplomat would not, as might be witnessed in the story of Soviet diplomatic disinformation surrounding the Cuban Missile Crisis.

Of the purges and show trials of Stalin's Russia, we have ample evidence in the Byzantine state. Theophanes notes Justinian's behavior after discovering a plot against him by one Herakleios, who

> was brought in bonds from Thrace along with all the other officers who were his comrades. Justinian hanged them all on the wall. He also sent men into the interior who rooted out many more officers and killed them, those who had been active against him and those who had not alike. . . . Justinian blinded the patriarch Kallinikos and exiled him to Rome. . . . [He] destroyed an uncountable number of political and military figures; many he gave bitter deaths by throwing them into the sea in sacks. He invited others to a fine meal and hanged some of them when they got up; others he cut down. Because of all this everyone was terrified.[83]

If one were to change the names from Herakleios and Kallinikos to Tukachevsky and Zinoviev, and substitute Stalin for Justinian, this story retains a frightening degree of fidelity. Such Soviet-sounding stories are repeated in Comnena's *The Alexiad*, who notes even her adored father's use of torture to uncover plots against him.[84]

The Russians and Byzantines also share a penchant for disposing of dissidents in particularly brutal fashion. As with the assassination of Georgi Markov in London by the Bulgarian secret police, or the assassination of Leon Trotsky in Mexico by the NKVD, so the Byzantines were willing and able to destroy enemies of the state abroad. After making a peace treaty with the Bulgarians, Emperor Constantine V "sent men into Bulgaria who seized Sklabounos the ruler of Sebereis, a man who had worked many evils in Thrace. Christianos, an apostate from Christianity who headed the Skamaroi, was also captured. His hands and feet were cut off at the mole of St. Thomas. . . . [He was eviscerated] and then he was burned."[85] Look at what is described here: Imperial agents did not just execute a traitor, they also kidnapped him and returned him to imperial territory so that he could be executed *spectacularly*. Examples of such "extraordinary rendition" are noted several times in Byzantine texts. The poisoning of Alexander Litvinenko, as it is suggested, by his former Chekist peers would not seem strange to the Byzantines in any aspect other than the particular method.[86] They would likely heartily agree with the assassination's necessity.

For the Byzantines, various populations along the borders were troublesome, and so they were forcibly uprooted and moved to parts of the empire where they had less opportunity to cause harm. The heretical Athenganoi, the Paulicians, and much of the Armenian aristocracy were relocated between the eighth and tenth centuries "to remove recalcitrant elements which, if left in their homeland, might have become serious sources of trouble."[87] Such forced movements of populations, most often minority groups perceived as security risks, were a frequent recourse of Stalin, who took thirteen entire minority nations that "totaled more than 2 million people [and] deported [them] to internal exile."[88] This has even occurred in post-Communist Russia, though to a much smaller degree.[89] Beyond these, however, is a general climate of security. Like the Byzantines, Russia has for most of its political existence viewed itself as being surrounded by threats. As George Kennan put it in his famous "Long Telegram," at bottom a "neurotic view of world affairs is [a] traditional and instinctive [part of the] Russian sense of insecurity."[90] Causation and correlation are hard to distinguish here. Do the Byzantines and the Russians look alike simply because they share, randomly, a similar worldview? Or do they share a similar worldview because of a shared religious/ideological background? Here the "layer cake" of culture and the thickness of the intervening centuries of history make it hard to give a definitive answer.

One of the most curious aspects of the current Russian security environment is the resurgence of religion. In the 2000 National Security Concept, the Putin administration stated, "assurance of the Russian Federation's national security also includes protecting the cultural and spiritual-moral legacy and the historical traditions and standards of public life, and preserving the cultural heritage of all Russia's peoples. There must be a state policy to maintain the population's spiritual and moral welfare, prohibit the use of airtime to promote violence or base instincts, and counter the adverse impact of foreign religious organizations and missionaries."[91] Here we have the highest authority directly relating the health of Russia's traditional religion, Orthodoxy, to the security of the state. Several significant works of scholarship have identified that this "tendency to see religious difference as, at least in part, a potential security threat is shared" by both the Orthodox Church and Vladimir Putin, and presumably the current government.[92] Equally interesting is the fact that Putin, an apparently practicing Orthodox Christian himself, ensured that in 2002 the Federal Security Agency (FSB) rededicated its traditional Orthodox chapel in the Lubyanka. This, wrote Julie Elkner, "set the seal on the special relationship between the FSB and the Russian Orthodox Church (Moscow Patriarchate)." Deputy FSB director Vladimir Shul'ts hailed the consecration of the church as a "truly emblematic event," which, Elkner suggests, should be "viewed in the light of the complex and dramatic history of relations between the secret police and the Orthodox Church."[93] One commentator has convincingly described how the Russian Foreign Ministry has been harnessing the Orthodox Church as a tool to control expatriate Russian communities outside Russia via the reuniting of the Russian Orthodox Church Outside Russia with the Patriarchate in Moscow.[94]

Although John Anderson relates this increasing state Orthodoxy to the politicized Patriarchate under Peter the Great, it is clear on review that the tradition of politicized state religion has a longer pedigree indeed, and one can note the similarity to Byzantine views on the subject going back nearly a millennium. What will be interesting to see is if this view continues with the current degree of energy once Putin has left the political scene. Regardless, that Orthodoxy should be so resurgent in Russia after seventy years of enforced atheism shows the resilience of cultural habit over the longer term. It reinforces our argument in the conclusion of this volume that culture is an indicator not of *what* but *how*.

Echoes of Empire

By no means is it the case that Russia is solely bound by its Byzantine heritage, for though there are many similarities, differences abound as well. As was noted in the introduction to this volume, there are simply too many unaccountable variables that scholars simply cannot untangle. At each stage of Russia's history since the founding of the Kievan and Muscovite states, the Russians as a people have been a unique and independent force in European and Asian history. There have been many influences on Russia over the centuries, each piling on top of the other like layers in a cake: Byzantine, Mongol, Western European, and the powerful rules of men like Ivan IV, Peter the Great, Lenin, and Stalin, who shaped history and culture with sheer force of personality. But just as biblical scholars and paleographers seek the "ur-text" as they trace their work's history, so in the field of intelligence and security one can seek some original source of behaviors that predate any future evolutions. In Russia one has a clear source of this in the history of the Byzantine Empire.

The importance of this particular argument can neither be overstated nor ignored. As explained above, it must be clear that the Russians are their own people, with a political and social volition beyond their cultural antecedents. When the nations of the West, conversely, try to understand the behavior of the Russian state—or the historic behavior of its Soviet or Tsarist predecessors—some keys need to be provided to unlock the behavior and make sense of it. Especially when dealing with the behavior of Russia in its security culture and its manifestation in intelligence, a heritage significantly different from that of the Western European and Anglo-Saxon states is clearly at work. It is in the parallels to the great empire of Constantinople where one may begin to see inside, or rather deeply behind, many Russian behaviors.

Can one extend the argument made here about Russia's Byzantine inheritance to other states of the Byzantine Commonwealth, such as Romania, Bulgaria, Serbia, and the closest inheritor, Greece? Perhaps to some degree. Here one would also need to account not only for the reimported Russian influence of the Communist era but also for more than five hundred years of the Ottomans' occupation—and the latter featured rule by their *dragoman* and *hospodar* client rulers, often Phanariote Greeks, which, though strongly Hellenic, was more clerical in tone.[95] Greece under the colonels was strongly authoritarian and had all the features of a police state, and Bulgaria and Serbia have clearly had their troubles with authoritarian security cultures since their post-Communist independence; yet just as clearly, states such as Romania (noted for its strong Phanariote political culture as late as the nineteenth century[96]) have altered their political culture radically since the end of communist rule and cut a hard course toward democracy and an accountable security structure in a Western European mold.[97] Ultimately, as quoted elsewhere in this volume, as W. Somerset Maugham asserted, it is clear that "tradition is a guide and not a gaoler."

Epigraph and Acknowledgment

Dimiter G. Angelov, "Byzantinism: The Imaginary and Real Heritage of Byzantium in Southeastern Europe," in *New Approaches to Balkan Studies*, edited by Dimitris Keridis, Ellen Elias-Bursać, and Nicholas Yatromanolakis (London: Brassey's, 2003), 3. The author acknowledges that an earlier version of this chapter was published as "Echo of Empires," *Journal of Slavic Studies* 23, no. 4 (2010): 574–96.

Notes

1. Dimitry Obolensky, *Byzantium and the Slavs* (Crestwood, NY: St. Vladimir's Seminary Press, 1994).

2. Edward Lucas, *The New Cold War* (New York: Palgrave, 2008).

3. Reuel Marc Gerecht, "A Rogue Intelligence State? Why Europe and America Cannot Ignore Russia," *European Outlook* (American Enterprise Institute), no. 2 (2007): 1.

4. Olga Kryshtanovskaya and Stephen White, "Putin's Militocracy," *Post-Soviet Affairs* 19, no. 4 (2003): 289.

5. See Amy Knight, *Spies without Cloaks: The KGB's Successors* (Princeton, NJ: Princeton University Press, 1998), in passim; Gerecht, "Rogue Intelligence State?"; and Kryshtanovskaya and White, "Putin's Militocracy."

6. Knight, *Spies without Cloaks*, 244.

7. Obolensky, *Byzantium and the Slavs*, 83.

8. G. Ostrogorsky, *History of the Byzantine State*, translated by J. Hussey (New Brunswick, NJ: Rutgers University Press, 1957), 509.

9. For a less sanguine view of Byzantine influence on early Russia, see J. L. I. Fennell, *Ivan the Great of Moscow* (New York: Macmillan, 1961), 319–20.

10. Cornelius Krahn, "Messianism-Marxism," *Journal of Bible and Religion* 31, no. 3 (July 1963): 211.

11. F. L. Cross and E. A. Livingstone, eds., *Oxford Dictionary of the Christian Church*, 2nd ed. (Oxford: Oxford University Press, 1983), 218. See also Edward Luttwak, *The Grand Strategy of the Byzantine Empire* (Cambridge, MA: Belknap Press, 2009), 137.

12. Dimitri Stremoonkhoff, "Moscow the Third Rome: Sources of the Doctrine," *Speculum* 28, no. 1 (January 1953): 85.

13. Obolensky, *Byzantium and the Slavs*, 79.

14. J. S. Duncan, *Russian Messianism: Third Rome, Revolution, Communism and After* (London: Routledge, 2000), 11.

15. Stephen Schenfield, *Russian Fascism: Traditions, Tendencies and Movements* (London: M. E. Sharpe, 2001), 29; Richard Pipes, *Russian Conservatism and Its Critics: A Study in Political Culture* (New Haven, CT: Yale University Press, 2007), 148–49.

16. Obolensky, *Byzantium and the Slavs*, 101.

17. John J. Dziak, *Chekisty: A History of the KGB* (Lexington, MA: Lexington Books, 1988), 4.

18. Arnold J. Toynbee, *A Study of History*, 2nd ed. (London: Oxford University Press, 1948), 320–408; on Caesaro-Papism, see 164–83.

19. Dimitri Obolensky, *Byzantine Commonwealth: Eastern Europe 500–1453* (London: Phoenix, 2000).

20. Zoe Katerina Knox, *Russian Society and the Orthodox Church: Religion in Russia after Communism* (London: Routledge, 2004), 170–71.

21. Nikolas Oikonomides, "The Role of the Byzantine State in the Economy," in *The Economic History of Byzantium*, edited by Angeliki E. Laiou (Washington, DC: Dumbarton Oaks, 2007), 973, www.doaks.org/resources/publications/doaks-online-publications/byzantine-studies/the-economic-history-of-byzantium/ehb44-state-and-the-economy.

22. Dziak, *Chekisty*, 2.

23. Ibid., 1.

24. Ibid., 2.

25. Branko Milanovic, "An Estimate of Average Income and Inequality in Byzantium around Year 1000," *Review of Income and Wealth* 52, no. 3 (September 2006): 450. See also Angeliki E. Laiou and Cecile Morrisson, *The Byzantine Economy* (Cambridge: Cambridge University Press, 2007), chap. 4 passim.

26. John Haldon, *Byzantium at War* (New York: Osprey, 2001), 74.

27. Luttwak, *Grand Strategy*, 416.

28. Haldon, *Byzantium at War*, 74.

29. Dziak, *Chekisty*, 2.

30. Procopius, *Secret History*, xxx.

31. Alexander Kazhdan, ed., *Oxford Dictionary of Byzantium* (Oxford: Oxford University Press, 1991), 37. See also Louis Bréhier, *Les Institutions de l'Empire Byzantin* (Paris: Editions Albin Michel, 1949), 327.

32. William J. Sinnegen, "Two Branches of the Roman Secret Service," *American Journal of Philology* 80, no. 3 (1959): 238–54.

33. John Bagnall Bury, *Philotheus: The Imperial Administrative System of the Ninth Century, with a Revised Text of the Kletorologion of Philotheos* (London: Oxford University Press, 1911), 106.

34. Anna Comnena, *The Alexiad*, translated by E. R. A. Sewter (New York: Penguin, 2004), 186, 261, 282.

35. Comnena, *Alexiad*, 201, 384.

36. Michael Psellus, ed., *Fourteen Byzantine Rulers*, translated by E. R. A. Sewter (New York: Penguin, 1996), 43.

37. Comnena, *Alexiad*: "was not unaware," 184, 202, 278, 297; "reliable information," 130; "informants," 142.

38. Kekaumenos, *Strategikon*, para. 78. www.acad.carleton.edu/curricular/MARS/Kekaumenos.pdf.

39. Peter Edbury, "Crusader Sources from the Near East," in *Byzantines and Crusaders in Non-Greek Sources 1025–1204*, edited by Mary Whitby (Oxford: Oxford University Press, 2007), 29.

40. Kazhdan, *Oxford Dictionary*, 1248.

41. Michael Antonucci, "War by Other Means: The Legacy of Byzantium," *History Today* 43, no. 2 (1993): 11–13.

42. Theodosius II, *Novitia*. 21.

43. Bury, *Philotheus*, 93.

44. Anonymous, *On Strategy*, in *Three Byzantine Military Treatise on Strategy*, edited by George T. Dennis (Washington, DC: Dumbarton Oaks, 1985), para. 43/p. 125.

45. Liudprand of Cremona, "The Embassy of Liudprand of the Cremonese Bishopric to the Constaninopolitan Emperor Nicephoros Phocas on Behalf of the August Ottos & Adelheid," in *The Complete Works of Liudprand of Cremona*, translated by Paolo Squatriti (Washington, DC: Catholic University of America Press, 2007), 238.

46. Warren Treadgold, "Notes on the Numbers and Organisation of the Ninth-Century Byzantine Army," *Greek, Roman, and Byzantine Studies* 21 (1980): 269.

47. Bréhier, *Institutions de l'Empire*, 307.

48. *On Strategy*, para. 43/p. 126.

49. Theophanes, *The Chronicle of Theophanes*, translated by Harry Turtledove (Philadelphia: University of Pennsylvania Press, 1982), para. 384/p. 80.

50. Bréhier, *Institutions de l'Empire*, 316; author's translation.

51. Obolensky, *Byzantium and the Slavs*, 19.

52. Procopius, *De Bello Gothico*, 4.17. Cf. David Jacoby, "Silk Economics and Cross-Cultural Artistic Interaction: Byzantium, the Muslim World, and the Christian West," *Dumbarton Oaks Papers* 58 (2004): 198.

53. Theophanes, *Chronicle of Theophanes*, para. 430, 119.

54. Constantine Porphyrogenitus, *De Administrando Imperio*, edited and translated by G. Moravcsik and R. J. H. Jenkins, book 46, 50–60.

55. John Meyendorff, *The Byzantine Legacy in the Orthodox Church* (Crestwood, NY: St. Vladimir's Seminary Press, 1982), 93. See also A. Laiou, "On Just War in Byzantium," in *Studies in Honor of Speros Vryonis Jnr*, edited by S. Reinert, J. Langdon, and J. Allen (New Rochelle, NY: Aristide D. Caratzas, 1993), I, 153–74; N. Oikonomides, "The Concept of 'Holy War' and Two Tenth-Century Byzantine Ivories," in *Peace and War in Byzantium: Essays in Honor of George T. Dennis S.J.*, edited by T. S. Miller and J. Nesbitt (Washington, DC: Dumbarton Oaks, 1995), 62–86.

56. Meyendorff, *Byzantine Legacy*, 8.

57. Obolensky, *Byzantium and the Slavs*, 109.

58. Dimitri Obolensky, *Six Byzantine Portraits* (Oxford: Oxford University Press, 1988), 12–13.

59. John Haldon, *Byzantium in the Seventh Century* (Cambridge: Cambridge University Press, 1990), 208ff.; some scholars say it was established under Emperor Heraclius, by 640.

See Treadgold, "Notes," passim; and Romilly Jenkins, *Byzantium: The Imperial Centuries* (London: Weidenfeld & Nicolson, 1966), 16.

60. J. F. Haldon and H. Kennedy, "The Arab-Byzantine Frontier in the Eighth and Ninth Centuries: Military Organisation and Society in the Borderlands," in *The Byzantine and Early Islamic Near East*, edited by H. Kennedy (Aldershot, UK: Ashgate, 2006), 79–81.

61. Luttwak, *Grand Strategy*, 5–6, 416.

62. Maurice, *The Strategikon*, translated by George T. Dennis (Philadelphia: University of Pennsylvania Press, 1984), book XI, para. 1, 113.

63. Constantine VII, 13.

64. Constantine VII was first under the regency, then the rule, of the former admiral Romanus Lecapenus, who made himself emperor and ruled from 922 to 940. Only on Romanus's death did Constantine VII rise to be sole emperor.

65. Nikephoros Phokas, attrib., *On Skirmishing*, in *Three Byzantine Military Treatises*, translated by George T. Dennis, 163.

66. Anonymous (ca. 960 CE), *Campaign Organisation*, in *Three Byzantine Military Treatises*, 293.

67. *On Strategy*, para. 42, 123.

68. *On Skirmishing*, para. 7, 163.

69. Ibid.

70. Leo the Deacon, *The History*, translated by Alice-Mary Talbot and Denis Sullivan (Washington, DC: Dumbarton Oaks, 2005), book VII, para. 5, 168.

71. *Campaign Organization*, para. 18, 293.

72. Luttwak, *Grand Strategy*, 416–17.

73. Francis Dvornik, "Byzantine Influence on the Kievan State," *Dumbarton Oaks Papers* 9 (1956): 76.

74. Daniel Tarschys, "Secret Institutions in Russian Government," *Soviet Studies* 37, no. 4 (October 1985): 528.

75. Tarschys, "Secret Institutions," 529.

76. Ibid., 532.

77. Christopher Andrew and Oleg Gordievsky, *KGB: The Inside Story* (London: Hodder & Stoughton, 1998), 28.

78. Knight, *Spies without Cloaks*, 221.

79. Andrei Soldatov and Irina Borogan, *The New Nobility: The Restoration of Russia's Security State* (New York: PublicAffairs, 2010), 28–29.

80. Len Scott, "Secret Intelligence, Covert Action and Clandestine Diplomacy," *Intelligence and National Security*, 19, no. 2 (2004): 335.

81. Ibid., 323.

82. Richard Shultz and Roy Godson, *Dezinformatsia: The Strategy of Soviet Disinformation* (New York: Berkley Books, 1986), 16.

83. Theophanes, *Chronicle of Theophanes*, para. 375, 71–72.

84. Comnena, *Alexiad*, 384.

85. Theophanes, *Chronicle of Theophanes*, para. 436, 125.

86. See Alex Goldfarb and Marina Litvinenko, *Death of a Dissident: The Poisoning of Alexander Litvinenko and the Return of the KGB* (London: Free Press, 2007).

87. Peter Charanis, "The Transfer of Population as a Policy in the Byzantine Empire," *Comparative Studies in Society and History* 3, no. 2 (January 1961): 151.

88. J. Otto Pohl, "Stalin's Genocide against the 'Repressed Peoples,'" *Journal of Genocide Research* 2, no. 2 (2000): 267.

89. B. Nahajlo, "Forcible Population Transfers, Deportations and Ethnic Cleansing in the CIS: Problems in Search of Responses," *Refugee Survey Quarterly* 16, no. 3 (1997).

90. George Kennan, "The Long Telegram," cable, Embassy in Moscow to State Department, February 22, 1946.

91. Vladimir Putin, "2000 Russian National Security Concept," www.russiaeurope.mid .ru/russiastrat2000.html.

92. John Anderson, "Putin and the Orthodox Church: Asymmetric Symphonia?" *Journal of International Affairs* 61, no. 1 (2007): 195.

93. Julie Elkner, *Spiritual Security in Putin's Russia*, History and Policy Paper 26, July 2005, www.historyandpolicy.org/papers/policy-paper-26.html#summ.

94. Daniel P. Payne, "Spiritual Security, the Russian Orthodox Church, and the Russian Foreign Ministry: Collaboration or Cooptation?" *Journal of Church and State* 52, no. 4 (2010).

95. L. S. Stavrianos, *The Balkans since 1453* (London: Hurst, 2002), 270. The Phanar was the neighborhood in Constantinople left to the Greeks after the conquest of 1453, and repopulated in the decades after by Greek speakers from other parts of the Ottoman Empire, often traders. Their language skills were harnessed by the Ottomans, and the term "Dragoman" means "translator," the representative of the Ottoman governor, who himself would remain distant from the local population.

96. Ibid., 692.

97. Larry L. Watts, "Intelligence Reform in Europe's Emerging Democracies: Conflicting Paradigms, Dissimilar Contexts," *Studies in Intelligence* 48, no. 1 (2004).

CHAPTER 6

Origins of an Arab and Islamic Intelligence Culture

Abdulaziz A. Al-Asmari

In his epistle "Secret Keeping and Mincing Words," the prolific ninth-century Arab writer and philosopher Al-Jahiz says that it is human nature "to seek news and intelligence."[1] According to Al-Jahiz, humanity's search for news is as old as history. The reason is not difficult to see. Life, or rather survival, requires constant responses to questions and queries that must be answered if one is to protect oneself and prepare for unforeseen eventualities. Arabs, like other nations of the world, used intelligence and engaged in a variety of espionage activities during peacetime as well as wartime. Understanding the religious and ideological basis of any given society is a prerequisite for any effective engagement with that society. This is no less true of the Arab and Islamic worlds than of anywhere else, especially given that, though religion underlies basic beliefs in most parts of the world, "it is not normally toxically linked with politics in the same way as it is in the Middle East."[2] It is also essential in a broader context than the Middle East because Islam is a global religion, and many communities and governments in Africa, Asia, the Trans-Caucasus, and other regions are as much inheritors of an Islamic intellectual and intelligence legacy as they may be of indigenous, pre-Islamic influences.

This chapter demonstrates that there is an Arab concept of intelligence that dates back long before the rise of Islam in the first half of the seventh century, more specifically to the Age of Jahiliya (Ignorance) of the second and third centuries and beyond. During those ancient times the Qahtani tribes of

Southern Arabia, like all inhabitants of the northern and central parts of the Arab Peninsula, had their own networks of spies and secret agents, who were quite active during both war and peace. In the early stages of Islam,[3] the Prophet Muhammad (pbuh) and his followers first made use of and later enriched and developed those intelligence notions and practices that they had inherited from their Arab predecessors.[4] As Richard Gabriel has observed, the Prophet Muhammad was not merely "a tactician, military theorist, organizational reformer, strategic thinker, operational-level combat commander, political-military leader, heroic soldier and revolutionary, inventor of the theory of insurgency and history's first successful practitioner"; he was also "a master of intelligence in war, and his intelligence service eventually came to rival those of Rome and Persia, especially in the area of political intelligence."[5] That being said, a pre-Islamic Arab tradition underpins the subsequent Islamic approach to intelligence, which has since spread with that religion well beyond the Arab world.

Arabic Intelligence Terminology

The Arabic equivalent of the English word "intelligence" is *mukhabarat* or *istikhbarat*, both of which are derived from the same Arabic triliteral root, *khabar*. As a noun, this word can be used in a wide variety of contexts, meaning, for instance, any of the following: "news," "account," "advice," "hearsay," "message," "rumor," "knowledge," "answer," "response," "reply," "report," and "story." It can also be used to mean "having a great deal of news" or "having great depth of knowledge and expertise." This noun may also refer to one's final story or news, that is, death. The subject noun *mukhbir*, a derivative of *khabar*, means "he who transmits news" or "he who spies on others" for whatever reason, although the term is normally associated with state-sponsored agents.[6] The present-day term *mukhabarat* is almost exclusively used to mean "intelligence," although it was also used during the Umayyad and Abbasid Caliphate (seventh to fifteenth centuries) to mean "correspondence," "reports," "letters," "writing," and "contacts."[7] In the Arab world today, both *mukhabarat* and *istikhbarat* may be used interchangeably to mean "intelligence," although the latter is commonly reserved for military intelligence, whereas the former is used for all types: domestic, foreign, military, nonmilitary, and counterintelligence.[8]

Although in English the word "spy" can variously be used to describe foreign or local agents who observe, investigate, or engage in secret observation, Arabic makes a clear distinction between those who spy for their own people, state, or interests and those who are employed by an enemy, a rival, or a foreign power. The Arabic word *jasous* is reserved primarily for those who are employed as agents and spies for foreign rivals. Colloquially, it is used to describe those who seek unflattering, debasing, or embarrassing information about others, for the purpose of defamation, embezzlement, or blackmail, or any such ignoble purpose.[9] In the collective consciousness of the Arabs, the word is therefore laden with negative and derogatory implications. *Namous*, conversely, is normally, although not exclusively, reserved for those who are especially aware, conscious, knowledgeable, and cognizant of the deep and hidden secrets of others. In its broader implications *namous* is used to describe men of wisdom, learning, and sagacity. The word is sometimes used as a synonym for "integrity" and "honor." In a special sense, in Islam, it is universally used to denote the greatest source of "news" and "intelligence," the Angel Gabriel, whom Muslims believe to have been sent by Allah to the Prophet Muhammad in order to convey Divine commands and reveal the words of the Quran.[10]

To distinguish spying for a good cause from "sniffing out" information for evil ends, Arabs use two different words. *Tajassasa* is normally used to describe the act of attempting to acquire any secret or covert information. Although the noun *jasous* (spy) does not appear in any Quranic text, its root, the verb *tajassasa*, appears in a verse in the *surah* (chapter) of *Hujurat* (Chambers), where Muslims are enjoined not to engage in this activity; it is normally associated with, but not confined to, the undercover work of anyone who spies for someone else, especially for an enemy or a foreign power.[11] *Jasous* is also used to refer to the act of detecting private information for selfish reasons, material gain, or any other nonbenevolent purpose. *Tajassasa* is used in the Quran to admonish believers to "avoid suspicion (as much as possible), for suspicion in some cases is a sin; and not to spy on each other, or speak ill of each other behind their backs."[12] Conversely, the verb *tahassasa* is used specifically to denote the act of acquiring information for one's own use, for a good cause, or for some generally benevolent or benign purpose. It is in this sense that Jacob uses the verb in the Quran when he asks his other sons to search for their brother Joseph, enjoining them to "Go ye and *inquire about* Joseph and his brother, and never give up hope of Allah's Soothing Mercy."[13]

Throughout Arab history, a spy, whether a foreign agent or a local operative, has most commonly been referred to as *ain* (pl., *uyoun*), which literally means "eye." The resemblance, both semantically and figuratively, between the Arabic word and its English counterpart, the verb "espy," is quite apparent. *Ain*, which has been in circulation for the last two millennia in Arabic, is still used extensively in a variety of contexts, chief among which is the intelligence field. It refers, among other things, to a herald, to a person who is dispatched to explore a situation, to one who brings back tidings, to a secret observer, and to a collector of information. Arab historians and lexicographers such as Muhammad Murtadha Al-Zabeedi argue that *ain* (which also means "a bird of prey" and, by extension, "having very keen vision") was applied to spies and informers because much of their work depended on what they observed, particularly with their eyes.[14]

Other Arabic terms denoting spies or undercover agents include *dasees, daleel, talee'ah, rabee'ah, muharwil, hawas, fuyouj, sheefa,* and *baghiyah.* The noun *dasees* is derived from the verb *dasa,* which may be used to mean any of the following: "creep in," "encroach unnoticed," "blend in," and "intervene." In general, *dasees* means "he who is involved in clandestine reconnaissance," who "intervenes" or "who enters any territory (literally or figuratively) without the knowledge or consent of others." The link between this sense and "espionage" is self-evident.[15] *Daleel,* conversely, is most commonly used in the sense of "guide," "scout," "lookout," or "herald," but it is also quite often used euphemistically to mean "spy." The term was originally applied to those who possessed accurate knowledge not only of the intricate network of overland routes across the desert, and the locations of wells, springs, and pastureland, but also the rivalries and alliances between different tribes.

Rabee'ah, which denotes a hilltop or an elevated place, is used figuratively for scouts whose missions would naturally become easier when they operated from a high vantage point. The term was quite common, appearing frequently in a number of ancient Arabic documents, especially in poetic texts antedating Islam by some decades. The pre-Islamic poet warrior Urwa bin Al-Ward (d. 594) illustrates the vital role played by the *rabee'ah* in the deserts of Arabia, when, in one of his poems, he writes: "Before we stealthily descend upon a watering place, we (normally) dispatch a *rabee'ah* [scout], who, like a tall tree, stands erect to keep a proper lookout."[16] In a reference to the terrible conditions under which the *rabee'ah* operated, another poet, Aws bin Hajar (530–620), describes a dejected lover as "lurking behind the curtains of nature like a spying *rabee'ah,* parched, and frightened."[17] An interesting category of *rabee'ah* was the "naked scout."[18] This somewhat odd title derives from what such scouts normally did in an emergency when they discovered an imminent danger but had no time to communicate a warning to their fellow tribesmen. They would remove their clothes and then, mounted on their horses, would wave them as improvised warning flags.

The term *taleah,* which is derived from the verb *tala,* may refer to any of the following: "pioneer," "he who is at the front," "pathfinder," "forerunner," "explorer," and "reconnoiter." This could be extended to include a "person who knows [secrets] first," presumably through espionage. The task of the *talee'ah,* which may be translated into English as "advance scout" or "secret herald," involved infiltrating enemy ranks in order to collect as much tactical information as possible about the targets, their exact location, state of preparedness, terrain, provisions and water resources, and the numbers of camels, horses, and other livestock, and their strengths or weakness. The *talee'ah* enjoyed some sort of recognition as an elite group, in that they carried out their duties independently and reported directly to the commander of the army. Their most desired qualities were speed and sharp eyes; they did not have to be master horsemen or swordsmen. The duties of the *rabee'ah*, conversely, involved observing enemy movements and reporting any developments to the army commanders. Such observations were normally carried out from a vantage point such as a hill in a neutral zone or no man's land. The *rabee'ah* would then send reports to his commanders through the use of a variety of methods such as drums, fire, or smoke signals.[19]

Fuyuj literally means "he who walks fast or runs from one place to another." Because speed is of vital importance in the transmission of intelligence, the term has come to be applied to spies and agents. A related Arabic term is *muharwil*, which literally means "runner," "one who moves briskly," or "scrambler," but was also used for a spy. *Sheefa* is derived from the verb *shafa*, which originally meant "yearn for something," but with the passage of time came to refer to lifting one's head in order to see clearly, and to being at the front and in a position to see more clearly than others. The connection between "yearning to know secrets" and "spying" is self-evident. This word is reserved for civilian uses, whereas *rabee'ah* is intended for military purposes. Because the primary duty of a spy is to seek and acquire classified information, the Arabic term *baghiya*—which means "the seeker," "he who is on a special quest," or "he who demands to know or possess something"—was occasionally used to refer to clandestine collectors of information.[20] Another word that was widely associated with spies is *munafiq*, which is reserved specifically for Arab and non-Arab but putatively Muslim spies who operate under the guise of Islam in order to subvert it from within through the dissemination of disparaging rumors and falsehoods. The Quran uses the word in this sense several times.[21]

To ensure that they were fully aware of the arrival of newcomers to their communities, especially under cover of darkness, the ancient Arabs entrusted the task of monitoring arrivals and departures to special night sentinels or watchmen, called *suh-har*. This Arabic word is derived from the verb *sahara*, which means "stay wakeful" or "watchful," especially during the night. The vigilant *suh-har* frequently lurked in the dark, usually at the approaches to a market town, a crossroads, or any location where it was believed that a stranger or suspect would be arriving.[22] It was customary for the feuding tribes of Arabia to employ *uyoun* in order to spy on competitors or rivals. Before executing a raid or a reprisal attack, a tribe would, as a matter of course, deploy a number of lookouts in order to reconnoiter the situation. However, spying was not limited to gathering military intelligence in times of war; agents would also provide valuable security and economic information in peacetime.

On the domestic front, the *uyoun*—sometimes called *ruwwad* (pioneers) in this context—were responsible for inspecting property and for finding pastureland and water, especially during droughts.[23] Intelligence relating to the availability of water and pastureland suitable for grazing livestock has always been of vital importance throughout the arid peninsula. Many wars across history have been waged by the tribes of Arabia for no other reason than to control or monopolize wells and water resources. Scouting for water and pastureland was not only customary but necessary before a Bedouin group could fold camp and move on.

Special mention must be made of the early Arabic term *bareed*. This widely used word—which has always denoted "news reporting" or, more broadly, "post" or "mail"—signifies the interest shown by the early Arabs in this activity. The term appears in a number of ancient documents and poems, most famously in a poem written by the sixth-century Arab poet Imru' al-Qais. The Prophet Muhammad also used this word in one of his sayings when he enjoined his followers to give earnest and careful consideration to such reporting.[24]

Early Arab Records of Espionage

With the weakening position of the Eastern Roman Empire in Syria and northern Mesopotamia during the mid–second century, early migrants from the Arabian Peninsula gradually built the independent state of Manathira (or Lakhmidi) along the Euphrates River.[25] They also succeeded in establishing another state known as the Ghassanids in Syria, where Jafnah bin Omar was the first of a long line of kings who ruled over this northwestern corner of Arabia. The Byzantines (as we may now call them, see chapter 5 in this volume; the Arab word for Byzantium was *Rūm*, or Roman[26]) did not view the emerging state of the Ghassanids as a rival power but as an ally against the Persians, with whom they were for a long time locked in a continual state of warfare. The Persians, conversely, considered the Manathira state, which stretched along their western and northwestern frontiers, as a kind of buffer zone against their Byzantine enemies. For strategic reasons, the Persians nurtured the new state of the Lakhmids and ensured that it would not easily fall prey to foreign invaders. In short, both the Byzantines and Persians saw the strategic benefits of maintaining what John Glubb would later call "a system of Arab satellite princedoms guarding the desert flanks of both empires."[27]

It was inevitable that rivalries and conflicts of interest would arise between the two Arab states, supported as they were by the two rival powers in the region. Relations continued to deteriorate, and the two sides often found themselves locked in engagements that were in most cases proxy battles fought on behalf of the Persians and Byzantines. The most famous of these confrontations was one in which the Ghassanid, Al-Harith bin Jabalah, scored a decisive victory over Munthir III, who was killed. The Byzantines considered this outcome a victory for their own cause.[28]

Despite the close military links between these two Arab states and their patron empires, there is very little documented evidence of cooperation between them in the field of intelligence. One of the earliest references to intelligence activities carried out by the Arab states appears in the multivolume anthology and encyclopedia *Kitab al-Aghani* (Book of Songs), which was compiled in the tenth century by Abu Faraj al-Asbahani. According to al-Asbahani, the most important task of the *uyoun* was to provide personal security for their monarchs and superiors. Al-Asbahani relates the story of a Manathira spy who was able to save the life of his king, Al-Naman bin Al-Munthir (AD 582–610).[29] The spy, who was based deep inside the Ghassanid state in northern Arabia (Syria), wrote to his master, warning that a rival had sent an agent for the purpose of assassinating the king. With this vital intelligence, Al-Naman bin Al-Munthir ordered his men to track down and shadow the newly arrived would-be assassin. He was caught preparing for his deadly mission and killed before he could carry it out.[30]

There is evidence that the Qahtani Arabs of southern Arabia engaged in intelligence activities as early as the second century BC. Extant inscriptions from the time contain references to such activities, which, despite the primitive methods and tactics, were in many ways quite well organized. A recent study in old south Arabian epigraphy shows that a high proportion of the ancient Qahtani army was charged with intelligence-related duties. Ten percent of all fighting men were assigned to such activities as skirmishing, scouting, and reconnoitering. As A. F. Beeston has shown, the Qahtanis recruited nomadic Bedouins and a variety of mercenaries to carry out espionage missions, despite the fact that these sources were not fully trusted or deemed reliable by their handlers.[31]

With the possible exception of those living in Mecca and Medina, who mainly worked as traders, the majority of the population of Arabia comprised nomadic Bedouins, who moved from one place to another in search of water and pasture. The early war records of the Bedouins of central Arabia contain numerous references to the use of *ain*,[32] *rabee'ah*,[33] and *talee'ah*.[34] This indicates the existence of some sort of tactical intelligence, albeit in an undeveloped and primitive form. The general system that governed Bedouin social relationships was based on total allegiance to the leader of the tribe or clan. These tribal communities—whose main occupation was keeping camels, goats, and sheep—lived "in semi-isolation from the rest of the world . . . in a state of perpetual war."[35] Because these nomads were totally unmindful of the outside world, they produced a culture in which, as Philip K. Hitti has put it, "the raid or *ghazwa*, . . . otherwise considered a form of brigandage, [was] raised by the economic and social conditions of desert life to the rank of a national constitution." It lay "at the base of the economic structure of Bedouin pastoral society," in which "the fighting mood [was]a chronic mental condition" and "raiding is one of the few manly occupations." Hitti further quotes a poet of the period who observed that "our business is to make raids on the enemy, on our neighbor and on our own brother, in case we find none to raid but a brother!"[36] Although not on the scale of a general war, the raids were so common that a new Arabic term, *su'louk*, was coined to describe those involved in this specific form of attack, in which numerous Arab poets took part. These poet brigands often boasted about their exploits, which frequently involved scouts and spies.

Scouting and intelligence gathering were always an organic part of the skirmishes and clashes of *su'louk*. Before an attack was launched, one or more *rabee'ah* elements would be called upon to scout the area and report any sightings of the targets or any unusual happenings. The work carried out by desert scouts and reconnoiters was considered more critical and perilous than that of the ordinary fighting men. Severe punishments were meted out to those captured. The poet Aws bin Al-Hajar describes the *rabee'ah* as living "in perpetual fear, chronically thirsty. So scared are they of the light, that when the sun shines, they turn their faces the other way."[37] The *rabee'ah* agents were so central to these conflicts that one such conflict, the Basous War (494–534) between the Taghlib and Bakr tribes, is also remembered as the "Days of the *Rabee'ah*." In his mammoth anthology of Arabic prose and poetry from pre-Islamic times until the tenth century, Al-Asbahani writes of the efforts each tribe involved exerted to trace and uncover the spies working in its midst. He also recounts how the agents of the tribe of Bakr bin Wa'el managed to infiltrate the ranks of the Ka'ab bin Rabee'ah tribe during the Falj War.[38]

Precisely because of the Bedouin raiding tradition, spies were also entrusted with the vital task of protecting the commercial caravans across the vast deserts of Arabia.[39] Intratribal routes, overland arteries between the Bedouin areas and urban centers, and the communication lines between the northern parts and the southern frontiers of the Arab Peninsula were all under the close watch of those early intelligence pioneers.[40] The use of *uyoun* was sometimes dictated by the need to honor the Quraishis' treaty obligations with the many tribes whose commercial caravans bound for Mecca or the north normally passed through what was then a trading town called Yethrib but would later become the city of Medina. To ensure that caravans and travelers might pass peacefully and without incident in the vicinity of Medina, or indeed across the entire region controlled by them, the Quraishis made extensive use of scouts, spies, and watchmen. Chief among their targets were those who violated agreements, conspired against their implementation, or sought to incite other tribes to transgress and breach the accords.

The early spies of Arabia underwent vigorous training in a range of arts and skills. Above all else, they were trained to be patient and resilient, to bear unexpected physical or psychological hardships, and to blend in with the target community. Camouflage became an essential part of espionage. Significantly, the chronicler and commentator Muhammed Ibn Al-Tabari (d. 923) speaks of some undercover agents who carried dedication to their profession to great lengths, when they underwent voluntary surgery in order to mask their identities, deceive the enemy, and be in a better position to carry out their duties. Tabari explains how primitive surgical or noninvasive procedures were sometimes performed to alter the shape of the nose or ears of such agents.[41]

Prospective agents were also trained in survival and communications skills. To communicate with their base or with each other, the early *uyoun* used fire at night and smoke during the day. They also exchanged coded messages in order to circumvent detection or exposure. An important and regular source of information came from concubines and slaves,[42] who were used to gather general information and to provide valuable and accurate details about their masters' plans, movements, contacts, and close associates.[43] For verification purposes, the early Arabs normally dispatched two spies on any particular mission.[44] Spies were also used to entrap rivals and also in starting disinformation campaigns designed to dispel specific perceptions and rumors and to frustrate enemy efforts. Poison was occasionally used to eliminate enemies or those deemed to pose a grave danger to the community.[45]

The Prophet Muhammad's *Sunnah* and Intelligence

Many ideas, regulations, and practices relevant to intelligence that were enshrined in the principles and injunctions of the Quran are further articulated in the *Hadith* and *Sunnah*. The Quran contains the holy scriptures of Islam and is considered by Muslims, Arab and non-Arab alike, to be the most authoritative and revered document in their history. Quranic legislation includes rulings that can be applied to the practice of espionage and intelligence with concepts of that which is ethically acceptable (*sadar*), such as surveillance of potential threats, or forbidden (*haram*), such as prurient intrusions into personal privacy. Just as the Quran is the most important source of intelligence legislation, the Prophet Muhammad's *Hadith* (sayings) and *Sunnah* (way of life) constitute the second most important source. From Islam's earliest days, the *Hadith* have been carefully collated, studied, indexed, and discussed by various Islamic schools of thought. They have also been thematically and chronologically catalogued. Although scholars and religious authorities are not unanimous as to the authenticity of some of the sayings attributed to the Prophet Muhammad, the bulk of these have, as far as the available sources would permit, been minutely checked, verified, and carefully written down by specially trained scribes, giving Islamic religious texts an apparent rigor and credibility matched by few other religions—an important consideration when understanding the strength of both the moral and intellectual authority that these texts hold for believers.

And these in turn rest upon the Quran, which goes well beyond laying down the general principles and rules. The Quran actually provides numerous examples of intelligence work drawn from history and the lives of the prophets, in which it is not difficult to see the intelligence cycle at work. In the Quran, some references tend to suggest that intelligence operations carried out against the enemies of Islam and in the interests of Muslims at large are quite legitimate and admissible. This explains why contemporary Islamic groups—which base their ideology on Islam and which strive to achieve a specific aim in the interest of Muslims, such as liberating occupied lands, expelling colonialists, and spreading Islam—view any attempt at undermining the enemy as not only legitimate but also a religious duty. Conversely, spying on the private lives of individuals is illegal and inadmissible according to the Quran. Islam also accentuates the negative impact of espionage against the Muslim Umma (community), describing those planted amid the Muslims who work for the enemies of Islam as *munafiqoon*, who are to be detested and severely punished.

These intelligence methods constituted part of the cultural heritage of the Arabian Peninsula before the advent of Islam. The Muslims who inherited them in turn developed them to serve their own needs and requirements. Clandestine methods and organizational approaches have a particular relevance to Islamic doctrines because of the role of covert activity in the earliest years of the religion's development. During these years, when the Prophet Muhammad was at risk from potentially violent persecution by the established Quraishi political and religious leaderships of the day, his call to the new faith was shrouded in secrecy. In particular, in the first three years, known in Islamic history as the Secret Stage, all his movements, contacts, and meetings with his followers were carried out clandestinely. This difficult period was followed by what Arab historians call the Open Stage, when Muslims embarked upon a vigorous, open campaign aimed at spreading the word of Allah to their fellow Arabs. These changes also reflect a shift from covert to overt conflict and from cold to hot warfare.

The formative impact of clandestinity on Islam is reflected in the articulation of moral regulations concerning espionage and practical, almost instructional exemplars of intelligence activities, especially human intelligence and paramilitary special activities. In terms of what might be called concepts and doctrines of intelligence, these latter activities are particularly instructive. The Open Stage, of course, involved open conflict, and Muhammad's organizational skills and leadership proved quite competent and innovative here, especially in his use of what may be called military intelligence, including the appointment of one of the earliest recognizable dedicated intelligence (in modern parlance) cells, which was headed by Umar bin Al-Khattab. The *Haddith* and *Sunnah*, in conjunction with early Islamic historical narratives, provide an extensive and detailed body of guidance on the conduct of clandestine human intelligence; the exploitation of intelligence sources, including early materials exploitation; and human source reporting and organization, and the implementation of operational and tactical military intelligence.

The Prophet Muhammad on Organization, Doctrine, and Tradecraft

In Islamic history, clandestine activity dates back to the inception of the new religion. The Prophet Muhammad started his call to Islam by patiently and silently collecting information on those whom he was hoping to win over to Islam. Chief among the qualities which he was seeking in prospective converts were honesty, trustworthiness, and the ability to keep a secret. Besides his wife, Khadeejah, the Prophet Muhammad's young cousin, Ali bin Abi Talib, and his closest friend and confidant, Abu Bakr, were the first to respond surreptitiously to his call and provide him with much-needed moral and material support. During the early period of Islam, the theater of covert operations extended far beyond Mecca and Medina to include areas as far as Yemen to the south and Abyssinia (present-day Ethiopia) to the west. It was of course only natural that in the beginning covert activities faced myriad problems. As Richard Gabriel has noted, the Prophet Muhammad's followers were "mostly townspeople with no experience in desert travel."[46] Thus, on some of the early operations, the Prophet Muhammad had to rely on desert dwellers and Bedouin guides. Then, as his foothold in Medina grew firmer, "his intelligence service became more organized and sophisticated, using agents in place, commercial spies, debriefing of prisoners, combat patrols, and reconnaissance in force as methods of intelligence collection." Muhammad himself, as Gabriel points out, seems to have possessed a detailed knowledge of clan loyalties and politics within the insurgency's area of operations and used this knowledge to good effect when negotiating alliances with the Bedouins."[47]

The first Muslim to carry out clandestine collection was Abdullah, son of Abu Bakr, whose secret reports in the first days of the Hijra, the journey made by the Prophet and his companions to Medina, were of paramount significance to the survival of the Prophet Muhammad and Abu Bakr. This young man was directed by the Prophet Muhammad to mingle with the Quraishis of Mecca during the day and then report to him at night on what he saw and heard in the then hostile land. For three successive nights, this young *ain* would slip out quietly from Mecca to the cave where the Prophet Muhammad was hiding following the attempt on his life. There, Abdullah "would go to see [Muhammad and Abu Bakr] after dusk, stay the night there, apprise them of the latest situation in Mecca, and then leave in the early morning to mix with the Meccans as usual and not to draw the least attention to his clandestine activities."[48]

Abdullah was assisted in his mission by two people: his sister, Asma bint Abu Bakr, and a trusted shepherd named Amir bin Furaihah. Besides updates on the situation in Mecca, Furaihah, who tended his master Abu Bakr's flock, offered the Prophet Muhammad and his master an additional vital service. He would "steal away unobserved, every evening, with a few goats to the cave and furnish its inmates with a plentiful supply of milk."[49] During the day, Furaihah would mix with other shepherds in the area, carefully listening and memorizing details of the stories and rumors they related to each other. These details would reach the Prophet Muhammad and Abu Bakr by nightfall. Abdullah's sister, Asma, may be said to be the first female *ain* spy in Islamic history, as she too carried out clandestine collection and reported to the Prophet Muhammad, when her brother was for one reason or another unable to deliver his reports.

Informants included people from all walks of life—men and women; young and old; rich and poor; close relatives and freed slaves; Muslims, Jews, and polytheists; Arabs and non-Arabs. Despite the many differences among these precursors of modern intelligence, what united them all was dedication to the cause, adherence to secrecy, and respect for the unity of command.[50] The reporting network in Mecca, for example, was headed by the Prophet Muhammad's own uncle, Abu Al-Fadhl Al-Abbas, and was undoubtedly the most important source of intelligence during the period before its conquest by the Muslims. But many other intelligence-gathering stations, as we would say in modern parlance, were dispersed over most parts of Arabia. There was indeed hardly a tribe or a clan that did not have a secret *ain* agent reporting on its general affairs, alliances, and intentions. But the Prophet Muhammad had other sources of information: recent converts to Islam and traveling Copts and Syrians, as well as local merchants and traders. These often acted as valuable sources of information, either voluntarily or for some form of material reward, such as cash or weapons. The early Muslims also resorted to envoys and couriers to gather information on the lands and people to whom they were dispatched. The immunity conferred upon these men afforded them an opportunity to move from one place to another with relative ease and to mingle more freely with their targets.[51]

The Prophet Muhammad's clandestine operators were also important in the economic war that the Muslims launched against hostile Mecca. During the period when the Prophet Muhammad was planning to impose a total economic blockade on his religious adversaries, he did all he could to hinder and intercept caravan routes linking Mecca to the outside world, especially the desert overland routes from Mecca and Syria in the north to Yemen in the South. When he once learned of the approach of a Mecca-bound caravan belonging to Abu Sufyan, one of the wealthiest and most influential Quraishi chieftains and the main rival of the Prophet Muhammad on the battlefield, he immediately ordered three men to go to Mecca in order to seek details of its exact destination.[52] To tighten the grip around the Meccan polytheists, the Prophet Muhammad had to rely on the reports of lookouts and agents who were well dispersed in and around Mecca and Medina. The raiding operations that were planned and executed on the strength of their reports brought all Meccan foreign trade to a standstill. Describing the tight blockade on Mecca, Thumamah bin Athal al-Hanafi told his fellow Meccans: "By Allah, not a single grain of wheat reaches you unless the Messenger of Allah, peace be upon him, permits it."[53]

On the eve of the Battle of Uhud, the Prophet Muhammad sent two agents to scout the area around Medina and Mount Uhud and to collect as much information as they could on the Quraishis, especially the number of fighting men deployed against him and the areas in which they were concentrated. They reported that the enemy had arrived at a place called Al-Aridh, northeast of Medina, famous for its wide expanse of rich agricultural soil, but that its fields and orchards had almost vanished and that the green areas had turned into a wasteland. The sudden disappearance of the rich foliage, which was devoured by the livestock and draft animals of the Quraishis, provided a clear indication as to the size of the Quraishi battalions. Because the number of beasts of burden and other animals was directly proportional to that of the advancing armies, the Prophet Muhammad and his men concluded that they were facing a very large army. Even after the end of fighting at Uhud, the Prophet Muhammad continued his intelligence activities when he ordered that the Quraishi retreat be closely monitored. He specifically wanted details of the means of transportation used by the Quraishis, especially the numbers and types of draft animals they employed. He instructed his agent Saad bin Abi Waqqas to "bring us news of their movements. If they have mounted the camels rather than the horses, then this signifies that they have decided to depart. But if they have mounted their horses rather than their camels, then most likely they are bent on attacking Medina."[54]

Besides the deployment and operation of human intelligence sources, there was also guidance on the validation and analysis of this intelligence. On the eve of the Battle of Badr, the Prophet Muhammad dispatched three of his close confidants and eminent companions—Ali bin Abi Talib,[55] Al-Zubair bin Al-Awwam,[56] and Sa'd bin Abi Waqqas[57]—to reconnoiter the area that was to witness the first major armed confrontation with his Quraishi enemies. The three men headed toward a place known to be water-rich and frequented by caravans as well as inhabitants of nearby lands. The scouts spotted two young boys drawing water from a well, captured them, and led them to the Prophet Muhammad's headquarters, where it was hoped that the Prophet would extract useful information from them. Finding that the Prophet was busy performing his prayers, the three men began interrogating the captives. When asked for whom they were carrying the water, the boys gave what sounded like an evasive answer, saying that they were working for the Quraishi army advancing toward Medina. This answer was not to the liking of the Prophet's companions, who had been under the impression that the boys belonged to Abu Sufayan's caravan, which had suddenly changed course and vanished in the desert. To force the boys to tell the truth, they started to beat them severely.[58]

These beatings compelled the young boys to say that they were in fact work-ing for Abu Sufyan, leader of the richly laden Quraishi caravan, which was on its way from Syria to Mecca. Upon this admission, they were then left alone.[59] When the Prophet Muhammad finished his prayers, he was advised of what had happened and how the boys had changed their story. Examining the details carefully, the Prophet disapproved of what the three scouts had done to the boys and felt that something was amiss. Censuring his companions, the Prophet said: "When the boys utter the truth, you beat them, and when they tell a lie, you release them!" He then decided to conduct the interrogation of the water carriers himself. Without resorting to violence or the threat of force, the Prophet Muhammad managed to extract crucial information about three areas of interest to the Muslim army: the whereabouts of the Quraishi army, the number of fighting men deployed by Quraish, and the names of their command-ing officers.[60]

The Prophet Muhammad started by asking the boys where the Quraishis had camped. He was told that they were behind the sand dunes at Adwa Quswa. When he asked them how many fighting men there were, they said that they did not know. To extract this vital information, the Prophet then asked the young boys how many camels were slaughtered each day. They said "9 on one day and 10 on another." Given that camels were the main source of sustenance for tribesmen during raids and battles, and that it was common knowledge among all desert dwellers that a camel can feed between 90 and 100 people, the Prophet indirectly learned that the advancing army numbered between 900 and 1,000 men. He then inquired about the leaders of the Quraishi army. He was told that among the commanding officers were Utbah bin Rabee'ah, Shee-bah Akhah, Umayya bin Khalaf, Al-Abbas bin Abdul-Muttalib, and Sahl bin Amru. These names gave the Prophet a relatively clear picture of what to expect, for he knew these men, their backgrounds, their points of strength, and their tribal connections. The Prophet also realized that the opposing army was three times larger than his own. When he finished the interrogation, the Prophet turned to his companions and said: "Mecca has deployed the cream of Quraishi fighters against you." He then made his battle plans in the light of the information obtained from the water carriers.[61]

Agents were also used for tactical and operational deception. This may clearly be seen in what is now known as the Hamra' Al-Asad operation. One result of the Battle of Badr was the growing awareness among the Quraishis that their commerce and caravan routes were under constant threat as long as Medina remained in Muslim hands. Despite successes scored by the Quraishis against the Prophet Muhammad's army, the Battle of Uhud was far from deci-sive. Both sides suffered heavy losses and retreated from the battlefield, the Muslims toward their base in Medina and the Quraishis toward Mecca. But each side kept a watchful eye on the other; just as the Muslims had numerous *uyoun* in Mecca, the Quraishis had their own among the Muslims.

When the leader of the Quraishis, Abu Sufyan, ordered his troops to camp at a place called Al-Rawha', 14 kilometers from Medina, his military command- ers met to discuss and review the events at Uhud.[62] According to Al Tabari:

> One group said to another: "You did nothing. Although you broke down their [the Muslims'] force, you made no use of your achievement. . . . There are still some distinguished men among them who will probably gather people up to fight you again. So let us go back and annihilate them and crush their forces." It was in fact a hasty decision taken by shallow-minded people who misjudged the potential power and morale of both parties, which is why an eminent leader of Quraish, Safwan bin Omaiyah, tried to dissuade his people from pursuing that venture, saying: "O people. Do not do such a thing! For I fear that he [Muham- mad] will gather up those who had stayed behind and did not fight in Uhud. Go back home as victorious." I am not certain about the outcome or about the turn events might take if we return to reengage the Muslims in the battlefield.[63]

Through his own network of *uyoun*, details of these deliberations reached the Prophet Muhammad. Fearful that a second Quraishi assault might have an undesirable result, he decided to launch a campaign aimed at shaking the morale of the Quraishis and deterring them from launching an assault. To this end, he summoned all his troops and, following on the heels of the Quraishi army, he led them to a place called Hamra' Al-Asad, where he met one of his *uyoun*, Ma'bad Al-Khuzai.

Ma'bad was well chosen for his role. He was not a Muslim and came from a very large tribe that occupied much of the land between Mecca and Medina. His presence in the area was therefore quite normal and did not raise any suspicion. Furthermore, as an ordinary non-Muslim tribesman, unrelated to the Prophet Muhammad or his tribe, he was likely to be believed. Ma'bad was commanded to catch up with Abu Sufyan's army in order to pass on some disinformation and propaganda reports about the Prophet's preparedness for war, the condition of his troops, their psychological state, and their impatience to avenge themselves. According to one traditional account, when he found the opportunity to speak to Abu Sufyan, Ma'bad reported that

> "Muhammad . . . is marching to meet you with a large host of fighters; I have never seen anything similar before. He has mustered all the troops who have tarried and did not join in [the Battle of] Uhud. They surely regret what they have missed and want to compensate for it now. Their hearts are filled with hate and resentment." Abu Sufyan said: "Woe to you! What do you suggest?" He said: "By Allâh, I see that you would not leave till he comes and you see the heads of their horses; or till the vanguard of his army appears from behind that hill." Abu Sufyan said: "By Allâh, we have reached a common consent to crush the Muslims and their power." The man, once more with an implied warning,

advised to the contrary. In the light of this news, the resolution and determination of the Meccan army failed. Panic and terror took firm hold of them. They consequently deemed it safest to fold camp and complete their withdrawal to Mecca.[64]

Agents were also employed in paramilitary operations, particularly in assassination efforts against influential opponents and critics of the Prophet Muhammad and the Muslim cause. As Gabriel points out, "Political maneuver and negotiation, intelligence, propaganda, and the judicious use of terror and assassination were employed to wage a psychological warfare campaign against those potential sources of opposition that could not yet be won by calculation of self interest or ideology."[65] To silence detractors and eliminate instigators and those whom the Prophet Muhammad considered enemies to Islam, he launched many covert operations, which were also intended to boost the morale of the Muslims, influence the military decision of their enemies, and deceive his enemy's intelligence.[66]

Among the first to be targeted by the early Muslims were the poets, whose role was equivalent to that of journalists, publicists, or public relations officers today and who were greatly venerated by their fellow Arab tribesmen and townsfolk alike, as great men of eloquence and sagacity. Islam, however, at least during the early stages, placed certain constraints on poets and ultimately denigrated their status. In pre-Islamic Arabia, each tribe had at least one poet, who, more than the national bards or poets laureate of the West, acted as a general spokesman of his tribe. The role of the ancient Arab poet was quite complex. Besides promoting and defending the tribe's image, the poet was also a military spokesman. His judgments would sometimes "assume the strength and authority of the judiciary," and his influence might occasionally exceed that of the tribal leader himself.[67] On account of the rhyme, rhythm, and other musical and linguistic devices used, a poet's utterances were strongly etched on the collective memory of the tribe. The Quraishi leaders, who were intent on wiping out the new faith and countering the Prophet Muhammad's increasing popularity, naturally enlisted the help of their tribal poets, who obliged by writing various poems attacking the Prophet and fueling hatred against Islam. At first, the Muslims tried to win those eloquent men and women over to their side, or at least to avoid being the object of their attacks. When these efforts failed to produce the desired results, and when the damage inflicted upon the Muslims was too great to tolerate, the Prophet had to respond violently. He decided that those who attacked Islam and sought to undermine it should be physically eliminated.

One such poetess was Asma' bint Marwan, who belonged to the Aws tribe in Medina and was especially outspoken in her tirades against the Prophet Muhammad and the Muslims. Her razor-sharp jibes against the new religion gained wide popularity among the tribes. In one of her poems she attacks Muslims and those tribes that embraced Islam; ridicules the character of the "stranger," the Prophet Muhammad; and calls upon her fellow tribesmen to end the Muslim question by murdering the Prophet:

> I despise Banu Malik and al-Nabit
> And Auf and Banu al-Khazraj.
> You obey a stranger who is none of yours,
> One not of Murad or Madhhij.
> Do you expect good from him
> After the killing of your chiefs
> Like a hungry man waiting for a cook's broth?
> Is there no man of pride who would attack him by surprise?
> And cut off the hopes of those who expect aught from him?[68]

The man who eliminated this sharp-tongued satirist was Omeir bin Wahab Al-Awsi, who managed to enter her home and stab her while she slept.[69] This assassination had not, however, been authorized in advance by the Prophet Muhammad. When Al-Awsi met the Prophet and asked if he would be taken to task for what he did to the poetess, however, he was assured that "no two goats would butt over her death."[70]

Among the first poets to be silenced on the Prophet Muhammad's instructions was Abu Afak, who had reportedly attained the age of 120 years and was notorious for incitement against the person of the Prophet, for his venomous denunciations, and for his denigration of Islam and Muslims. A very intricate plan was prepared to silence him in the courtyard of his own house.[71] The man assigned to carry out the operation was one of the poet's own tribesmen, so that when the murder was uncovered, it would not lead to any tribal repercussions or start an endless cycle of revenge.

Covert action was not confined to poets and influential figures; it was also conducted against leaders of rival religious movements. Among those who were assassinated for propagating what the Muslims considered a revisionist brand of Islam was Al-Aswad al-Ansi, who claimed to be a prophet sent by Allah.[72] The Prophet Muhammad's followers, however, considered him to be nothing more than a magician or a fortune-teller:

> But he was no minor magician or fortune-teller. . . . He was powerful and influential and possessed a strange power of speech that mesmerized the hearts of his listeners and captivated the minds of the masses with his false claims. With his wealth and power he managed to attract not just the masses but people of status as well. . . . Al-Aswad's tribe were the first to respond positively to his claims to prophethood. With this tribal force he mounted a raid on San'a. He killed the governor, Shahr and took his wife to himself. From San'a he raided other regions. Through his swift and startling strikes, a vast region in southern Arabia,

from Hadramawt to At-Taif and from al-Ahsa to Aden came under his influence.[73]

To silence Al-Aswad al-Ansi and stop his movement before any further damage occurred, the Prophet Muhammad ordered his execution.[74] He commanded Wabrah bin Yahnus to head for Yemen secretly in order to prepare an assassination plan. Wabrah devised an intricate plan in which a number of Muslims of Persian origin were to take part. Most crucial was the role played by al-Ansi's wife, Mirzabanah, who was known to harbor nothing but disdain and hatred for Al-Ansi, who had killed her first husband and forced her to marry him. Mirzabanah provided vital intelligence on Al-Ansi's movements and facilitated the killers' entrance to her castle, where the operation was successfully carried out.[75]

Some covert action was intended to boost the morale of Muslims. An illustrative example of this may be seen in the operations aimed at retrieving the body of Khabeeb bin Uday. Khabeeb was among the early Muslims who vigorously supported the Prophet Muhammad and fought under his banner in the decisive Battle of Badr, where he was reported to have killed a number of Meccan polytheists. Soon after this battle, the Prophet sent him on a reconnaissance mission to observe the movements of the Quraishis and check whether they were, as reported, engaged in any military preparations. But Khabeeb and his nine fellow scouts were discovered, tracked, and surrounded. Seven of them died in the engagement that followed while Khabeeb and two other men were tricked into surrendering in the hope that they would be set free. Instead, they were sold to the Meccans, who, in order to exact revenge on Khabeeb for killing so many of their men at Badr, crucified him and left his corpse to rot in the desert.

Khabeeb's fate grieved the Prophet Muhammad, who immediately ordered one of his *uyoun*, Amru bin Ummaya Al-Dhamiri, to head for Mecca and retrieve his body. As long as the decomposing corpse of the renowned fighter remained on the cross, the morale of the Muslims was low, whereas that of the Quraishis was boosted. Amru stealthily went to the spot where Khabeeb's cross had been erected, scaled it, and hastily detached the crucified corpse. He then sped back to Medina, stopping only briefly to provide a proper burial for his fallen comrade. When the Quraishis later discovered that the corpse had vanished, they were at a loss as to what had happened. The operation had a negative impact on their morale while boosting that of the Muslims.[76]

Muhammad's Meccan enemies, however, did not lag behind the Muslims in terms of intelligence. When Abu Sufyan inquired if anybody had spotted strangers or heard of any spies working for the Prophet Muhammad, he soon learned about two men who had been sent to spy on him. When he was shown the spot where the two men had tied their camels, Abu Sufyan ordered his men to bring him a sample of their dung, in which he discovered some palm date stones. "This," he declared, "is the fodder of [Medina]. The two men must be the Prophet Muhammad's spies." He then ordered the caravan to change course and make haste.[77] Successive attempts at the life of the Prophet were also made. One such attempt, which proved futile, was that of Omeir bin Wahab Al-Jamhi. Consequently, counterintelligence and protective security were at a premium in the Prophet's intelligence operations.

Although the Prophet Muhammad himself was the overall commander-in-chief of state security in Medina, Umar bin al-Khattab was effectively in charge of running what we would call today the counterintelligence machinery, implementing day-to-day orders and following up on security policies.[78] In a more productive application of robust interrogation than that of the two water carriers referred to above, a suspected spy was taken to Umar who started to interrogate him by asking him first to identify himself and say where he came from and what he was after. The man was quite economical in his responses. But after a while he was pressured into revealing that he was actually a spy.[79] He also told his interrogators that he was carrying a message from the Ghaftanis to the Jews of Khaibar in order to barter military help for palm-tree dates. When asked if there were any fighting men on their way to succor Khaibar, the spy then told them that there were two hundred men under the command of Wabar bin Oleim. To avoid death, the man then cooperated with the Muslims and led them to the area where they had kept their cattle. He led them to the Ghatfan camp, but when the members of the Muslim detachment, led by none other than Muhammad's cousin Ali, arrived, they discovered that the camp had been totally deserted.[80]

In another case, the Prophet Muhammad's agents in the Islamic stronghold of Medina unmasked an elaborate Byzantine plan to spy on the Muslims. Just nine years after the Prophet had established his rule in Medina, the Byzantines instructed one of their priests, Abu Amie Al-Khazraji, to declare that he had converted to Islam. He was also directed to build a new mosque in order to provide a secure venue for his agents. The choice of its location was quite significant, in the same neighborhood and very close to the Qiba' mosque, which the Prophet's men had constructed earlier. The "Muslim" monk asked the Prophet to inaugurate the place of worship and bless it with his presence. The Prophet responded by saying that he was quite busy and requested postponement of the ceremony until he had accomplished a mission with which he was preoccupied at the time. Meanwhile, the Prophet's men, whose suspicions had been raised, watched closely what happened in and around the newly built mosque. When sufficient evidence was obtained, the Prophet ordered the mosque to be demolished.[81]

Conclusion

The intelligence activities that were practiced by ancient Arabs constitute part of the cultural heritage of the Arabian Peninsula. The Muslims who benefited from the rich legacy left them by their forebears in turn ameliorated and developed them to serve their own needs and requirements in accordance with their own topography and circumstances.

The Prophet Muhammad, from the start of his mission, was fully aware of the vital role of intelligence in securing success for his operations and in achieving tactical and strategic goals. Throughout the various stages of his call to Islam, the Prophet carried out all sorts of intelligence activities. During the early Secret Stage of his mission, which lasted three years, he felt it necessary to keep his movements and contacts quite confidential. To this end, he approached only those whom he knew well and trusted. Good character and personal qualities as well as certain strict criteria had to be met before a person was invited to embrace the new faith. Once he had secured their allegiance, the Prophet would embark on training and educating new recruits in the ways of Islam, without fearing that he would be betrayed. This period was characterized by extreme secrecy, alertness, and caution so that the new religion would not be crushed before it could grow.

During the subsequent Open Stage, the tactic of secrecy was abandoned. Having established a small but firm base in Meccan society, the Prophet Muhammad took fewer precautions and openly advocated his new faith, not only to his fellow Meccans but also to those who came to Mecca for business, religious, or personal reasons. The third stage began with the Prophet's emigration to Medina, where he succeeded in establishing the first Muslim state. This last stage witnessed intense and bloody confrontations between those who responded to his call and adopted the new faith and those who adhered to their ancestral religions and sets of values. It was during this stage that Islamic intelligence work may be said to have come of age. New tactics and methodologies were employed to protect the fledgling state and spread the new faith outside the confines of Medina.

These intelligence activities—entirely conforming with Roy Godson's classic "elements of intelligence" formula entailing clandestine collection, analysis, counterintelligence, and covert operations—strongly affected the course of Islamic history, especially in the struggle between the Prophet Muhammad and his followers on one hand, and the enemies of Islam on the other hand.[82] The Prophet appears to have managed within a relatively short time to rejuvenate Bedouin society and to create a new state based on the new faith. If we exclude the spiritual dimension and divine intervention to which the Muslim faithful attribute the Prophet's successes, Muslim intelligence activities may be seen as having played a decisive role in instilling, nurturing, and spreading Islam in the deserts of Arabia. The activities, operations, and tactics employed during the three stages of Islam have firmly established themselves in Islamic history as part of the *Sunnah* and the heritage of Islam. And as part of the Quranic and Islamic tradition, they represent a deeply rooted body of principles and practice of intelligence that will inevitably inform the norms, values, and activities of governments and substate actors who define themselves in terms of this tradition. If one is to properly understand the intelligence cultures of the Arab and wider Islamic worlds, it is beneficial and indeed necessary to understand the pre-Islamic Arab legacy of intelligence and the formative experience of intelligence at the birth of Islam.

Notes

1. Fatih Abdul Salam Haroun, ed., *Rasa'el Al-Jahiz* (Al-Jahiz's Epistles) (Cairo: Maktabat al-Khanji, 1964), 1:145.

2. John D. Stempel, "The Impact of Religion on Intelligence," *International Journal of Intelligence and CounterIntelligence* 18, no. 2 (2005): 282.

3. A. F. L. Beeston, *Warfare in Ancient South Arabia*, in Studies in Old South Arabian Epigraphy Series 3 (London: Luzac, 1976), 7–11.

4. Muslims are enjoined to use the honorific appendage "pbuh" (peace be upon him) every time the name of the Prophet Muhammad is mentioned, whether orally or in writing. Since the seventh century, this has become an established tradition in all manner of writings, religious tracts as well as academic research and journalism. Its omission would imply not only an anticlerical attitude but would also suggest disbelief atheism or apostasy.

5. Richard A. Gabriel, *Muhammad: Islam's First Great General, Campaigns and Commanders* (Norman: University of Oklahoma Press, 2007), xviii–xix.

6. See Lisan Al-'Arab Lexicon, 2:1090, under "*khabar.*" The word is often used in the Quran in the form of "*khabeer*" as in the Surah of "Fatir," verse 14: "None can inform you like him who is aware" and the Surah of the "Ant," verse 88: "And thou seest the hills thou deemest solid flying with the flight of clouds: the doing of Allah Who perfecteth all things. Lo! He is informed of what ye do."

7. See entries under (خبر) in the following dictionaries and lexicons: Taj Al-'Arūs, Lisan Al-'Arab , Al-Qamūs Al-Muhiṭ, and Al-Aghani.

8. However, some countries, such as the kingdom of Saudi Arabia, have adopted the term "Istikhabarat" to refer to what the other Arab countries call "Mukhabarat."

9. See entries under (جاسوس), "Jasous," in Lisan Al-'Arab.

10. See entries under (ناموس) in Lisan Al-'Arab, Al-Qamūs Al-Muhiṭ, and Al-Aghani.

11. Muhammed bin Ali al-Shawkani, *Fatah Al-Qadir* (The Almighty's Bestowment of Victory) (Beirut: Dar Al-Fikr, n.d.), 40.

12. Surah of "Chambers," verse 12.

13. Surah of "Joseph," verse 87.

14. See Taj Al-'Arūs, 13:303; 6:38.

15. See "دسيس" in Jaj Al-'Arūs, Lisan Al-'Arab, and Al-Aghani lexicons.

16. Urwa Bin Al-Ward Al-Abssi, *Diwan Urwa Bin Al-Ward* (Collected Poems of Urwa Bin Al-Ward) (Beirut: Dar Al-Ketab Al-Arabi, 1994), 55.

17. Aws Bin Hajar, *Al-Diwan* (Collected Poems), edited by Muhammed Yousuf Najm (Beirut: Dar Sadir, n.d.), 66.

18. Ali Izz Al-Din Ibn Al-Athir, *Al-Kamil Fi Al-Tarikh* (The Complete History) (Beirut: Dar Sadir, 1982), 1:492.

19. Ibid., 33.

20. See entries in Taj Al-'Arus, Lisan Al-'Arab, and Al-Qamus Al-Muhit.

21. Surah of "Women," verses 144–45.

22. Ali Izz al-Din Ibn al-Athir, *Al-Kamil Fi Al-Tarikh*, 1:116.

23. Abu 'Ubayd 'Abd Allah Ibn 'Abd Al-'Aziz Al-Bakri, *Mu'jam Ma Ista'jam* (Lexicon of Foreign Words) (n.p., n.d.), 1:80.

24. Lisan al-Arab, 16:5750.

25. Ali Izz al-Din Ibn Al-Athir, *Al-Kamil Fi Al-Tarikh* (The Complete History) (Beirut: Dar Sadir, 1982), p. 139.

26. See chapter 5 in this volume, by Kristian Gustafson.

27. John Glubb, *A Short History of the Arab Peoples* (London: Hodder & Stoughton, 1969), 23–24.

28. Mohamed Bayoumi Mehran, *Studies in the History of the Ancient Arabs* (Alexandria: Dar Al-Ma'rifa Al-Jami'iyya, 2005), 503–5, 508ff.

29. Kheireddine Zrcelli, *Figures* (Beirut: Dar Al-'Ilm Lil-Malayin, 2002), 2:153–54.

30. Abu Al-Faraj Al-Isbahani, *Kitab Al-Aghani* (The Book of Songs) (n. p., n.d), 12:158.

31. Beeston, *Warfare*, 7–11.

32. Abu 'Ubayd 'Abd Allah Ibn 'Abd Al-'Aziz Al-Bakri, *Mu'jam Ma Ista'jam*, 1:181.

33. Ibid., 1:882.

34. Ibid., 1:586.35. Glubb, *Short History*, 25.

36. Philip K. Hitti, *The Arabs: A Short History* (London: Macmillan, 1950), 13.

37. Aws bin Hajar, *Al-Diwan* (Collected Poems), edited by Muhammed Yousuf Najm (Beirut: Dar Sadir, n.d.), 66.

38. Al-Asbahani, *Al-Aghani*, 5:22.

39. Abu Ubaidah Muammar Bin Al-Muthana, *Ayyam Al-Arab Qabl Al-Islam: Naqa"Idh Jareer Wa Al-Farazdaq* (Days of the Arabs before Islam: The Satires of Jareer and Farazdaq) (Beirut: Dar Al-Kitab al-Arabi, 1908–9), 2:650–75, 781–84.

40. Rad Mahmud Ahmad al-Barhawi, *Al-'Uyūn Wa-Al-Jawasis fi Al-Dawlah Al-Islamiyah Mundhu 'ahd Al-Rasūl Wa-Ilá Nihayat Al-'Aṣr Al-Umawi* (Spies and Agents in the Islamic State) (Irbid, Jordan: Dar Al-Mutannabi, 2002), 26.

41. Abu Ja'far Muhammed Ibn Jareer Al-Tabari, *Tarikh Al-Umam wa Al-Mulook* (History of Nations and Kings) (n.p., 1960), 1:617–25.

42. Uthman bin Amru al-Jahiz, *Al-Bayan wa al-Tabyeen* (Eloquence and Poetic Devices), edited by Abdul Salam Haroun (Kuwait: Al-Maktab Al-Arabi, 1968), 1:98.

43. Al-Bakri, *Mu'jam*, 1:92.

44. Ibid., 2:411.

45. Muṣ'ab ibn 'Abd Allah Al-Zubayri and Évariste Lévi-Provençal, *Kitab Nasab Quraysh* (Book of Quraish's Descendants) (Al-Qahirah: Dar al-Ma'arif lil-Ṭiba'ah wa-al-Nashr, 1953), 210.

46. Gabriel, *Muhammad*, xxv.

47. Richard A. Gabriel, "Muhammad: The Warrior Prophet," *Quarterly Journal of Military History* 47 (Summer 2007): 4.

48. Saifur Rahman al-Mubarakpuri, *Ar-Raheeq Al-Makhtoom* (The Sealed Nectar) (Al-Riyadh: Darussalam, 1979), 80.

49. Ibid.

50. Al-Barhawi, *Al-Uyoun wa Al-Jawasees*, 82.

51. Ibid., 59.

52. Al-Tabari, *Tarikh*, 2:296.

53. Ibn Hisham, 1:420.

54. Muḥammad ibn 'Umar Al-Waqidi and J. M. B. Jones, *Kitab Al-Maghazi = the Kitab Al-Maghazi of Al-Waqidi* [*Kitab al-maghazi*] (London: Oxford University Press, 1966), 1:298.

55. Ali bin abi Talib, the first of the *fedayeen* in Islam, was Muhammad's paternal cousin and confidant. He took part in all the battles during the lifetime of Muhammad. Ali was the fourth and last of the Rashidi caliphs, who ruled the state of Islam after Muhammad. His caliphate lasted four years, eight months, and twenty-two days.

56. Al-Zubair bin Al-Awwam was the son of Muhammad's aunt Safiya. He embraced Islam at the age of seventeen and was one of the six-member Shura Council, who elected Omar bin Khattab to be the second Rashidi caliph after Abu Bakr.

57. Saad bin Abbi Waqas was also one of Muhammad's relatives on his mother's side. He too was one of the earliest converts to Islam and known in Islamic history as the first warrior who used his arrows and spears to further the cause of Islam.

58. Al-Waqidi, *Kitab Al-Maghazi*, 1:52.

59. Abu Sufyan was one of the most cunning minds in Arab history. He was ten years older than Muhammad and died aged ninety, almost twenty years after Muhammad's death. He had fought against Muhammad until the conquest of Mecca, when he embraced Islam.

60. Al-Waqidi, *Kitab Al-Maghazi*, 1:52.

61. Ibid., 1:53.

62. Al-Tabari, *Tafsir Al-Tabari* (Al-Tabari's Commentaries) (Dar al-Maarifa, 1990), 4:68.

63. Al-Mubarakpuri, *Ar-Raheeq Al-Makhtoom*, 129–30.

64. Ibid., 130.

65. Gabriel, *Muhammad*, xxi.

66. From a purely nonreligious standpoint, the Prophet Muhammad has been judged to be a very astute leader, as has been attested to here by Gabriel, and by others elsewhere. However, Muslims believe him to be a prophet, and in that context, it would only be right to say that terminologies such as "assassination," "maneuver," "propaganda," "psychological warfare," and others found elsewhere in this treatise must never be seen in separation from his religious role. The things he performed would have been instructed to him by God, or deemed by the prophet to be religiously correct. Seen under that light, and notwithstanding his abstract brilliance as a commander, these deeds performed by the prophet have a deeper meaning and a wider implication than what the mere military or intelligence analysis implies.

67. Hanna Al-Farkhouri, *Tarikh Al-Al-Adab al-Arabi* (History of Arabic Literature), 8th ed. (Beirut: Al-Matba'a Al-Bulsiya, 1961), 59. Commenting on the impact of the poets on ordinary people, a Muslim scholar, Ibn Taimiya, points out that poetry, unlike prose, can popularize anti-Islamic feelings and drive people away from the path of Allah. See Abu Al-Fath Al-Shahristani, *Mosuat Almell wa Madaheb* (Encyclopaedia of Peoples and Sects), 1st ed. (Beirut: n. p., n. d), 84.

68. *Ibn Ishaq: Sirat Rasul Allah* (A. Guillaume's Translation of *The Life of Muhammad*), 675–76.

69. Al-Waqidi, 1:173. See also Sirat Ibn Hisham ([Muhammad's] Biography by Ibn Hisham, *Al-Marji"Al-Akbar Lil-Turath al-Islami* (Greatest Primary Sources of Islamic Heritage), 1:414ff.

70. Sirat Ibn Hisham ([Muhammad's] Biography by Ibn Hisham, *Al-Marji"Al-Akbar Lil-Turath al-Islami* (Greatest Primary Sources of Islamic Heritage), 1:418.

71. Yusuf ibn 'Abd Allah Ibn Abdul Barr, *Al-Isti'ab fi ma'rifat Al-Ashab* (Comprehension in Knowing Friends) (Al-Qahirah: Dar Al-Maarifah, 2006), 3:1218; Ahmad ibn Yahyá and Muhammad Hamidullah Baladhuri, Ansab Al-Ashraf (Ancestry) (Al-Qahirah: Dar al-Ma'arif, 1987), 1:373.

72. Ali Muhammed Al-Sallabi, *Sirat Abu Bakr Al-Siddiq: Shakhsiyatuhu wa Asruhu* (A Biography of the Life and Times of Abu Bakr Al-Siddiq) (Cairo: Muasasat Iqra, 2006), 162ff.

73. See "Fayruz Ad-Daylami," at Department of Islamic Affairs and Charitable Activities, Government of Dubai, website, www.dicd.gov.ae/vEnglish/detailnewspage.jsp?articleID=3627&page Flag=1.

74. Al-Tabari, *Tarikh*, 3:185.

75. Ahmad ibn Yahyá Baladhuri, *Futūh Al-Buldan* (Conquests of Countries) (Beirut: Dar al-Nashr lil-Jami'iyin, 1958), 125–26.

76. Yusuf ibn 'Abd Allah Ibn Abdul Barr, *Al-Isti'ab fi ma'rifat Al-Ashab*, 3:1383–85.

77. Battle of Badr, www.johina.net/vb/t13799.html.

78. Al-Barhawi, *Al-Uyoun wa Al-Jawasees*, 99–102.

79. The Arabic word used in the original text is شدوا عليه. This can also be translated as meaning "they were rough or severe with him."

80. Al-Waqidi, *Kitab Al-Maghazi*, 2:562.

81. Ibid., 3:1047.

82. See, for example, Roy Godson, *Intelligence Requirements for the 1980s: Elements of Intelligence* (Washington, DC: National Strategy Information Center, 1979).

PART III

Current Practice and Theory

CHAPTER 7

Pakistan's Inter-Services Intelligence

Robert Johnson

In September 2011, ten years after the attacks in New York and Washington by al-Qaeda, and the initiation of United States–led operations in Afghanistan, the US chairman of the Joint Chiefs of Staff, Admiral Mike Mullen, announced that a truck bomb attack against a NATO post south of Kabul, an assault on the US Embassy, and a similar high-profile raid on the Intercontinental Hotel in the Afghan capital had been planned and conducted by the militant Jihadist Haqqani network with the support of the Directorate of Pakistan's Inter-Services Intelligence (ISI).[1] This accusation, he argued, was based on "credible evidence." Rehman Malik, Pakistan's interior minister, stated: "I categorically deny it," suggesting "we have no such policy to attack or aid attack(s) through Pakistani forces or through any Pakistani assistance."[2] Prime Minister Yusuf Raza Gilani added that "we strongly reject assertions of complicity with the Haqqanis or proxy war."[3] Turning the accusations back against the Americans, he continued: "The allegations betray a confusion and policy disarray within the US establishment on the way forward in Afghanistan. . . . Pakistan cannot be held responsible for the security of US–NATO–ISAF [International Security Assistance Force] forces in Afghanistan." When it was hinted the Americans might enforce a principle of "hot pursuit" against Haqqani fighters across the Afghan border, Malik reiterated that "the Pakistan nation will not allow the boots on our ground, never," citing Pakistan's existing cooperation with the United States in return for respect for national sovereignty.

These bad-tempered exchanges have deepened a popular anti-American sentiment within Pakistan, but, curiously, they have not answered questions about the exact role of the ISI nor enamored the organization to the Pakistani people. During the years 2010–11 Pakistan had expelled some US military trainers and had periodically prevented NATO logistics containers from crossing the border. The Americans responded by suspending $800 million in military aid from its usual budget of $2 billion. The Pakistan army and government insisted that the Americans were dependent on them, not least with respect to future negotiations in Afghanistan, but they also argued that Pakistan was fragile. Many Pakistanis privately confide this fragility is caused by the policies pursued by its own national elites, including the army and the ISI. The Pakistan security forces state they are willing to cooperate with the United States against al-Qaeda, but resource constraints prevent them from defeating the Taliban. Those in the political establishment in Pakistan fear that the Americans will demand too much and "humiliate" the country.[4] Demands for cooperation against Haqqani—coming close behind the US Special Forces raid that killed Osama bin Laden, which appears not to have had any consent from the Pakistan government or security forces—were deeply unpopular. Concerns that, following the inevitable Western withdrawal from Afghanistan, India might exploit its relationship with Kabul prompted a disclosure from General Ashfaq Parvez Kayani, the chief of the army. He expressed his anxiety that Pakistan might be squeezed on both its eastern and western borders. American assessments are that the Pakistan army would like to maintain close ties with Haqqani as a tool against pro-Indian elements in Afghanistan. President Karzai is seen as a pro-Indian leader, who, for his part, blames the ISI for the death of his father.[5] The detonation of a powerful vehicle-borne bomb adjacent to hostelries used by Indian aid workers and businesses in Kabul in 2010 increased suspicions that the ISI lay behind an attempt to drive out Indian influence.

Lieutenant General Ahmed Shuja Pasha, the director of the ISI, admitted there was "contact" with Haqqani, but not command and control.[6] Some American security personnel argue that the Pakistan army has been fought to a standstill by Jihadist militants like Haqqani, but it is more likely that the army has decided that it cannot fight all the militant groups of the border areas at once, and a deal, the Shakai Agreement, was struck with Haqqani in 2004. Under its terms, Haqqani was to act as an interlocutor with Jihadist groups in South Waziristan and all "foreign fighters" were to be registered in tribal areas, while being given funding support and a free hand to operate, which in effect meant turning a blind eye to cross-border attacks in Afghanistan.[7] Although the 2004 agreement broke down and was renegotiated several times, the ISI was in the front line of both talks and the fighting in the border areas.[8] At Miram Shah in North Waziristan, the truces have enabled Haqqani and army bases to be colocated in the town without dispute.

More important, from the American perspective, Haqqani is a force that cooperates with the Quetta Shura, the senior leadership of the Afghan Taliban. Nevertheless, the existence of the sanctuary for the Haqqani network inside Pakistan is denied by Islamabad, fueling accusations of deliberate duplicity. Afghan officials, eager to retain American support, are more blunt. Hanif Atmar, the former minister of the interior, noted: "I think this is absolutely well understood that the Afghan terrorists with support from the ISI and al-Qaeda are purposefully and deliberately targeting Afghan politicians, government sites and foreign forces."[9] Afghans regularly argue that rather than insurgency in their country threatening to spill over into Pakistan, it is Pakistan that is intentionally destabilizing Afghanistan.

The ISI has a reputation for brutality, arbitrary violence, the sponsorship of terrorism, and interference in domestic politics, yet Western policymakers often refer to its crucial, frontline role in combating al-Qaeda.[10] The ISI has been regarded as a renegade organization with rogue agents, but also as a critical interlocutor with militant Jihadist organizations on the Afghanistan–Pakistan border. It has been accused of intimidating democratic politicians and even of the murder of former prime minister Benazir Bhutto, but it is regarded as a vital component in the preservation of Pakistan that can prevent the country's nuclear arsenal from falling into the wrong hands. It was accused of harboring Osama bin laden until his death in a US Special Forces operation in May 2011, despite cooperation with the West against elements of al-Qaeda that had taken refuge in South Waziristan.[11] Given the fragility of Pakistan's democracy, insurgency in Waziristan and in neighboring Afghanistan, and the consequences of violent militancy in the country, the ISI's involvement in each of these areas is of significant international interest.

The current Western concern is twofold. One, how loyal is the ISI to the civilian democratic government of Pakistan, and would the failure of cooperation open the way to the collapse of the Pakistan state? Two, how sincere is the ISI in its cooperation with Western intelligence agencies against the broad coalition of Jihadists that threaten the West or the coalition forces operating in Afghanistan? Assessments of the ISI are notoriously partisan, and some analysts, particularly in India, have been eager to blame Pakistani intelligence for terrorist operations across the region. Although some argue that the ISI is the eminence grise of covert operations by militant Jihadists, some Pakistani officers argue that their country is practically under siege and the ISI should work closely with the army in trying to contain the threat. Less charitable critics maintain that this situation is the result of the ISI's own policies, a form of "blowback" after years of sponsoring and fostering violent groups. The sense that the army and ISI are engaged in staving off each new threat as it emerges as they struggle for the state's survival is palpable in their vocabulary, but may reveal only the tactical situation rather than a strategic agenda. If Pakistan's true strategic ends were its desire to survive a variety of threats and challenges—economic, environmental, and military—then its use of the ISI to make agreements, to co-opt allies, and to neutralize rivals would provide a persuasive alternative explanation to that advanced by those apt to see only conspiracy. The absence of reliable evidence fuels suspicions of complicity in terrorist outrages, although the absence of empirical evidence is a situation not unfamiliar to scholars of intelligence elsewhere. Despite the problems of fragmentary evidence, the ISI's past record offers a glimpse of the organization's track record and might offer the opportunity to assess its culture in terms of ethos, methods, and approach. Understanding the habitual, normative culture of the ISI might move us toward a better appreciation of how its strategy and priorities are shaped, although we should acknowledge that the culture of the ISI remains subordinate to its primary function: the preservation of state power.

The ISI is directed by the senior figures of the Pakistan Army to serve the interests of the state and the armed forces. The supremacy of the ISI mirrors the paramountcy of the Pakistan army in the country's political arena and the economy. The ISI is a servant of the armed forces with a degree of its own "agency," which is the result of its distinctive mission, and it has evolved through a history of clandestine operations and the requirement to manage intermediate groups or individuals. Despite sharing the ISI's objective of preserving the state, the army officer corps has often had a somewhat strained relationship with its intelligence wing; service in it is sometimes seen as a career-end appointment, detrimental to the unity of the army's chain of command in operational planning and, formerly, too involved in religious or political conspiracies. To many army officers, it has also lacked the prestige and honor of other, more conventional appointments. However, the ISI has often been at the forefront of efforts to confront Pakistan's chief regional rival, India, and it is seen as a useful tool for the formulation of military and strategic plans. It has a great deal of experience working with leaders on the Pakistan frontier and among insurgents from Afghanistan, which gives the Pakistan army "reach" beyond its own frontiers. It is therefore considered a useful organization for the projection of Pakistan's national interests into Afghanistan and Central Asia. It has been an indispensable instrument for coercion in domestic politics in order to protect the army's interests and therefore those of the state, and its actions are justified by rhetoric that gives the impression that it is able to preserve the nation against a variety of existential threats.

Since the 1980s the ISI has built up a cadre of well-trained operatives who are experienced in working alongside Jihadist organizations. Those hired by the ISI as intermediaries operate with a great deal of independence. Despite officially distancing themselves from Jihadist movements, the militants are still seen as potential allies in the pursuit of Pakistan's national interests.[12] In Kashmir the ISI fostered militant Jihadists to fight there when operations in Afghanistan throughout the 1980s were being wound down. Impressed by the utility of proxy paramilitaries with a successful outcome against the Soviets, it was a natural extension to fight the Indian government at its point of greatest vulnerability. Although Kashmir has the potential to become a battleground again, operations there diminished in importance because of insurgencies in Afghanistan and in Pakistan's North West Frontier Province and Federally Administered Tribal Areas after 2001. The ISI is deeply involved in the process of negotiation, recruitment, and sometimes "direction" of militant groups, but external pressures generate a national defense reflex in the Pakistan army and the ISI. Coalition cross-border drone strikes and the covert mission that ended with the death of Osama bin Laden in Abottabad fuel domestic debates about how far Pakistan should cooperate with the West without jeopardizing its national sovereignty and independent freedom of action.

It is clear that Pakistan security forces regard al-Qaeda as a threat.[13] Although the Jihadist defense of Pakistan might appeal to the more idealistic and ideologically inclined within the armed forces—a feature, incidentally, that is vigorously denied officially—there is no affinity with the internationalism of al-Qaeda. Fears that pro–al-Qaeda elements in the armed forces, following the arrest of Jihadist sailors, had facilitated an attack on the Mehran Naval Air Station in June 2011 led to dismissals but also public denials that there were any al-Qaeda sympathizers within the services.[14] Since 2001 there has been some continuity in the decision to treat various militant groups in different ways. The priority has been to manage its own internal militancy problem, to deflect groups where necessary against external powers, but to neutralize those that posed a threat to the state. Between 2003 and 2004 the ISI cooperated with the United States to bring about the arrest of certain al-Qaeda operatives. Despite accusations that the ISI harbored Osama bin Laden, there is as yet no evidence of collusion, and it may have been unaware of his exact location. Conversely, new evidence has emerged that the ISI was aware of the Lashkar-e Toiba attack plan against Mumbai, at least in principle, if not its precise details.[15] Its "links," at least in terms of its ability to communicate if not direct operations, and its coerciveness have given rise to the image of an organization that is nefarious and double-dealing. Syed Saleem Shahzad, a journalist murdered in 2011, alleged that some former ISI and military personnel have joined militant Jihadist groups, and that one, Major Haroon Ashiq, encouraged the ISI and Lashkar-e Toiba to execute the Mumbai attacks in 2008 in order to realign Pakistan's attention against India and relieve pressure on militants in the tribal areas of the North West.[16]

Yet, for all its reputation, the ISI has been a failure. Frequent setbacks and miscalculations have encouraged the ISI to turn to coercion as a means to compensate for its inability to control events, and the level of violence in Pakistan indicates just how much it has struggled to manage the consequences of its own policies.

Organization, Strategy, and Culture

The literature on the existence and influence of "military culture" is extensive, although the discourse on intelligence culture remains embryonic.[17] Assessments of culture are often at risk of overgeneralizing responses to specific historical circumstances, attributing distinctions that are fallacies, or constructing relativist judgments that actually tell us more about the observers themselves than the subjects they claim to have examined. A more reliable means to assess culture might begin with an assessment of strategic objectives, the organization of the institution, and some reference to its longer-term historical conditioning, although the available space in this chapter precludes a full exposition of the latter.

The official role of the ISI is to serve as the first line of defense by providing the government with intelligence about threats to national security. Pakistan's strategy has been dominated by the desire to hold India's vast armed forces at bay, to maintain independence against foreign powers (requiring closer relations with China as a counterweight to dependence on the United States), and to prevent further partitioning or separatism where, perhaps, "Pashtunistan" or Baluchistan might follow the Bangladeshi model.[18] Perceived threats to national security from India, but also from internal separatist or democratic movements that might reduce the power of the elites, particularly the army itself, meant that the ISI extended its reach into the political life of the country in the interests of national defense. The result was that its loyalty to those civilian administrations of which it did not approve was sometimes in doubt, whereas operations might be initiated in Kashmir or Afghanistan to preempt a perceived emerging threat. The ISI has acted as one of the means to achieve Pakistan's strategic ends, and it has made use of militant groups as a cheap and effective source of information and action. Alignment with militants has also given the army Islamist credentials and legitimacy against "corrupt," secular politicians. The ways of achieving strategy via the ISI have been the most controversial. Given the power of the United States and neighboring India, a culture of deniability has developed. Foreign Minister Hina Rabbani Khar flatly denied that the ISI had links with the Haqqanis in North Waziristan following allegations by Admiral Mike Mullen, the chairman of the US Joint Chiefs of Staff, that the Jihadist faction was "the veritable arm" of the ISI inside Afghanistan. Khar argued that such allegations would compel Pakistan to abandon its alliance with the United States, arguing that "you cannot afford to alienate Pakistan; you cannot afford to alienate the Pakistani people."[19] Aside from the emotions raised by what Pakistanis feel is an arbitrary breach of their sovereignty, Javed Hussein, a former Pakistan army brigadier working as a security analyst, was perhaps more revealing in his response. He argued that US operations in North Waziristan against Haqqani would be a "strategic blunder" in that it would stir up a hornet's nest at a time when the United States could not afford to open another front against Jihadist militants.[20] Rather than revealing a conspiracy, the comment suggests perhaps that Pakistan is unable to contain the militancy in its frontier districts.

In the 1980s and 1990s, during Pakistan's sponsorship of insurgency in Afghanistan and Kashmir, the ISI worked alongside Islamic extremists. When the West withdraws from Afghanistan and its interest in the region diminishes, then Pakistan will want to reassert itself and may use the same type of nonstate actors to further its influence, to develop its strategic depth, and to keep India distracted. The ISI is likely to be at the forefront of that effort. Pakistan is working on developing closer relations with Iran and China while gaining what it can through its somewhat strained relationship with the United States. It is concerned about India's interest in Afghanistan and believes that it is in its strategic interests to have a compliant, pro-Pakistan regime in Kabul.

The ISI was the conduit through which Western support for the Afghan Mujahideen was deployed during the Soviet occupation of Afghanistan, and this cooperation occurred at a time when the ISI was increasingly influenced by radical Islamist thinking, a fact that was officially sanctioned by General Zia ul Haq and by successive chiefs of the ISI. During the Afghan Civil War (1989–2001), the ISI played a key role in promoting Pakistan's interests— namely, establishing a regime in Kabul favorable to Islamabad so as to create an imaginary "strategic depth" in any struggle with India. Its role was not limited to intelligence gathering or the processing of neutral "product," but took the form of overt political sponsorship and covert operations. The ISI was also active in the ultimately disastrous Kargil Operations against India in 1999.[21]

With Pakistan's sudden abandonment of the Taliban and cessation of its sponsored insurgency in Kashmir in light of 9/11 and Operation Enduring Freedom in 2001, President General Pervez Musharraf cut militant personnel gradually from the armed forces and intelligence services and cooperated with the West in counterinsurgency operations in South Waziristan in 2004 following insurgent attacks astride the Afghanistan–Pakistan border. Although Musharraf was publicly critical of the Islamist agenda of previous governments, it was the ISI that brokered deals with the militants in the frontier areas. The ISI facilitated the Shakai Agreement. In return for a cease-fire by insurgents and intelligence on "foreign fighters," the Pakistan government agreed to offer funds to the Pakistani Taliban, the Tehrik-i Taliban Pakistan. The agreement failed in 2009 when "Uzbek" fighters clashed with the Pakistan army, which also involved South Waziristan local insurgents. The Tehrik-i Taliban Pakistan leader, Beitullah Mehsud, nevertheless miscalculated, and after renewed fighting he was killed in August that year.[22] The threat of fragmentation of the militant movement was nevertheless prevented by the intervention of Sirajuddin Haqqani, the Taliban leader based in North Waziristan, who was, ironically, the chief interlocutor for the Pakistan Army. The ISI has tried to foster allies among the Waziristan militants to take on Jihadist factions and foreign fighters, and count on the support of the Abdullah Mehsud group, Mullah Nazir and Turkistan Bhittani, as well as the Punjabi Taliban in Wana. In light of militancy in Swat and unrest in the major cities—including the so-called Lal Masjid (Red Mosque) uprising of 2007—the ISI and the Army feel that national security is again at stake.[23] The civilian government has struggled to come to grips with an array of domestic problems, namely, insurgency in the frontier districts, violent sectarianism, a long-standing low-intensity conflict in Balochistan, the consequences of the Indus River's flooding in 2011, and the global economic downturn.

The ISI is today responsible for the gathering and processing of foreign and domestic intelligence, and the coordination of intelligence between the armed forces' own branches. The ISI trains agents, provides security for its senior officers, and protects the country's nuclear weapons program. The ISI has also been involved in more aggressive activities in the past, including foreign espionage, counterintelligence, and "covert operations." Its functions have included telephone tapping and other signals interception, surveillance, the monitoring of extremists, and interference in the democratic process, including election rigging and the intimidation of politicians. It has also been alleged that it has indulged in assassination, narcotics smuggling, and the sponsorship of terrorism, although these are often impossible to verify. There have been accusations that it carried out the assassination of Benazir Bhutto because she wanted to reduce the political power of the armed forces in the country, and the ISI has been regarded as the mastermind behind the 2008 attacks in Mumbai.[24]

The key point, in terms of the ISI's role and culture, is that senior army officers believe that the ISI and the army are there to "protect national security," a broadly defined concept that includes not only the defense of the sovereignty of Pakistan but also the interests and institutions of the army, navy, and air force, which regard themselves as the central pillars of the nation and the very embodiment of its culture. They believe that, without the armed forces playing a central role in the life of the state, the nation would be weakened and broken up by separatist forces, and, in that condition, would be overrun by India. India's size and proximity loom large in the minds of Pakistan's commanders, and the involvement of India in the breaking up of East Pakistan and West Pakistan in 1971 and in the protracted conflict in Kashmir has strongly influenced their views of the country's vulnerabilities.

There is no doubt that the political culture of a country affects the activity of its intelligence services. In Pakistan, though the ISI has a professional ethos and serves its commanders loyally, it regards civilian politicians with suspicion, if not contempt, and it has frequently operated outside the law to achieve its objectives. It regards its mission of national security as a higher calling, above the authority of politicians and lawyers. It uses secrecy and the concept of national security as the means to avoid infringements of its freedom of action. Indeed, the intelligence services are a key component of the semimilitarized state of Pakistan. The ISI has the role of coordinating the armed services' intelligence machinery as well as gathering, analyzing, and assessing foreign intelligence, both military and nonmilitary. However, despite the existence of the Intelligence Branch, the civilian intelligence organization under the Interior Ministry with responsibility for internal security, the ISI has often processed and acted on intelligence in domestic affairs. The ISI's director-general is always a serving officer of lieutenant general rank, as are the three deputy directors-general, and even the Intelligence Branch is led by serving or retired military officers.[25] The ISI also has specialist units for its tasks that extend beyond a purely "intelligence" function: The Joint Intelligence North supported insurgents that crossed the border into Indian Jammu and Kashmir, and was the agency that backed the Taliban in the 1990s. The division also maintained links with Islamist organizations inside Pakistan, including Harkat-ul-Mujahideen, Lashkar-e Toiba, Al Badr, and Jaish-e-Mohammad. The Joint Intelligence Miscellaneous is also thought to have played a role in acquiring nuclear technology and carrying out covert action. As in other intelligence services, specialist branches appear, are retitled, and are reabsorbed depending on their tasks.

The Islamization of the ISI in the Afghanistan-Soviet War

In Pakistan in the 1970s, when national cohesion and political legitimacy were so fragile, Islamist views gained currency as a way of generating national unity, but also of justifying state decisions that could not then be questioned. This was a distinctive feature of the country's political culture, and Pakistan's ISI primarily still used the "national security" argument to justify its activities and to conceal its failures.

When military rule came to an end in 1973, Zulifqar Ali Bhutto used the rhetoric of radical Islam to win over the Pashtuns of the North West Frontier Province and the Balochis in elections. In the Constitution he framed in 1973, article 227 laid down that no law would be permitted that was "repugnant to the injunctions of Islam." Additionally, an Islamic Council was established (although its powers were not defined), Islamiyat was placed on educational curricula, and Bhutto replaced Sunday with Friday as the weekly holiday. However, Bhutto was more interested in the preservation of his power and the cultivation of his image as *quaid-i-awam* (leader of the people) in the style of Mao Zedong or Kim Il-sung than in trying to be a religious icon.[26] He was at heart a secularist, and he thus invoked the concept of Muslim unity at the Lahore Islamic Summit to win favor.

As his popular support ebbed away, Bhutto turned to a closer alliance with the Islamists, purging the administration of certain secularists who threatened national cohesion. Haunted by the specter of separatism, he exploited India's first nuclear weapons test to call for the creation of an "Islamic bomb" for Pakistan.[27] In the elections of 1977 Bhutto used the ISI to check all the candidates and blocked certain opposition members from standing through police orders. Protest rioters were attacked by the Federal Security Force. However, the ISI and the Pakistan army, especially the junior ranks, were strongly influenced by Islamist arguments that, in fact, Bhutto was *undermining* Islam and was insincere in his politics. In July this cohort informed its senior officers that they would no longer support the prime minister, despite a last-minute decree that favored Islamist demands. The commander of the army, Zia ul Haq, therefore seized power in a coup d'état. Zia ul Haq continued the trend toward Islamization for much the same reasons as Bhutto, although he was genuinely more devout than the former prime minister. Zia established a Federal Shariat Court and a Council of Islamic Ideology to decide on what, in legal terms, was "repugnant to Islam," and he encouraged, promoted, and supported an Islamist agenda.[28] The decision to elevate theocratic forces to positions of constitutional authority in the service of unifying political ideas severely damaged Pakistan's intelligence and security forces.[29] At the tactical level Islamist thinking has long been a strong motivational force for intelligence operatives and troops. But, as so many other ideologically driven forces around the globe indicate, it is this very thinking that clouds analysis, strategic calculation, and economy of effort. Nowhere was this demonstrated more clearly than in the operations in Afghanistan and Kashmir.

For Pakistan, controlling Afghanistan or at least having a compliant regime there apparently offered "strategic depth" for two reasons: One, it held out the possibility that Pashtuns of the region would assist in any conflict with India; and, two, it neutralized the threat of an independent "Pashtunistan" being created, a potential separatist phenomenon that threatened the territorial integrity of Pakistan.[30] The Soviet invasion of Afghanistan in 1979 created the opportunity of American assistance and thus support for the Zia regime. The Americans regarded the containment of the Soviets as a far higher priority than any concerns about Pakistan's internal politics. Nevertheless, the United States could not be seen to be supporting the Afghan resistance directly, and so assistance to the Mujahideen was channeled through the ISI. To avoid detection, funds, arms, and supplies were handled exclusively by the ISI's Afghan Bureau, with few checks on who received them.[31] American personnel were not permitted inside Afghanistan, so all guidance, munitions distribution, and advice also fell to the ISI. The ISI's director-general, Lieutenant General Akhtar Abdur

Rahman, was a "no-nonsense officer with a singular vision of fighting the Soviets and clearing them out of Afghanistan." According to Shuja Nawaz, he "brooked little interference—even from the Americans—in the internal operations of the ISI."[32] In addition, the ISI and Special Services Group trained 83,000 Afghan Mujahideen in bases inside Pakistan between 1983 and 1997. In turn, ISI agents of the Covert Action Division received training by the Central Intelligence Agency (CIA) in the United States.

Mohammad Yousaf, a former ISI officer, wrote that the relationship between the ISI and the CIA had been close, especially in the Reagan era, and there was cordiality with the Saudi intelligence service, which was also backing the Afghan effort, although there were no associations with the other Arab backers or the Arab volunteers inside Afghanistan. However, it was not a relationship without problems. Despite the huge amount of American funding, some $30 billion in 1987, most of the money was spent on arms purchases, so the ISI was left struggling to support the Mujahideen in the country. The stores to support the training camps cost $1.5 million every month in 1987, and there were significant costs in providing trucks, mules, fodder, fuel, and rations across the border. CIA operatives also displayed their ignorance of conditions inside Afghanistan in terms of the equipment they sometimes supplied.

Yousaf noted that it was American intelligence that was the most valued. Signals intelligence was particularly useful in assessing the morale and performance of Soviet and Afghan government forces. Satellite photography assisted in the selection of targets. CIA demolitions advice was a great asset. In terms of a relationship with the United States, clearly some ISI officers had little sympathy with American values, but Yousaf believes that, despite the suspicions of their generous donors, there were few episodes of corruption.[33] This can be explained partly through the professional ethos of the organization, but also a growing sense of affinity with the Mujahideen and its embattled cause, which was often expressed in religious terms. Some regular Pakistani army personnel operated inside Pakistan as members of the ISI. They tended to be men recruited from the North West Frontier Province who were fluent in Dari, Pashto, or Afghan Farsi, and, though styled "volunteers," they were not always as enthusiastic as their title suggests. They had strict instructions not to reveal their identity if captured and were informed that they would be denied anyway.[34]

The ISI and General Zia not only bypassed the Pakistan Foreign Ministry on the Afghanistan issue; the army command was also not consulted. This may have been due, in part, to their desire to get an Islamist government into power in Kabul after the Soviets withdrew, to which the United States would not have agreed.[35] It also suggests that the ISI and its leadership will always put national interests ahead of Pakistan's alliance relationships, and will seek to avoid accountability at home.

The ISI and the Hezb-e Islami/Gulbuddin

The ISI expanded during the Afghan conflict to circa 26,000 personnel, and its financial autonomy meant that it developed a habit of independence in its activities. Moreover, its ability to dictate which Afghan factions received supplies and support meant that it was in a powerful position. Pakistan favored Gulbuddin Hekmatyar as its protégé in Afghanistan. Hekmatyar, in fact, commanded little loyalty among the Pashtuns, even in Paktia, and his effect on Soviet forces was minimal compared with other warlords, but what impressed the ISI were his ruthlessness, the fact that he controlled territory close to the border, and his Jihadist credentials.[36] Moreover, Lieutenant General Hamid Gul, the ISI's director-general, was himself an Islamist and regarded the Jihadists as protégés of Pakistan. Mindful of the post-Soviet war dispensation, Hekmatyar carefully stockpiled his weaponry, insisted on the exclusion of Afghan rivals from the refugee camps, and concentrated on cultivating his allies inside Pakistan. The irony was that Hekmatyar, a declared anti-American militant, was a recipient of arms, equipment, and supplies shipped via the ISI from the United States. Despite Hamid Gul's efforts to professionalize the Afghanistan operations, the ISI's autonomy and its support for Hekmatyar marked a further erosion of its secular values and were to have major consequences.[37]

When the Soviets withdrew, Hekmatyar was proactive in trying to gain power. One of his men, Syed Jamal, murdered thirty of Massoud's leaders in the so-called Farkhar Massacre in a clear attempt to neutralize a rival faction. When the resistance captured Khost in March 1991, the ISI was quick to claim that Hekmatyar's faction had been responsible, even though it was not, in order to attract Afghan popular support. However, these moves suggested that Pakistan's main proxy was not as powerful as he had seemed initially, even to the ISI.[38] When an Afghan military leaders' joint *shura* met in Pakistan in 1991, there was a new determination to cooperate against the successor regime in Kabul, and the United States agreed to support this military effort by supplying the Mujahideen factions directly rather than through the ISI as in the past. This removed the ISI's ability to fund Hekmatyar using external means. Pakistan turned instead to the support of another emerging Pashtun militia, the Taliban, and this organization, backed by ISI intelligence, weapons, and logistics, gradually rolled back the other factions.[39] The Taliban established its own regime in Kabul, imposing Islamist doctrine and providing a secure platform for ISI intelligence gathering on Central Asia.[40] Only pockets of resistance survived in the form of the United Front in the north and the Shias in the west. The ISI participated in a major offensive against the northern Afghan allies in the late

1990s in an effort to secure a military victory for its faction. By contrast, the Pakistani civilian government just wanted an end to the war. Nevertheless, it was clear that the ISI and the army had developed an appetite for proxy operations using its Pashtun allies.

In 1993 the United States placed Pakistan on the watch list of states suspected of supporting terrorism because Lieutenant General Javed Nasir, then the head of the ISI, had made it impossible for the Americans to buy back the FIM-92 Stinger surface-to-air missiles given to the Mujahideen during the Soviet–Afghanistan conflict, and it was known that the ISI was supplying the terrorist Harkat ul-Ansar organization, and possibly funding the radical madrassa Markaz Dawa Al Irshad. Six months after America's designation, Nasir was retired and Pakistan was removed from the watch list. American focus switched away from Pakistan and Afghanistan to threats in the horn of Africa, Southeastern Europe, and the Middle East.

The ISI and Kashmir Operations

India has long accused Pakistan's ISI of fueling insurgency in Kashmir, and it is worth noting that the internal security problem worsened once the ISI's operations in Afghanistan had been scaled down. Indian analysts assert that—with the recovery of identification details from militants who have been killed, to the forensic examination of improvised explosive devices, communications equipment, and weaponry—there is evidence that Pakistan directly supported the insurgency. Indian officers remarked that there was a "step change in the degree of sophistication in the insurgents'" attacks and in their capabilities after 1989.[41] Pakistan has always denied any support, but Indian analysts believe that General Zia ul Haq initiated a proxy war using the ISI and that there was a transfer of experienced personnel (under the euphemism "resources") from the Afghan theater.[42] An Indian Joint Intelligence Committee report in 1995 claimed that Pakistan spent 240,000 rupees per month on the insurgency campaign, supporting about six major groups with a combined strength of between 5,000 and 10,000.[43] There seemed to be a calculation by the ISI that covert action would allow Pakistan to achieve its objectives without a more costly, conventional war. The aim was to drain India of military resources and force it to cut back on conventional war spending—thus reducing the threat on the central front. Insurgency offered the opportunity to demoralize the Indian security forces, and to precipitate heavy-handed reactions and thus drive the Muslim Kashmiri population into the arms of Pakistan. India accused the ISI of orchestrating a parallel political campaign, with propaganda, agitation, funding of radical groups, and the deliberate provocation of communal violence.[44]

India also believes that the ISI was behind Sikh agitation for an independent Khalistan, and even unrest in the North East.[45] To some extent, it is easy to assume that conspiratorial agencies, like the ISI, are responsible for all epi-sodes of unrest and terrorism inside India. However, after the recent bombings of Mumbai, the available evidence suggested that "homegrown" Jihadists, operating independently of Pakistan, were capable of carrying out attacks of this nature. Much of the unrest in the North East of India is centered on specific local and regional issues rather than a deliberate Pakistani policy of Balkaniza-tion to reduce India's power.

As so often is the case, intelligence agencies, particularly those with an emphasis on covert action, create an exaggerated sense of their power and a formidable reputation. This reputation, and their secrecy, serve to project their influence and conceal their mistakes. The fact is that the sponsorship of insur-gency in Kashmir did not achieve the ISI's objectives, although it created more misery for those who endured it and exasperated the Indian security forces. The failure of covert action led to a far more dangerous escalation of the Kashmir conflict in 1999. The Kargil operations of that year in turn generated calls for nuclear deployments and necessitated urgent American diplomatic interven-tion. Ironically, the escalation of the threat persuaded the ISI that it was the key agency in the defense of national security. It could argue that it was taking the fight to the enemy, but the operations in Afghanistan and Kashmir had also rather conveniently given it the opportunity to obtain more funding, expansion of its personnel, and greater freedom of action. It is important to note that, for the Pakistan army and the ISI, the scale of the Indian threat has been a key driver in its strategy for Kashmir and for the projection of its influ-ence in Afghanistan.

The ISI and Nuclear Proliferation

When it was revealed that the Pakistani scientist Abdul Qadeer Khan was the mastermind behind the sale of nuclear secrets to Iran, Libya, and North Korea in 2004, it suggested the ISI had either failed to monitor its own scientists or it had been complicit in the whole operation.[46] Despite much anxiety about Iran's nuclear program, Pakistan asserted that there could be no investigation by the International Atomic Energy Agency into its own role in the development of Iranian capabilities, which appeared to be a blunt attempt to conceal its tracks.[47] Musharraf acknowledged that considerable nuclear expertise and equipment were dispatched between 1987 and 2003, but he claimed that the twelve "greedy scientists" had acted alone. The International Atomic Energy Agency was not permitted to interview those who were detained. Nevertheless, it is difficult to accept that the armed forces, and the ISI's Joint Intelligence Miscellaneous, which were responsible for the nuclear program, did not know of the sales and transfers, particularly when a Pakistani C-130 aircraft was pho-tographed in Pyongyang alongside missile parts in 2002.[48] Khan alleges that Musharraf had full knowledge of the transfers.

There were concerns that the United States had turned a blind eye to Pakistan's nuclear program until the matter came to light from Libyan sources. However, the Americans were quick to seize on the intelligence from Libya, so it is possible that the full extent of the illegal sales may not have been known to the United States until they got the Libyan tip-off.[49] The Americans were able to intercept a German vessel carrying centrifuge parts en route to Dubai in October 2003. However, it has also been alleged that the CIA had protected Khan from prosecution in Europe (for the theft of nuclear secrets from the Netherlands), and that their reassurances that they had him "under surveillance" was really an excuse to give him a free hand, although no motive has been advanced for this action. The Dutch judge, Anita Leeser, who oversaw the case against Khan in 1983, remarked that key documents had "disappeared." However, there was evidence to suggest that the ISI had set up front companies in Europe to conceal Khan's activities, and they had intermediaries working for them in Dubai. It also appears that China was also assisting in the sale and transfer of technical knowledge, following ISI requests. Even though he was questioned about the alleged sale of secrets, Khan maintained that his operations had to be kept secret to avoid detection by the Americans. Shuja Nawaz, who consulted army archives and interviewed leading officers, believes that "either the army was complicit in Khan's activities or it had been derelict in its security and surveillance duties."[50] It seems inconceivable that the ISI did not know about Khan's dealings; but if it did not, then it reveals another failure of considerable magnitude. There was some alarm in the West when Khan, who had been under house arrest, was granted immunity from prosecution and released in February 2009, while all eleven of his colleagues were released from prison by May 2006.[51] Pakistan's attitude toward the Khan case reveals not only the culture of security that pervades the establishment but also the culture of secrecy that gives rise to accusations of double-dealing from its allies.

The ISI since 9/11

The United States' approach to Pakistan is not a simple matter. There have been genuine concerns not just about the sale of nuclear secrets but also with the numbers of Jihadist organizations in the country and the degree of Islamist infiltration in state institutions. Washington believed that Musharraf was a critically important ally in the global war on terrorism, that Pakistan was a "front-line state" that had access to the Taliban, and that the Pakistan security services had a unique opportunity to roll up members of al-Qaeda. The Americans needed Musharraf's help; but at the same time, they could make demands on him to cooperate. In 2001, following the terrorist attacks of 9/11, George W. Bush insisted publicly that Pakistan withdraw its support for the Taliban in Afghanistan and assist in the apprehending of al-Qaeda's members via the ISI.

The deputy secretary of state, Richard Armitage, used "strong language" to insist that Pakistan relinquish its support for the Taliban.[52] Musharraf was forced into a volte-face of policy, and, as a result of the unrest that followed, all parties in Pakistan lost confidence in him.

Despite Musharraf's change of policy, many in the ISI felt that Pakistan had to act in its national interests against the United States. Some ISI officers were advising the Taliban on American tactics and plans as late as October 2001.[53] The ISI moved to protect Jalaluddin Haqqani, whom it regarded as a key strategic asset, by sheltering him in Pakistan's Federally Administered Tribal Areas. Nighttime airlifts were organized for Pakistani nationals within the Taliban ranks from Kunduz.[54] General Hamid Gul, the former director-general of the ISI, even remarked that the "attacks on New York and Washington [9/11] were an Israeli-engineered attempt at a coup against the government of the United States." He posited: "The destabilization of Pakistan is part of the US plan because it is a Muslim nuclear state."[55] Such ideas were surprisingly common-place among both Islamists and educated "moderate" Pakistanis. This may have been, in part, because they wanted to displace the horrific nature of terrorism from any association with Islam and their own country, but also because it has become ideological shorthand to blame the United States, or the CIA, for every ill affecting society. Accidents, unrest, and even environmental problems are frequently attributed to the American intelligence service.[56] ISI–CIA complicity is sometimes invoked as part of this fabric of conspiracy in Pakistan civil society. After 9/11 many Islamists in Pakistan demanded to see evidence of Osama bin Laden's involvement. Once the Americans and their coalition allies had secured Afghanistan, videotape and written evidence was provided, but by then the Islamists had already been convinced by their own conspiracy theories. The death of Osama bin Laden has further strengthened the suspicions about the Americans and the degree to which the ISI is a coconspirator.

To reinforce the new direction of strategy, Musharraf purged the ISI and leadership of the army of certain Islamists. The ISI director-general at the time, Lieutenant General Mahmood Ahmed, was replaced by Lieutenant General Ehsanul Haq.[57] In addition, 40 percent of the ISI was cut, partly a consequence of the end of ISI activities in Afghanistan, but also because of a scaling back of the Kashmir operations. Some senior officers objected, including the deputy chief of the ISI, Mohammed Aziz Khan, but they were "retired" or, in the case of Khan, promoted to the "ceremonial" post of the chairman of the Joint Chiefs of Staff Committee. In addition, there were 2,000 arrests of leading Islamists.[58]

However, there were some concerns. By May 2002 many militants had been released without charge, and attempts to seize the assets of Islamist organizations were halfhearted, because of misplaced confidence in being able to control these elements. Banned organizations reappeared under different titles or went underground, where they continued fund-raising or training fighters. Without doubt, some of the rank-and-file members of the ISI were still sympathetic to their Islamist allies, and they shared a deep disquiet about any association with America.[59] Musharraf admitted, when pressed about a lack of commitment to the war on terror, that renegade or "retired" ISI officers and agents may indeed have been supporting the Taliban. However, he was at pains to point out that Pakistan was playing a proactive role in defeating the Taliban and capturing al-Qaeda. In South Waziristan in 2004, attempts by the Pakistan army to root out foreign fighters caused defiance and then active resistance. As the army proceeded with its operations, it came under attack from local insurgents, many of whom were Taliban veterans.[60] There were heavy casualties, but the troops were withdrawn because of the impossibility of achieving any political success with a military campaign.

Jalaluddin and Sirajuddin Haqqani and the ISI

The Haqqani network in North Waziristan became a crucial interlocutor for the army and the ISI. Although the elder Jalaluddin, the experienced Mujahideen commander, compelled a great deal of respect on both sides of the border, his son, Sirajuddin Haqqani, was requested to act as the intermediary with tribal groups in South Waziristan, and in return he was given a free hand to operate inside Afghanistan against the Americans. The Pakistan army and the ISI were only too pleased to displace the insurgency from their own territory into the American sphere. Fighting has not ceased for long, however. Foreign fighters in South Waziristan created their own dynamic, and rival tribal groups made use of the army, al-Qaeda, or the Haqqani network for their own ends. The ISI does not seem to be able to control events and has been targeted by the insurgents. The Pakistan army and its security service have paid a high price in lives lost in the struggle with Jihadists; so, too, has the civilian population caught in the crossfire.

After the attack on the Indian Parliament on December 13, 2001, and bombings in Kashmir shortly after, India mobilized forces and made accusations that the state of Pakistan was behind the outrages. Musharraf argued that the ISI and the army were fully under his control, and serving personnel certainly had vested interests in supporting the military head of state. The outbreak of violence at the Red Mosque and fighting in Swat, close to Islamabad, coupled with mounting losses among the security forces in frontier districts, made this statement more credible.[61] The expressions of support for militancy tended to come from the retired ISI officers, such as Khalid Khwaja. He stated that "we have done the worst possible thing. We have been responsible for the miseries of our brothers and sisters because we didn't believe in God, but we believed in Bush and Blair."[62]

It is not just the outbursts of Islamists that cause doubts amongst Western governments. The cease-fire and negotiations with the Tehrik-i Taliban Pakistan (TTP) and allied tribal groups in Waziristan caused disappointment in the International Security Assistance Force (ISAF). Coalition forces in Afghanistan were unable to pursue the insurgents across the border into Pakistan and turned to strikes by unmanned aerial vehicles (i.e., drones) instead. Effectively, Pakistan frontier areas provide a "safe haven," and attacks are still launched across the international border. There have been disturbing reports that, in October 2006, Coalition troops had to fight not only entrenched Afghan Taliban south of Kandahar but also their Taliban reinforcements, who had arrived in pickup trucks "waved on by Pakistani border guards."[63] The Pakistan army's conclusion of its military operations in South Waziristan in 2004 certainly gave the Taliban a crucial respite, but more active support of the Haqqani network represents direct aid against American and Western interests.[64] Shelling across the Pakistani border into Afghanistan appeared to have been carried out with the connivance of Pakistani troops or the ISI and seemed to be retaliation for unmanned aerial vehicle operations and the strike against Osama bin Laden's compound in Abbottabad. In July 2011 the United States withheld a third of its military aid to Pakistan in protest.

The United States–led coalition believed that it could trace Taliban support to Pakistani training camps run by members of the ISI, with munitions dumps and new weapons caches along the border and a Taliban headquarters based near Quetta. It is estimated that in the battle with the ISAF in southern Afghanistan in mid-2006, the Afghan Taliban fired a staggering 400,000 rounds of ammunition, 2,000 rocket-propelled grenades, and 1,000 mortar shells— quantities that in fact seemed likely to have come from outside Afghanistan. Moreover, madrassas in Pakistan are dominated by the Jamiat-e-Ulema Islam, a group that provided the spiritual impetus to hundreds of Taliban before 2001. Migrant Pakistani laborers, who looked to get employment in the opium harvest in the south of Afghanistan, were recruited at the end of every season to participate in the Jihad against Western forces and the Afghan National Security Forces. The cost of the weapons stocks overrun by NATO in southern Afghanistan were estimated to be £2.6 million. This suggests that narco-dollars, or perhaps vigorous fund-raising, was supporting the insurgency.

The Pakistan government nevertheless insisted that it had nothing to do with supporting insurgency, and it is fair to say that the border areas have rarely been firmly under Islamabad's control. In 2004, the Pakistani army deployed up to 80,000 troops in the region, while NATO had just 31,000 in Afghanistan. Moreover, the ISI carried out more than 700 arrests of prominent Jihadists and members of al-Qaeda, including Khaled Sheikh Mohammed, the architect of 9/11. Pakistan's casualties from militancy totaled 3,600 in 2007, 8,400 in 2008, and more than 4,000 in 2009, with a similar trend thereafter. Nevertheless,

Matt Waldman asserted, through a report based on interviews with several Taliban, that the ISI was so complicit in supporting the Taliban that it was as evident, in the fighters' words, as "the sun in the sky."[65] Musharraf was quick to dispute the report, arguing that the Taliban could not have a headquarters at Quetta and that it was contrary to the ISI's interests to support the Afghan insurgents. He was prepared to accept that "rogue elements" of former ISI officers could have been active. Some of those who worked for the ISI had the same ethnic background and worldview as their Taliban comrades and had many years' experience sharing their hardships and cultural ethos, so the extent to which they could be considered "renegade" seemed doubtful.[66] However, without explaining the motive, critics believe that the regular ISI could be using these "rogue elements" as a convenient cover for its operations. When a large vehicle-borne bomb was detonated outside Indian hostelries in Kabul in 2010, many local Afghans believed that it was an ISI operation delivered by Haqqani.[67] Musharraf had in fact tended to target al-Qaeda and foreign fighters in Pakistan, rather than the Afghan Taliban, which enjoyed a strong following in some of the frontier districts. This may have been due in part to the question of limited resources, but it is also true that Musharraf had to tread a delicate course between his Western allies and his own disaffected people, particularly the Islamists, who were a useful political counterweight to the opposition.

The ISI may also have an eye on the future. It suited Pakistan's national interests to displace the focus of the TTP and Afghan Taliban into Afghanistan and away from Pakistan. Grooming the Haqqani network offered the opportunity for potential pro-Pakistani Afghan leaders in the future. At the very least, the Haqqani could offer to continue to act as negotiators for the ISI, especially in South Waziristan. Many in Pakistan expect the Western forces to pull out of Afghanistan in 2014, and this begs the question of what political dispensation will exist there. Some clearly feel that, once the ISAF has gone, some sort of accommodation with the Taliban will be necessary, and this affects the current handling of them.[68] Equally, some, especially Indian analysts, believe that extremists within the armed forces, following Musharaf's resignation in 2008, could effectively "Talibanize" Pakistan. However, this is a misconception. Although a few of the senior officers subscribe to a conservative brand of Islam, Tableeghi Jamaat, the vast majority of the officer corps are secular, professional, and loyal. Since 2002, whenever the Pakistan army was attacked by the Taliban and their allies in South Waziristan, the sympathies for Jihadists were no longer guaranteed. Attacks on patrols in the area were seen as an attack on the institution of the army and the state. The army "closed ranks" against this threat. Where there were episodes of indiscipline, they came from the Frontier Constabulary, an organization with familial and ethnic ties to the tribesmen of the region. The priority for the army and the ISI remains the preservation of the state and the ruthless pursuit of Pakistan's national interests.

Assessments

The army has been eager to contain Islamism, while pension, financial, or land rewards ensure loyalty.[69] The army and the ISI were always reliable agencies for Musharraf, despite episodes of sectarian or communal conflict that broke out in most major cities and tribal areas after 2001. The ISI will, no doubt, continue to operate in its traditional roles, protecting the nation's "security" by preserving the power of the armed forces, and projecting its influence beyond the borders of Pakistan and treating Islamist proxies as secondary to its strategic interests. However, as its record shows, it has not always been successful in suppressing popular unrest, providing accurate intelligence on the threat, or containing Islamism. Whether it is able to do so in the future, therefore, remains in doubt. Democrats are nevertheless deeply disturbed by the effect of such a powerful intelligence service. *The Nation* captured the complaint in an editorial: "[The ISI] is a government within a government—the intelligence agencies . . . [have a] virtually autonomous role in the political affairs of the country. The baneful influence of the intelligence agencies has spread its malign shadow over the political destiny of the country."[70]

This anxiety resurfaced with the assassination of Benazir Bhutto on December 27, 2007. Although the government was at pains to point out that the assassins were members of the al-Qaeda-affiliated Lashkar-e-Jhangvi, led by the militant Beitullah Mehsud, members of the *Pakistan People's Party* argued that the ISI was behind the murder.[71] Bhutto had written a letter herself on October 16, 2007, which named four men who intended to kill her, and they included the head of the Intelligence Branch, Ijaz Shah, and Hamid Gul, the former chief of the ISI. *The Times* subsequently carried a story of alleged renegade ISI involvement in the assassination.[72] Perhaps the tragedy is that a number of groups had motives to kill her, including the TTP and the Jihadist militants of the Punjab.

Religion is easily recognizable as a badge of identity, and therefore "culture" appears to be the most important element in dictating the radicalized fortunes of the ISI and its support for Jihadist organizations in the 1980s and 1990s. But state power is the real root of the ISI's raison d'être. In Afghanistan, in Kashmir, and the North West Frontier Province of Pakistan, though religious rhetoric could be invoked to win popular support, it was Pakistan's preservation or projection of power that mattered most. The ISI's support for the Afghan Taliban was motivated by the realpolitik of dominating the region on Pakistan's western and northern approaches, rather than the "other worldly" cultural concerns of building a caliphate based on the Sharia. As the free press and democratically minded have already recognized, it is not Islamism but the ISI's arbitrary exploitation of power that is most feared. It is the elements that operate on the fringes of the ISI, and independent extremists, that pose the most deadly menace.

The ISI became an important element in Pakistan's politics and strategy when it became financially independent and developed a habit for action that was not subject to independent scrutiny. Nevertheless, despite its influence, it remains a tool of the state and its military elite; it is not independent. In recent years it has tapped into business and banking to sustain its wealth and independence, and it still monitors politicians at home and overseas. These trends suggest that it will continue to interfere in domestic Pakistani politics on its own initiative and when directed by anxious military leaders. Current officers claim that the army and the ISI "obey the government," but this is unlikely to last long, because they will become impatient with a civilian administration unable to "solve" the financial crisis affecting the globe and which seems weak in the face of destabilizing Islamist militancy. The army leadership is still very conservative and not fully infected with Islamism, but there is a concern that a new generation of officers might, like Gul and Nasir, be more willing to accommodate the TTP within Pakistan and other militant groups, particularly in light of indecisive military operations on the frontier. Ahmed Rashid notes that Pakistan army and ISI judgments about the near future are wrong, which will precipitate a national crisis. He argues that debt and inflation will increase, relations with the United States will continue to deteriorate, but, worst of all, they will delude themselves that they can continue to manipulate militant groups, crack down on "miscreants," and keep the Americans at arm's length while maintaining their aid dependency.[73]

Despite its fearsome reputation, the ISI has been a singularly unsuccessful organization: It lost control of the Taliban, Haqqani, and its other Islamist protégés; it has periodically ruined Pakistan's relationship with India over covert operations in Kashmir; it has courted the most militant Islamist factions, only to see its cities plagued by sectarian violence; and it has so damaged the credibility of civilian politics that the army cannot escape its responsibility as kingmaker. In terms of its tactics, it has a long record of illegal actions: Its abuses have either been the result of a lack of control, oversight, and accountability, or desperation and survival. If Pakistan ever becomes a "failing state," many Pakistanis believe that the army and the ISI will be largely to blame for it. The ISI and the Pakistan army need to develop a more responsible and accountable ethos, but they are unlikely to accept Western assistance in this regard because of a passionate desire to avoid external interference, a point underscored by difficult bilateral relations even with Pakistan's most supportive ally, the United States. Admittedly, the available and accessible sources make drawing a conclusion extremely difficult and limited. However, until there is a substantial reexamination of the ISI and the Pakistan army's recent operations, and a better understanding of Pakistan's context and imperatives, it seems they are likely to go on failing and, as in the past, turn to coercion and violence to compensate for their lack of strategic success.

Notes

1. "Pakistan's Spy Agency Is Tied to Attack on US Embassy," *New York Times*, September 22, 2011.

2. Ibid.

3. "Pakistani PM Gilani Hits Back at the US Accusations," Reuters, September 24, 2011.

4. "Pakistan Scorns US Scolding on Terrorism," *New York Times*, September 23, 2011.

5. "Pakistan Spat Highlights Bitter Truths Facing the US in Afghanistan," *Time*, September 26, 2011.

6. Thomas Ruttig, "The Haqqani Network as an Autonomous Entity," in *Decoding the New Taliban: Insights from the Afghan Field*, edited by Antonio Giustozzi (London: Hurst, 2009); "Pakistan Scorns US Scolding"; Carlotta Gall, "Former Pakistani Officer Embodies a Policy Puzzle," *New York Times*, March 3, 2010.

7. "Afghanistan Warns Pakistan against Border Fighting," *USA Today*, September 25, 2011.

8. Cases in point are the February 2005 Srarogha agreement, the treaty with the Utmanzai Waziris in September 2006, and separate agreements with the TTP in South Waziristan.

9. "The Endgame in Afghanistan: How Do We End the Proxy Wars?" *Time.com*, September 23, 2011.

10. On the fear and sensationalism that the ISI generates in India, see Lal Bhure, *The Monstrous Face of ISI: The Real Story behind the Inter-Services Intelligence Agency of Pakistan* (New Delhi: Siddharth, 2000); and Srinkanta Ghosh, *Pakistan's ISI: Network of Terror in India* (New Delhi: A. P. H., 2000).

11. Imtiaz Gul, *The Most Dangerous Place* (New York: Viking, 2010); Abdel Bari Atwan, *The Secret History of Al-Qaeda* (Berkeley: University of California Press, 2006).

12. Steve Coll, "Don't Look Back," *New Yorker*, March 1, 2010.

13. Author's interview with Jason Burke, October 18, 2011.

14. Dexter Filkins, "The Journalist and the Spies," *New Yorker*, September 19, 2011.

15. Jason Burke, "Mumbai Spy Says He Worked for Terrorists, Then Briefed Pakistan," *The Guardian*, October 18, 2011.

16. Hasan Zaidi, "The Changing Face of the Taliban," *InPaper Magazine*, *Dawn*, September 2011; Dexter Filkins, "The Journalist and the Spies," *New Yorker*, September 19, 2011.

17. Military culture has been much-debated as a concept; see Theo Farrell and Terry Terriff, *The Sources of Military Change: Culture, Politics, Technology* (Boulder, CO: Westview Press, 2002), 3–21; Theo Farrell, "Culture and Military Power," *Review of International Studies*, 24 (1998): 407–16; Ann Swidler, "Culture in Action: Symbols and Strategies," *American Sociological Review* 51, no. 2 (April 1986); and Peter Wilson, "Defining Military Culture," *Journal of Military History* 71, no. 1 (2008): 11–43.

18. "Endgame in Afghanistan."

19. "Pakistan Warns That US Accusations May Cost Washington," *Los Angeles Times*, September 24, 2011.

20. Ibid.

21. For details of accusations of the degree of clandestine involvement in terror in India, see Rajeev Sharma, *Pak Proxy War: A Story of ISI, Bin Laden, and Kargil* (New Delhi: Kaveri Books, 1999).

22. Imtiaz Ali, "Beitullah Mehsud: The Taliban's New Leader in Pakistan," *Jamestown Terrorism Focus*, January 9, 2008.

23. Zaidi, "Changing Face."

24. The allegation from India was that the ISI had orchestrated the Mumbai attack by facilitating Lashkar-e Toiba, but Jason Burke argues that the ISI, though informed of the operation in principle, did not know its details. Their interlocutor was "David Headley," alias Daood Gilani, and the handler, allegedly, was Major Iqbal of the ISI. Stephen Tankel suggests that the ISI would have liked to direct Lashkar-e Toiba but failed to control it. Divisions and schisms within Lashkar-e Toiba emerged from interrogations of Gilani, and it seems the operation became a "martyrdom" mission quite late in the planning stage. See Jason Burke, "Mumbai Spy Says He Worked for Terrorists."

25. The ISI commanders are designated deputy director-general–political, deputy director-general–external, and deputy director-general–administration. The ISI is further subdivided into specialist divisions. The Joint Intelligence Bureau is responsible for both internal and external open sources intelligence and human intelligence. The Joint Counter-Intelligence Bureau also has both internal and external responsibilities. The Joint Signals Intelligence Bureau monitors all communications intelligence. Joint Intelligence X administers accounts; Joint Intelligence Technical examines technical intelligence and emerging technologies, and the Special Wing is responsible for intelligence training in the armed forces and for liaison with foreign intelligence agencies.

26. His desire to preserve power was in part due to a sense of siege. The ISI actually assisted him in locating and thwarting a coup by military officers in 1972 that led to the Attock Conspiracy Trial. The tribunal was led by General Zia ul Haq, who sympathized with the accused officers.

27. Gorden Carrera, *Shopping for Bombs* (London: Hurst, 2006), 8–9.

28. Abdus Sattar Ghazali, "Islamic Pakistan: Illusions and Reality," August 14, 1999, www.ghazali.net/book1/chapter11a/.

29. After Zia, religious affiliation reports on each officer were dropped but the ISI still briefed corps commanders on the political situation in the country, which created a habit and expectation of interest.

30. This assumption seemed to have ignored the obvious point that the greater depth would create a drain on already-stretched national resources.

31. The Afghan Bureau's finances were not supervised. Proper accounting was not established until Lieutenant General Hamid Gul took over. The Afghan Bureau consisted of three branches—Operations, Logistics, and Psychological Warfare. It was supported by a department for clothing and funds and for sending food and matériel to officers operating inside Afghanistan.

32. Shuja Nawaz, *Crossed Swords: Pakistan, Its Army, and the Wars Within* (New York: Oxford University Press, 2008), 372. Gul took much the same line and wanted to keep the Americans out.

33. The so-called Quetta Incident, where three officers were court-martialed in 1983 for accepting bribes to give arms to one faction above its quota, was an exception according to Yousaf. Mohammad Yousaf and Mark Adkin, *Beartrap: Afghanistan's Untold Story* (London: Leo Cooper, 1992), 31. That said, early attempts to recruit Jihadists from refugees was a failure because of rampant corruption. Ibid., 29.

34. Nawaz, *Crossed Swords*, 375.

35. Ibid., 392.

36. Alex Strick van Linschoten and Felix Kuehn, *An Enemy We Created: The Myth of the Taliban–Al Qaeda Merger in Afghanistan, 1970–2010* (London: Hurst, 2011), 72.

37. Nawaz, *Crossed Swords*, 383.

38. The turning point seems to have been Hekmatyar's failure to take Jellalabad. Bhutto claimed it was an ISI-inspired plan, formulated by the director-general of the ISI, Lieutenant General Hamid Gul. Nawaz, *Crossed Swords*, 4–32 (based on an interview with Benazir Bhutto).

39. Much has been written on the alleged creation, direction, and control of the Taliban by the ISI, but evidence from the field suggests the movement had a long gestation, was given support by the ISI once it had begun to establish itself in Kandahar, and was never under the ISI's control. See Linschoten and Kuehn, *Enemy We Created*, 120–21.

40. According to interviewees among the Taliban, while ISI officers and agents accompanied the Taliban and were colocated with them, relations were fragile. Linschoten and Kuehn, *Enemy We Created*, 122.

41. "Dangerous Game of State-Sponsored Terror," *The Guardian* www.guardian.co.uk/kashmir/story/0,2763,722049,00.html.

42. Nawaz, *Crossed Swords*, 431.

43. John Pike, "Directorate for Inter-Services Intelligence," July 25, 2002, www.fas.org/irp/world/pakistan/isi/.

44. Benazir Bhutto was clearly not part of this, and the ISI acted independently. When she called for a cross-party meeting to deal with the issue, Nawaz Sharif called for a strike in support of Kashmir. Her colleague, Sheikh Rashid, said he had set up a training camp for Jihadists. Nawaz, *Crossed Swords*, 432.

45. B. Raman, "Pakistan's Inter-Services Intelligence," SAAG.

46. The testing of Pakistan's first nuclear weapon occurred in a chaotic and anxious atmosphere. It is believed that the ISI invented the canard of an imminent joint Israeli–Indian air strike, which pushed the civilian authorities to agree to the tests. See Shahid ur Rehman, *Long Road to Chagai: The Untold Story of Pakistan's Nuclear Quest* (Islamabad, 1999).

47. Brahma Chellaney, "A Quiet Burial of a Scandal That will Haunt Washington," *Japan Times*, May 13, 2006.

48. Nawaz, *Crossed Swords*, 490.

49. Gordon Correra, *Shopping for Bombs* (London: Hurst, 2006), 106ff.

50. Nawaz, *Crossed Swords*, 555.

51. At the time of writing, Khan was free to move around Pakistan and meet with friends and family, but he is accompanied by a security team and it seems that he may not be permitted to leave the country.

52. US Department of State, cable, "Deputy Secretary Armitage's Meeting with General Mahmud: Actions and Support Expected of Pakistan in Fight against Terrorism," September 14, 2001, Secret, redacted, National Security Archive, www.gwu.edu/~nsarchiv/NSAEBB/NSAEBB325/doc04.pdf.

53. Linschoten and Kuehn, *Enemy We Created*, 237.

54. See Ahmed Rashid, *Descent into Chaos: The US and the Disaster in Afghanistan, Pakistan, and Central Asia* (New York: Penguin, 2009), 89; and Ahmed Rashid, *Taliban: Militant Islam, Oil, and Fundamentalism in Central Asia* (New Haven, CT: Yale Nota Bene Books, 2001). Also see Ahmed Rashid, *Pakistan on the Brink: The Future of America, Pakistan and Afghanistan* (New York: Viking, 2012); Tim McGirk, "Rogues No More?" *Time*, April 29, 2002; and Linschoten and Kuehn, *Enemy We Created*, 244.

55. Arnaud de Borchgrave (United Press International editor), *Newsweek*, September 14, 2001.

56. The Pakistan army argued that Pashtuns were forced to retaliate against American occupation and drone strikes; they blamed the United States for the energy crisis in Pakistan, citing the delay to the Turkmenistan–Pakistan pipeline project caused by American operations in Afghanistan; they stated that drug abuse is increasing in Pakistan because of the Afghan conflict, fueling domestic crime. The increase in attacks on the security services, the rise in kidnapping as a tactic from Afghanistan and the ability of India to exploit a potential "second front" against Pakistan are all attributable to the United States' policies. Author's interviews, 2011.

57. Mahmud Ahmed had told the Taliban's ambassador, Abdul Salam Zaeff, in 2001: "We want to assure you that you will not be alone in this Jihad against America. We will be with you." Allegedly, President Zardari had addressed Taliban prisoners in a similar manner in 2010: "You are our people; we are friends; and after your release we will of course support you to do your operations." Matt Waldman, "The Sun in the Sky: The Relationship between Pakistan's ISI and Afghan Insurgents," Crisis States Discussion Paper, London School of Economics and Political Science, June 2010, 8.

58. Robert Johnson, *A Region in Turmoil: South Asian Conflicts since 1947* (London: Reaktion Books, 2005), 231.

59. There were continuing supplies of weapons to the Taliban in September 2001. Owen Bennett Jones, *Pakistan: Eye of the Storm* (New Haven, CT: Yale University Press, 2003), 241.

60. Anand Gopal, Mansur Khan Mahsud, and Brian Fishman, "The Battle for Pakistan: Militancy and Conflict in North Waziristan," New America Foundation, available at Counter-terrorism.newamerica.net.

61. Imtiaz Gul, *Most Dangerous Place: Pakistan's Lawless Frontier* (New York: Penguin, 2009), 171; Linschoten and Kuehn, *Enemy We Created*, 298.

62. Rory McCarthy, "Dangerous Game of State-Sponsored Terror That Threatens Nuclear Conflict," *The Guardian*, May 25, 2002.

63. Ahmed Rashid, "Nato's Top Brass Accuse Pakistan over Taliban Aid," *Daily Telegraph*, October 6, 2006.

64. Steve Schippert, "Pakistan Cedes North Waziristan to Taliban," September 6, 2006, http://inbrief.ThreatsWatch.org/2006/09/pakistan-cedes-north-wazirista/.

65. Waldman, "Sun in the Sky." For reactions, see "Pakistani Agents Funding and Training Afghan Taliban," BBC, June 13, 2010.

66. Antonio Giustozzi, *Koran, Kalashnikov and Laptop* (London: Hurst, 2007), noted there were those with long-standing experience of working in Afghanistan or with militants on the frontier; Seth Jones referred to elements of the Frontier Corps and the ISI who were engaged in supporting insurgents in Afghanistan; Seth Jones, "Counter-Insurgency in Afghanistan," RAND Counter-Insurgency Study 4 (Santa Monica, CA: RAND Corporation, 2008); Waldman, "Sun in the Sky," 5.

67. Author's interviews, March 2010.

68. Ayesha Siddiqa, "Between Military and Militants," *World Today: Chatham House* 63, no. 4 (2007): 6.

69. Ibid.

70. *The Nation*, editorial, June 28, 1997.

71. Syed Faisal Shakeel, "PPP Demands Probe Based on Benazir's Letter," *Dawn*, December 30, 2007.

72. Jeremy Page, "Main Suspects Are Warlords and Security Forces," *The Times*, December 27, 2007.

73. Ahmed Rashid, interview at King's College London, June 2011.

CHAPTER 8

Iranian Intelligence Organizations

Carl Anthony Wege

The Islamist government of Iran is rooted in a vision of Twelver (Ithna-Ashari) Shi'ism, which traditionally asserted that any government other than that of the hidden imam[1] was necessarily illegitimate.[2] Clerical authorities came to govern Iran directly without intervening or parallel political structures only following the historically unique 1979 Revolution.[3] To paraphrase Gabriel Almond, as quoted by Stephen Welch in chapter 2, the 1979 Revolution changed the "pattern of orientations to political action" wherein "every political system is embedded." Revolutionary Iran became a neotheocracy ideologically driven by a radicalized Shiism to foster regional revolution.[4] The structure of Iran's intelligence establishment derived from the imperatives of this revolutionary state, whereas Persia's renewed ambitions to further a Shi'a Islamist imperium transformed political dynamics across the region.

Iran's Security Architecture

Iran, like other governments across the Near East, relies on multiple overlapping security organs to sustain its regime. Tehran's Shi'a regime is characterized by an interwoven network of competing security organs and clerical factions. These security organs are often associated with individual clerics or specific clerical factions, which are differentiated by varying degrees of adherence to Ayatollah Ruhollah Khomeini's original version of Islamic jurisprudence (*velayat-e faqih*).[5] The distinctive characteristic of Iranian intelligence is the Islamist veneer that overlays both the structure and function of its intelligence bureaucracies in their association with these clerical factions.

Iran's prerevolutionary National Intelligence and Security Organization (Sazemn-i Ettela'at Va Amniyat-I Kishavr, SAVAK), which was created by the shah in 1957 with assistance from the US Central Intelligence Agency and Mossad,[6] is the antecedent institution of the modern Iranian intelligence establishment.[7] Its orientation, focus, organization, and approach to the intelligence enterprise were entirely secular. Although postrevolutionary Iranian intelligence institutions go to great lengths to deny any association with the old SAVAK, it nonetheless influenced the initial configuration of the Revolution's successor intelligence entities.

The Khomeini government in its first months relied on the Palestine Liberation Organization for intelligence support.[8] However, by August 1979 a Ministry of Intelligence and National Security (Sazamaneh Etelaat va Amniateh Mihan, SAVAMA) had been created by Hojatolislam Mohammed Mufateh.[9] SAVAMA was the immediate SAVAK successor organization developed under General Hussein Fardust. Fardust, although closely associated with the shah, organized the new service using the remnants of SAVAK, and he recovered most of the SAVAK files on political dissidents.[10] The institutional responsibility of SAVAMA was foreign operations (the Revolutionary Guards were responsible for internal security during the first years of the Islamic Republic of Iran).[11] The postrevolutionary intelligence establishment developed on the foundation of both the Ministry of Intelligence and Security (MOIS, now called the Ministry of Intelligence and National Security) and Mohsen Rezaii's Iranian Revolutionary Guard Corps (IRGC; Pasdaran or Pasdan-e Inqilal-e Islami).[12] MOIS functioned more as an executive entity than an actual ministry, in that it was directly responsible to the supreme leader of the Islamic Republic (Ayatollah Ali Khamenei) and not to the Islamic or Islamic Consultative Assembly (Majlis-e Shora-ye). Iran's intelligence services, as they were maturing through the 1990s, established relationships with foreign services such as the Russian Foreign Intelligence Service (Sluzhba Vneshnei Razvedki, SVR).[13] The SVR trained hundreds of Iranian intelligence personnel and was allowed to station Russian personnel on Iranian soil.[14] The traditional emphasis of the Russian services on disinformation and the placement of agents of influence, particularly during the time of the Soviet KGB, were continued by the modern SVR and are sometimes reflected in MOIS's operations. Illustrative of this practice is the argument made by some scholars that Iranian disinformation operations successfully persuaded the Western powers before the 2003 invasion that Iraq was engaged in a significant program of weapons of mass destruction aimed at its neighbors.[15] Iran could thereby have used the United States to get rid of Saddam Hussein and have thus removed a major military obstacle to Iranian expansion. The maturation of the Iranian services also resulted in especially close relations with the services of Syria, and important relations with the services of Sudan, Libya, and Tajikistan.[16]

The Ministry of Intelligence and Security (Vezarat-e Ettela'at va Aminat-e Keshvar, VAVAK) was the successor organization to SAVAMA and was created in August 1984, with Mohammed Rayshahri as the first minister of intelligence. VAVAK instituted a system of regional bureaus, which created an internal Iranian security matrix administered by the rapidly growing security services.[17] Structurally, the early-twenty-first-century iterations of VAVAK boasted sixteen separate directorates, of which three had direct responsibility for terrorist operations. The Directorate of Overseas Affairs was responsible for MOIS branches abroad, with special emphasis on operations against the Peoples Mujahidin Organization.[18] The Directorate of Foreign Intelligence and Liberation Movements participated in typical foreign espionage operations. The Directorate for Security ostensibly engaged in internal security but was primarily responsible for overseas assassinations of regime opponents.[19] The French Center for Research on Intelligence claims the MOIS staff numbers roughly 15,000, with between 2,000 and 8,000 deployed outside the country at any one time either covertly or under cover of official Iranian organizations (including government corporations, embassies, etc.).[20] Overseas VAVAK residents under embassy cover are said to have served three- to five-year terms.[21] More recently, the second tier of VAVAK was divided into five elements: Analysis and Strategy, Homeland Security (protecting state institutions), National Security (responsible for monitoring overseas opposition movements), Counterintelligence, and Foreign Intelligence (with analytical departments and geographic regional divisions).[22]

VAVAK's cofounder, Abu al-Kassam Misbahi (sometimes called Farhad), defected to Germany's Federal Intelligence Service (Bundesnachrichtendienst, BND) in 1996, which opened an analytic window for the West on early iterations of VAVAK's internal organization.[23] Iran's German networks were its most important in Europe, because they were derived from the special political relationship between Iran and Germany that has existed since the nineteenth century. Germany led Europe in what was called critical dialogue, which sustained an important German–Iranian commercial relationship and allowed German political influence entrée into the Near East. Consequently, the working intelligence relationship between Germany and Iran was one that both parties made efforts to maintain.[24] This German–Iranian relationship gave the German BND insight into the Iranian government, but it is unlikely that much of that information was shared with other Western powers.[25] Before 1999, VAVAK operationally engaged in a regular practice of assassinating regime dissidents.[26] This practice became less frequent after the purge of relative hard-liners following the conviction of supposed rogue agents of VAVAK in the so-called chain murders of dissident Iranian writers and intellectuals during the presidency of

Mohammed Khatami (1997–2005).[27] VAVAK, during the 1990s, also came into competition with the al-Quds element of the IRGC in establishing relations with various militant Shi'a organizations outside Iran.[28]

Although the IRGC's initial 1979 mission was to defend the regime from internal enemies, it also acted directly in furtherance of the Islamic Revolution's foreign policy goals.[29] The Pasdaran, after attaining the status of an independent ministry in 1982, emerged as a Praetorian Guard for both the Islamic Republic of Iran and the clerics leading it. The IRGC and the regular armed forces (Artesh), though integrated at the level of the national command, remain competitor organizations. The rivalry was analogous with both Germany's Waffen SS of the Nazi era and the modern Chinese People's Liberation Army. The IRGC, like the Waffen SS, constituted an ideologically anchored security force in political competition with the regular army for both resources and political influence respecting national security policy. The Pasdaran, like the People's Liberation Army, had also entered the state economy at nearly all levels, which created economic interests that the IRGC had to protect at the policy level.

Within the IRGC the al-Quds security apparatus, consisting of about 1,000 men, undertook both intelligence gathering and covert action outside Iran.[30] This was distinct from the larger al-Quds special operations forces, which numbered several thousand and served in Lebanon, Bosnia, Sudan, and elsewhere. The Islamic Republic of Iran, following Syria and using the instrument of al-Quds, expanded the use of state-supported terrorism as an instrument of foreign and intelligence policy.[31]

A litany of public domain al-Quds operations outside Iran is unnecessary except to note that the IRGC al-Quds demonstrated a global reach in support of Iran's national foreign policy goals. The African hub that Tehran established in Sudan illustrates this global reach. Iran's efforts began early, when Hassan al-Turabi's National Islamic Front's successful 1989 Islamist coup in Sudan caused Iranian president Akbar Hashemi Rafsanjani, joined by the IRGC along with Hezbollah's Imad Mugniyah, to visit Khartoum.[32] The result of the 1991 meeting was the transfer of approximately 2,000 IRGCs into Sudan, where they organized twelve terrorist training camps in the eastern part of the country while reorganizing the country's security services.[33] Sudan became a focal point that allowed Iranian intelligence to co-opt and service networks of Sunni Islamists. Iran understood early on that cooperation with Sunni Islamists would be in its interests. The utility of these Islamist assets for al-Quds is truncated by the degradation of operational management and the flexibility intrinsic in politically quasi-independent entities. The operational skill set of the Sunni networks are also limited compared with those available to al-Quds professionals. Sudan, by the end of the twentieth century, and now ruled by Omar Hassan al-Bashir, became a refuge for Palestinians from Hamas, the Palestinian Islamic

Jihad, and Fatah operatives who were wanted by Israel. Sudan also facilitated a method whereby some wanted terrorists could return to the fight by going from Khartoum first to Iran and then infiltrating back into operational areas of the Middle East.[34] Sudan by the late 1990s still had hundreds of IRGC members in the country training foreign terrorists in addition to engaging in other military missions.[35] In the early twenty-first century Sudan developed a significant role in Iran's global arms-smuggling networks as a regional center for larger Iranian arms-trafficking efforts.[36] Hezbollah members, acting on Iran's behalf, bought weapons and transported them north through Egypt and into the Sinai, where Bedouin smugglers moved them on into Gaza. In 2009 Israel was concerned enough about the volume and quality of weapons moving north to risk an international incident by attacking a convoy ferrying Iranian weapons that were en route to Gaza via Egypt.[37] At the end of the day, however, what remains is that a substantive Iranian-facilitated arms-smuggling network, aided by Hezbollah operatives, is moving large quantities of arms through Africa into the Middle East. Some of these arms are smuggled to Hezbollah in Lebanon, some to Hamas in Gaza, and some furthering other Iranian interests in Africa.

In 1992 the global reach of al-Quds, using intelligence networks through Iran's embassy to coordinate local operational support, facilitated attacks in Argentina against the Israeli Embassy and in 1994 a Jewish Community Center in Buenos Aires.[38] Some Argentine Islamist organizations sympathetic to Iran were used for initial surveillance and target designation. Such preplanning sometimes uses Iranian veterans of the Afghanistan war against the USSR, who have high status among Islamists, to assist local sympathizers in creating target packages. These targets may later be attacked using professionals following a political decision in Tehran.[39]

In the Palestinian theater of war, Iran used Lebanon's Hezbollah as a surrogate. Iranian overtures to Hamas, both directly and through Hezbollah, allowed Iran to directly confront Israel. This began with Israel's ill-advised deportation of roughly four hundred Hamas and Islamic Jihad activists to the Marj al-Zahour area of Lebanon in 1992, which inadvertently furthered Iranian-inspired Sunni Shi'a cooperation in the anti-Israeli Resistance (Muqawama). Although it was a failure in hindsight, as a proposal Israel's deportations must have initially appeared to have some merit in that Sunni religious and political activists would be marooned in a region dominated by the Shi'a and with a history of friction with the Palestinians. The hope, if there was a specific hope articulated within Israeli councils of government by the Shin Bet, would be that these activists would never return to Israel. They would be limited to voicing anti-Israeli propaganda while kept on a very short leash by their new hosts. Alas, the result was a textbook example of blowback. Rather than living as unwanted guests, the Palestinians were taken under the wing of Hezbollah and tutored in the arts of the Muqawama. Imad Mugniyah, assisted by Abdallah

Safi-Id-a-Din, coordinated such instruction between Hezbollah, Hamas, and Islamic Jihad.[40] Those Sunni Palestinian Islamists, housed and operationally indoctrinated through Hezbollah, are now exploited by Iran in both the West Bank and Gaza. The institutionalization of the "Lebanese Model" in Gaza—and, to a lesser extent, in the West Bank—served Iranian interests and left the Israelis preoccupied with an enemy stronger than they had heretofore faced in the territories. This sublimation of Shi'a jurisprudential interest to Iranian political interests continues to widen its scope. This was most recently demonstrated by the movement of an entire Fatah faction from the Ain Hilwa camp near Sidon, Lebanon, to shelter with Hezbollah under Pasdaran tutelage in the spring of 2010.[41]

Iran's ambivalence concerning, if not outright support for, the Muslim Brothers (Ikhwan), particularly in their Egyptian incarnation but also in Jordan, likewise serves Shi'a interests. The Egyptian Revolution in 2011 created a political opening for the Ikhwan to directly participate in the government. The Freedom and Justice Party formed by the Egyptian Ikhwan won a plurality in the 2012 parliamentary elections and constituted a legislative coalition with other Islamist parties, and the Freedom and Justice candidate, Mohammed Morsi, won the presidency. If Egyptian society continues to move in a more overtly Islamist direction, the resultant decrease in American influence inherently works to Iran's advantage.[42]

The IRGC and its intelligence apparatus took advantage of opportunities presented by cooperation between radical Islamists. The Pasdaran supported an infrastructure of Islamist terrorist organizations oriented toward both Sunni and Shi'a through a national system of training camps. These camps are considerably more substantial than those that had been maintained by various Palestinian factions in Lebanon or what had been available in Libya or Syria. Groups trained in the Iranian camps could sometimes function as proxies advancing Iranian interests. Iran's camp system was configured to support different terrorist organizations and to focus on differentiated skill sets. In Qom, for example, the Fatah Ghani Husseini camp was used primarily by Turkish Islamists, whereas in Qasvim the Abyek camp was used for training in political assassination. Thousands of trainees have now passed through this system, and about 10 percent have been selected for more extensive training.[43] This system of training camps was fashioned quite early in the Islamic Republic of Iran and continues to this day. Nowadays, regular groups of Hamas activists from Gaza continue to cycle through the Iranian camp system.[44]

The Shatterbelt

In Iran itself, the revolutionary bureaucracy was Islamicized, so that the instruments of authoritarian control all manifest a Shi'a veneer that reflects the direct clerical role pioneered by Khomeini. The vulnerability of the region's Sunni governments to Iran's revolutionary Shi'a imperium results from the region's weak state system. These weak states characteristically lack intermediating social-political institutions that link state and society, which thereby creates a vacuum that Iranian-supported or -created organizations can exploit. Civil bureaucracies could function as intermediating social-political bodies but rarely do. Weberian-style bureaucratic administrative organization was historically premised on an existing civil society, which is the very thing lacking across the region.[45] Consequently, the effort to graft a European-style state system into the Near East region became as problematic as similar efforts in Africa. Near Eastern governments—whose administrative bureaucracies overtly claim participation, delegation, and power sharing yet fail to do these things—only foster a perception of weakness in a political culture characterized by patrimonial leadership.[46]

Although Farsi-speaking Persians (and Azeris) dominate Iran's government and society, myriad ethnic groups, which constitute more than a third of the country's population, live on its periphery. This creates a latent "shatterbelt" of potential access points for Iran's enemies. According to the *Asia Times* this center/periphery division has always characterized the modern Iran's national state.[47] The center/periphery divide has sometimes been manifested in social unrest, as in the disputed presidential elections of 2009. In that instance President Mamoud Ahmadinejad clearly benefited from an electoral process that was rigged against his opponent, Mir-Hossein Mousavi. President Ahmadinejad then used the Mobilization of the Oppressed (Basij-e Mostaz'afin or Basiji) militias drawn from outside the urban centers to overwhelm dissenters. The troops of the Basiji militia, which was under the command of the Pasdaran after 2008, were generally poorly educated and uniformly drawn from rural areas. A similar organization, the Helpers of God (Ansar e-Hezbollah), sometimes cooperated with the Basiji, and these became the primary instrument of suppression used against street protesters in Iran's urban centers. This Basiji along with the Ansar e-Hezbollah ultimately crushed opponents of the 2009 election results. Nonetheless, the social unrest did seriously alarm the regime, and thus it created some uncertainty with respect to the ultimate loyalty of the security agencies. Consequently, Khamenei reshuffled the intelligence structures so as to more effectively confront any future unrest. The Pasdaran incorporated some of the internal security functions of VAVAK and the Security Directorate of the Basiji into a new entity that included Khamenei's personal organization, known as Department 101, to create a new organization.[48] The significance of the new organization—called the Intelligence Organization of the IRGC and headed by Hossein Taeb, who previously ran the Basiji—was mitigated by the fact that the administration of its constituent agencies was necessarily drawn from existing intelligence management. Therefore, though antiregime political collusion within the intelligence establishment became less likely, concomitantly administrative efficiencies were degraded as the new entities developed functionality within the larger existing regime political structures. The result was a greater number of security agencies, which decreased the likelihood of an antiregime conspiracy but also undermined national coordination of security policy.

The long border from Turkey and Central Asia to Afghanistan creates a herculean border protection task for Iran's security services and VAVAK's Khorassan Department, which is responsible for Afghanistan and Central Asia. In Afghanistan the United States has free rein to establish electronic listening posts and safe areas from which to conduct covert operations against Iran.[49] Afghanistan also confronts Iran with a generally hostile Taliban movement aided by both Pakistan's Inter-Services Intelligence (ISI) and Saudi Arabia's al Istikhbarat al A'amah.[50] Iran's relationship with the ISI and Pakistan is historically multifaceted and problematic. In chapter 7 of this volume, Robert Johnson notes that Pakistan helped to jump-start Iran's nuclear program. Yet the ISI, apparently acting under US patronage, has also attempted to place moles in this same nuclear program.[51] Although Pakistan tries to improve political and diplomatic relations with Tehran, the ISI works against Iranian interests in Afghanistan. Likewise, Baluchistan has proven particularly difficult for the Iranian services, with the Sunni-oriented Soldiers of God (Jundallah) organization emerging as a significant threat, as demonstrated by its devastating bomb attack in October 2009 in Pisheen that killed a number of senior Pasdaran leaders.[52] Afghanistan and also Iraq nonetheless constitute theaters of conflict where Iran can practice tradecraft against the United States in an operational environment.

The fall of Saddam Hussein in Iraq, from Iran's perspective, constituted something of a foreign policy success. The United States conveniently removed Saddam's military barrier against al-Quds and VAVAK operations into Shi'a communities in adjacent states. However, the loss of Saddam's Iraq, from a Sunni perspective, resurrected the threat of a renewed Persian Empire astride the Gulf. Saddam, although a domestic and international bad actor, was a military bulwark preventing Iranian expansionism throughout the region. VAVAK had four departments located in the west and southwest of the country responsible for coordinating activities in Iraq. These included the Kurdistan, Kermanshah, Ilam, and Khuzestan departments.[53] Likewise, Iraq's security environment allowed al-Quds to gain experience in widespread covert action across an entire theater of operations. Al-Quds Department 9000 initially supported local Iraqi entities such as the Mahdi Army, Kata'ib Hezbollah, Qazali (a splinter Mahdi entity), and the Shebaini networks with money and training.[54] Iran also configured an Iraqi command element that it called the Ramzan Corps (subdivided into Nasr, Zafar, and Fajr commands), which facilitated operations against coalition forces.[55] Concomitantly, MOIS established stations in Baghdad,

Najaf, Karbala, Kut, Basra, and Kirkuk.[56] In the geographic area of Iraqi Kurdistan, the Iranians are faced with a more difficult problem. The Kurds, although carrying a tragic history of betrayal by the Western powers, are nonetheless a point of access into Iran. Israel's Mossad has maintained a substantive presence in Kurdistan since at least the early 1970s, and American penetration expanded following the first Gulf War.[57]

Central Asia presents an opportunity for VAVAK—albeit one mitigated by both the traditional Turkish/Iranian rivalry reborn in Central Asia and the resurgence of Russian power in the region. Nations contiguous with Iran, such as Azerbaijan and Turkmenistan, offer the most significant prospects. The Iranian security services are increasingly essential as Iran forges its place in the sun in the Near Eastern milieu. The shah-era "triple alliance" of the non-Arab states of Iran, Turkey, and Israel hemming in the Sunni Arabs has been reduced to a bilateral Turkish–Israeli relationship, which is further deteriorating as the Turks face the rise of their own Islamist political parties. Nonetheless, the maturing Iranian services have some established level of stability with respect to their relationships with foreign services. There are even instances of communication between Iranian services and the US intelligence community through the good offices of the Jordanians,[58] whose military intelligence component has maintained relations with MOIS.[59]

Assessing the Persian Security Establishment

An assessment of Iranian intelligence organizations must presume that formal institutional arrangements do not accurately reflect the actual organizational relationships between the Iranian services. Political authority flows through Iran's clerical–security matrix using traditional lines of kinship that are characteristic across the Near East.[60] Iran differs from Arab states in that the corrosive influence of patronage and kinship on the organizational effectiveness of its intelligence establishment is mitigated by the remaining revolutionary élan that still motivates many serving the institutions of Iran's government. It is worth noting that every minister of intelligence since 1984 has been a cleric, carrying this revolutionary élan, rather than a technocrat.[61] The remaining revolutionary fervor of this Islamist imperium also creates strategic goals for Iranian policy that animate the government intelligence bureaucracies.

Iranian collection disciplines vary in their efficiency but can be graphically represented as a series of concentric circles surrounding Iran, with the effort more productive in areas geographically closer to Iran. Tehran's extraterritorial clandestine operational skill set is focused on covert weapons acquisition programs in Europe and state-sponsored terrorism. Postrevolutionary Iranian agencies are at least adequate at internal security, although they confront regular spasms of social unrest, with the most serious previously discussed deriving from the disputed presidential election of 2009.[62] The violent suppression of these disturbances necessarily has an impact on the security services. Security service factions less loyal to the regime become ripe for exploitation by hostile services, irrespective of how those services have been reorganized. Illustrative of this was the defection of General Ali Asgari, a former deputy defense minister who commanded the Pasdaran in Lebanon during the 1980s.[63] Among the most critical collection arenas for Iran is in the area of nuclear technologies. Iran's nuclear program is an extraordinarily sensitive internal arena, and the combination of defections, assassinations, and penetrations in 2005 led to the creation of Oghab-2, a specialized counterespionage agency with a core mission to defend the nuclear program. Initially housed within the Pasdaran intelligence framework, Oghab-2 began to expand rapidly, so by 2007 it was said to have upward of ten thousand persons employed.[64]

Iranians' collection of electronic intelligence (including signals, measurement and signature, communications, and imagery) is limited by challenges rooted in both technology and inadequate human resources (electrical and software engineers, mathematicians, linguists, etc.). Iran faces particular challenges in the area of advanced intelligence applications of nanotechnologies and quantum computing. Most information and network technologies must be covertly imported, which limits their availability. Moreover, internal instability has reduced Iran's ability to domestically educate a sufficient number of persons with the relevant technological skills. The need to import commercial computer chips and related hardware, even covertly, leaves the most sensitive areas of Iran's intelligence enterprise open to covert infiltration through compromised hardware.[65] The virtual world created by information technologies covering the globe does allow Iran's security services entrée into Iranian expatriate communities. The traditional requirement to access the West by traveling through Ankara, Larnaca, or Beirut is now supplemented by network access to Iranian communities overseas. Conversely, such technologies provide a portal, although a more limited one, into Iranian society and government. Tehran's access to other states is increased, albeit with much potential remaining unrealized due to Iranian domestic limitations in relevant technologies and human resources. And the ability of Israel and the United States to technically exploit the limited electronic portal into Iran puts Iranian electronic intelligence disciplines in an untenable situation attempting to defend the country.[66]

The work of the intelligence enterprise is still anchored in analysis and dissemination of that analysis to policymakers. In the Iranian context such analyses are necessarily skewed toward threats to internal security. The bilateral balance of VAVAK and the Pasdaran (to include the Basiji and associated entities) thus focuses on internal security to an extent unknown in democratic countries. The core structure of this security matrix creates a balance precluding concentrations of power in the security organs fostering a limited rivalry used to ensure their rectitude in loyalty to the Islamic Republic of Iran. This approach is effective when the rivalries are contained, yet the Persian house has fundamental social cleavages that have been papered over with a praetorian state. Stresses on these cleavages accentuated by rivalry between the security organs in the context of larger social unrest may lead to events cascading out of control.

As we have seen previously in this volume, a number of scholars have sought to develop a concept of intelligence culture, and in chapter 6 Abdulaziz Al-Asmari characterizes how aspects of the early Arabian intelligence practice were absorbed into much of Islam. Iranian intelligence culture finds the analytical capacity of the regime's services challenged by the need to report within the scope of an Islamist facade characterizing the consumers of that intelligence. Shi'a clerics whose worldview is colored by jurisprudential filters govern Iran. These clerics accept technology but understand neither modernity nor social science. They therefore do not appreciate nuance and analytical methodologies concerning target countries, governments, and personalities. The blending of human analysis augmented by information technologies in Western intelligence bureaucracies has further degraded Iran's relative analytical capacity. This comparative difference has been accentuated with the rapid expansion of Western intelligence bureaucracies since 9/11 and the increasing incorporation of information technologies into Western analytical products. In the context of these information technologies, the cliché that "you can't do much carpentry with bare hands, and you can't do much analysis with bare brains" is apt.[67] Shortcomings in intelligence analysis are expected in most authoritarian regimes for obvious political and ideological reasons. Yet such assessment is also sometimes problematic in technologically advanced democratic regimes. In chapter 10 Ken Kotani notes that cultural biases within the Japanese policy-making establishment, for example, discount the value of intelligence assessment in favor of operations. Japanese policymakers, like their Iranian counterparts, are thereby less informed, which leads to a corrupting of diplomatic and political maneuverability for these governments in international relations.

The major strategic threat to Iran is the tectonic plates of modernity itself. Khomeini's majestic vision of an unfolding Shi'a revolution has now deteriorated into profane efforts to further Iran's national foreign policy goals under an Islamic veneer. Iran's clerical government has become internally corrupted by power and fractionalized. It is sustained by multiple security services in competition for political power and social status. Nonetheless, Iran's various intelligence agencies now sustain a regional Islamist imperium that reflects Tehran's goal of attaining regional dominance. The interlocking networks of clerical factions and security organs have institutionalized the pursuit of this foreign policy goal.

Archie Roosevelt argued long ago that a lust for knowing, seeking understanding unclouded by worldview, must animate the intelligence enterprise.[68] The Shi'a worldview of the clerics leading the Tehran government substantially undermines the Iranian intelligence enterprise to the detriment of the Islamic Republic of Iran.

Notes

1. The twelfth imam recognized by the Shi'a, Muhammad al Mahdi, was hidden from the world by divine intervention in AD 874. It is expected that his return will usher in the Day of Judgment. The Shi'a community also includes Zaydis or Fivers, who claim five true imams, and Seveners or Ismailis, who now live primarily in an arc from Central Asia and Afghanistan to Western China.

2. Iran's sixteenth-century Safavid Dynasty circumvented this problem by asserting that the Shah and associated institutions derived their authority from Allah. The seventeenth-century creation of the office of Mullabashi (chief mullah) precipitated ongoing contention between religious and secular power in Iran. See Roger M. Savory, "The Problem of Sovereignty in an Ithna Ashari ("Twelver") Shi'i State," in *Religion and Politics in the Middle East*, edited by Michael Curtis (Boulder, CO: Westview Press, 1981), 135–37.

3. Azar Tabari, "The Role of the Clergy in Modern Iranian Politics," in *Religion and Politics in Iran*, edited by Nikki R. Keddie (New Haven, CT: Yale University Press, 1983), 72.

4. Mir Zohair Husain, *Global Islamic Politics* (New York: HarperCollins, 1995), 227–35.

5. Wilfred Buchta, "Ideological Factions within the Power Apparatus," in *Who Rules Iran?* (Washington, DC: Washington Institute for Near East Policy, 2000), 14.

6. Mahammad Amjad, *Iran: From Royal Dictatorship to Theocracy* (Westport, CT: Greenwood Press, 1989), 65.

7. See Abbas William Samii, "The Shah's Lebanon Policy: The Role of SAVAK," *Middle Eastern Studies* 33, no. 1 (January 1997): 66–91.

8. Robin Wright, *In The Name of God: The Khomeini Decade* (New York: Touchstone, 1989), 110.

9. Edgar O'Balance, *Islamist Fundamentalist Terrorism, 1979–1995: The Iranian Connection* (New York: New York University Press, 1997), 38. Relations between Khomeini and Arafat deteriorated following the latter's support for Saddam Hussein during the Iran–Iraq War of the 1980s.

10. Gholam R. Afkhami, *The Iranian Revolution: Thanatos on a National Scale* (Washington, DC: Middle East Institute, 1985), 114. Also see Ervand Abrahamian, *The Iranian Mojahedin* (New Haven, CT: Yale University Press, 1989), 50.

11. Haleh Afshar, "The Iranian Theocracy," in *Iran: A Revolution in Turmoil*, edited by Haleh Afshar (Albany: State University of New York Press, 1985), 191.

12. There is technically a coalition of law enforcement forces under the authority of the Ministry of the Interior consisting of city police, countryside police, and the gendarmerie and various revolutionary committees. These entities are of limited intelligence significance.

13. The SVR was the Russian Foreign Intelligence Service established in 1991 as a follow-on to the old KGB First Directorate.

14. The Russians provided training in intelligence collection methods using three-month training cycles under the direction of the Russian Interior Ministry and under the auspices

of Yevgeni Primakov. See "Russian Agents Teach Iranians How to Spy," *Washington Times*, September 11, 1995.

15. "Iran's Spies," *Sunday Herald*, December 24, 2006. This was allegedly accomplished by feeding false information to various Iraqi opposition organizations infiltrated by MOIS.

16. "The Iranian Intelligence Services," *Note for News* (French Centre for Research on Intelligence), no. 200, January 5, 2010, available at www.cf2r.org.

17. *Intelligence Newsletter*, no. 286, April 18, 1996.

18. The Peoples Mujahidin Organization is a Marxist organization founded in 1965 and dedicated to the overthrow of the Islamic Republic of Iran. Although considered a terrorist organization by the United States, it has nonetheless provided apparently accurate information on Iran's nuclear program.

19. "MOIS Structure," February 28, 2006, www.iranterror.com/content/view/176/66.

20. "The Iranian Intelligence Services," *Note for News*, no. 200, January 5, 2010, available at www.cf2r.org.

21. Precision in this sort of thing is always problematic due to everything from definitional differences respecting what constitutes a ministry employee to active disinformation efforts on the part of the ministry.

22. "Iranian Intelligence Services."

23. The German courts referred to Misbahi as witness "C" in German terrorism trials involving a VAVAK-sponsored assassination. Misbahi, in addition to being a close aide to Rafsanjani and cofounder of VAVAK, managed intelligence networks in Iranian expatriate communities in Europe. See "Former Official Disclosed Iran's Complicity in Murders," *Washington Post*, April 12, 1997.

24. Indicative of this was the visit of Iranian intelligence minister Fallahian with Germany's BND chief Bernd Schmidbauer. The meeting allegedly dealt with humanitarian issues. See "Iran's State of Terror," *Time*, Atlantic Edition, November 11, 1996. Schmidbauer returned the favor by visiting Tehran secretly in 1996. See *Brief on Iran*, no. 462, July 25, 1996. Germany has also supplied computer equipment and training to the Iranian services. O'Balance, *Islamic Fundamentalist Terrorism*, 157.

25. Although given the close post–World War II relationship between Germany and Israel and Israel's close pre-Revolution relationship with the shah of Iran, it is likely that the old access channels between Israel and Iran and current channels among Germany, Israel, and Iran have yielded a significant amount of back-channel interaction.

26. This was particularly applicable to cadre from the Peoples' Mujahidin and Iranian Kurdish Democratic Party.

27. Douglas Jehl, "Killing of Three Rebel Writers Turns Hope into Fear in Iran," *New York Times*, December 14, 1998.

28. Frederic Wehrey, Jerrold D. Green, Brian Nichiporuk, Alireza Nader, Lydia Hansell, Rasool Nafisi, and S. R. Bohandy, *Rise of the Pasdaran* (Washington, DC: RAND National Defense Research Institute Intelligence Policy Center, 2010), 10.

29. O'Balance, *Islamic Fundamentalist Terrorism*, 41. The IRGC ceded this role to MOIS in 1983 but regained it following the election of President Khatami in 1997.

30. Buchta, *Who Rules Iran?* 69.

31. See Grant Wardlaw, "Terror as an Instrument of Foreign Policy," in *Inside Terrorist Organizations*, edited by David C. Rapoport (New York: Columbia University Press, 1988). Libya also attempted to use state-sponsored terror but proved not very competent at it.

32. Sudan's Islamic Front was a local version of the Ikhwan; by 2011 the Islamic Front had evolved into something called the National Congress Party. Al-Turabi would himself be

imprisoned and released multiple times between 2004 and 2011 by one-time allies in Sudan's Islamist government. Mugniyah would be assassinated in Damascus Syria, presumably by Mossad's Kidon element.

33. The number of Iranian personnel would swell to 3,000 in 1996, decline to about 1,500 by the turn of the century, and numbers a few hundred today. See "Sudan Is a Surrogate for Iranian Terrorism," *Washington Times*, April 27, 1994; and "Elite Iran Unit Said to Control Sudan's Security," *Washington Times*, August 28, 1993. It is also worth noting that Iran had named Majid Kamal as its chargé d'affaires in Khartoum. He had previously served in Beirut in the early 1980s assisting in the creation of Hezbollah. Administratively, a committee including al-Turabi's aide, Ali Othman Taha, and General Rahim Safavi of the IRGC was responsible for the particulars of Iranian intelligence-related assistance under the auspices of Ali Manshawi. Many of the camps in the early 1990s training foreign terrorists were run by Ali Alhaja, a close associate of al-Turabi. See Shaul Shay, *Somalia between Jihad and Restoration* (New Brunswick, NJ: Transaction Publishers, 2008), 63. Initially, the major terrorist training camps were Al-Shambat and Al Amzraa, later including camps at Khadolfi, Al-Grif, Benda, Karda, and Bahra. See Shaul Shay, *Red Sea Terror Triangle: Sudan, Somalia, Yemen, and Islamic Terror* (New Brunswick, NJ: Transaction Publishers, 2006), 47. Nearly two dozen additional camps existed for training terrorists under the tutelage of Osama bin Laden Salafists. These camps basically dissolved after 9/11.

34. "Israeli, US Intelligence Report Says Sudan Becoming Haven for Hamas, Hezbollah," BBC Summary of World Broadcasts, March 14, 2001.

35. See Amir Taheri, "Sudan: An Expanding Civil War with an Iran Connection," *International Herald Tribune*, April 9, 1997. Sudan also allowed mooring facilities in Port Sudan to service Iranian submarines.

36. Smuggling is sustained in part by tribal relationships and religious affiliations that are centuries old and stretch across a geographic arc from East Africa all the way around to Pakistan. See Annette Hübschle, "Unholy Alliance? Assessing the Links between Organized Criminals and Terrorists in Southern Africa," ISS Paper 93 (Paris: Institute for Security Studies, 2004), 9.

37. Israeli Air Force assets including Hermes drones out of Palmachim Air Base near Tel Aviv, accompanied by an Eitan unmanned aerial vehicle (i.e., drone), carried out at least two separate operations in January and February 2009. They attacked two separate convoys carrying Fajr 3 rockets intended to be smuggled from Egypt for use by Hamas in Gaza. It appears that dozens of smugglers and Iranian escorts were killed in the operation. See "Israeli Drones Destroy Rocket-Smuggling Convoys in Sudan," *Sunday Times*, March 29, 2009. US Department of Defense Special Operations Task Forces (88/145) also covertly engaged al-Qaeda across the Horn of Africa following the 1998 Embassy bombings. See Donovan C. Chau, *US Counterterrorism in Sub-Saharan Africa: Understanding Costs, Cultures, and Conflicts* (Carlisle, PA: Strategic Studies Institute of the US Army War College, 2008), 18.

38. "Iranian Diplomats Said to Be Suspects in Blast at Argentina Jewish Center," *Washington Post*, July 29, 1994.

39. "The Iranian Hand on the Plunger," *Yediot Ahronot*, July 29, 1994; and Foundation for Democracy in Iran, *Weekly News Update*, May 27, 1996.

40. "The Changing Colors of Imad Mugniyah," *Jerusalem Report*, December 3, 2002, 4. In one of the region's many ironies, Israel had been tolerant of Hamas in the Gaza during the early 1980s as a counterweight to Fatah.

41. Musa Keilani, "Another Split with Worrisome Repercussions," *Jordan Times*, March 21, 2010. The two thousand or so fighters under the command of Colonel Muir Maqdah,

formerly of Fatah's Force 17, had a history of auctioning themselves to the highest bidder, deep involvement in alleged corruption in the Ain Hilwa refugee camp, and Maqdah was on the losing end of a political dispute with Palestinian president Mahmoud Abbas.

42. "The Muslim Brotherhood in Egypt: Hurdles on the Way to Power," Center for Security Studies, Zurich, October 2011.

43. "Iran Builds Up Network of Terror Schools," *Electronic Telegraph*, July 8, 1996. Additional camps have included the Nahavand camp in Hamadan for Lebanon's Hezbollah, and the Imam Ali camp in east Tehran, which is the largest camp and used by Saudi opposition groups. Iranian exile groups have also named Bahonar Barracks, Mostafa Kohomeini Barracks, Ghayoor Asli Barracks, Imam Sadegh Camp, Korreit Camp, Lavizan and Abyek training centers, etc. See "Terrorist Training by the Quds Force and the VEVAK," February 28, 2006, available at www.iranterror.com.

44. See "Iran's Al-Quds Octopus Spreads Its Arms," *Jerusalem Post*, October 27, 2008.

45. See Nazih Ayubi, "Arab Bureaucracies: Expanding Size, Changing Roles," in *The Arab State*, edited by Giacomo Luciani (Berkeley: University of California Press, 1990). A civil society is here understood in Lockean terms, whereby government is created by a social contract among individuals to protect individual rights to life, liberty, and property.

46. Bill and Leiden have commented; in the patrimonial style of Middle Eastern leadership, the leader becomes the fount of all important ideas and strategies. Policies and programs emanate from him. See James A. Bill and Carl Leiden, *Politics in the Middle East* (Boston: Little, Brown, 1984), 151–52.

47. "Iran's Lurking Enemy Within," *Asia Times*, January 8, 2006.

48. "Iran Exile Group: Khamenei Tightens Intelligence Grip," Reuters, November 12, 2009. Khamenei was assisted by Ali Asghar Hejazi. Hejazi was directly involved in creating the MOIS and has coordinated intelligence agencies under Khamenei since 1989.

49. In this context Dubai has become a Near Eastern version of Vienna during the Cold War, and Oman functions as a major covert asset of the United States, as does Jordan.

50. See Abedin Mahan, "The Iranian Intelligence Services and the War on Terror," *Terrorism Monitor* 2, no. 10 (May 19, 2004), www.jamestown.org/programs/gta/terrorismmon itorgta/.

51. "Major Personnel Boost for Oghab-2," *Intelligence Online*, May 11, 2007.

52. Pisheen is on the Baluchistan–Pakistan border with Iran near the Persian Gulf. See "Iran's Lurking Enemy Within." The United States has apparently attempted to exploit what amounts to a tribal militia, albeit one with its own ties to al-Qaeda, to conduct operations against Iran. In February 2010 Iran managed to capture the leader of Jundallah, Abdol Malek Rigi, following a visit to a US facility in Pakistan. It was a significant blow to the Jundallah organization.

53. "MOIS Structure," February 28, 2006, www.iranterror.com/content/view/176/66.

54. Department 9000 was apparently established to act as a liaison between local Iraqi Shi'a militants and al-Quds. See "Tehran's Secret Department 9000," *Newsweek*, May 28, 2007.

55. Bill Roggio, "Iran's Ramazan Corps and the Ratlines into Iraq," *Long War Journal*, December 5, 2007, www.longwarjournal.org/archives/2007/12/irans_ramazan_corps.php.

56. See "The Iranian Intelligence Services," January 5, 2010, *Note for News* (French Centre for Research on Intelligence), no. 200, available at www.cf2r.org.

57. Eliezer Tsafrir, who had been a senior Mossad official, revealed that Israeli–Kurdish relations were so good that Israel had military advisers in Iraqi Kurdish regions during the

period 1963–75 and the Kurds had assisted in the movement of Jews from the area to Israel as far back as the 1950s. Reuters, February 21, 1999.

58. "The Iranian Intelligence Services and the War on Terror," *Terrorism Monitor* 2, no. 10 (May 29, 2004), www.Jamestownfoundation.org.

59. "Iranian Intelligence Services," *Note for News*.

60. See "Revolutionary Disintegration," *Time*, June 26, 1995.

61. See "Iran's Clerical Spymasters," *Asia Times*, July 21, 2007. Likewise, there is what amounts to a "commissar system" of clergy in every entity of governance that reports directly to the supreme leader. It is also relevant that much of the leadership in MOIS have attended the Madrase-ye Haqqani theological school in Qom. See Buchta, *Who Rules Iran?* 166. The Haqqani school itself was founded by the Hojjatieh, a semisecret anti-Sunni society that technically rejects the *velayat-e faqih* of postrevolutionary Iran. See "Shi'ite Supremacists Emerge from Iran's Shadows," *Asia Times*, September 9, 2005.

62. See "Daily Update," *Intelligence Watch Reports* 3, no. 116 (April 26, 1996). E.g., Iran managed to dismantle a network of American collection assets by 1989, and in 1995 it broke up five espionage networks set up by Turkey within the country. This continued to the 2010 detention of several American "hikers" who entered Iran via Kurdistan and were finally released in 2011. See "US Hikers Arrested at Iran Border," *Guardian*, August 2, 2009.

63. "Defector Spied on Iran for Years," *Sunday Times*, March 11, 2007.

64. "Major Personnel Boost for Oghab-2," *Intelligence Online*, May 11, 2007. IRGC management was evident in Oghab-2's first iteration under General Gholam Mohrabi but is still anchored in the Pasdaran with the top tiers, including General Ahmad Wahidi and his second, General Akbar Dianatr, coming from the IRGC. The third level does begin to diversify with Ali Naqdi formerly of the Tehran police. Major efforts have apparently been made to excise moles in the nuclear program from Pakistan's ISI acting under US auspices.

65. Iran's experience with the weaponized software called the Stuxnet worm perfectly illustrates the problem. The worm exploits vulnerabilities in the commercial Microsoft Windows computer operating system.

66. A cybersecurity unit within the IRGC, the "Control Center for Internet Activities," is relatively small with quite limited resources as compared with their Western counterparts. It was initially headquartered in the Firouzeh Palace (Ghasreh Firouzeh) district of Kamali Township. See "Iran Exile Group."

67. Tom Armour, DARPA Tech Symposium 2002, Information Awareness Office, Cognitive Amplification, citing Bo Dahlbomand and Lar-Erik Janlen.

68. Archie Roosevelt, *For Lust of Knowing: Memoirs of an Intelligence Officer* (Boston: Little, Brown, 1988).

CHAPTER 9

Intelligence and Security-Sector Reform in Indonesia

Peter Gill and Lee Wilson

I n the past thirty years throughout Europe, the Americas, and more sporadically elsewhere, the issue of how to institute some democratic control over security intelligence agencies has steadily permeated the political agenda. This shift has been a central, and sometimes painful, aspect of the democratization of formerly authoritarian regimes, both civilian and military. For example, the death of the dictator Francisco Franco in 1976 precipitated democratization in Spain that included the demilitarization of intelligence. Military rule ended in Brazil in 1985, though the military-dominated National Intelligence Service was not replaced until 1990 as part of a continuing process of demilitarization. During the years 1993–94, a more rapid transformation of formerly repressive security agencies was attempted in South Africa. In the countries of the former Soviet bloc, no agency has been immune from the changes—although the amount of real, as opposed to nominal, reform varies widely. Even in what might be described as the "old" democracies of North America, Western Europe, Australia, and New Zealand, legislative or judicial inquiries into scandals involving abuses of power and rights by the agencies have resulted in new legal and oversight structures for the agencies.

Such changes have been less common in Asia, though there are exceptions, such as South Korea.[1] In this chapter we examine the situation in Indonesia, where the first law on state intelligence was passed in 2011. We discuss the competing approaches to the analysis of intelligence democratization; provide an account of the development of intelligence since the country achieved independence; and analyze the current prospects for democratization given the social, economic, and political context of the country's state and security networks.

What Do We Mean by Intelligence Democratization?

Elsewhere, one of us has suggested that *intelligence* can be defined as "mainly secret activities—targeting, collection, analysis, dissemination, and action—intended to enhance security and/or maintain power relative to competitors by forewarning of threats and opportunities."[2] But our interest is in how to define *democratic* intelligence. We suggest that it can be defined by adding the following: "These activities will be subject to control and oversight in the interests of effectiveness, efficiency, legality and respect for rights." In general, the characteristics of intelligence under authoritarianism include the lack of any legal mandate; a plurality of agencies; repression of regime opponents, including frequent human rights abuses and public fear mongering; and secret budgets and involvement in corruption. Democratization requires more than elections; it can only be achieved through interrelated political and legal mechanisms capable of maintaining accountability in this most secretive area of states' activities. Analysis in this area deploys two main models; in the Americas it is most likely to be civil–military relations (CMR), whereas in Europe it is more likely to be security-sector reform (SSR).[3] Bruneau and Boraz argue that intelligence "can best be conceptualized as a subset of civil–military relations," and therefore that intelligence reform should be studied via three fundamental issues of CMR: democratic civilian control, effectiveness in achieving roles and missions, and efficiency.[4] In most "new" democracies, they suggest, intelligence is still almost a monopoly of the military yet is often overlooked as reformers concentrate on the establishment of new civilian agencies, while in the "old" democracies the military is still often predominant. The research focus must be on state intelligence institutions and those providing direction and oversight.

SSR has differing definitions with varying degrees of inclusiveness. Its narrower definition is really no different from that given above for CMR, because it refers to state security forces and their civilian management and oversight bodies; but, reflecting the more fundamental concern with "human" rather than traditional "national" security, a broader definition is more widely used. For example,

> The OECD DAC (Organization for Economic Cooperation and Development, Development Assistance Committee) Guidelines on Security System Reform and Governance agreed by ministers in 2004 define the security system as

including: core security actors (e.g., armed forces, police, gendarmerie, border guards, customs and immigration, and intelligence and security services); security management and oversight bodies (e.g., ministries of defense and internal affairs, financial management bodies and public complaints commissions); justice and law enforcement institutions (e.g., the judiciary, prisons, prosecution services, traditional justice systems); and nonstatutory security forces (e.g., private security companies, guerrilla armies, and private militia).[5]

Bruneau and Matei argue that this variety of definitions and the inclusion of nonstate bodies reduces the utility of the SSR concept, but, conversely, the CMR model risks unduly privileging the military mode of intelligence; we can find almost as many cases of civilian as of military intelligence abuse.[6]

The other strength of the SSR model is that it invites us to look at intelligence "beyond the state." Conventional intelligence studies have been too dominated by the examination of state agencies, despite wide variations between countries in terms of where the locus of intelligence activity lies.[7] This may be the consequence of the general underdevelopment of modern state institutions, but it can also be observed in older democracies with well-established state institutions where the corporate intelligence sector has grown in significance since the end of the Cold War. As we shall see, the need to examine intelligence beyond the state is especially important in the Indonesian case, even though the continuing dominance of the military in domestic government and politics might suggest the superiority of the CMR framework. The SSR perspective is preferred precisely because it facilitates the study of the many different types of security actors operating at the neighborhood, regional, and national levels. Given the European origin of SSR, applying it to an Asian country will provide an interesting test of its utility for comparative research—including its shortcomings. Whichever model is deployed, note that democratization is a process, not an event, and, as such, may progress or regress.[8]

Security and Intelligence in Indonesia: From Independence to New Order

From the perspective of a small but quite crowded island off the northwest of the European mainland, it is actually quite difficult to imagine Indonesia as a nation at all. It is an archipelago of about 17,500 islands, of which 6,000 are inhabited across a distance, from west to east, of about the same as that from Iceland to central Turkey. It has 238 million citizens, 45 percent of whom are Javanese, and 87 percent are Muslim—the country has the largest Muslim population in the world. Although the official language is Bahasa Indonesia, which today most Indonesians speak, there are more than seven hundred languages across the islands and their multiple ethnic groups. The fear that the country is not yet firmly established as a unified state leads to the emphasis in policy on national unity, economic development, political stability, and the sanctity of borders.[9] It took the newly independent Indonesia until 1949 to finally secure its autonomy from postwar attempts by the Netherlands to reestablish its control.[10] At the risk of oversimplifying, the next fifty years can be described as falling into three main periods.

From 1949 until 1957 was a period of "political liberalism" and a series of coalition governments, usually short-lived because of the unwillingness of excluded ethnic groups to accept the legitimacy of governments that were normally dominated by Javanese. The military steadily increased its influence as successive central governments paid little attention to state building across the islands and failed to maintain order to the satisfaction of the military.[11] The first formal intelligence organization of the newly independent country was the Secret Agency of the State of Indonesia (*Badan Rahasi Negara* or "Brani"), which was set up in May 1946 as "an umbrella for a diverse spread of ad hoc units established by field commanders across Java," including counterintelligence and "field preparation" for reconnaissance.[12] Presaging what has been a permanent feature of intelligence in Indonesia—self-funding—some funds were raised by selling what had been Dutch opium reserves to Chinese merchants. Over the next few years, the military and civilian Ministry of Defense struggled to establish intelligence and the police also maintained their own intelligence desk, but there was no national coordination. The United States first came on the scene in 1952, when a small number of civilians were selected for paramilitary and intelligence training by the US Central Intelligence Agency (CIA) under the label of the Security Bureau.[13]

Between 1958 and 1966 liberalism gave way to "guided democracy," which included martial law, as the military adopted its "dual function" of both protecting and helping to run the state under Sukarno's increasingly personalized rule.[14] He sought to reinstate the 1945 Constitution (which gave more power to the executive than the provisional 1950 Constitution, which favored the assembly) and authorized the creation of the Intelligence Coordination Agency (*Badan Koordinasi Intelegen* [BKI]) to help with this. The agency's contribution was not very significant, but once the 1945 Constitution was reinstated by decree, Sukarno enhanced the BKI's budget and renamed it the Central Intelligence Agency (*Badan Pusat Intelegen* [BPI]). As such, it remained largely a coordination body for contributions from the military, the police, and Attorney General's Office.[15]

The precise events around the September 1965 coup attempt by a group of Indonesian Communist Party (*Partai Komunis Indonesia* [PKI] members and sympathetic military officers, apparently with the knowledge of Sukarno and Subrandio, the head of the BPI, are not clear—but the aftermath certainly is. The plotters were quickly put on the defensive, and Suharto, encouraged by Sukarno, created the Operational Command for the Restoration of Security and Order (Kopkamtib) three days after the coup attempt to mobilize the armed forces against the PKI. Since the start of Indonesia's "Confrontation" with the United Kingdom over Malaysia in 1963, propaganda had been deployed by both sides, but the United Kingdom took advantage of the coup to intensify its attack on Sukarno and Subrandio, helping to damage their image, inciting people against the PKI, and undermining support for the Confrontation campaign.[16]

As the commander of Kopkamtib, in the name of national security, Suharto proclaimed a need to forge a chain of intelligence to monitor community activities considered to be a danger to the government. In 1966 he created the State Intelligence Command (*Komando Intelegen Negara* [KIN]), a strategic body responsible directly to him, incorporating all intelligence agencies to report on foreign and domestic security issues.[17] Opsus (special operations), which was responsible for covert political and diplomatic operations, had worked for Suharto since the West Irian campaign in 1960 and continued its work. When Sukarno was forced to delegate government authority to Suharto in March 1966, the army attacked the BPI headquarters building and detained everyone there. In March 1967 KIN became the State Intelligence Coordination Agency (*Badan Koordinasi Intelijen Negara* [BAKIN]), with essentially the same mandate, and BAKIN immediately formed close ties with the CIA because BAKIN wanted help with its domestic anticommunist campaign and in foreign communist countries; likewise, the CIA wanted regional help given the mire in which it was becoming steeped in Vietnam. In 1968 a special unit was created for foreign counterintelligence—the Special Intelligence Unit, eventually known as Satsus Intel, which received CIA funding and also support from other Western agencies, including training from MI-6 and Mossad. By 1973 Satsus Intel employees were considered honorary employees of BAKIN but remained separate.[18]

The failed coup was the pretext for the initiation of the New Order by means of the mass slaughter over the next six months of anywhere up to 1 million people by military and intelligence agencies led by Suharto and orchestrated by Kopkamtib.[19] Such extensive violence became a theme of the regime, which justified killings by reference to the need to eliminate ever-present threats to the security of the state. As Tony Day suggests, it is hard to imagine the New Order without the constant threat of disorder.[20] Lindsey notes the ways in which informal systems of violence and extortion became institutionalized under the New Order, in which "the territorialized system of the *preman* [gangsters] as urban standover criminals was writ large as the state used violence, systematic terror, and intimidation to extract the *japrem* [illegal rent] that funded the crony capitalism of the New Order. This led also to a proliferation of *dekking* or *bekking* ('backing'), the mechanism by which state officials protected street-level *preman*. Rival criminal 'gang' structures linked political and business elites through the military to *preman*, who sometimes mutated into private armies or militias linked to political and business leaders."[21]

And yet this excessive violence, it can be argued, resulted also from the felt need of the security apparatus to show that it was more in command than it necessarily was. Much of the ceremony surrounding the New Order drew upon the attempted coup of 1965, the September 30 Movement (Gestapu, *gerakan September tiga puluh*, G30S). The official version of events is retold in books and films in which the events of G30S assume the role of foundational myth for the New Order. Commemorative events served to reify and instantiate the threat of the PKI, thus underlining the Suharto administration's ability to restore and maintain order after cataclysmic social upheaval and appalling slaughter.[22] National vigilance courses were introduced to make citizens aware of the alleged threats to the social order.[23] Although the security apparatus could display ruthless efficiency in specific places at certain times, the very nature of Indonesia meant that it was unable to actually maintain control everywhere, though it certainly was able to intimidate enough to deter serious threats.[24] The first quarter century of the New Order coincided with the Cold War, when the concern of the older democracies with interests in the region, especially the United States and Australia, was with anticommunism. Moreover, for the international order, based upon the recognition of the monopoly of a state's absolute authority within its domain, the appearance of a strong centralized state—whether police state or military dictatorship—able to provide security was important.[25]

In 1970 BAKIN was reorganized into two main departments, one foreign, the other domestic, plus a third for Special Operations, though most of these were still carried out via Opsus, for example, ensuring election victories for Suharto and the growth of the Golkar electoral machine that underpinned the New Order.[26] Infighting between Opsus and BAKIN during the years 1973–74 eventually led to the former being merged within BAKIN's third department, which was now tasked with "conditioning"—that is, molding public opinion especially in five areas: Muslims, military, mass media, students, and business leaders.[27] However, during the late 1970s BAKIN was essentially subordinated to military intelligence. Following a fundamentalist-inspired aircraft hijack that was successfully thwarted by military special forces, military intelligence used its suspicions of BAKIN's involvement to virtually emasculate the agency. The military's own Strategic Intelligence Center now expanded into the Strategic Intelligence Agency (*Badan Intelegen Strategis* [BAIS]), which absorbed many of the investigative and enforcement powers of Kopkamtib. One of few areas where BAKIN held its own was in counterintelligence against foreign espionage, much helped by continuing support from the CIA.[28]

Democratization in Indonesia: The Context for SSR

There is inadequate space here to consider in detail the extensive literature on "transitions," but our position is that there is "no way around a detailed study of the interplay of actors and structure in concrete settings."[29] Although events such as the fall of the Berlin Wall in 1989 or Suharto resigning in 1998 symbolize what seem rapid transitions, they may actually be the culminations of long, uneven, and fragmentary processes. Unsurprisingly, given their function of sustaining regimes, intelligence services themselves may play a key role, in either facilitating change or, more commonly, inhibiting it.[30] In Indonesia, however, by the mid-1990s BAKIN bordered on irrelevance and played no significant role in the May 1998 riots that presaged the end of Suharto's rule.[31]

If a country exists within a "democratic region," then "clustering" improves the prospects for reform—but this was hardly a condition in Southeast Asia.[32] More broadly, some powerful players within the international order promote and enhance democracy, but Asia has no real equivalent for the carrots and sticks of European Union–NATO membership that have been used to encourage democratization in Europe. Foreign aid to SSR in Indonesia—mainly to state actors but also to civil-sector organizations—had grown to something like $30 million a year by the end of 2004, with more aid going to police reform, given the hesitations over directly aiding a military that was not exactly embracing the ideas that came with it.[33] However, the main thrust of this has been to further US and Australian security interests, especially since 9/11, which are not always simply consistent with democratization per se.

Linz and Stepan suggest that there are five interconnected and mutually reinforcing arenas of "modern consolidated democracy": the rule of law, economic society, political society, civil society, and the state apparatus.[34] The first four are crucial elements of the context for SSR, and we discuss the fifth in more detail. Given that the security sector is certainly the hardest to change in former military regimes, our conclusions should not be taken as necessarily applying to other aspects of Indonesian society.

The Rule of Law

Underlying more specific questions of the democratization and the impact of Western support is the fundamental question of the applicability of Western standards to Indonesia. For example, both Suharto and Prabowo Subianto often made recourse to culturalist arguments in defense against critiques of human rights abuses.[35] The defense of national unity and sovereignty has been key to military and intelligence claims that they must be unhindered in their activities; yet all nations (Asian or not) would claim the same—the point is that these activities should be subject to civilian control and the law. In terms of political culture, there is clearly a difference in emphasis between the liberal individualism of Europe and the Americas and the communitarianism that is widespread in Asia, but the idea of "community" and people's obligations thereto can too quickly be conflated into obligations of loyalty to a predatory state by authoritarian governments and their allied elites. Indonesia signed the International Covenant on Civil and Political Rights in 2006, and the key question is the extent to which national legal reforms stay within the "margin of appreciation" permitted by rights conventions to all countries.

The Indonesian Criminal Code provides a legal basis for the control of police and security operations but is widely ignored, in part because of an inadequate judiciary that is still subject to de facto control by the executive and the failure to enforce even those rare sentences of rights violators that are passed.[36] In the immediate post–New Order period a number of factors combined to bring about a worsening rather than any improvement of human rights, including the entrenched elites' corruption, the collapse of the economy, and local independence movements. In such a context the military and security forces rested on their accustomed role as guardians of national unity and security and committed widespread atrocities with impunity.[37] Although the tragic circumstances of the 2004 tsunami precipitated some resolution of separatist claims in Aceh, in other cases autonomy disputes persist. For example, in Papua the People's Council resolved that all candidates in district-level elections should be indigenous Papuans, but this measure has been rejected by Jakarta as discriminatory and in violation of national law.[38]

The case that has come to symbolize the apparent impunity with which the State Intelligence Agency, now known as *Badan Intelijen Negara* (BIN), is able to operate, however, is the murder of Munir Said Thalib, one of Indonesia's most respected human rights lawyers and founder of the Commission for Missing Persons and Victims of Violence (Kontras) and the Indonesian Human Rights Monitor (Imparsial). He was poisoned with arsenic on a flight from Jakarta to Amsterdam in September 2004. The only person so far convicted of his murder is a former Garuda Indonesia airline pilot who was traveling on the plane and was known to have close links with BIN; for example, his mobile telephone records showed more than two dozen calls in the days before and after the murder with a top BIN official. However, a former BIN deputy chief, Muchdi Purwopranjono, was acquitted in December 2008 of all the charges eventually brought against him. Actions in both district courts and the Supreme Court have left many entirely dissatisfied with the failure to conduct a thorough investigation of Munir's murder, and its anniversary remains a rallying point for human rights campaigners.[39]

Economic Society

In Indonesia there is considerable resistance to capitalism and there is also a residual mistrust of market forces for several reasons, including a rejection of the Dutch colonial legacy and disenchantment with the large (often foreign) firms that benefited under Suharto. Yet economic performance was good during the three decades of the New Order; annual growth averaged 7.4 percent, which posed something of a paradox for Duncan and McLeod because the usual requirements for an effective market economy—secure private property rights, impartial enforcement of contracts, and a neutral bureaucracy—were absent. Rather, firms and individuals were vulnerable to extortion from *preman*, the military, the police, and rent-seeking by bureaucrats. However, though this contributed to minimal change or innovation in the informal or traditional economy, the more modern and dynamic sector did benefit from the security of property and enforceability of contracts. This resulted from the symbiotic relationship between Suharto, his ministers, key bureaucrats, and the military and the conglomerates, large foreign firms, and "first-family firms." Here the wealth generated was shared to mutual advantage under relatively secure conditions enforced by the police, the military, the judiciary, and private militias. By contrast, "outsider" firms were subjected to relatively predatory behavior by the regime.[40]

With the collapse of this "Suharto Franchise" after 1998, economic performance weakened because there was no rapid adoption of new business practices to match that of electoral politics.[41] A law was passed in 2004 requiring military disengagement from business, but this has been resisted by the military.[42] Corruption remains endemic, though it is quite "orderly"; for example, although some rackets have been pushed out of the state system since 1998, they have gone "private" and now operate against the government, which is, of course, harder for the state to control; and this danger is aggravated by any decline in state capacity as a result of shrinking budgets.[43] Or, to put it another way, one Suharto has been replaced by many rent-seeking "mini-Suhartos."[44]

Political Society

Because Suharto resigned in 1998, there have been a series of more or less free multiparty elections—the most recent in 2009—that are the clearest manifestation of a more democratic Indonesia. However, it is not clear that the transition has gone much beyond establishing an "electoral democracy." The 1945 Constitution includes the five principles of *Pancasila*:

- protect the citizens of Indonesia,
- protect the land of Indonesia,
- attain public prosperity,
- educate the nation, and
- participate in global security efforts based on independence, eternal peace, and social justice.

All state intelligence agencies are established to protect the country's Constitution, but what is more significant is that the Indonesian Constitution is based on a rejection of Western "liberal governance" in favor of an "integralist" state—an amalgam of its component citizens—and therefore there is no need for checks to be placed on the state. (For European readers, this will be reminiscent of French political culture and the reason why parliamentary oversight of intelligence there came about much later than elsewhere in Europe.) The 1945 Constitution's Second Amendment, which was passed in 2000, allows for significant personal protections and provides for legal regulation of the military and police; but given their mandate for national security and state sovereignty, there is plenty of room for significant differences in interpretation.[45]

Recent ethnic conflict in Kalimantan, religious conflict in Maluku and Poso, increased religious intolerance elsewhere in Indonesia, and the prevalence of civil militias ostensibly representing ethnic and religious identities throughout Indonesia all underline the degree to which the New Order managed to keep a lid on internecine conflict by enforcing the ethical code of SARA—*suku, agama, ras, antar golongan*; that is, ethnicity, religion, race, and class—in which the public discussion of such matters was forbidden.[46] Again, it must be emphasized how important this is to understanding the perception of security threats; despite some talk of foreign sponsors of terrorism, almost all are seen as internally driven.[47]

One element of the post-Suharto regime (both authoritarian and centralist) was decentralization beginning in 2001 throughout thirty provinces, two special regions (Aceh and Yogyakarta), and Jakarta (the capital district), down to districts and municipalities. The impact of this has varied widely; significant reform has been achieved where leaders have been able to secure public policies from capture by private interests, through some combination of stable political coalitions or support networks in civil society.[48]

However, other networks will work contrary to democratization; one result of the 1945 Constitution was the Sidoarjo Intelligence System—a parallel network of bureaucratic, military, and industrial elites.[49] Further parallelism between state and criminal organizations characterized the New Order, and if, as reform progresses and/or state budgets shrink, paramilitary gangs compensate for the loss of state support by forming their own private alliances with business, "insecurity networks" may prevail.[50]

The plethora of security actors extends below the level of the central government and across all walks of life. For example, *siskamling*, police-controlled networks of neighborhood security systems, *hansip*, civil defense units, and civil service police units were founded in 1990 but since 1999 have increased decentralization, come under the control of local regencies, and interact in different ways with national military and police.[51] Further, in 2002–3 *kominda* were created as local intelligence groups organized by local governments, within which police, military, and BIN would share information. Although these all reflect the desire to increase the "reach" of the state among highly dispersed communities, they also provide the opportunity for local interests to dominate security governance. These will include gang leaders, or *preman*, who have now entered local government or Parliament and are legally representing their "communities."[52] It is easy to see these groups as illegitimate, but it is not, in our view anyway, so clear-cut. There is a gray zone of legality that is being constantly negotiated, that might be viewed as a process of de facto sovereignty, and that needs to be acknowledged alongside more conventional notions of constructing "democratic" states.

Civil Society

Active and politicized civil society groups are an important element of democratization. But although the 1997–98 economic crisis, including the collapse of the rupiah, saw genuine popular resistance to Suharto after he was "reelected" in March 1998, forcing his resignation two months later, civil society remains underdeveloped with only a small number of active organizations.[53] Thus, Makaarim refers to the lost momentum of SSR because civil society never replaced the military in controlling the direction of reform: "SSR is no longer a process that is influenced by the direction that comes from civil society, instead it is fully dependent on how much the ideas can be compromised with the interests of security elite and actors."[54] However, it must be noted that there are a number of active civil society organizations, such as Pacivis and Lesperssi, which, as is shown below, have intervened directly in the debate on intelligence reform. In the last decade a more pluralist civil society has developed, though critical media, including television channels, and media access to conflict areas such as Papua and Aceh, are normally blocked and freedom to report on security service abuses is limited.[55]

The State Security and Intelligence Apparatus since 1999

A relatively autonomous state that is not under elite domination and adequate state capacity are other factors facilitating democratization.[56] The military had been distancing itself from the increasingly personalized nature of Suharto's rule and his family enrichment throughout the 1990s, but its leaders still saw themselves as guardians of stability and "guided" the transition, although new limits to their influence were indicated by their subsequent "loss" of police and intelligence primacy to civilian agencies.[57] But state institutions are still dominated by relatively narrow military and economic elites. The adequacy of state resources for law enforcement remains an issue; but of equal or greater concern are the extraordinary heterogeneity of the country in terms of ethnicity and geography and the endemic police corruption. Decentralization, proffered as a prerequisite for transition to democratic forms of governance, often lays itself open to the very forces of separatism regularly used to justify continued military intervention or local elites' control of violence that defies democratization.[58]

The main state intelligence actors are the Strategic Intelligence Agency (BAIS) of the Indonesian National Armed Forces (*Tentara Nasional Indonesia* [TNI]), BIK Polri within the national police, and BIN. All three maintain a domestic intelligence capability. As we saw above, a weak BAKIN played little role in Suharto's downfall, and its weakness was aggravated by the lack of funds in the wake of the economic collapse, the fact that its Cold War targets (as for other Western agencies) had diminished, and by Habibie's (Suharto's immediate successor) purging of the Christians in senior posts who had been preferred by Suharto. However, Abdurrahman Wahid (a.k.a. Gus Dur) became president in October 1999, and in 2000 he sought to revamp intelligence by creating the State Intelligence Institute, which answered to the minister of defense and had the authority to oversee military intelligence. This direct assertion of civilian control was not appreciated by the military.

BAKIN was redesignated BIN in January 2001, and its budget was expanded at the expense of military intelligence.[59] The series of Christmas Eve 2000 church bombings in Indonesia exposed BIN's "scanty knowledge" of the Jemaah Islamiyah network that was responsible, and very shortly the insignificance of internal intelligence (other than for the purposes of repression) was to be reversed. First, when Megawati Sukarnoputri (Sukarno's daughter) was made president by the National Assembly in July 2001, she appointed a new BIN chief—A. M. Hendropriyono—who was also given ministerial status;[60] second, after the 9/11 attacks in the United States and the Bali bombing in October 2002, BIN was not only given more responsibility for the coordination of intelligence but also increased its operational focus. In part this was indicated by the opening of offices in the provinces, regencies, and municipalities to which government powers were devolved in the hope that BIN would provide coordination between military and police at local level.[61] The first civilian head of BIN was appointed in 2009, but he was replaced by another military head in 2011 immediately after the passage of the Intelligence Law.[62]

The military had maintained an administrative structure parallel to that of the state during the New Order, and even though the new law on TNI 2004 sought to reduce the military's role, it still included "assisting in local governance" as one of its responsibilities "other than war."[63] Thus, the links between the military, police, and intelligence run from the top to the bottom of Indonesian government—but only with a great deal of organizational friction. There are specific policy areas in which these links become more crucial, such as counterinsurgency and counterterrorism, in which they are all involved. For example, in a well-meaning effort to civilianize counterinsurgency, responsibility was shifted in 2000 from the military to the police—specifically to its paramilitary unit, Brimob—but for various reasons, including inadequate training, the move was unsuccessful.[64] Kopassus (*Komando Pasukan Khusus*), Indonesia's military Special Forces, have their own intelligence capacity, and became synonymous with human rights violations; its Detachment 81 was deeply implicated in the carnage in East Timor and routinely engaged in sabotage, kidnapping, and murder.[65] Yet, despite the police having had formal counterterrorism primacy since 2000, in the wake of the 2002 Bali bombing and the 2003 Marriott Hotel bombing, the government was reportedly seeking ways to increase Kopassus's role as a counterterrorist squad.

Friction between the police and the military increased further when Detachment 88, which was under police command but was funded and trained by the United States, began to be involved in counterterrorism investigations in 2004, apparently duplicating the similar skills of Detachment 81. In July 2010 President Susilo Bambang Yudhoyono ordered the formation of the National Anti-Terrorism Agency (*Badan Nasional Penanggulangan Terorisme* [BNPT]), led by a two-star police general, Ansyaad Mbai. The BNPT is charged with formulating policy and the coordination and implementation of counterterrorist efforts by the respective civil and military agencies, and it answers directly to the president. Concerns remain about the concentration of too much power in the hands of the BNPT, a lack of clarity in threat definition, the operational management of army and police intelligence agencies, and coordination with BIN.[66] This innovation may compound intelligence management problems in Indonesia: multiple agencies, the lack of regulation, and a general lack of coordination between agencies themselves and with the police and the military.[67]

Intelligence Reform in Indonesia: Establishing Democratic Control and Oversight?

As far as intelligence is concerned, democratization is usually discussed in terms of the control and oversight of agencies. "Oversight" is defined as a means of ensuring public accountability for the decisions and actions of security and intelligence services. It must be distinguished from control, which refers to the "act of being in charge of the day-to-day management of the intelligence services."[68] An indispensable precondition for democratization of intelligence is "legalization" via legislation. The president must gain approval of the People's Representative Council (*Dewan Perwakilan Rakyat* [DPR]) to make laws and determine the budget, but he or she is not accountable to the assembly.[69] Executive dominance of the DPR is the major challenge of intelligence reform;[70] for one thing, members have very little knowledge of intelligence, and the chance to develop expertise is minimized because parties shuffle members around commissions twice a year.[71] Commission One for foreign, defense, and security relies almost entirely on former military/security officers for advice, and before 2009 few members showed much interest in the issue.[72] The lawmaking process in Indonesia is quite distinctive; the commission would assign an ad hoc working committee (*panja*) to discuss the bill with government representatives. If inter-party differences represented on the *panja* can be settled, there will be no voting when the bill goes back, neither in the full commission nor in the subsequent plenary session.[73]

There have been at least three official draft laws on intelligence. The first was dated January 2002 and was leaked, having been prepared by BIN after 9/11. It proposed extensive powers of arrest and detention along with restrictions on legal representation and the right to silence, but it was dropped after a barrage of criticism from the chief justice, the police, and human rights organizations. However, in the wake of further bombings, including that of the Australian Embassy in September 2004, another draft law began circulating, which again included extensive arrest powers.[74] Nongovernmental organizations responded to this in the form of a 2005 draft law prepared by the Global Center for Civil Society Studies (*Pusat Kajian* Global Civil Society [sic] or PACVIS) based at the Universitas Indonesia. Although still drawn in broader terms than the intelligence legislation typically found in Europe and the Americas, this was certainly an improvement on that written by BIN. For example, it proposed that a separate body be established for strategic foreign and defense intelligence and that there be a body for the coordination of intelligence assessments separate from BIN itself, and it set out procedures for the external authorization of the use of covert information gathering and for the control and oversight of intelligence by the executive branch and the DPR.[75]

These proposals did not seem to have had much impact on official thinking, judging from the next government draft published in March 2006, which retained an extremely broad grant of discretionary powers to the agencies with little in the way of control or oversight.[76] BIN retained overall coordinating authority (article 8), and arrest powers and covert information gathering would not require external authorization (article 12). Further, as well as enumerating the main intelligence agencies, it said that "other performers of intelligence functions" could be established by presidential decree (article 7[2]), which rather missed the point as to why legislation is seen as important for democratic control. (This provision was not included in the 2010 redraft, but it is a moot point as to whether the president would regard himself or herself as prevented from appointing other agencies.)

The 2010 redraft of the law was distinctive,[77] in that it was initiated by a group of new members of Parliament on Commission One who had experience of and interest in legislating for intelligence.[78] After amendment, this became law in October 2011, and it included signs that some of the provisions most criticized in the 2006 version had been addressed; for example, the preamble referred to a fairly conventional series of security threats "such as terrorism, espionage, sabotage, subversion, theft of natural resources, and interstate organized crime" and the consequent "need for professional state intelligence, improvement of intelligence cooperation and coordination, in addition to establishing rule of law, democratic values and principles as well as acknowledgement and respect for human rights." This is a sign of at least rhetorical acknowledgment of the significance of rights because it did not appear in the equivalent section of the 2006 draft.[79] BIN's powers are defined more specifically, but in other respects much discretion is retained or actually extended. BIN is to retain its authority for both domestic and foreign intelligence. With respect to BIN's powers, article 13 (1) reads: "In addition to the powers mentioned in Article 12 [to conduct investigations], on the basis of this Law, State Intelligence Agency (BIN) has a special power to intercept communication and investigate any financial undertaking that is suspected to fund terrorism." We also need to note, however, that the draft required no external authorization for this special power, as is regarded as a sine qua non for democratic control and as had been suggested by the PACIVIS 2005 draft (article 14). During the legislative process a provision was added requiring district court approval before interceptions of communications, which sounds like progress until the unreformed nature of the judiciary is taken into account. Even the credibility of the special regional corruption courts established since 2006 has been undermined by allegations that poor screening of judges has led to many dubious acquittals.[80]

Another of the main criticisms of the 2006 draft (article 12) was its grant of arrest powers to BIN, and these have been omitted—this is important and suggests that civil society criticisms have had some effect.[81] However, article 13(2) of the 2010 draft introduced a new concept of "intensive investigation": "In addition to the special power mentioned in paragraph (1), State Intelligence Agency (BIN) has the power to intensively investigate a person who is strongly suspected to be a terrorist in an investigation to uncover his/her activity." Precisely what this means is not defined in the draft, but the explanatory memorandum provides further information: "BIN's special power for intensive investigation is preventive in nature, in contrast to the power exercised by law enforcement, in which case it is based on Criminal Code. The special power is given with the intention of gathering information as well as acting swiftly for the purpose of protecting the rights of the citizenry and public, which are more important than the rights of a person who has the potential to rob the rights of the former—in addition to protecting other national interests." We should not be surprised that the power is preventive, because that is the precise raison d'être of intelligence, but it is easy to see how "intensive investigation" will include detention for the purposes of interrogation.

Oversight Tasks

Since 1999 the DPR has had much-enhanced legislative, budgetary, and supervisory functions, including the right to investigate. Parliamentary commissions have become very active in requesting information from the government and in holding hearings, but so far this has had little impact on intelligence matters (which, to be fair, is also the case in many much older democracies). The development of serious intelligence oversight is hardly advanced by the custom of representatives and journalists accepting money from ministers to ask the "right" questions.

As noted above, Commission One covers foreign, defense, and security matters, but its members have been preoccupied with the first of these. On the face of it, Commission One has achieved much by means of its control of the budget; for example, the actual figures earmarked by its budget committee for counterterrorism and intelligence were published in 2002 in the wake of the first Bali bombing, and the total was actually less than proposed by BIN. However, it is not clear how significant this is, given that BIN is still able to raise money from its own businesses, for example, its newspaper. A key element of democratic control is that agencies may only spend money allocated by parliament—this is still lacking from the new law.[82] Article 43 of the new law provides only for supervision of BIN by unspecified internal mechanisms and a special commission within the DPR. This will have some potential influence by means of endorsing the president's appointments of agency heads and is empowered to question them.[83] However, civil society organizations fear that the law's provisions for severe penalties for "leaking intelligence information" could be used to hinder oversight by civil society and media organizations.[84] This, the lack of provision for citizens to complain, and the uncertainty surrounding the powers of the parliamentary commission all suggest that oversight of even this one intelligence agency will remain very weak.[85]

Conclusion

The literature on postauthoritarian regimes in Europe and Latin America suggests there are broadly three main ways of describing the situation in these regimes: democracy is "consolidated,"[86] and all politically significant groups adhere to democratic "rules of the game"; second, early change is at a "standstill,"[87] where change has stopped at, for example, "feckless pluralism"[88] or "pseudodemocracy";[89] and third, there may be "regression," and Putin's Russia is often cited as an example.[90] Although the passage of the new Intelligence Law represents a significant milestone in Indonesia, it cannot really be characterized as any of these three. Defects in the law itself and uncertainties as to what change it will make in practice certainly do not permit the conclusion that democracy in Indonesia has been consolidated. Conversely, it is clearly not an indicator of regression. However, to describe the country in terms of feckless pluralism or pseudodemocracy is not necessarily more helpful.

Indonesia may still be struggling with what has been described in Europe as the first "generation" of SSR—legislation for the intelligence mandate, and procedures for control and oversight.[91] However, drawing this conclusion makes assumptions about the nature of the state and power in Indonesia that might not be warranted. As we have argued, Indonesia is not only a postcolonial state in which the role of violence plays a key role in the maintenance of authority. It is a neopatrimonial state in which the exercise of authority relies as much on the maintenance of relations that are mutable, personal, and precarious as it does on the actual control of territory.[92] Most often it relies on being able to give the appearance of being in control; if necessary, through the application of extreme violence, directly or via proxies. Democratic process in the form of national electoral systems, as Trocki notes, often predicates the rise of "violent and predatory local figures," while in the longer term serving to consolidate national unity and transparent political process.[93] In postauthoritarian Indonesia there is a public desire for change, for the contestation of authority and greater empowerment of civic power. The recent *cicak-buaya* case—in which Police General Susno Duaji sparked public outcry when he compared the Corruption Eradication Committee's attempts to investigate senior members of the police as akin to a lizard confronting a crocodile—can be seen as evidence at least of a growing public intolerance of abuses of power.[94] Yet there is a long way to go if popular sovereignty as an ideal is to be achieved. Although there may be support for sharpening the instruments of civic society, a decentralized state with multiple, competing sites of authority, blurred jurisdictional boundaries, and the continued rent-seeking of entrenched military and economic elites in the context of periodic terrorist attacks suggest that there will be little significant intelligence democratization in the foreseeable future.

We have not attempted any systematic consideration of the applicability or otherwise of CMR/SSR models outside the Americas and Europe, but it is clear that Indonesia's experience cannot be adequately explained via the CMR model because, though there is more civilian control of the military (e.g., the police have been civilianized), the problems of inefficiency, corruption, and human rights abuses are as likely to derive from civilian elites as from residual military influence. But we have shown that the nature of state and society in Indonesia is such that conventional notions of democratization in terms of the democratic control of *state* agencies are inadequate to deal with the complexities of Indonesia, where the legitimacy or otherwise of many corporate and community organizations performing intelligence functions and security roles must also be considered.

Given post–New Order configurations of authority and power, it is inconceivable that the Indonesian state will become centralized in such a way as to ensure that greater control and accountability of the intelligence sector can be addressed. In a decentralized state with networks of multiple security actors in each area, the idea of parliamentary oversight is somewhat fanciful. This issue can only be addressed through the education and empowerment of civil and political societies locally, bearing in mind that currently some of these actors may be more of a security problem than its solution. Thus, the broader notion of SSR provides a better analytical perspective, but both the process and the outcomes will be very different from those envisaged in Europe.

Notes

1. Jonathan Moran, "The Role of the Security Services in Democratization: An Analysis of South Korea's Agency for National Security Planning," *Intelligence and National Security* 13, no. 4 (1998): 1–32.

2. Peter Gill, "Theories of Intelligence: Where Are We, Where Should We Go, and How Might We Proceed?" in *Intelligence Theory: Key Questions and Debates*, edited by Peter Gill, Stephen Marrin, and Mark Phythian (London: Routledge, 2009), 208–26, at 214.

3. The intellectual origins of CMR are described by Samuel P. Huntington, *The Soldier and the State* (Cambridge, MA: Harvard University Press, 1957). Its object was to maximize national security with least sacrifice to other social values by balancing the power of civil and military groups. SSR is a paradigm for good governance that sprang from the need for normative order in Central and Eastern Europe following the collapse of socialism and the reconstruction of the Balkans. Miroslav Hadžić, "The Concept of Security Sector Reform," in *Sourcebook of Security Sector Reform: Collection Papers*, edited by Philipp Fluri and Miroslav Hadžić (Geneva and Belgrade: Geneva Centre for the Democratic Control of Armed Forces and Centre for Civil–Military Relations, 2004), 11–44, at 12. SSR is a constantly evolving and hotly debated concept that has rapidly become a central plank in EU foreign policy, part of a democratizing agenda in which progress is measured in accordance with the extent to which public control is exercised over the various state and nonstate actors that constitute the "security system."

4. Thomas C. Bruneau and Steven Boraz, "Intelligence Reform: Balancing Democracy and Effectiveness," in *Reforming Intelligence: Obstacles to Democratic Control and Effectiveness*, edited by Thomas C. Bruneau and Steven Boraz (Austin: University of Texas Press, 2007), 2–6.

5. See Organization for Economic Cooperation and Development, *The OECD DAC Handbook on Security System Reform (SSR) Supporting Security and Justice* (Paris: Organization for Economic Cooperation and Development, 2007), www.oecd.org/dataoecd/43/25/38406485.pdf; cf. Timothy Edmunds, "Security Sector Reform: Concepts and Implementation," in *Towards Security Sector Reform in Post–Cold War Europe: A Framework for Assessment*, edited by W. N. Germann and T. Edmunds (Geneva and Bonn: Geneva Centre for the Democratic Control of Armed Forces and Bonn International Center for Conversion, 2003), 11–25, at 11–12; Heiner Hänggi, "Conceptualising Security Sector Reform and Reconstruction," in *Reform and Reconstruction of the Security Sector*, edited by Alan Bryden and Hänggi (Münster: Lit Verlag, 2004), 1–9, table 1.1.

6. Thomas C. Bruneau and Florina Cristiana Matei, "Towards a New Conceptualization of Democratization and Civil–Military Relations," *Democratization* 15, no. 5 (2008): 909–29, at 914.

7. Adda Bozeman, "Knowledge and Method in Comparative Intelligence Studies," in *Strategic Intelligence and Statecraft*, edited by Adda Bozeman (Washington, DC: Brassey's, 1992), 180–212, at 196.

8. Charles Tilly, *Democracy* (Cambridge: Cambridge University Press, 2007), 50.

9. Leonard Sebastian, "Domestic Security Priorities, 'Balance of Interests' and Indonesia's Management of Regional Order," in *Order and Security in South East Asia: Essays in Honour of Michael Leifer*, edited by R. Emmers and J. Liow (London: Routledge, 2006), 175–95, at 191.

10. Although there was continuing conflict over Western New Guinea/Irian Barat until 1962. The intelligence implications of this are recounted by Wies Platje, "Dutch Sigint and the Conflict with Indonesia, 1950–62," *Intelligence and National Security* 16, no. 1 (2001): 285–312.

11. Joseph L. Derdzinski, *Internal Security Services in Liberalizing States: Transitions, Turmoil and (In)security* (Farnham, UK: Ashgate, 2009), 83–84.

12. Ken Conboy, *Intel: Inside Indonesia's Intelligence Service* (Jakarta: Equinox Publishing, 2004), 18.

13. Ibid., 17–27. During the 1950s the United States became increasingly disenchanted with President Sukarno, and in November 1957 President Eisenhower approved direct CIA aid to rebel colonels on Sumatra who planned to overthrow him. The following February, the colonels declared themselves to be the government when Sukarno was visiting Japan but he successfully resisted the coup. More bizarrely, the CIA sought to exploit Sukarno's reputation as a womanizer and purported to show him in a fabricated pornographic film and photographs. John Ranelagh, *The Agency: The Rise and Decline of the CIA* (New York: Simon & Schuster, 1987), 332–35.

14. Derdzinski, *Internal Security Services*, 84–85.

15. Conboy, *Intel*, 27–30.

16. David Easter, "British Intelligence and Propaganda during the 'Confrontation' 1963–66," *Intelligence and National Security* 16, no. 2 (2001): 83–102, at 98.

17. Haryadi Wirawan, "Evolusi Intelijen Indonesia," in *Reformasi Inteligen Negara* (Jakarta: PACIVIS, 2005), 23–49, at 34.

18. Conboy, *Intel*, 43–60.

19. Robert Cribb, ed., *The Indonesian Killings: Studies from Java and Bali* (Clayton, Victoria: Centre of Southeast Asian Studies, Monash University, 1990).

20. Tony Day, *Fluid Iron: State Formation in Southeast Asia* (Honolulu: University of Hawaii Press, 2002).

21. Tim Lindsey, "The Criminal State: *Premanisme* and the New Indonesia," in *Indonesia Today*, edited by Grayson Lloyd and Shannon Smith (Singapore: Institute of Southeast Asian Studies, 2001), 283–97, at 285.

22. E.g., "*Hari Kesaktian Pancasila*" (Sacred Pancasila Day), an annual event at which tribute was paid to the generals murdered by the PKI on September 30, 1965, as heroes of the state. Staged at a monument and museum complex built at the site of the well into which the bodies of the murdered generals were thrown, the event served to establish the official history of the attempted coup. Emphasis was placed upon the brutality of the deaths of the generals at the hands of the PKI, and served to magnify the communist threat to the social order. Katherine E. McGregor, "Commemoration of 1 October, '*Hari Kesaktian Pancasila*': A Post Mortem Analysis," *Asian Studies Review* 26, no. 1 (2002): 39–72, at 52.

23. National vigilance refresher courses (*tarpadnas, penataran kewaspadaan nasional*) were introduced by the National Defense Institute (Lemhannas, Lembaga Pertahanan Nasional)

to brief both the military and the civil administration on the possible threats to national stability. A joint project between Lemhannas and the Operational Command for the Restoration of Order and Security (Kopkamtib, *Komando Operasi Pemulihan Keamanan dan Ketertiban*), *tarpadnas* was instigated following the crackdown of the student movement against Suharto in 1978. Jun Honna, "Military Ideology in Response to Democratic Pressure during the Late Suharto Era: Political and Institutional Contexts," *Indonesia* 67 (April 1999): 77–126, at 79–82.

24. Derdzinski, *Internal Security Services*, 87–88.

25. Adrian Vickers, "The New Order: Keeping Up Appearances," in *Indonesia Today*, ed. Lloyd and Smith, 72–84. In political theory and international relations, sovereign statehood is typically predicated on the supreme authority of the government of a populated territory within its jurisdiction. International recognition of domestic authority by other governments thus assumes a normative aspect in which sovereignty is presumed to be coherent and to reside in the state. Internationally this then becomes "a necessary condition of outward agency." Jens Bartelson, *A Genealogy of Sovereignty* (Cambridge: Cambridge University Press, 1995), 26.

26. Adrianus Harsawaskita and Evan A. Laksmana, *Rethinking Terrorism in Indonesia: Lessons from the 2002 Bali Bombing*, UNISCI Discussion Paper 15 (Madrid: Research Unit on International Security and Cooperation, 2007), 74–75, www.ucm.es/info/unisci/revistas/UNISCI15_Harsawaskita-Laksmana.pdf.

27. Conboy, *Intel*, 65–87.

28. Ibid., 150–56.

29. Georg Sørensen, *Democracy and Democratization: Processes and Prospects in a Changing World* (Boulder, CO: Westview Press, 2008), 33.

30. Peter Wilson, "The Contribution of Intelligence Services to Security Sector Reform," *Conflict, Security and Development* 5, no. 1 (April 2005).

31. Conboy, *Intel*, 199.

32. Renske Dorenspleet and Petr Kopecký, "Against the Odds: Deviant Cases of Democratisation," *Democratization* 15, no. 4 (2008): 697–713.

33. International Crisis Group, *Indonesia: Rethinking Internal Security Strategy*, Asia Report 90 (Jakarta and Brussels: International Crisis Group, 2004), 20–22.

34. Juan Linz and Alfred Stepan, *Problems of Democratic Transition and Consolidation: Southern Europe, South America and Post-Communist Europe* (Baltimore: John Hopkins University Press, 1996), 7–15.

35. See Douglas E. Ramage, *Politics in Indonesia: Democracy, Islam, and the Ideology of Tolerance* (London: Routledge, 1995); and Elizabeth Fuller Collins, "Indonesia: A Violent Culture?" *Asian Survey* 42, no. 4 (2002): 582–604. For a robust defense of the notion of universal human rights against claims of "Asian values," see Jack Donnelly, *Universal Human Rights in Theory and Practice*, 2nd ed. (Ithaca, NY: Cornell University Press, 2003), 107–23.

36. Derdzinski, *Internal Security Services*, 101–4.

37. Ibid., 112–14; Elizabeth F. Drexler, *Aceh, Indonesia: Securing the Insecure State* (Philadelphia: University of Pennsylvania Press, 2008).

38. International Crisis Group, "Indonesia: The Deepening Impasse in Papua," press release, August 3, 2010, www.crisisgroup.org/en/publication-type/media-releases/2010/asia/indonesia-the-deepening-impasse-in-papua.aspx.

39. *Jakarta Post*, September 7, 2010.

40. Ron Duncan and Ross McLeod, "The State and the Market in Democratic Indonesia," in *Indonesia: Democracy and the Promise of Good Governance*, edited by Ron Duncan and Ross McLeod (Singapore, ISEAS Publishing, 2007), 73–92, at 75–78.

41. Ibid.; see also Natasha Hamilton-Hart, "Government and Private Business: Rents, Representation and Collective Action," in *Indonesia*, ed. Duncan and McLeod, 93–114.

42. Damien Kinsbury, "Indonesia," in *PSI Handbook of Global Security and Intelligence: National Approaches*, vol. 1, edited by Stuart Farson, Peter Gill, Mark Phythian, and Shlomo Shpiro (Westport, CT: Praeger Security International, 2008), 247–62, at 258.

43. Lindsey, "Criminal State," 285.

44. B. Ghoshal, "Democratic Transition and Political Development in Post-Soeharto Indonesia," *Contemporary Southeast Asia* 26, no. 3 (2004): 506–29, cited by Derdzinski, *Internal Security Services*, 93.

45. Cf. Derdzinski, *Internal Security Services*, 98–101.

46. International Crisis Group, *"Christianisation" and Intolerance*, Asia Briefing 114 (Jakarta and Brussels: International Crisis Group, 2010).

47. International Crisis Group, *Indonesia: Debate over a New Intelligence Bill*, Asia Briefing 124 (Jakarta and Brussels: International Crisis Group, 2011), 4–5.

48. I Ketut Putra Erewan, "Tracing the Progress of Local Governments since Decentralisation," in *Indonesia*, eds. Duncan and McLeod, 55–69.

49. Derdzinski, *Internal Security Services*, 99.

50. Richard Robison, Ian Wilson, and Adrianus Meliala, *"Governing the Ungovernable": Dealing with the Rise of Informal Security in Indonesia*, Policy Brief 1 (Perth: Asia Research Centre, Murdoch University, 2008).

51. Stein Kristiansen and Lambang Trijono, "Authority and Law Enforcement: Local Government Reforms and Security Systems in Indonesia," *Contemporary Southeast Asia* 27, no. 2 (2005): 236–54.

52. Loren Ryter, "Their Moment in the Sun: The New Indonesian Parliamentarians," in *State of Authority: The State in Society in Indonesia*, edited by Gerry van Klinken and Joshua Barker (Ithaca, NY: Cornell University Press, 2009); International Crisis Group, *Indonesia: Debate over New Intelligence Bill*, 3.

53. Jean Grugel, *Democratization: A Critical Introduction* (London: Palgrave, 2002).

54. Mufti A. Makaarim, "Civil Society and Security Sector Reform," in *Journey of Reform: Security Sector Reform in Indonesia*, edited by Beni Sukadis and Eric Hendra (Jakarta: Lesperssi, 2008), 135–43, at 137.

55. Derdzinski, *Internal Security Services*, 107–8.

56. Grugel, *Democratization*, 45.

57. Derdzinski, *Internal Security Services*, 88–92.

58. E.g., see Vedi Hadiz, *Localizing Power in Post-Authoritarian Indonesia: A Southeast Asian Perspective* (Stanford, CA, and Singapore: Stanford University Press and Institute of Southeast Asian Studies, 2011).

59. Conboy, *Intel*, 203–5.

60. Ibid., 213–14.

61. Derdzinski, *Internal Security Services*, 96–97.

62. *Jakarta Post*, October 23, 2011.

63. International Crisis Group, *Indonesia: Rethinking Internal Security Strategy*, 11.

64. Ibid., 5.

65. Ken Conboy, *Kopassus: Inside Indonesia's Special Forces* (Jakarta: Equinox, 2003); International Crisis Group, *Indonesia: Rethinking Internal Security Strategy*, 5–6; Kingsbury, "Indonesia," 251–52.

66. Fatima Astuti, "In Focus: Indonesia's National Counter Terrorism Agency (BNPT)," *Counter Terrorist Trends and Analysis* 2, no. 20 (2010): 1–3; International Centre for Political

Violence and Terrorism Research, S. Rajaratnam School of International Studies, Nanyang Technological University, 2010.

67. International Crisis Group, *Indonesia: Debate over a New Intelligence Bill*, 6; Aleksius Jemadu, "Accentuating the Coordination in Indonesian Intelligence Reform," in *Journey of Reform*, eds. Sukadis and Hendra, 102–10, at 108–9.

68. Hans Born and Loch Johnson, "Balancing Operational Efficiency and Democratic Legitimacy," in *Who's Watching the Spies? Establishing Intelligence Service Accountability*, edited by Hans Born, Loch Johnson, and Ian Leigh (Washington, DC: Potomac Books, 2005), 225–40, at 226.

69. Derdzinski, *Internal Security Services*, 99.

70. Jemadu, "Accentuating," 106.

71. M. Fajrul Falaakh, "The Framework for Intelligence Reform in Indonesia," in *Journey of Reform*, eds. Sukadis and Hendra, 111–16, at 114.

72. This is from personal information. Also see Derdzinski, *Internal Security Services*, 105.

73. International Crisis Group, *Indonesia: Debate over a New Intelligence Bill*, 7.

74. International Crisis Group, *Indonesia: Rethinking Internal Security Strategy*, 14.

75. Indonesian Working Group for State Intelligence Reform, *Bill of Law on State Intelligence* (Jakarta: PACIVIS, 2005).

76. Indonesia, Draft Law of the Republic of Indonesia Number . . . Year 2006 on State Intelligence, March 10. 2006.

77. We are grateful to Beni Sukadis at Lesperrsi for making this draft available and facilitating its translation into English.

78. International Crisis Group, *Indonesia: Debate over a New Intelligence Bill*, 8.

79. In the "explanatory provisions" of the 2006 draft, included among the usual enumeration of global threats to security such as terrorism and subversion was "neoliberalism." In the wake of the 2008 financial crisis, one might suggest that other countries would do well to adopt this definition. However, it has been omitted from the list of threats attached to the 2010 draft.

80. Donny Syofyan, "Restoring Public Trust in Corruption Courts," *Jakarta Post*, November 29, 2011, www.thejakartapost.com/print/361217.

81. Cf. International Crisis Group, *Indonesia: Debate over a New Intelligence Bill*, 10.

82. Budgetary allocation is perhaps the most important mechanism by which parliaments establish control over executives. The immensity of the challenge of SSR in Indonesia can be gauged from the fact that the military has historically been largely independent of the government, receiving around 70 percent of its income from a wide spectrum of business activities, both legal and illegal; Kingsbury, "Indonesia," 248. The BIN budget for its 1,800 personnel plus administrative staff for 2011 has been reported as $140 million; Bagus Saragih, "Intel Law Is New Dawn for RI Spies," *Jakarta Post*, October 12, 2011.

83. Ridwan Max Sijabat, "Who's Afraid of the BIN Bad Wolf?" *Jakarta Post*, October 5, 2011,

84. Saragih, "Intel Law."

85. E.g., Fitri Bintang Timur, "The New Intelligence Law: Not Smart Enough," *Jakarta Post*, October 12, 2011.

86. Grugel, *Democratization*, 67; Bruneau and Boraz, "Intelligence Reform," 11–12.

87. Sørensen, *Democracy*, 55.

88. Thomas Carothers, "The End of the Transition Paradigm," *Journal of Democracy* 13, no. 1 (2002): 5–21.

89. Larry Diamond, *Developing Democracy: Towards Consolidation* (Baltimore: John Hopkins University Press, 1999), 15.

90. Andrei Soldatov, "Russia," in *PSI Handbook*, vol. 2, eds. Farson et al., 479–97.

91. Edmunds, "Security Sector Reform," 16–19.

92. Lee Wilson, "Beyond the Exemplary Centre: Knowledge, Power and Sovereign Bodies in Java," *Journal of the Royal Anthropological Institute* 17 (2011): 301–17.

93. Carl A. Trocki, "Democracy and the State in Southeast Asia," in *Gangsters, Democracy and the State in Southeast Asia*, edited by Carl A. Trocki (Ithaca, NY: Cornell University Press, 1998), 7–16. Although, as Ryter points out, attempts to evaluate governance in Indonesia on the basis of the degree to which democratic principles are implemented runs the risk of assuming a "categorical abstract"—democracy—as the baseline against which a state is assumed to be succeeding or failing and disregarding quite different configurations of authority and power. Ryter, "Their Moment in the Sun," 215.

94. Also of the power of social networking media in civil society discourse. Detective Chief Commander General Susno Duaji rather naively coined the phrase "*cicak lawan buaya*," or "lizard versus crocodile," in reference to the corruption eradication committee's investigation (KPK, *Komisi Peberantasan Korupsi*) into impropriety amongst senior police officers. The phrase became emblematic of the attempts by the KPK, a small and under-resourced commission, to attempt to tackle the huge issue of endemic corruption in the police force. After the police arrested KPK officials Bibit Samad Rianto and Chandra M. Hamzah on alleged corruption charges, more than 1 million members joined a Facebook campaign calling for their release.

CHAPTER 10

A Reconstruction of Japanese Intelligence

Issues and Prospects

Ken Kotani

On April 4, 2009, the Japanese government mistakenly announced that North Korea had launched a Taepodong-2 ballistic missile. The false news was distributed around the world. This incident does not mean that Japan always has a tendency to cry wolf, but it is true that Japanese intelligence has been much more vulnerable to these types of incidents compared with other countries. After World War II, Japan failed to build an overseas intelligence apparatus or develop an institutionalized intelligence community, something regarded as an imperative for modern states in developing and building a proper security and foreign policy. Instead of developing these tools, successive Japanese governments have been able to rely on US intelligence gathering, a situation that is fostered and maintained in the United States–Japan Alliance. Another factor that made the development of an intelligence community in Japan problematic was the country's pacifist Constitution, specifically its prohibition of overseas military operations. These factors resulted in a vulnerable and late-developing intelligence function within the Japanese government.

A number of times during the Cold War, the Japanese government did actually try to establish intelligence service and antiespionage laws, but the plans usually faced strong opposition from liberal public opinion and bureaucratic sectionalism in Kasumigaseki (the administrative district of Tokyo), and all attempts eventually failed. Following the Cold War, the government was shocked enough by the North Korean ballistic missile test, which was fired over Japan in August 1998, to restart a discussion of Japanese intelligence reform, which continues to this day. This chapter focuses on Japanese bureaucratic and cultural issues influencing the country's intelligence development by reviewing a number of different reform discussions after World War II.

A Brief History from World War II to the Cold War

During World War II Japan had a strong intelligence apparatus and antiespionage laws. Intelligence was managed by intelligence sections of the Imperial Japanese Army and Imperial Japanese Navy. They were able to collect a significant amount of foreign intelligence through their human networks in Siberia, Manchuria, China, and Southeast Asia, and to also intercept and break some diplomatic and military signals traffic of the United States, the United Kingdom, the Soviet Union, and China.[1] Although the intelligence agencies could collect valuable intelligence, the operations staffs sometimes neglected the fruits of this intelligence gathering, which resulted in a number of disastrous defeats, like the Battle of Midway in 1942 and the Battle of Leyte Gulf in 1944. The estrangement of operations staffs from intelligence was mainly caused by long-standing Japanese bureaucratic bias, which gave policy and operations much higher status than intelligence, a bias that carried over in postwar Japanese bureaucracy.

After the Japanese surrender in August 1945, the intelligence organizations were dismantled by the Allies. In those dark days of Japanese defeat and surrender, a rumor spread that officers who had been engaged in intelligence work would be sentenced to life imprisonment; and due to the rumor, the intelligence officers of the Imperial Japanese Army and Imperial Japanese Navy destroyed most of their secret documents and have kept their silence since the end of war.[2] This systematic destruction of Japanese intelligence caused a discontinuity between prewar and postwar intelligence that stood in sharp contrast to the Allied support of General Reinhardt Gehlen's organization in West Germany.

In the early part of the 1950s, Japan tried to set up a new intelligence body starting from scratch, under the auspices of the then–prime minister, Shigeru Yoshida; the chief cabinet secretary, Taketora Ogata; and Jun Murai, chief of the security section of the National Police Agency. These men were intent on establishing for Japan a central intelligence machinery similar to the US Central Intelligence Agency (CIA).[3] They understood that the lack of central intelligence machinery in the Japanese government during the war caused serious bureaucratic infighting about information sharing between the Imperial Japanese Army, Imperial Japanese Navy, and the Ministry of Foreign Affairs. However, the press bitterly opposed the plan, and Yoshida was obliged to compromise, establishing the Research Center (later, the Cabinet Intelligence Research Office) in the Cabinet Office headed by Murai in April 1952.[4] The center was given a staff of only thirty and an inadequate legal basis as "its duty is to collect and analyze information relating to the policy of cabinet."[5] It was expected to collect and analyze open-source information and aggregate information of other ministries and agencies, but the shortage of staff and legal restraints resulted in a body that barely functioned as an intelligence apparatus throughout the Cold War period.

Intelligence Organizations of Japan

At present, Japan possesses a number of self-contained intelligence institutions: the Cabinet Intelligence and Research Office, the Public Security Intelligence Agency, and the various ministry-embedded apparatuses: the Defense Intelligence Headquarters of the Ministry of Defense, the Public Security Department of the National Police Agency, and the Intelligence and Analysis Service of the Ministry of Foreign Affairs. To all appearances, these institutions form a Japanese intelligence community.[6] However, this community is very small and lacks the unifying force for coordinating all the various intelligence services.

The Cabinet Intelligence and Research Office

The Cabinet Intelligence and Research Office (CIRO) is Japan's central intelligence agency based in the Cabinet Office. CIRO's staff numbers about 170, but 100 of them are on loan from other ministries and agencies, and most chief positions are occupied by police officers. CIRO's duty is to collect open-source information and coordinate with other intelligence agencies, but the shortage of staff makes these duties difficult to execute. The head of CIRO is required to advise the prime minister weekly, but according to Andrew Oros, "many experts give CIRO poor marks on its primary mission of dealing with intelligence on national strategy, particularly in the post Cold War period."[7] In 2004 the Cabinet Office launched a plan to expand the staff of CIRO from 170 to 1,000, but the plan was abandoned.[8] CIRO did grow with a new department, the Cabinet Satellite Intelligence Center, as a subordinate organization, which was set up in 2001. The center employs a staff of 320 (100 of whom are imagery intelligence analysts) and has four optical satellites and one radar satellite. The newest version of satellite (IGS-6A) was launched in September 2011 and is said to have 60-centimeter resolution.[9]

The Ministry of Foreign Affairs

The Ministry of Foreign Affairs (MOFA) has a long tradition of collecting intelligence overseas compared with other agencies. The Investigation Department was established in 1934 and was absorbed in 1991 into the International

Intelligence Department, which has now become the Intelligence and Analysis Service. In the absence of a foreign intelligence-collecting agency, MOFA's service is regarded as a kind of overseas intelligence. However, because all MOFA personnel are trained and employed as diplomats, they cannot function as true intelligence operatives. It is prohibited, for example, for MOFA personnel to engage in intelligence and covert activities in foreign countries. It is said that about eighty staff members are allocated to MOFA's intelligence section. Logically, this section can collect diplomatic information through hundreds of embassies and consulates all over the world, but actually overseas embassies can bypass the Intelligence Department and send information directly to MOFA's policymaking departments. MOFA has a counterpart to the US State Department's Bureau of Intelligence and Research called the Intelligence and Analysis Service. This organization has long been regarded as a backwater in the ministry, although attempts are under way to overhaul MOFA intelligence analysis.[10]

The Defense Intelligence Headquarters of the Ministry of Defense

The Defense Intelligence Headquarters (DIH) of the Ministry of Defense (MOD), which was set up in 1997, is the largest intelligence apparatus in the Japanese intelligence community, with more than 2,400 staff members, most of them coming from the various military service arms. The DIH is under the direct control of the defense minister, and each week the director of DIH briefs his chief. Until the founding of the DIH, Japanese military intelligence was handled separately by the Japan Ground Self-Defense Force (JGSDF), the Japan Maritime Self-Defense Force (JMSDF), and the Japan Air Self-Defense Force (JASDF) intelligence sections, and for a long time it was difficult to break the departmental walls and stovepipes among them.

The DIH's main intelligence role has been to collect and analyze signals intelligence through six intercepting facilities in Japan. The DIH also possesses an imagery intelligence section, an analysis section, and a joint intelligence section, all of which work together with the JGSDF, the JMSDF, and the JASDF. The DIH's precursor was the Second Investigation Bureau of the JGSDF, which focused primarily on attacking Soviet traffic during the Cold War. The Second Investigation Bureau's most famous case was the interception in September 1983 of the communications between the Su-15 interceptor that shot down a civilian Boeing 747, Korean Airlines Flight 007, and the fighter's command-and-control base in the eastern USSR. The Soviet Union did not officially admit its involvement in this accident, but a recording of the communications was subsequently released by the US government. This strongly suggests that the recording had been passed to the Americans by the Second Investigation Bureau.

The Public Security Intelligence Agency

The Public Security Intelligence Agency (PSIA) is an internal investigation agency, much like the British MI-5. Its staff is estimated at 1,500. The PSIA was established as a division of the Ministry of Justice in 1952 to monitor nationalistic and communist activities in Japan. Unlike the police, the PSIA has no equivalent of subpoena powers to compel individuals or organizations to comply with an investigation. In fact, the PSIA is thought to be nothing more than an enforcement organization of the Subversive Activities Prevention Law, which aims to prevent radical groups from carrying out terrorism and violent activities on Japanese soil. The law, which is regarded by many analysts as toothless, has been applied only in very limited cases in the past and was not invoked even in the case of the March 1995 sarin gas attack on a number of Tokyo subway stations by the cult Aum Shinrikyo. The Public Security Examination Commission took the view that the Subversive Activities Prevention Law did not apply to the Aum Shinrikyo case, which prompted public debate about the PSIA's future existence. Since then, the PSIA has been struggling for its survival, and it has moved its focus to new and emerging threats, such as drug dealing and terrorism threats. Since its reorganization of 1996, the PSIA has also increasingly shifted its efforts from internal investigations to foreign intelligence collection.

The National Police Agency

The National Police Agency (NPA) is responsible for policing the entire nation and protecting it against foreign espionage and terrorism, like the Federal Bureau of Investigation in the United States. In fact, the NPA is the most influential intelligence apparatus in the Japanese intelligence community. The NPA's capabilities rest not only on its 300,000-member police force (a number greater than Japan's military services) but also on its links with the other chief intelligence positions of other agencies. The NPA regularly sends senior police officers to the director of cabinet intelligence, CIRO, the deputy director of the Cabinet Satellite Intelligence Center, the head of the signals intelligence section of the DIH, and the director of the first intelligence department of the PSIA. The highly centralized NPA can collect information through these intelligence sections of the other agencies. The Public Security Department, the NPA's main intelligence component, is responsible for counterintelligence duty in Japan. It consists of a Foreign Affairs Section, an International Terrorism Section, and a Public Security Section.

After World War II Japanese intelligence was rebuilt for monitoring communist activities in Japan, and the police were suitable for these duties. Moreover, the role of the Japanese military forces was very limited in the Cold War period, and the police took over the role of the military services. For example, in 1976 when Soviet air force lieutenant Victor Ivanovich Belenko flew his MiG-25 jet fighter to Hakodate airport in order to defect, the Japanese police force tried to keep military officers out of the airport. It was a typical dispute over bureaucratic turf, and a humiliating incident for the military specialists who were not allowed to examine the MiG during the initial phase of the incident.[11]

The NPA also shows interest in international cooperation, including increased exchanges with foreign agencies to fight common threats. After Japan's signing of the Mutual Assistance Treaty with the United States, South Korean, Chinese, EU members, and Russian governments, the NPA was able to share information directly with police forces of those countries over the head of MOFA. Despite this growth of influence, the NPA remains essentially a law enforcement organization collecting information for their own investigations, not for shaping foreign and security policy. In other words, the NPA is the most efficient collector of information in Japan, but that information is kept in dead storage.

Current Issues in Japanese Intelligence Reform

The end of the Cold War had a large impact on the Far Eastern security environment, and the Japanese government started to discuss the organizational reform of security and intelligence matters facing international and internal difficulties, only to be overtaken by events. In 1995 there were, as we have seen, the Tokyo subway gas attacks killing thirteen people, severely injuring fifty, and injuring thousands more. Both the NPA and the PSIA failed to uncover or prevent these attacks. Then, in August 1998, the Japanese intelligence community was shocked by the North Korean test launch of a Taepodong-1 intermediate-range ballistic missile, officially to try and launch a satellite into orbit. Japanese intelligence failed to detect and warn the country's leaders about this impending missile launch, and this incident led to the decision by the prime minister to launch reconnaissance satellites. The 9/11 attacks on the United States by al-Qaeda further pushed the discussion for security reform onto the agenda, and thus prompted a succession of discussions and reports concerning Japanese intelligence and security reform. In recent years the Cabinet Office, MOFA, the Liberal Democratic Party, and the PHP Research Institute (a Japanese private institution) have all published different plans for intelligence reform.

In October 2004 the Council on Security and Defense Capabilities (a panel of ten experts) submitted the report *Japan's Visions for Future Security and Defense Capabilities* (Araki Report) to Prime Minister Junichiro Koizumi.[12] As the title suggests, the report is a comprehensive vision of Japan's security policy for the twenty-first century, which also covers intelligence reform (1) to improve information gathering in line with the policy-side requirement, (2) to enhance CIRO's control on information flow and urge intelligence sharing among ministries and agencies, (3) to effectively utilize human intelligence (HUMINT), (4) to foster intelligence specialists, (5) to set up security procedures and penalties, and (6) to build up international cooperation in the intelligence field. In September 2005 MOFA published the *Report of Enhancement of Overseas Intelligence Activities* (the "First Machimura Report").[13] In this report MOFA indicated that it wanted to set up HUMINT apparatus under the control of the foreign minister, as with the British Secret Intelligence Service. This report only referred to intelligence reform within MOFA, however.

In June 2006 the PHP Research Institute released the report *Japanese Intelligence: A Road Map to Transformation*, which provided a comprehensive survey of the issues on Japanese intelligence, which also made a proposal for reform.[14] The report advocated the establishment of an intelligence community in the Japanese government, along the lines of that in the United Kingdom: (1) to establish a Cabinet Intelligence Committee/Joint Intelligence Committee in the Cabinet Office for strengthening intelligence gathering and the analysis structure of the Cabinet Office, (2) to promote intelligence sharing within the intelligence community based on exchanges of personnel and network development, and (3) to overhaul security systems for further information sharing among ministries and agencies. This report still serves as the basis for intelligence reform discussions in Japan.

In the same month the Liberal Democratic Party published its own *Report of Enhancement of National Intelligence* (the Second Machimura Report).[15] This investigation was influenced by the so-called Shanghai incident, in which a Japanese diplomat in Shanghai committed suicide in the wake of a Chinese honey trap in 2004. MOFA had failed to prevent the Chinese secret police from blackmailing the diplomat. The Second Machimura Report recommended an overhaul of Japan's central intelligence machinery, with a focus on improving the intelligence capability of the Prime Minister's Office (Kantei). It proposed that the Japanese government should (1) set up an intelligence committee staffed by cabinet members, (2) upgrade the position of the director of cabinet intelligence (the position is currently just an assistant of deputy chief of the cabinet secretary), and finally, (3) set up an assessment staff to produce analytic papers for the Cabinet Intelligence Committee to circulate to top-level officials in the Japanese government.

In February 2008 the Cabinet Office published a new report, *The Improvement of Intelligence Functions of the Prime Minister's Office*, which reached conclusions largely similar to those of the Second Machimura Report.[16] It recommended (1) establishing equal relations between policymaking and intelligence elements in the Cabinet Office, (2) enhancing intelligence-gathering activities, (3) promoting intelligence sharing among ministries and establishing the Prime Minister's Office's control over information flows in the Japanese government, (4) developing a more coherent intelligence infrastructure, and (5) overhauling the entire Japanese security system. It would be fair to say that this report sought to establish a collegial machinery modeled on the United Kingdom's Joint Intelligence Organization. This built on an earlier Cabinet Office paper, *Improvement of Counter-Intelligence Functions*, in August 2007, on the basis of which CIRO had set up a Counter-Intelligence Center by the subsequent April.[17] The conclusions of these two papers were brought together by CIRO in February 2009 for the Fourth Council on Security and Defense, held in the Prime Minister's Office.[18]

Ultimately, the various reports and investigations converged on relatively similar diagnoses of the difficulties and shortfalls of the current Japanese intelligence system. These dysfunctions include a lack of overseas HUMINT-collection capabilities, the absence of an effective centralized intelligence machinery and poor intelligence sharing among ministries, problems in tasking and direction, and an inadequate protective security system. Another issue, which stretches back more or less to World War II, is the low status of the intelligence function and its consequent vulnerability to politicization.

The Lack of Overseas Human Intelligence Collection Capabilities

Although Japan did build HUMINT networks in its overseas territory and Asian countries before World War II, practically none of these human sources remained after the war. In general, it could be fair to say that the Japanese island-nation mentality is not suitable for HUMINT activities in foreign countries. Although the role of HUMINT has often been criticized as pertains to reliability and slow response times, it is essential against nonconventional threats; as Paul Maddrell has pointed out, "transnational intelligence collection on today's threats forces spy agencies to engage in global collection," and Japanese intelligence has been left behind in the world trend to update HUMINT activities.[19]

Currently, Japanese diplomats play a central role in overseas information gathering, collecting information through their diplomatic networks and open sources in the host country, but they are not allowed to engage in covert activities. In the economic field, the Japan External Trade Organization, which is supervised by the Ministry of International Trade and Industry, collects economic and industrial information from abroad, sometimes collecting information on military technologies. The NPA, PSIA, and MOD also send their staffs as secretaries or military attachés of the Japanese embassy abroad, and one of their duties is to collect political and military information.

HUMINT should provide information that is usually unavailable from diplomatic means, but the Japanese government's agents cannot collect overseas information beyond diplomatic information in foreign countries. It is almost impossible for them to collect information about those countries that do not have diplomatic relations with Japan, such as North Korea. The Japanese government recognizes that there are seventeen abducted Japanese citizens in North Korea, but it has been impossible to learn anything about their status, and this situation has deeply frustrated the government.[20] MOFA was planning to set up a HUMINT section and send their intelligence officers to foreign countries, but the plan seems to have been frustrated.

The Lack of Central Machinery and Poor Information Sharing

Under the present Cabinet Office, there are two different frameworks in place—one based on the American CIA–styled CIRO, and the other based on the British Joint Intelligence Committee–styled Cabinet Intelligence Committee/Joint Intelligence Committee, which was set up in 1986. However, the US and UK intelligence systems are entirely different, as Philip Davies points out: "Despite the existence of similar joint bodies for collating similar raw information, and with a common combined assessment as the goal, the two [US/UK] systems can be seen as moving in different directions."[21] Basically, the Japanese bureaucratic culture is similar to that of the United States, marked by strong sectionalism, which causes rivalry and friction among ministries; but the Japanese political system is similar to that of the United Kingdom, being based on consensus-oriented cabinet agencies that hold a parliamentary mandate. The result has been a hybrid intelligence system, under which the Japanese Cabinet Office is trying to manage both bureaucratic and collegial intelligence methods simultaneously, with the result that neither system works effectively.

The Japanese government system is built on the basis of individual ministries and agencies, with high walls that cannot be broken; in other words, stovepipes among Japanese bureaucracy prevent them from sharing information with each other or with the Cabinet Office. The former director of cabinet intelligence, Yoshio Omori, wrote that he was not given any intelligence from MOFA and MOD, even though he was the head of central intelligence.[22] He struggled to break the walls between CIRO and the other ministries, but he failed. Throughout Japanese modern history, the government has never succeeded in managing the central intelligence system effectively. In 1940 the Japanese government tried to set up the Cabinet Intelligence Bureau for sharing national intelligence, but the army and navy unraveled the plan before it even got off the ground.[23]

The absence of this machinery caused many troubles during the Pacific War. One example of this was when, in the Battle of Leyte Gulf in October 1944, the Japanese Navy suffered heavy losses from the US Navy but falsely announced to the public that the Imperial Japanese Navy had sunk eleven aircraft carriers, two battleships, and three cruisers, leading some army planners to conclude that the US Navy had been driven out of the area. In actual fact, no US ships had been sunk in the battle and the Japanese Army, relying on the false figures of the navy, changed its strategy accordingly. Its officers believed that Japan had succeeded in taking air superiority in the area. The army had planned to wage a decisive battle against the US troops on Luzon Island, but the false reports of the destruction of the US task force caused the army to attempt a new campaign to take Leyte Island, which was located hundreds of miles south of Luzon. The army then tried to redeploy its main force by sea from Luzon to Leyte, with the net result that most of its troops were annihilated by US air attacks during transit.[24]

After the war, the Japanese government reflected that the lack of central intelligence machinery had caused disastrous situations in war planning and set up CIRO, taking the CIA as its model. Despite this promising start, the Japanese government did not understand the CIA effectively and CIRO's intelligence duty was very restricted without the authority to force other bureaucratic apparatuses to share information. In other words MOFA, MOD, and NPA were not and still are not obliged to pass information to CIRO. These ministries continued to send their staff to the Prime Minister's Office as aides and personal secretaries to the prime minister and were able to bypass CIRO and deliver information personally and directly to the prime minister himself.[25] The information-gathering and analyses processes are subsequently not to be considered equal across the board. As a result, the situation became Balkanized, and the secretaries of the prime minister and the chief cabinet secretary became buried under piles of intelligence and information documents, which are not in an order of priority, have not been sufficiently evaluated, and sometimes contradict each other.

CIRO is also under the influence of the NPA, with many chief positions being held by ex-members of the police force, so there is a strong image of a police-style detective culture, rather than an intelligence-gathering and assessment culture.[26] MOD and MOFA are afraid that giving information to CIRO means giving information to the NPA, which is well-known in Kasumigaseki for its secrecy. Legend has it that it has never shared any information with MOD and MOFA.[27] Unless the underlying situation changes, however much CIRO is strengthened, it is hard to see the information-gathering problem being resolved. In the half century that has passed since CIRO was established after World War II, it has been Japan's central intelligence organization, yet its function has not been adapted to meet the demands of the present day, and it is now in a state where it is necessary to make serious changes.

In the 1980s the Japanese government had begun to realize that centralization was not working well. Initially, senior officials simply thought that an American-style system did not fit Japan, so there was an attempt to introduce the British system in 1986 without dissolving CIRO. The result was the creation of the Cabinet Intelligence Committee, which is made up of deputy secretaries and chief secretaries and which has only two meetings a year, with each meeting lasting only about an hour, which clearly does not provide any dynamic or responsive capability.[28] In contrast, there are the twice-monthly meetings of the British Joint Intelligence Committee at the level of bureau chiefs, who are much more involved in actual operations. The British committee system is fundamentally based on the idea of collegiality, but the strongly turf-minded Japanese bureaucrats did not welcome the committee system. As a result, the reality of the committee is like a table talk rather than a discussion of national intelligence. This is because the committee does not possess a permanent secretariat staff; nor does it have an assessment staff that can write papers for the committee. In April 2008 CIRO appointed five cabinet intelligence analysis staffs to draft a National Intelligence Estimate in order to assist in better managing national intelligence.

Problems in Tasking and Direction

In general, the Japanese intelligence community usually needs political guidance on the priorities of the agenda so that its collection and reporting can be relevant to policymakers' decision needs.[29] However, no effective system for formulating and issuing intelligence requirements and priorities has ever been articulated by the Japanese government, and thus the agencies have been forced to work without explicit tasking. Japanese political leaders are usually more concerned with negotiating a policy consensus between political factions and interests than with carefully examining intelligence and factoring it into the foreign policy decision-making process. In other words, Japanese politicians or policymakers tend to put political considerations ahead of intelligence or information on the ground. This was one of the reasons that Japan waged a war against the United States in 1941, although it was known by Japanese military leaders that the United States' military power was far greater than Japan's. The Japanese government, army, and navy spent a lot of energy moving toward a consensus before the Pacific War and finally reached a consensus after one particularly grueling, continuous, sixteen-hour meeting on November 1, 1941, which resulted in war against the United States.[30]

Too much time is expended in Japanese policymaking because of the need to build a consensus. Another result of the consensus system is that new information is actually undesirable. This has also led to information being suppressed, even when it looks accurate. In their policymaking process, politicians do not need information from the intelligence services; they think much of reaching a consensus in their political group, and as a result they sometimes ignore overseas intelligence when the intelligence no longer serves their political goal.

Before World War II there was no center of power in the Japanese political arena. Even the prime minister was no more than a first among equals, and he faced difficulties in building a consensus on Japanese foreign policy. For example, before World War II the prime minister, Fumimaro Konoe, who was not enthusiastic about the war against the United States, failed to persuade the military leaders and finally abdicated his role as prime minister. After the war the position of the prime minister was strengthened, but consensus building remained important. Article 65 of the Japanese Constitution states, "administrative power is vested in the Cabinet." In other words, the Japanese prime minister cannot decide anything without obtaining the consent of other cabinet members and the cabinet is usually managed on the basis of unanimity. The Japanese prime minister sometimes spends much of his energy persuading the minister of education or the minister of health on overseas and security matters. In this decision-making process, the prime minister does not need secret intelligence for deciding overseas policy. Richard Betts wrote that "the importance of successful intelligence ultimately varies with the policies it has to support," but Japanese intelligence has been generally forsaken by political leaders.[31]

In 1986 the prime minister was granted the authority to convene the Security Council of Japan in case of an emergency. The council is made up of nine ministers who engage in overseas and security matters, but the role of the council is to consider the situation, not to be a decision-making body. The council fell into abeyance during the Cold War period, because Far Eastern international circumstances were relatively stable under US dominance in the region, and Japanese politicians' need for secret information remained very low. Not until 2006, under Prime Minister Shinzo Abe, was there any attempt to regularize such interdepartmental coordination. Abe had plans to set up a new National Security Council (NSC) in the Cabinet Office that would supersede the largely moribund Security Council. The new NSC was to be composed of inner cabinet members and would allow for swift foreign and security policy decision making.[32] The NSC was also expected to give direction to the intelligence community by issuing national requirements and incorporating the intelligence produced in response directly into its policy deliberations. Thus the NSC was intended to effectively implement an intelligence cycle between the Prime Minister's Office and intelligence community. Unfortunately, the sudden resignation of Abe in September 2007 preempted these plans.

Weak Protective Security

Beyond problems managing the intelligence interagency function, the lack of common and robust protective security standards across the Japanese government has also contributed to the reluctance of the various intelligence agencies to share intelligence with one another. Japan has neither an official secrets statute nor a single, consistent security clearance system. Each intelligence apparatus has different security standards and procedures. For instance, MOD has a relatively strict security procedure, whereas MOFA does not have any system at all. If MOD were to pass top secret information to MOFA, MOFA would not need to treat the information as top secret. As a result, MOD hesitates to share information with other ministries.

The long-term problem with poor protective security policy and a weak counterespionage system is less the extent of compromise of specific sensitive items in relation to an adversary or rival than the degree to which this inadequate policy and system undermines trust between the intelligence community's organizations. And trust is essential for effective information sharing and operational cooperation. But since 1945, Japan has struggled with an almost ineffectual counterintelligence and security system.

Before World War II, under the Military Secrets Law and the National Defense Security Law, foreigners involved in spying activities or their Japanese agents could be punished "with the death penalty or unlimited penal servitude with a minimum of three years."[33] This was considered an adequate deterrent, despite the damage done by the Soviet-controlled agent Richard Sorege. However, at the end of the war, when these laws were abolished, there was no legislation put in place covering a counterintelligence structure. When the Rastropov incident came to light in 1954, and the deputy head of MOFA was prosecuted for collaboration, the fact that the prosecution was brought under the National Public Service Law concerning the duty of civil servants to maintain secrecy, which had a maximum sentence of no more than one year's imprisonment, showed that the existing legislation was inadequate. Actually, Japan was a "Spy Heaven" for Soviet spies during the Cold War period. The inadequacy of both the security system and available punishments was further demonstrated over a decade with a succession of spy scandals, including the Kononov (1971), Miyanaga (1980), and Levchenko (1982) Soviet espionage cases, among others.[34]

After KGB major Stanislaw Levchenko's 1982 defection to the United States, he testified that a number of Soviet-controlled agents remained active in Japan. This prompted something of a spy fever within the Japanese government. Prime Minister Yasuhiro Nakasone tried to pass a State Secrets Bill in June 1985, but he abandoned the effort as a result of furious public opposition.[35] The need to deal effectively with foreign espionage was proving hard to reconcile with the legacy of World War II and a keenly felt distrust of anything redolent of a "secret state" reminiscent of Imperial Japan among liberal voices in the press and electorate. Unsurprisingly, contemporary Japanese politicians hesitate to discuss security issues openly.

It is weaknesses such as these in the intelligence security system that act as a barrier to the promotion of the exchange of intelligence between Japan and other countries. The US deputy secretary of state, Richard Armitage, published a famous report in 2000, *The United States and Japan: Advancing towards a Mature Partnership*, which set the tone for the strengthening of United States–Japan security cooperation as well as promoting the idea of US–Japanese cooperation in the intelligence arena. This report also called for increased intelligence sharing within the Japanese government, increased participation by the Japanese parliament in intelligence operations, and increased public and political support for legislation concerning an Official Secrets Act or similar type of legislation.[36]

Legislation concerning intelligence security relates to the duty of civil servants to maintain the secrecy of the National Public Service Law. As was mentioned above, the maximum penalty of national civil servants law is no more than one year's imprisonment; the November 2001 amendments pertaining to military secrets to the Self-Defense Force Law, which covers government institutions as well as private corporations, set the maximum prison sentence at no more than five years; and in connection to intelligence this law was received from the United States within the framework of the Mutual Support Agreement concerning Special Military Intelligence (Secrets Protection Law), and the maximum sentence was set at no more than ten years.

The need for effective and resilient security policy has remained a difficult issue. When Japan signed the General Security of Military Information Agreement with the United States in August 2007, there was some hope that its effects would reach beyond military secrets and help drive the development of a comprehensive intelligence security system. Presently, according to expert indications, at least 1,000 people are involved in activities within Japan on behalf of China.[37] The NPA officially warned about Chinese activities in Japan: "The way of Chinese information gathering is quite slick at hiring Japanese agents, while they are creating friendly Sino-Japanese relations on a superficial level."[38] It is likely that several incidents could have been avoided if an effective counterintelligence system had been in place.

There remains some hope that some form of antiespionage statute may yet take shape. In August 2011 the Council of Advisers for Legislation on Security Law submitted its report to the government. According to the report, the Japanese government would introduce the Special Secrets Law, which covers national security and secrets, and in case of an intentional leak of a secret, the offender would be penalized with five or ten years of imprisonment.[39] However, the ruling party finally gave up its effort to enshrine the plan into law in March 2012.

The Weak Status of Intelligence and Politicization

Within the Japanese bureaucracy, intelligence duty has been undergraded and has been considered an easy job for a long time. There is a common joke in which intelligence officers of Japanese military forces are sometimes asked "Is there anything wrong with your health?"—implying that able-bodied men do not do such work. During World War II there may have been intelligence departments that existed to assess foreign intelligence in principle, but, in fact, operational elements conducted their own intelligence appreciations with little or no reference to the specialist intelligence cells. The best and brightest of the army and navy were usually deployed to the operations branches, and the second best were deployed to intelligence duties. Moreover, though both departments often had the same information sources, the operations staff members believed that their assessment was superior to that of the intelligence staff.[40] This trend was caused by the ambiguousness of the Japanese word commonly used to denote "intelligence."

This problem has been exacerbated by the fact that the Japanese term for "intelligence" suffers from much the same ambiguity as the English term. In Japanese the term *joho* can mean, variously, information in general, a finished intelligence assessment, and intelligence from secret sources. The resulting ambiguity has led to both confusion and conflict in Japanese intelligence practice. For military operations staffs, *joho* is taken to refer generically to "information," leading them to take the view that the job of an intelligence department was to gather raw, mainly open information or data, such as newspaper clippings. Operations elements had an exaggerated perception of their own role in the Imperial Japanese Army and believed that they should perform the analytic function. Conversely, intelligence staff took *joho* to mean analytic work and the production of finished intelligence. They therefore believed that it was their duty to analyze information and produce the finished appreciations that would be incorporated into operational decision making and war planning. The gap between the operations staff and the intelligence staff was so serious that the chief of the army's Intelligence Department was completely alienated from the army's war planning throughout much of the Pacific War. During the battle of Guadalcanal, Major General Seizo Arisue, chief of army intelligence, realized that his intelligence assessments had been neglected by the operations staff and he resented integrating the Operations and Intelligence departments.[41] This failure to both integrate and exploit intelligence in the command process contributed in significant part to the decisiveness of the Allied defeat of Japanese forces during this campaign.

The situation has changed very little since the end of the war. Current operations and policy personnel retain much the same primacy over intelligence personnel in the Japanese bureaucracy, and intelligence assessments are hardly used by policymakers. This unequal relationship can lead to both the marginalization and politicization of intelligence in the making of Japanese foreign policy. For example, in September 1994 MOFA ignored the overseas information that public security in Rwanda was getting worse, which resulted in significant delays in instructing MOD and the Self-Defense Forces to send peacekeeping troops to the country.

Attitudes and Pace of Change

It has not been difficult to carry out several reform phases of the Japanese intelligence machinery. Many officers understand the specific problems of Japanese intelligence, but they are not willing to reform it rapidly. The biggest problem is the serious friction among ministries and, most important, which ministry can take the initiative to set up new intelligence machinery. Currently the NPA is the most influential power in Japanese intelligence circles, covering not only internal intelligence but also overseas intelligence, signal intelligence, and imaginary intelligence, as well as controlling CIRO. CIRO, MOFA, MOD, and the PSIA are concerned that the current round of intelligence reforms would not be seen by the police as being in their interests, resulting in intense resistance from the strongest element of the Japanese intelligence community. It is unlikely that any effective intelligence reform can take shape until the sectionalism and bureaucratic infighting have been resolved.

The other problem is the attitude of politicians toward intelligence. Intelligence has been nothing more than a role fulfilling successive prime ministers' intellectual curiosity. They do not need intelligence analysis in their policymaking; nor do they trust this analysis, and they prefer to get information from newspapers than from the intelligence services. For example, at the end of November 1941, two weeks before the Pearl Harbor attack, Japanese political and war leaders expected that the United States would be willing to compromise diplomatically with Japan. The Japanese prime minister and foreign minister had obtained supposedly "secret" information from a November 25 *New York Times* article, but the source of this article was the Chinese ambassador to the United States, whose purpose was to confuse diplomatic talks between the United States and Japan; the next day, the United States submitted a sort of ultimatum to Japan that gave the optimistic Japanese leaders a terrific shock. And Japan's intelligence practice has improved little since then. Moreover, Japanese leaders also place a great deal of weight on public opinion, which is typically apathetic when not actively averse to intelligence matters. Nonetheless, the spy scandals of the 1980s have had a lasting impact on the thinking of Japanese political leaders vis-à-vis intelligence.

The pace of Japanese intelligence reform is very slow, but there are signs of some steady progress. At last, in April 2008, CIRO assigned five intelligence analysts to the Japanese Joint Intelligence Committee, taking the British Assessment Staff as its model. The Joint Intelligence Committee's analytic team is allowed to access any intelligence of the government and is tasked to produce National Intelligence Estimates for the Cabinet Intelligence Committee. CIRO has also set up the Counter-Intelligence Center, whose duty is to supervise the national security activities of the Japanese government. It appears likely that the Japanese government will resolve its tangle of bureaucratic interests through collegial system models based on the United Kingdom's Joint Intelligence Organisation. But the success of this effort will depend fundamentally on the Japanese government's ability to grapple with the internecine rivalries and running disputes that have characterized the Japanese intelligence community since its inception.

Notes

1. Ken Kotani, *Japanese Intelligence in World War II* (Oxford: Osprey, 2009), 12–71.

2. Kazuo Kamaga, "Daitoa Senso ni Okeru Ango-sen to Gendai Ango" (Covert War in the Pacific War and Modern Code), *Dodai Kurabu Keizai Konwakai* (Tokyo) 2 (1989): 186–90.

3. Hajime Kitaoka, "Sengo Nihon no Interijensu" (Japanese Intelligence after World War II), in *Interijensu no 20 Seiki* (Intelligence in the 20th Century), edited by Terumasa Nakanishi and Ken Kotani (Tokyo: Chikura Shobo, 2007), 166–78.

4. Mikio Haruna, *Himitsu no Fairu; CIA no Tainichi Kousaku (Jou)* (Secret Files; CIA's Covert Activities in Japan, vol. 1) (Tokyo: Kyodotsusin, 2000), 521–30.

5. Order for the organization of the Cabinet Office, no. 219, July 31, 1952, www.cas.go.jp/jp/hourei/seirei/naikaku_s.html.

6. Oros's article is a comprehensive study of the present Japanese intelligence community; Andrew Oros, "Japan's Growing Intelligence Capability," *International Journal of Intelligence and Counterintelligence*, 15, no. 1 (2002).

7. Ibid., 6.

8. *Sankei*, March 29, 2004.

9. *Asahi*, September 23, 2011.

10. Taigai Joho Kinou Kyouka ni Kansuru Kondankai (Committee of Enhancement of Overseas Intelligence), www.mofa.go.jp/mofaj/press/release/17/rls_0913a.html.

11. Yahiro Okoda, *Migu 25 Jiken no Shinsou* (The Truth of the MiG-25 Incident) (Tokyo: Gakushu Kenkyusha, 2001).

12. Council on Security and Defense Capabilities, *Japan's Visions for Future Security and Defense Capabilities*, www.kantei.go.jp/jp/singi/ampobouei/dai13/13siryou.pdf.

13. "Taigai joho no kinou kyouka ni mukete," www.mofa.go.jp/mofaj/press/release/17/pdfs/rls_0913a.pdf.

14. PHP Research Institute, ed., *Nihon no Interijensu Taisei: Henkaku heno Rood Mappu* (Japanese Intelligence: A Road Map to Transformation) (Tokyo: PHP Research Institute, 2006), http://research.php.co.jp/research/risk_management/policy/data/seisaku01_teigen33_00.pdf.

15. Liberal Democratic Party, *Kokka no joho kinou kyouka ni kansurr teigen* (Report of Enhancement of National Intelligence), www.jimin.jp/jimin/seisaku/2006/pdf/seisaku-016.pdf.

16. Cabinet Office, *Kantei ni okeru joho kihou no kyouka no houshin* (The Improvement of Intelligence Functions of the Prime Minister's Office), www.kantei.go.jp/jp/singi/zyouhou/080214kettei.pdf.

17. Cabinet Office, *Kaunta interijyensu kinou no kyouka ni okeru kihon houshin* (Improvement of Counterintelligence Functions), www.cas.go.jp/jp/seisaku/counterintelligence/pdf/basic_decision_summary.pdf.

18. "Anzenhosyou to boueiryoku ni kansuru kondankai (Dai 4 kai)," www.kantei.go.jp/jp/singi/ampobouei2/dai4/gijisidai.html.

19. Paul Maddrell, "Failing Intelligence: US Intelligence in the Age of Transnational Threats," *International Journal of Intelligence and Counter Intelligence* 22, no. 2 (2009): 215.

20. "Abduction of Japanese Citizens by North Korea," www.rachi.go.jp/index.html.

21. Philip Davies, "Intelligence Culture and Intelligence Failure in Britain and the United States," *Cambridge Review of International Affairs* 17, no. 3 (2004): 518.

22. Yoshio Omori, *Nihon no Interigensu Kikan* (Japanese Intelligence Agency) (Tokyo: Bunshun Shinsho, 2005), 37–38.

23. Shiro Inoue, *Shogen Senji Bundan-shi: Joho-kyoku Bungeika-cho no Tsubuyaki* (Witness on a Literary World: A Memoir of the Chief of Literature Section of the Intelligence Bureau) (Tokyo: Ningen no Kagakusha, 1984), 8.

24. Yuzuru Sanematsu, *Joho Senso* (Intelligence War) (Tokyo: Tosho Shuppansha, 1972), 232.

25. PHP Research Institute, *Nihon no Interijensu Taisei*, 22.

26. Oros, "Japan's Growing Intelligence Capability," 6–8.

27. PHP Research Institute, *Nihon no Interijensu Taisei*, 28.

28. Ibid., 23.

29. Mark Lowenthal, *Intelligence from Secret to Policy*, 2nd ed. (Washington: CQ Press, 2003), 144.

30. Bouei Kenshujyo Senshisitsu hen (National Institute for Defense Studies, Military History Department), ed. *Senshi So-sho, Daitoua Sensou Kaisen Keii*, 5 (Military History Series, The Process of the Outbreak of the Pacific War, War History, vol. 5) (Tokyo: Asagumo Shuppansha, 1974), 569–70.

31. Richard Betts, *Enemies of Intelligence: Knowledge and Power in American National Security* (New York: Columbia University Press, 2007), 192.

32. Hitoshi Yuuichirou, *Nihon ban NSC no Kadai* (Issues of Japanese NSC), Issue Brief 548, National Diet Library, 2006, 8–9, www.ndl.go.jp/jp/data/publication/issue/0548.pdf.

33. Minoo Hidaka, *Gunki Hogo-ho* (Military Secret Act) (Tokyo: Haneda Shoten, 1937), 24.

34. Gaiji Jiken Kenkyu Kai (Study Group for Spy Incidents), *Sengo no Gaiji Jiken* (Spy Incidents after World War II) (Tokyo: Tokyo Hourei Shuppan, 2007); Stan Levchenko, *On the Wrong Side: My Life in the KGB* (Dulles, VA: Potomac Books, 1988).

35. Masashi Kaneko, "Nihon no intelligence community" (Japan's Intelligence Community), in *Sekai no Intelligence* (World Intelligence) (Tokyo: PHP Shuppan, 2007), 123.

36. Institute for National Strategic Studies, "The United States and Japan: Advancing towards a Mature Partnership," INSS Special Report, 2000, http://se2.isn.ch/serviceengine/FileContent?serviceID=10&fileid=DF76B344-40F0-95E9-10AB-431693ADE1A7&lng=en.

37. PHP Research Institute, *Nihon no Interijensu Taisei*, 25.

38. "The 50 Years of Security Police," *Shouten* (Focus), no. 269 (September 2004): 43.

39. "Report of the Council of Advisers for Legislation on Security Law," http://202.232.146.151/jp/singi/jouhouhozen/housei_kaigi/konkyo.pdf.

40. Kotani, *Japanese Intelligence*, 103–8.

41. Itsiji Sugita, *Joho Naki Senso Shido* (Conducting War without Intelligence) (Tokyo: Hara Shobo, 1987), 127.

CHAPTER 11

The Processes and Mechanisms of Developing a Democratic Intelligence Culture in Ghana

Emmanuel Kwesi Aning, Emma Birikorang,
and Ernest Ansah Lartey

With the possible exception of South Africa, Ghana is one of the few states in Sub-Saharan Africa with a historical intelligence culture. This is unique in postindependence Africa, where the use and abuse of intelligence became more focused on regime protection and its sustainability. In Ghana, however, because of the particular nature of the leadership of the country's independence struggle, when it won its independence in 1957, a key focus of its leaders became establishing institutions, structures, and procedures for the use of intelligence to serve national interests—though certainly, in some instances, for the misapplication of intelligence to serve the regime. Admittedly, some of these structures had existed and been used by the colonial power against the independence struggle. Nonetheless, this tradition and institutionalization of the processes and mechanisms for the application of intelligence to serve multiple interests has continued throughout all phases of Ghana's political development. Over the past fifty years these unique processes have been developing, yet very little scholarly work has been undertaken to appreciate the complexities, challenges, and milieu within which Ghana's intelligence community has functioned and, over time, developed a particular culture.[1]

This chapter examines the history and practice of intelligence in Ghana by analyzing the context within which such practices have become an ongoing aspect of Ghana's political culture. Although the chapter is not necessarily a straightforward historical account, there is no doubt that any such exercise (especially within the context in which this analysis is being undertaken) must review the historical/regime epochs in Ghana and discuss what was unique in those periods. But even more critically, though different regime types have used intelligence for multiple purposes, the reintroduction of democracy in Ghana under the Fourth Republican Constitution of 1992, after several years of military interventions in politics, contributed to the most dramatic change in public perception and appreciation of how intelligence is gathered and used, marked with the introduction in 1996 of specific intelligence guidelines. Almost two decades later, there have been few revisions. Part of this chapter's aims are to evaluate the extent to which the introduction of specific rules of engagement has contributed to a more effective and responsive use of intelligence in Ghana. Security and governance often go hand in hand in African politics. However, the extent to which these two political factors have contributed to the democratic development of most African states continues to remain a subject of controversy among African governments, policymakers, and scholars. Although a few African states have managed to establish positive connections between these two factors, the majority are still struggling to negotiate the appropriate synergies that will further catalyze the kind of security and governance structures that will ultimately promote the well-being of their populations.

In Ghana a critical observation of the postindependence political landscape reveals a rather tense, suspicious, and fractured "cooperation" between the security sector and the political administration until 1992, when the country made a democratic transition that has endured in open and competitive multiparty pluralism to this date. Hitherto, the country had experienced a protracted period of political instability with a systematic decline in key governance and security indicators such as human rights and multiparty pluralism. But the post-1992 constitutional era has seen a consistent deepening of these democratic norms such as human rights, the rule of law, multiparty participation, and a peaceful transfer of political power through democratic elections. Thus far there has been an expanding landscape in the political system, allowing for more political party inclusiveness and citizens' participation.

The last decade and a half have thus had encouraging implications for the continued growth of democratic developments vis-à-vis the security sector in Ghana. It requires that the security sector operates within a specific legal framework that authorizes their establishment, functions, and operations. As a result, it also means that they operate under civilian oversight structures that promote greater democratic principles such as transparency and accountability. To gain support from, and the loyalty of, the public, this also means forging closer synergies among the various actors in the sector, and adopting dynamic approaches that respond to human rights concerns while safeguarding the national interest.

One of the important challenges to attaining these goals is the question of the intelligence sector in Ghana and the extent to which it can be brought under effective, accountable, and transparent democratic oversight and freed from its historical baggage of intimidation and violence. Since 2009 the sector has come under severe public criticisms.[2] These criticisms have mostly centered on human rights abuses, which suggest in many ways that the intelligence services still retain some of their pre-1992 makeup that allowed them to intimidate and harass citizens and political opponents under the authoritarian regimes of the past.[3] The question is: Has the intelligence culture in Ghana always proved adversarial to the democratic development of the country? What impact have the democratic processes made on the intelligence services in Ghana? This chapter investigates the answers to these questions by tracing the history of the intelligence services in Ghana to the preindependence era, followed by an analysis of the evolving service since postindependence, through the various political dispensations that the country has experienced, and how these experiences and challenges have contributed to shaping the intelligence culture in Ghana.

Evolving an Intelligence Culture in Ghana

Ghana attained self-rule in 1951 and, eventually, independence from the British in March 1957. This was an occasion for optimism, great euphoria, and an abiding sense of national pride, when the prime minister, Kwame Nkrumah, declared Ghana's independence as a test case for the black man to demonstrate his ability to govern. Certainly for Ghana and now also for Africa, the one person whose name has been widely associated as being the most instrumental in rekindling the drive for independence was Nkrumah, Ghana's first prime minister and then president. Although this was a period of great optimism, it was also marked by grave antagonism, political hatred, and divisiveness between the different political groups that had fought the British for Ghana's independence. The two groups were the United Gold Coast Convention, which was transformed into the United Party, having led the renewed process for independence from the beginning of the 1940s under the slogan "Independence within the Shortest Possible Time," and Nkrumah's more radical Convention People's Party (CPP), which used the slogan "Self-Government Now."

Part of the source of tensions between these two parties—which had implications for the development of an intelligence culture in Ghana—was the fact that Nkrumah had been invited home from the United Kingdom by the United Gold Coast Convention to become its general secretary, but he had eventually broken away from his mentors. Such was the depth of this antagonism between the two parties that security and intelligence delivery in the immediate post-independence period also became tainted by it, and most liberal interpretations of intelligence and security during Nkrumah's stewardship between 1951 and 1966 have been examined through this lens.[4] For example, according to Kofi Quantson, even at independence, there were signs of the possible national security problems that the country could face: "These indications emanated from the fact that independence was not achieved with a general political unanimity. Very far from that. Independence was achieved in a poisonous atmosphere riddled with an acrimonious political divisiveness and unconcealed hatred between Nkrumah's CPP government and the combined opposition forces, the United Party. . . . Independence was attained on a virtually winner/loser basis with Nkrumah's CPP feeling openly buoyant and triumphant and opposition forces feeling naturally peeved, even frustrated and cheated."[5]

This situation set the tone for a particular type of divisive politics and national security challenges that confronted the country. In the face of this animus Nkrumah did not make any attempts at national unity, but further alienated himself from the opposition by employing the national security apparatus as a personal defense force for his regime against opposition elements. Also, in the period immediately preceding and following independence, there were at least four assassination attempts against Nkrumah; fingers were naturally pointed at his political detractors.[6] As a result of these persistent threats, the Security Services Bill was eventually passed in 1963. This resulted in counter-measures aimed at the opposition, and the strong security measures to deal with the menace would be loud enough to push for measures that could veer toward repression and suppression.[7]

It is widely acknowledged that even though intelligence activities were evident in Ghana before independence in 1957, it took the seminal events of the February 1948 riots—when veterans of World War II marched to Osu Castle, the official seat of the colonial administration—to demand from the British fulfillment of promises that had been made before their participation in the war. The spate of violence and stealth with which this march had been organized compelled the British colonial administration to establish a formal intelligence institution with surveillance, analysis, and data storage capability known as the Special Branch, which was an offshoot of the colonial police administration and the Reserve Unit. It became obvious that the colonial administration did not anticipate the intensity and spread of the 1948 riots given its existing security apparatus. A major security failure was perceived by the regular police service, leading to the establishment of the Special Branch, which was to focus on the collection of vital political and security information concerned with individuals thought to be indulging in subversive activities. The Reserve Unit was used to quell street protests and other demonstrations.

The intelligence structure and culture under Nkrumah were similar to what had existed during the colonial period. However, the exigencies of Nkrumah's Pan-Africanist outlook, as well as the Cold War confrontation between the Communist and Western political blocs, in 1958 necessitated the formation of an external intelligence capability, which was known as the Foreign Service Research Bureau and was attached to the Foreign Ministry.[8] As noted by Johnny Kwadjo, the primary reason for the bureau's formation was to acquire "reliable intelligence and counterintelligence capability" that would allow the regime to maintain its political independence while the East/West bipolar ideological hostilities raged on, as they might, and their protagonists came to have antagonistic or self-interested relations with the Nkrumah regime. As a result, the presidency "carved out an elite corps from the Foreign Ministry's Research Bureau to form the African Affairs Secretariat, which came under the administrative and operational control of the Presidency."[9]

In the early years of postindependence Ghana, the Special Branch also became a tool for general security appreciation in the country, and also increasingly for identifying and arresting persons who were perceived to be threats to the personal security of President Nkrumah. The Special Branch, together with several newly established institutions such as the Presidential Detail Department and the President's Own Guard Regiment, became the agencies responsible for the protection of the president. By 1958 there was a clear sense that a "new" and decidedly political form of intelligence was beginning to take shape—namely, the separation of intelligence into two facets: domestic intelligence dealing with internal matters, and external intelligence dealing with Nkrumah's obsession with the anticolonial struggle in Africa. As a result, a culture of limited oversight developed, whereby allocated funds were sometimes classified as available for broad "intelligence purposes" and placed under the personal control of trusted senior officials of the Ministry of Foreign Affairs.[10]

According to Kwadjo, the usage of intelligence for regime protection purposes started in the immediate postindependence period and became the focus of domestic intelligence across the colonial and postindependence eras. There was no difference between the outlook of the new intelligence services of this emerging, new postcolonial state and what had preceded it. Rather, it used the colonial police culture of heavy-handedness and harassment to intimidate the citizenry.[11] This period was marked, effectively, by the inappropriate use of the national security apparatus and the judiciary against opposition elements. According to Quantson, the direct intervention of the executive in the trial of cases against the opposition created security challenges, because this was regarded as the "crucifixion of due process for political expediency."[12] This was the beginning of a dangerous intelligence and national security culture in Ghana, in which the judiciary, intelligence services, and national security apparatus like the police and the military became extended arms of the executive, with minimal control and oversight. As a result, these agencies catered for regime security and not to the broader national security interest, such that with every new government that came to power, the first appointment focused on changes of the inspector general of police, the chief of Defense Staff, the national security coordinator, the chief of the Naval Staff, the head of military intelligence, the head of external intelligence (the Research Department of the Ministry of Foreign Affairs), and the head of the Bureau of National Investigation (BNI). This has become the accepted security culture in Ghana—that all top appointees in the security and intelligence services will be changed whenever there is a new political administration.

From 1958 onward, Ghana operated an elaborate intelligence system with an emerging culture with both internal and external capabilities, though with clear oversight differences. Proper coordination and coherence of culture among these capabilities remained doubtful because their collective efforts failed to uncover the coup d'état that eventually toppled the regime in 1966. Several questions arise with respect to the initial hesitant attempts at establishing institutions with their distinctive culture. In particular, what has been the impact of military coups and regimes on the intelligence and security sector in Ghana? To fully answer this question, we provide a chronology of key political developments in Ghana in table 11.1, which indicates a high level of political instability and the institutional hollowing-out that followed each change of government and its attendant divisiveness. In all these developments, the role of the security services, especially the military and the intelligence services, has critically contributed to either the attainment or retention of power by leaders or their abuse against Ghanaian citizens who have been perceived as enemies of the regime in power.

A closer look at the political past of Ghana indicates that there have been several instances where, for the sake of a perverted sense of national security, individual security and community security have been sacrificed. This has resulted in atrocities being committed against people merely upon suspicion of engaging in activities that were unilaterally deemed to threaten national security. National security has deliberately been confused with regime security. This phenomenon has enabled the ruling regime to subject opponents—real and imagined—to brutal treatment for committing acts of subversion. The BNI and the Military Intelligence Unit (MIU), the two foremost domestic intelligence agencies, have thus become synonymous with political brutality.

A major concern for the intelligence sector is that in the wake of military coups d'état, newly established regimes quickly take over to redirect the work of the intelligence services to their own safety and often subsume intelligence command and responsibility structures under the military leadership, creating a highly politicized and militarized intelligence sector that works solely toward

Table 11.1   Ghana's Political History and Regime Types

Date or Period	Regime Type	Name of Regime	Leader	Comment
1951–57	Self-government	Democratic, key functions of foreign, defense, finance, and intelligence under British colonial administration	Kwame Nkrumah (leader of government business)	Gained full independence for Ghana in 1957 and became prime minister and eventually president
March 6, 1957	Democratic	Convention People's Party	Kwame Nkrumah	Overthrown by military with Central Intelligence Agency support in 1966
August 29, 1969	Democratic	Progress Party	Kofi Abrefa Busia	Overthrown by military in January 1972
January 13, 1972	Military dictatorship	National Redemption Council	Ignatius Kutu Acheampong	Internal power play leading to change of name to Supreme Military Council I and II
June 4, 1979	Revolutionary military junta	Armed Forces Revolutionary Council	Jerry John Rawlings	Held power for four months and organized elections
September 24, 1979	Democratic	People's National Party	Hilla Limann	Overthrown by Jerry Rawlings in December 1981
December 31, 1981	Military/civilian dictatorship	Provisional National Defence Council (PNDC)	Jerry Rawlings	Ruled until 1992 when transformed PNDC into political party, National Democratic Congress and fourth Republication Constitution promulgated
January 1992	Democratic	National Democratic Congress	Jerry Rawlings	Served two terms until defeated in elections in 2000
January 2001	Democratic	New Patriotic Party	John Agyekum Kufuor	Served two terms and party defeated in 2008 elections
January 2009	Democratic	National Democratic Congress	John Evans Atta-Mills	Current president of Ghana

Source: Authors' data.

the protection of the regime.[13] After the 1966 coup, for instance, it was realized that most of the key elements within the Criminal Investigations Department of the Police Service and the Special Branch had been instrumental in staging the coup.[14] This became apparent when they took up key appointments in the new military government of the National Liberation Council (NLC). To ensure the protection of the NLC regime, the government established the MIU while disbanding the African Affairs Secretariat that had been functioning in the previous regime. This probably marked the beginning of the militarization of the internal intelligence architecture in Ghana.

The role of the MIU was to ensure that successive governments came into being through means other than the military. The paradox is that whereas the MIU was created to ensure regime security, it nevertheless became the focus for regime instability under subsequent military rulers. Kwadjo aptly asked: "Which was worse: repeated acts of conspiracy to overthrow the state perpetrated by elements in the security agencies or the persistent failure of the security establishment to thwart these coups?"[15] Between 1966, when the first coup took place, and 1979, when the Armed Forces Revolutionary Council took over power following a military uprising, the MIU had facilitated two military coups d'état that brought into power the National Redemption Council (NRC) in 1972 and the Supreme Military Council (SMC) in 1978.[16] Even though the Armed Forces Revolutionary Council ensured a smooth democratic transition of power, it later emerged again on the political scene as the Provisional National Defence Council (PNDC) following the 1981 coup that overthrew the civilian government it had initially installed.

In effect, not only did the emergence of the MIU trigger a spiral of military incursions into national politics in the country, it also ultimately led to a loss of trust and credibility in the entire intelligence services. The MIU was later disbanded after the 1981 coup d'état as a regime-protection strategy. It should be said that during all this, the focus of the internal intelligence continued to remain regime protection, with the increased politicization and militarization of the sector. The need to overhaul the entire security system became imperative not only as a political expediency but also to craft a new intelligence architecture that would remain independent of the military and police.

Predemocratic Era Regime Policies in Support of Intelligence Sector

In a bid to streamline and legitimize the endeavor to establish and operationalize Ghana's intelligence institutions, policies have been enacted to support the intelligence and security services in their activities. Even though such policies are not extensively discussed in this chapter, mention is made of them because they set the precedent for successive governments to modify them to suit their own purposes. These laws legitimized and became a justification for state security agencies to violate human rights, as "protection of national security" became the justification for the commission of acts of violence against citizens. Thus, a culture emerged in which, under the rubrics of "national security" and "national interest," anyone suspected of breaching the amorphous concept of national security automatically forfeited their human rights, and anything done to them became acceptable.[17] The frequency and ease with which these laws were passed demonstrate the lack of national consensus in their formulation, and were merely a tool employed by the executive to perpetrate violence against citizens. For example, the Preventive Detention Act, which had a five-year limit for detention without charge, was passed early in 1958 by the CPP to be used to curb the activities of those whose acts were perceived as dangerous to the security of the new state. Thus, persons could be arrested, detained, and questioned, but they would remain in detention even without trial if considered a national security threat by the regime.[18]

The Law on Protective Custody was passed by the government of the NLC, which overthrew Kwame Nkrumah in 1966. This law contained its own version of detention without trials. The passage of the Elections and Public Officers Disqualification Decrees in 1968 (NLCD 223) debarred persons associated with the CPP from holding any appointment in the public service for a period of ten years, starting January 10, 1968. This provision, as instituted by the NLC, not only deprived the persons concerned of their right to work in any field they chose, but also made them subject to public ridicule and impoverished them and their dependents.

The Subversion Decree of 1972 (NRCD 90), under which civilians were tried by military law and tribunals, continued under the government of the NRC. The Armed Forces (Special Powers) Decree of 1973 (NRCD 236) provided for the detention for an indeterminate period in military barracks, ordered by regional commissioners, for offenses involving financial loss to the state. The law on protective custody continued throughout the regimes of the NRC and the SMC I and II. During this period all functionaries, however lowly, were put in prison merely for having been officials of the ousted ruling political party; this law was used to intimidate and deter political opposition.

During the period of NRC rule there was no independent press, but the government found itself so much the subject of rumors that it passed the Prohibition of Rumours Decree of 1973 (NRCD 82). The decree was repealed a year later, however, because the government had acquired the image of an intolerant and repressive regime, fueling yet more popular discontent. The SMC passed another law, the Prohibition of Rumours Decree of 1977 (SMCD 92), in the heat of the anti-union-government campaign.[19] The Preventive Detention Law of 1982 (PNDCL 4), which was first introduced during Nkrumah's regime, would later be promulgated by the PNDC, which came to power by overthrowing President Hilla Limann in 1981. Under this law, persons classified as dangerous to national security could be arrested and detained for long periods without trial.

Another law, the Habeas Corpus (Amendment) Law of 1984 (PNDCL 92), was promulgated to prohibit the courts from examining the grounds upon which anyone had been detained. With these types of laws in effect, all manner of persons were therefore detained, often based upon mere allegation or suspicion of wrongdoing, and they were not given the benefit of a fair judicial review.

Building a Democratic Intelligence Culture in Ghana

To further strengthen the security sector in a way that conformed to democratic norms, a new legal regime was introduced in 1996, during the second elected administration of President Jerry Rawlings. The Security and Intelligence Agencies Act of 1996 (Act 526) became the reference point for all the intelligence sectors in the country. This new legislation effectively established the National Security Council (NSC) and outlined its composition as the president, the vice president, and the ministers in charge of foreign affairs, defense, the interior, and finance. The president may also appoint any other ministers whose portfolios may fall on a specific subject as may be deemed fit for security purposes. The rest of the members are:

- the chief of the Defense Staff and two other members of the Armed Forces;
- the inspector-general of police and two other members of the Police Service, one of whom shall be the commissioner of police responsible for the Criminal Investigations Department;
- the director-general of the Prison Service;
- the director of external intelligence;
- the director of internal intelligence;
- the director of the MIU;
- the commissioner of the Customs, Excise, and Preventive Service; and
- three persons appointed by the president.[20]

The NSC operates directly under the presidency. Act 526 further sets the functions of the NSC, one of which is its responsibility "for implementing government policies on security and attendant issues on or relating to the internal and external security of Ghana and to provide for related matters."[21]

Act 526 also provides for the appointment of a national security coordinator who will coordinate the intelligence agencies and their activities across the country. In particular, the coordinator will oversee the regional and district security councils, which also have compositions well spelled out in the act.[22] Under section III of the act, the BNI and the Research Department are responsible, respectively, for internal and external intelligence for the country. Their focus is crosscutting and touches on all facets and dimensions of national security as it pertains to country and its citizens.[23] The MIU also operates under the

Anti-Terrorism Act of 2008 (Act 762), and it is mandated to monitor terrorism-related activities (including smuggling and trafficking activities), money laundering, and the financing of terrorism. The Defence Intelligence Service also supports the National Security Agency. The intelligence service is making use of Ghana's navy and air force for its operations. There has also been established a Joint Intelligence Committee (JIC), which is an operational committee under the NSC (established by the Constitution) and chaired by the national security coordinator. The JIC meets weekly and oversees participation in meetings by the Ghana Police Service; the Bureau of National Investigation; the Narcotics Control Board; the Customs, Excise, and Preventive Service; the Ghana Immigration Service; the Serious Fraud Office; the MIU; the Fire Service Department; and the Ghana Prison Service.

The JIC, which has a twenty-four-hour operations room, is established under the NSC and operates using Israeli technology. In particular, the role of the national security coordinator is important. This position is appointed by the president in accordance with Article 195 of the Constitution, and the functions are to coordinate on a day-to-day basis the activities of the national, regional, and district security councils and the activities of the intelligence agencies; to collate and evaluate intelligence reports relating to national security, and to ensure dissemination of the information within the government as appropriate; to determine, in consultation with the director of the intelligence agencies, the human resources requirements of the intelligence agencies; and to assist the relevant intelligence agency to gather defense intelligence, both internal and external, and to use the information to detect and prevent threats to the security of the republic.

A security adviser is also attached to the government, and his or her office is located right at the heart of government, in Osu Castle in Accra. This position, which was created in 2009, is different from the national security coordinator. Closely related to the emerging complex institutional processes is the establishment of a Financial Intelligence Centre (FIC).[24] The FIC is located within the Ministry for Finance and Economic Planning, and its mandate under sections 4 and 6 of the Anti-Money Laundering Act of 2008 (Act 749) is to process, analyze, disseminate, and interpret information disclosed to or obtained by the center in terms of the act; to retain the information in the manner and for the period required under the act; to inform, advise, and cooperate with investigating authorities, supervisory bodies, the revenue agencies, and the intelligence agencies and their foreign counterparts; and to monitor and give guidance to accountable institutions, supervisory bodies, and other persons on the discharge of their duties and in compliance with the act. The FIC has the mandate under sections 28 and 29 of Act 749 to access information directly or indirectly from reporting entities, supervisory bodies, and public agencies. The FIC is operationally required to work closely with law enforcement agencies, the Attorney General's Department, and other government and private-sector agencies.

Parliamentary Oversight of the Intelligence and Security Sectors

Taking into consideration the history of the development of intelligence insti-tutions in Ghana and the manner in which these have been exploited for paro-chial and sectional interests, two critical questions emerge.[25] Does Ghana's Parliament have the necessary powers, capacity, and political will to provide effective oversight of the security sector? What roles can civil society organiza-tions play in relation to parliamentary oversight of the security sector? Here, we examine the functionality and effectiveness of parliamentary oversight of the security sector. It can be argued that though oversight of the security sector has improved since the return to democratic rule in 1992, the legacy of military control and the culture of secrecy still remain.

Parliamentary power in Ghana, even though constitutionally strong, remains weak relative to the executive. There are two main oversight commit-tees of Parliament whose work touches on the intelligence community. The first of these is the Parliamentary Select Committee on Defence and Interior (PSCD&I). The PSCD&I has 18 members out of the total parliamentary mem-bership of 230. Their responsibility is to "examine all questions relating to defense and internal affairs in Ghana."[26] The committee, however, has no clear-cut remit for oversight of the intelligence agencies. The committee has two key powers: (1) investigations; and (2) inquiries into the activities and administra-tion of ministries, departments, agencies, public organizations, and corpora-tions, as Parliament may determine. Such investigations and inquiries may extend to proposals for legislation.[27] Other powers conferred on the committee include all those of a high court for the purpose of enforcing the attendance of witnesses, compelling the production of documents, and the issuing of commis-sions for the examination of witnesses abroad.[28] Despite the fact that the PSCD&I has been vested with these powers, it seldom exercises them. There are, however, various gaps in the mandates of the different committees with direct and indirect oversight of the security sector. This becomes more glaring if one sets their current operations against their broad mandates. What it means, therefore, is that there is ample room for improving the oversight functions of the PSCD&I.

The function of the Public Accounts Committee (PAC), the second of the major oversight bodies, is "the examination of the audited accounts showing the appropriation of the sums granted by Parliament to meet the public expen-diture of the government and of such other accounts laid before Parliament." The PAC examines public accounts in general and discusses the report of the auditor-general. This activity provides the PAC with some measure of oversight over the expenses of the military and other security agencies. The PAC's mem-bers thus are empowered to question the rationale behind the use of funds, especially if funds are not being used according to the spirit and intent of their rationale. They can also question the policy, as their writ extends beyond fiduciary responsibility.[29] Based on emerging parliamentary praxis, the chairman of the PAC should be from the minority group in Parliament. This, to some extent, allows the chairman to discharge his or her duties dispassionately. The Finance Committee, another committee whose broad remit brings it into contact with the intelligence community, deals with matters related to finance and the economy generally, but it has the authority where "there has arisen an urgent or unforeseen need for expenditure . . . to authorize advances from the Contingency Fund to meet the need and report to Parliament." Furthermore, when such an advance has been made, the committee is bound to ensure that "supplementary estimates for replacement of the advance are prepared and laid before the House."[30] So far, however, the Finance Committee, like the PAC and the PSCD&I, has not flexed any muscle on intelligence oversight issues.

Parliament needs better institutional capacity to exercise its mandated oversight functions, together with the resources to enable and sustain such changes. Furthermore, existing legislation limits effective oversight, whereas frequent shifts in personnel and the excessive politicization of oversight institutions undermine an already weak human resource base. Parliament's oversight role needs to be complemented by the emergence of more security-conscious civil society actors. A critical study of the powers, capacity, and political will of these committees, and of the Ghanaian Parliament's ability to carry out effective oversight of the security sector, points to the following. First, the complex nature of the security sector presents a challenge for effective oversight; some issues are too technical for those without experience or training in security issues, and committees lack specialized support staff to overcome this problem. Excessive secrecy in national security matters frustrates effective parliamentary oversight, because security agencies often invoke national security to inhibit oversight of sensitive issues. There has also been a culture of self-censorship in Parliament. The Security and Intelligence Agencies Act of 1996, Act 526, only requires the executive to report to Parliament annually. However, it can be interpreted as providing a broader mandate for parliamentary oversight. Unfortunately, Act 526 does not provide for any systems of parliamentary oversight. It provides no guidance on the composition, mode of selection, mandate, or degree of access to sensitive information of oversight committees. In accordance with Act 526, the reporting arrangement seeks to hold the security agencies accountable and within the rule of law. However, the executive has often failed to meet its obligation to report to Parliament on security issues. Party loyalty and discipline limit oversight, because parliamentarians are unwilling to challenge members of government from their own party.

Toward Judicial Oversight

The role of the judiciary with respect to the protection of rights of individuals in the country has never been felt more vigorously. Even though more attention has been focused on the political class, recent judicial interpretations concerning certain actions by the BNI are instructive and provide the opportunity to consider the increasing role of the judiciary in the operations of the Ghanaian intelligence services from a more critical perspective. In the view of the judiciary, even though the BNI is legally bound to safeguard national security interests, it can only do so with proper recourse to legal procedures. Even though the intelligence sector has seen a considerable degree of reforms in recent decades, it does appear that the key institutions such as the BNI have yet to fully appreciate and respect the principles underpinning those critical reforms. This observation is evident in the recent judicial rulings on the actions of the BNI.

There are three critical areas where the interface between the BNI and the judiciary has produced some significant outcomes, the aim of which is to make the BNI's operations more responsive to human rights and the rule of law. The first instance borders on the extent to which the BNI can curtail people's freedom of movement when, indeed, such persons are suspected of corrupt practices. In the specific cases involving two former government officials who were both prevented from traveling outside the country by the BNI, the courts upheld that the BNI has no such powers to prevent such persons who are under criminal investigations from traveling. The ruling directed that their passports, which were hitherto seized by the BNI, should immediately be returned to them. The courts further enjoined the BNI to refrain from the practice of curtailing peoples' "free movement without recourse to the courts."[31]

Second, the BNI has been criticized widely for being obsessively covert when dealing with their potential political "clients." The process of interrogating clients without them having access to their lawyers during the interrogation is not uncustomary to the BNI. But as the country matures democratically, and the frontier of human rights expands, such traditional methods of conducting affairs in the intelligence services are increasingly being questioned. In another court case, in which a third former government official accused the BNI of refusing him access to a counsel during his encounter with them in 2009, the court clearly ruled in his favor. The court held that "it was unconstitutional for the BNI to deny . . . anybody access to a lawyer when in detention, a meeting or a 'friendly conversation' while in the offices of the BNI."[32] The court ruling touches on specific provisions of the country's Constitution. Thus the seizure of hand-held devices such as the mobile telephones of people invited to the BNI and not allowing them access to counsel during their interrogation were in breach of Article 14 of the 1992 Constitution on the right of accused persons to have access to counsel.[33]

Third, perhaps the most important dimension to this seemingly increasing role of the judiciary in the operations of the security and intelligence sector has to do with the internal reform processes that have been undertaken within the judiciary itself. Ultimately, the pursuit of any judicial reform processes should lead to faster adjudication of court cases, and thereby protect the human rights of individuals and make the practice of the courts the epitome of the rule of law. All these factors seem to be reflected in the recent encounters between the judiciary and the security and intelligence services. Indeed, the introduction of Fast Track High Courts has improved relatively the speed with which court cases, especially those involving the security and intelligence services, are conducted. Also, the Human Rights Division of the High Courts in Accra has, for instance, made some important judgments (including the cases discussed above) in which the human rights of the individuals involved have been upheld as against that of the intelligence institution. The implication is that even though the BNI is authorized by law to curtail an individual's freedom of movement, this can be done only if proper authorization has been sought from the court.[34] In the case of the ex-minister whose right to hold a passport was restored, the court demonstrated its adherence to the rule of law by asking him to notify it any time he wanted to travel abroad. Therefore, in both ways, the courts have sought to retain the centrality of their role in matters of the rule of law, especially between the security and intelligence services and the rights of the individuals involved.

Assessing the Compliance of the Intelligence Services with Judicial Oversight

Consequently, it is important to find out the extent to which the BNI has complied with these court rulings following its encounters with the courts. It is important to note that since these developments occurred, the BNI has responded positively to the decisions by the courts. In the first instance, it is instructive to realize that the BNI, including the Attorney General's Office, did not appeal these court rulings. This may suggest the admissibility of the violations they had committed under the pertinent circumstances. Second, the immediate return of the passports (as ordered by the courts) to those persons without further interfering with their freedom of movement is also a positive response by the BNI to the rule of law.

More significantly, subsequent to the ruling that the BNI must allow access to counsel during questioning of their clients, there has been some compliance with this ruling as well. Instances of this can be drawn from the recent cases involving Asamoah Boateng and Herbert Mensah, who went through questioning at the BNI office in the company of their respective lawyers.[35] In the case of Mensah, the government Information Ministry stated that he "had been questioned and his statement accordingly taken, in the company of his lawyer."[36] Such conduct by the BNI has been seen by many observers as a healthy development for the country's democracy and a deepening of the rule of law. However, there are still difficulties in the way the BNI operates. For instance, though the government argued that Mensah was questioned in the company of his lawyer, the client argued that "he was interrogated on two occasions without his lawyer and when he insisted on the presence of the lawyer, the BNI officials said it was an informal session and therefore did not require his lawyer."[37] The position of the BNI official in this particular instance was contrary to the court ruling, which enjoins the BNI to grant access to counsel when interrogating clients.

The Intelligence Services and the Media

Most often, the media plays a critical role in publishing stories about security and intelligence operations in Ghana. This media role was further enhanced with the repeal of the Criminal Libel Law in 2001. Hitherto, journalists were restricted in their reporting and could not publish certain stories for fear of being sued for libel. But given that the media landscape is now largely pluralist and diverse, with each newspaper or other outlet holding different ideological and political interests, there are occasions when some practitioners and press houses have published stories in which the substance undermines the dictates of fairness and objectivity. In a few instances those concerned with national security have had cause to view some publications as posing a national security threat to the country, and thus have triggered the arrest and detention of the publishers of such stories. For instance, in March 2011 the BNI accosted the editor of a newspaper for publishing a story alleging that the chief of the Defence Staff was soon to be replaced because he had fallen out of favor with the president.

This action by the BNI received wide condemnation by the media. The BNI was criticized for wrongful arrest and detention of the journalist. Put differently, "The editor was reported to have been handcuffed and bundled into a car by security officials . . . before being interrogated at the BNI in the absence of his lawyer."[38] A media expert described the action by the BNI as "unprofessional," stating that "under no circumstance . . . should a journalist be treated like a common criminal for publishing a story" deemed to be offensive to public sensitivity and also likely to destabilize the security and defense sector.[39] Further reports on this story painted the BNI as if it was still operating in the old military era. Thus the BNI, "by arresting this journalist, is simply behaving like the way they used to under the PNDC days when they went around after midnight, knocking people's doors and arresting them and just throwing them in the dungeon for years on end. If a journalist in our current democratic dispensation writes or publishes something that is even false, the aggrieved person or institution has the right to write a rejoinder."[40] The best place to seek redress is the National Media Commission and never the BNI. This statement aptly encapsulates the BNI's overzealous tendencies while also undermining the role of other key institutions such as the National Media Commission. The arrest and subsequent detention of the journalist prompted the Ghana Journalists Association to issue a statement, describing as "frightful" the involvement of the BNI in the manhandling of the journalist over his publication that claimed that there were going to be changes in the top hierarchy of the Ghana Armed Forces. It was further stated that even though journalists are not above the law, they must be treated humanely when arrested.[41] The security and the intelligence agencies contend that such stories in the media are fabricated to create insecurity in the security sector, and hence are the justification for the arrest and the interrogations of the editor in order to verify the authenticity of the reporting.

Conclusion

The growth and development of Ghana's intelligence services has been a slow and painful process. The intelligence service, just like the country's other security services, has been manipulated and used for the purpose of abusing the citizenry instead of protecting national security. From regime to regime, laws and principles governing the sector have been enacted; however, even these laws, for the most part, have served the interests of the rulers. The democratic dispensation of 1992, which brought along with it powers for the judiciary and legislature, has to some extent controlled some of the excesses of the intelligence services. The intelligence culture of Ghana originally developed over several decades preceding the independence period. Now that the country has experienced democratic rule continuously for twenty years, its intelligence service can be expected to develop a democratic culture that serves the national interests and not simply the narrow power interests of the ruling regime. In this context, a model for the effective and accountable functioning of Ghana's security sector would operate on several levels. In the first instance, and at the strategic level, Parliament should have complete oversight over security policy and objectives. At the tactical level, all operational issues should be examined only with the involvement of key stakeholders and experts. Civil society organizations should be brought in as an extraparliamentary source of oversight in order to offset suspicion between political elites and the security sector.

Notes

1. See, e.g., Sandy Africa and Johnny Kwadjo, eds., *Changing Intelligence Dynamics in Africa* (Birmingham: GFN/SSR, 2009).

2. Asante Fordjour, "A Review of the Conflicting Roles of the BNI and Ghana Police Service," 2009, www.ghanaweb.com/GhanaHomePage/features/artikel.php?ID=173175; Guure Brown Guure, "BNI: Bureau of National Intimidations—The Case for a National Security Strategy," 2010, www.ghanaweb.com/GhanaHomePage/NewsArchive/artikel.php ?ID=178496.

3. Bismark Bebli, "BNI Brings Back Dark PNDC Days" and "Dreaded BNI Arrest Editor," both *Ghanaian Chronicle*, March 18, 2011.

4. There has been a near industry of revisionist literature about this period. See, e.g., Dennis Austin, *Politics in Ghana 1946–1960* (Oxford: Oxford University Press, 1964).

5. K. B. Quantson, *Ghana: National Security* (Accra: Bestas Press–NAPASVIL Ventures, 2003), 1.

6. The immediate response to the fourth assassination attempt was the enactment of the Security Services Bill; see *Debates* 34 (November 25, 1963): 962–1012.

7. Quantson, *Ghana*, 9.

8. W. Scott Thompson, *Ghana's Foreign Policy, 1957–1966: Diplomacy, Ideology, and the Foreign Policy of a New State* (Princeton, NJ: Princeton University Press, 1969), 20ff.

9. Ibid., 100.

10. Ibid. One of the best books on this period; see esp. 59ff.

11. Ibid.

12. Quantson, *Ghana*, 9.

13. Hutchful Eboe, "Pulling Back from the Brink: Ghana's Experience," in *Governing Insecurity: Democratic Control of Military and Security Establishments in Transitional Democracies*, edited by Gavin Cawthra and Robin Luckham (London: Zed Books, 2003), 78–101.

14. It was identified after the 1966 coup d'état that the commissioner and deputy commissioner of the Criminal Investigations Department and the head of the Special Branch were part of those who staged the coup. Africa and Kwadjo, *Changing Intelligence Dynamics*, 100.

15. Ibid., 101.

16. Ibid.

17. Government of Ghana, *Ghana National Reconciliation Commission Report* (Accra: Government of Ghana, 2004).

18. For an interesting analysis of this act, see Ekow Nelson and Michael Gyamerah, "The Origins of Preventive Detention in Ghana," September 14, 2006, www.ghanaweb.com/Gha naHomePage/features/artikel.php?ID=110547.

19. "Union government," a concept brought forward by General Acheampong in 1977, sought to make Ghana a nonparty state. This was widely perceived as a ploy by the head of state to retain power.

20. Government of Ghana, Security and Intelligence Agencies Act (Act 526) of 1996, Section I:1.

21. Ibid., preamble.

22. Ibid.; see section II.

23. See, e.g., Kwesi Aning, "Security Sector Governance in Ghana," in *Security Sector Governance in West Africa*, edited by Osita Eze and Jens-U Hettmann (Abuja: Frederich Ebert Stiftung, 2005), 68–102.

24. See, e.g., Government of Ghana, Anti-Money Laundering Act, 2008 (Act 749); Government of Ghana, Economic and Organised Crimes Act, 210; Mutual Legal Assistance Bill, 2008.

25. This section draws on our earlier work; see Kwesi Aning and Ernest Lartey, *Parliamentary Oversight of the Security Sector: Lessons from Ghana* (New York: Centre on International Cooperation, 2009).

26. Standing Orders of Parliament, Order 158, under "Functions and Powers of Committees," November 2000.

27. Constitution of Ghana, Article 103 (3), 1992; Standing Orders of Parliament, 190, November 2000.

28. Constitution of Ghana, Article 103 (6), 1992; Standing Orders of Parliament, 155, November 2000.

29. Standing Orders of Parliament, Order 165 (2); see also Constitution of Ghana, chapter 13, 1992 and Article 187 (2), ibid. There seems to be some dissonance in the House of Parliament concerning the extent of PAC's oversight functions. According to the minority leader, Alban Bagbin, "It appears from the provisions of the Constitution and the Standing Orders so far mentioned that the committee's work is limited to examining only reports presented by the Auditor-General. This view is sometimes held by some of my colleagues but I hold a contrary opinion. I believe the committee, as a watchdog wing of Parliament in matters of public finance, can institute investigation into any matter of public interest where public funds are involved."

30. Standing Orders of Parliament, 169–70 (1) and (2), November 2000.

31. GhanaWeb, "BNI Cannot Seize Passports, High Court Declares," 2009, http://mobile.ghanaweb.com/wap/artcle.php? = 166710.

32. Modern Ghana News, "BNI Must Allow Access to Counsel," 2009, http://modernghana.com/print/233711/1/bni-munt-allow-access-to-co unsel.html.

33. Ibid.

34. Proper authorization could mean the BNI securing an arrest warrant from a judge.

35. Herbert Mensah is a close friend of former president Rawlings's family. He was invited to the BNI to assist in the investigation of a purported tape allegedly in his possession, the content of which revealed that the incumbent president, John Mills, intended to expend GH 90 million on the NDC presidential primaries in July 2011.

36. "Herbert Mensah Fails to Produce Tape," Graphic.com.gh, 2011, www.com.gh/print_article.php?news = 12963&link = /dailygraphic/page.php?n.

37. See "External Powers Are Influencing BNI-Herbert Mensah," 2011, www.multi tvworld.com.

38. "Prof Karikari Slams BNI for Arresting Editor," myjoyonline.com, 2011, http://news.myjoyonline.com/tools/printnesw.asp?contentid = 62897.

39. Kwame Karikari is the executive director of the Media Foundation for West Africa.

40. This comment was made by Kwame Karikari on Xfm, a local radio station based in Accra. See the comment at www.xfmnewscenter.com/news/news.php?cat = General&title = Media + Foundation + For + West + Africa + Condemns + Arrest + Of + Daybreak + Editor + #.

41. "GJA Warns BNI over Interference," http://vibeghana.com/2011/03/22/gja-warns-bni-over-interference/.

CHAPTER 12

Intelligence Community Reforms: The Case of Argentina

Eduardo E. Estévez

After decades of dictatorships and military influence in domestic politics, Latin America's new democracies faced the challenge to restore the respect for the rule of law and human rights. Intelligence is one of the issues with which they needed to deal. In fact, during the transition from the twentieth century to the twenty-first century, this challenge was twofold: to democratize the intelligence sector, and to adapt it to the threats and risks arising in a new and changing security environment. Significant progress in the democratization of intelligence can be verified in Latin American countries— for example, new legal frameworks, enhanced democratic control, revamped structures and professional education, and a tendency to openness through the interaction with scholars.[1] Yet the effectiveness and level of transparency the intelligence communities have achieved throughout the region are quite different and even questionable to some extent.[2] This situation can also be observed in other emerging democracies in the world.[3]

For decades, Argentina's intelligence community was heavily influenced and controlled by the armed forces, and it became engaged in political policing. The authoritarianism that dominated most of the twentieth century culminated in the military government that ruled from 1976 to 1983, which was widely known due to "the Dirty War," which was a period of state terrorism during the counterinsurgency struggle, and "the disappeared," that is, those people who were victims of repression. Since December 1983, however, Argentina has been living under stable democratic rule. A major goal for democratic leaders was to establish civilian democratic control over the traditionally highly autonomous military, security "police," and intelligence sectors. The main outcome was a set of pieces of legislation on intelligence, which included national defense and domestic security laws, within a major framework, the National Intelligence Law passed in December 2001. This chapter is about the process of the democratization of intelligence in Argentina from mid-1980s to the present; it explores the peculiarities of the governance of the intelligence sector as well as the pertinent issues, challenges, accomplishments, and results.[4]

Democratization and Path Dependency

The study of the process of intelligence democratization in Argentina focuses on knowing and explaining the pathway to change for a nondemocratic intelligence apparatus. This raises questions: How are intelligence services democratized in new democracies? What is intelligence reform? For some, democratization may mean the enactment of laws and decrees, to mandate reasonable levels of political control and transparency for the intelligence sector. However, reform has more to do with profound changes in organizational structures, culture, and practices. As a bureaucracy isolated by the requirements and constraints of secrecy, the intelligence services are "total institutions."[5] Formal and informal resistance to change may arise as a feature of their particular culture. Thus, the institutional impact of changes may be difficult to trace. Path dependence theory, with its focus on mechanisms that promote continuity or change, can be useful for explaining such processes.[6] The following are core concepts that inform this approach.

Path dependence processes involve conditions whereby legacies[7]— "decisions taken in the past, established ways of thinking and routines [that] have a decisive impact on the present"[8]—are relevant, thus tending to institutional stability.[9] Regarding institutional change, "layering," a type of gradual transformation of interest for this chapter, "involves active sponsorship of amendments, additions, or revisions to an existing set of institutions.[10] The actual mechanism for change is differential growth; the introduction of new elements setting in motion dynamics through which they, over time, actively crowd out or supplant by default the old system as the domain of the latter progressively shrinks relative to that of the former."[11]

The stability of path dependence may be disrupted by punctuated changes, described as "critical junctures" and as "significant changes."[12] Critical junctures are made of branching points, triggering events that initiate processes of institutional or policy change.[13] Other authors acknowledge the importance of other "starting points" (e.g., exogenous shocks) and advocate "periodizing based on important moments in those layers of the contextual environment that are likely to be most relevant to the process and outcome of interest."[14] The "process tracing method allows one to trace the operation of the causal mechanism(s)—for example, conversion, layering, increasing returns—at work in a given situation."[15] The reconstruction of the chronology of events that makes up the process is central.

Consistent with the expectations of path dependence theory, even under democratic rule the resilience of authoritarian legacies in the intelligence sector—including decision-making styles, doctrines, and practices—have resulted in significant institutional inertia.[16] Successive political actors committed to promoting change have tried to overcome this inertia.[17] Several tools may prove useful to evaluate the status of intelligence democratization and to assess the outcomes. It is relevant to detect critical junctures and significant events that trigger institutional change, as well as to identify the actors who were aware of such opportunities. Structural determinants—for example, strategic environment, politicization of security and intelligence, securitized domestic environment, and military influence—may shape the outcomes.[18] The levels of transparency, control, effectiveness, autonomy, and penetration are relevant indicators.[19] Certain relevant topics to consider are respect/violation of rights of citizens, use/misuse of secret expenses, intelligence failures endangering the democratic system, fully democratic regulations, effectiveness of parliamentary control, consistency between intelligence policy (determined by democratic authorities) and activities, access to archives of repression, media and judicial controls, evidence of change in the culture and practices of intelligence personnel, and intelligence-sector reliability in the international community.[20] This analysis also takes into consideration the recently described factors that either support or arrest progress in the process of intelligence democratization.[21] The next two sections trace the historical development of Argentina's intelligence sector and its democratization since the mid-1980s.

Origins, Legacies, and Challenges

Argentina's intelligence sector historically constituted a powerful intelligence service of the presidency, the services of each branch of the armed forces, and the smaller services of the federal police and security forces.[22] Most of the history of the Argentine intelligence and domestic security apparatus over four decades before the 1980s evolved under the influence of the military; as mentioned, the intelligence community engaged in political policing. The military coup of 1930 has been considered the starting point of a period characterized by the use of the coercive power of the state against the opposition, a period with long-lasting effects, such as the growth of a secret state within the state lacking external controls and accountability, which engaged in "surveillance, instigation, espionage, blackmail, and vetting."[23]

In 1946 the elected president, Juan Domingo Perón, created an office for the Coordination of Information of the Presidency and subsequently positioned it in the Ministry of War. In 1949 it was renamed the Office of Coordination of State Information. The State Information Service, under the presidency, replaced this office in 1951. The intelligence services of the army, the navy, and the air force had also been set up in 1946. The Federal Police, created in 1943, were also an active player, and the Federal Coordination Information Corps was its main intelligence element. For the historian Patricia Funes, 1956 represented a Gordian knot in the structuring of Argentina's twentieth-century intelligence sector,[24] when it was engaged in targeting communism and other extremisms.[25] That year, the State Information Secretariat (Secretaría de Inteligencia de Estado, SIDE) was set up under Decree 776 of the military government, named "Liberating Revolution." A decade later, in 1966, a new coordination and analytical body under the president, the National Intelligence Center (Central Nacional de Inteligencia, CNI), was established by law.

As Ana Lemos-Nelson puts it, a significant historical consideration in understanding the politics of Latin America is the presence of the military in internal law enforcement—domestic security—as a constant element since the prerepublican experience.[26] Argentina is no exception. During these decades under varied arrangements, military officers dominated the civilian intelligence agencies, and also the intelligence staffs of the police and security forces. For example, Secret Law 20,195 of 1973 specified that the secretary and undersecretaries of SIDE should be appointed from the senior ranks of the armed forces.[27]

The politically authoritarian but economically neoliberal military regime that ruled from 1976 to 1983 undertook the National Reorganization Process, which is remembered chiefly because of the "disappeared," the significant numbers of people eliminated by the government during that period.[28] The regime imposed changes aimed at promoting a market economy while executing the so-called Dirty War against supposed subversion, and became engaged in the South Atlantic conflict of 1982 with the United Kingdom over the Malvinas/ Falkland Islands.[29] The Dirty War entailed a powerful conjunction of state resources,[30] in which the intelligence agencies became essential instruments.[31] The scope of military intelligence activities during the dictatorship is illustrated by the scale of monitoring and infiltration of the education sector.[32] Significantly, Argentina was not acting entirely alone. At the regional level the military commanders of Argentina and other Latin American countries designed and implemented Operation Condor between late 1973 and early 1974. This operation was a broad and cooperative military and intelligence effort focused on counterinsurgency and counterterrorism.[33] The politicization of military intelligence also contributed to the South Atlantic conflict, of which it has been observed that "a crucial influence in the Argentine decision to invade the Malvinas Islands was the Argentine intelligence community's reluctance to interpret the available information appropriately; that is, in a manner that would contradict the military government's preconceived views and expectations."[34] This contributed to the miscalculation of the possible consequences of such an invasion.

During the 1970s both SIDE and the CNI were the major players in the intelligence community. Although the CNI tried to coordinate the community with varying degrees of success, SIDE usually prevailed. At the time the intelligence community was characterized by its weak legitimacy (it was regulated by decree—laws issued by military governments), by duplications and overlaps within SIDE, and also between diverse intelligence agencies, denoting a lack of coordination with the consequent squandering of resources. The public perception was that these bodies had a significant degree of autonomy, were not under effective political control, and were in constant collision with democratic values.

Since December 1983, Argentina's new democracy progressively accomplished fundamental improvements in the democratization of the intelligence and security services. To develop effective civilian democratic control, and break away from the pattern of the autonomy of the military, police, and intelligence sectors—and the monopoly of the military over the latter two sectors—Congress adopted specific legislation on defense, domestic security, and intelligence.[35] Beyond democratic transition, and as a general context, it is noted that during these twenty-seven years of democracy, the country experienced several military uprisings, domestic and international terrorist attacks, economic crises, political-institutional crises, and growing criminality.

Main Events in Democratization

When he was elected president of Argentina in 1983, Raul Alfonsín (who was president until 1989) appointed the first civilian head of SIDE, the lawyer Roberto Pena. During his fourteen-month term, Pena found resistance from the military and also from within the agency. He appointed civilian undersecretaries, performed a purging of military officers unprecedented in the history of the agency, and drafted a CNI reform proposal; as the proposal was unheard, Pena resigned.[36] The last intelligence chief of the Alfonsín administration, Facundo Suárez, also intended to empower the CNI as the main coordinator of the intelligence community.

A clean break with the past was a main item on President Alfonsín's agenda. Military junta members and guerrilla leaders were arrested, put on trial, and sentenced on human rights violations by a court of civilian judges. Alfonsín established the National Commission of the Disappeared, chaired by the well-known writer Ernesto Sábato. In November 1984, the commission issued its final report, "Nunca Más" (Never Again), which gave data on 9,000 disappearances during the military regime. After extensive debate and consensus, in 1988

Congress passed the National Defense Law 23,554. This law replaced the existing National Security Doctrine, which required internal security to be defined by an additional special law. The new law confined the armed forces to confronting external threats. Consequently, military intelligence was banned from conducting activities related to domestic political affairs. The analytical production of military intelligence would be carried out by an agency composed of the armed forces' intelligence agencies under the authority of the minister of defense.

Tense civil–military relations, including several military uprisings, characterized the period. In fact, "the insistence of the armed forces upon retaining their monopoly of intelligence and domestic security during the 1980s indicated that the military still regarded surveillance of domestic policies as a key reserved domain."[37] After the unexpected ultraleftist command attack on an army base in January 1989,[38] the reactive measures and short-lived decisions undertaken by President Alfonsín and later by President Menem—the creation of a Security Council,[39] and a Committee on Domestic Security[40]—raised concern about military involvement in domestic intelligence.

A number of intelligence scandals mushroomed during Carlos Menem's consecutive administrations (1989–95; 1995–99), and these were joined by issues such as the impact of the two international terrorist bombings and tendencies to involve the military in domestic intelligence and internal security.[41] The first intelligence chief of the Menem administration was the journalist Juan Bautista "Tata" Yofre. Curiously, retired general Carlos Alberto Martínez, former chief of intelligence during the military regime, was posted as director of the National Intelligence College (Escuela Nacional de Inteligencia, ENI).[42] Also curiously, Yofre's undersecretary, Carlos Cañón, who was also the CNI chief, supported the domestic use of military intelligence.[43] The dispute between the two chiefs became public, ending with Cañon's resignation in October 1989.[44] Intending to legitimize intelligence activities, Menem's second intelligence chief, Hugo Anzorreguy, tasked SIDE to support judicial criminal investigations, a matter that was open to question.[45]

The Internal Security Law 24,059 of 1992, which was also approved by consensus, established the civilian management of the police and security forces. It founded the National Congress Joint Committee for the Oversight of Internal Security and Intelligence Activities and Agencies and also the Internal Security Council within the executive, and it created the Directorate for Internal Intelligence under the Internal Security Secretariat of the Ministry of the Interior. This directorate, the first body on domestic intelligence with democratic legitimacy, was instituted as a permanent entity with an integrated staff trained in intelligence and active duty officers of the federal police, security forces, and provincial police agencies, as well as intelligence specialists, as deemed necessary.[46]

In June 1993 the so-called ideological surveillance scandal broke when an order to update intelligence files, issued by the Ministry of the Interior, was leaked to the press. Under the order, intelligence elements of the Police of the Buenos Aires Province and the National Gendarmerie had been conducting surveillance against students, teachers, and trade unionists.[47] The executive's Internal Security Council invited legislators from the Joint Committee for the Oversight of Internal Security and Intelligence to a meeting. A statement addressed to the police and security forces reiterated the strict prohibition on searching and collecting information, as well as producing intelligence concerning the inhabitants simply because of their race, religious faith or political opinion, or their adherence to principles of trade union, youth, student, cooperative, welfare and cultural movements, as well as the legitimate activity that they perform as members of organizations acting legally in the sectors mentioned above.[48]

In the meantime, a dialogue between Congress and the intelligence sector began to develop. In 1991 and 1992, the ENI held a special course for advisers of the legislative and executive bodies. In December 1993, the first International Seminar on Congressional Oversight of Intelligence Agencies and Activities took place, organized by two local nongovernmental organizations (NGOs) and the ENI, and sponsored by the Joint Committee for the Oversight of Internal Security and Intelligence.[49] Another international seminar took place in April 1995. In 1993, a bill on the intelligence system entered by majority senator Eduardo Vaca informally released for consideration of the executive reopened legislative debate. Although the majority draft followed a centralizing approach, similar to the system in force, the opposition draft proposed a decentralizing approach, clearly distinguishing between domestic intelligence and foreign intelligence, with ministerial and parliamentary controls, and judicial control of wiretappings. In August 1994, the Senate approved the majority bill, but in December 1995, because disagreements between the majority and the minority could not be overcome, the lower chamber disregarded the bill.

During the same interval Buenos Aires was hit by two terrorist bombings. The first one damaged the Embassy of Israel (March 17, 1992), and the second one damaged the Asociación Mutual Israelita Argentina, a Jewish community center building (July 18, 1994). In 1995, the Argentine government developed a strategy for counterterrorist cooperation at the regional level. The Tri-Border Tripartite Command was created in May 1996 to operate in the area between the cities of Puerto Iguazú (Argentina), Ciudad del Este (Paraguay), and Foz de Iguazú (Brazil). This command, which is composed of permanent members of the domestic security forces of the three countries, is in charge of the exchange of information and joint and combined counterterrorist actions.[50] A number of regional security initiatives also took shape under the auspices of Mercosur (Mercado Común del Sur, Common Market of the Southern Cone), chief among which was a program designated SISME (Security Information Exchange System).

In November 1998, the press revealed that air force intelligence personnel had been conducting surveillance activities on a number of journalists and a women's NGO. The officers responsible were prosecuted.[51] In June 2000, a judge discovered that Information Collection Center 141, under the Third Army Corps, was performing intelligence activities aimed at political parties, trade unions, and university groups in the province of Cordoba.[52] Fernando De Santibañes, the first intelligence chief of Fernando de la Rúa's administration (2000–2001), implemented several changes in SIDE: A thousand personnel were dismissed, the secret budget was cut, qualified and expert staff members were hired, and the organizational structure was refurbished.[53] An additional scandal in the Senate concerning the alleged payments of bribes in late 2000 prompted new disclosures about intelligence misconduct. The General Trusteeship of the Nation reported that SIDE had been declaring expenditures that had not in fact been made. The result was that the agency had retained a body of funding available to finance operations that could then be conducted outside any control or oversight. De Santibañes resigned on October 21.[54]

In 2001, eight intelligence bills were introduced to Congress, and the consensus-building process on intelligence legislation was thus reopened. After approximately eight months of discussion, a panel of about forty members—including legislators, intelligence experts, and parliamentary advisers—issued a consensus draft.[55] In August 2001, the executive referred the agreed-on bill to the Senate, and on November 27, Congress passed the National Intelligence Law 25,520. After sixteen years of democracy, Argentina's intelligence community stood on statutory footing for the first time. From 2002 until the present, there have been ongoing efforts to develop a systematic secrecy policy. President Nestor Kirchner (2003–7) issued at least eighteen presidential decrees waiving the legal obligation to preserve secrecy to permit disclosure of intelligence information on a case-by-case basis upon a formal judicial request.[56] The cases in question included human rights abuses during military regimes, corruption, the misuse of intelligence funds, terrorist-bombing investigations, and crimes committed by police officers. Known as the "Spy Law," the Data Retention Law 25,873, which was passed in December 2003 (and later regulated by Decree 1,563 of 2004), provoked concern in the media and public opinion.[57] Under this statute, telecommunications and Internet service providers were required to retain both personnel and the technical capability to intercept communications upon stated requirements of the Judiciary or the Public Ministry. In 2005, president Kirchner issued Decree 357, which suspended applications under the Spy Law. Finally, in February 2009, the Supreme Court of Justice declared the law unconstitutional.[58]

In 2005 a drug-trafficking scandal involved the National Aeronautical Police (Policía Aeronáutica Nacional, PAN), then under the Air Force Command.[59] President Kirchner transferred PAN from the Ministry of Defense to the Ministry of the Interior, renaming it the Airport Security Police (Policía de Seguridad Aeroportuaria, PSA).[60] A process of reform and institutional modernization began. Airport Security Law 26,102 of 2006, the legal framework for this new security force, was passed. The law stipulated that PSA contributes to the development of criminal intelligence within the National Intelligence System.

In March 2006, a human rights NGO, the Center of Legal and Social Studies (Centro de Estudios Legales y Sociales), reported that the navy was performing illegal domestic intelligence gathering at the Almirante Zar Naval Base, in Chubut Province.[61] President Cristina Fernández de Kirchner (2007–11; reelected in 2011) responded by conducting an extensive reform of military intelligence. Its doctrine was redefined. The Ministry of Defense took control of the entire military intelligence system through the National Directorate for Strategic Military Intelligence, proceeded to reformulate the cycle of military intelligence planning, and by Decree 1,076 of August 17, 2006, it was granted access to all military intelligence information.[62]

Matters were complicated by the fact that even democratic leaders had often used intelligence budgets for other purposes than those mandated by law. During the Menem administration, secret expenses were destined for the informal payment of extra salaries for ministers, secretaries, and undersecretaries. In December 2009, a federal court confirmed the prosecution of former president Menem, his economy minister Domingo Cavallo, and other former top officials on charges of embezzlement.[63] On a television program the evening of July 25, 2004, the justice, security, and human rights minister, Gustavo Béliz, further accused the Secretariat of Intelligence (Secretaría de Inteligencia, SI) of irregularities, and he showed a picture of one of its directors, whom Béliz said had real power and had overextended his competencies.[64] Although Béliz was subsequently prosecuted for revealing state secrets, in August 2011 he was acquitted.[65]

In 2010, President Kirchner issued Decree 4, which declassified information on the actions of the armed forces during the previous dictatorship in response to a request from a judge investigating violations of human rights. The decree excluded from declassification the information on the Falklands/Malvinas war and on strategic military intelligence. The press also published a list of personnel in Army Intelligence Battalion 601.[66] Given these examples and the other ones cited above, it is clear that the legislative oversight of intelligence was far more rigorous in the 1990s than in the 2000s.[67] Recently, the opposition proposed amendments to the intelligence law aimed at increasing democratic control and transparency still further.

Key Features of the Legal Framework

The National Intelligence Law 25,520 of 2001 established the juridical, organic, and functional basis of the current National Intelligence System. Three intelligence agencies are the leading bodies: the SI, the National Directorate for Criminal Intelligence (Dirección Nacional de Inteligencia Criminal, DINIC), and the National Directorate for Strategic Military Intelligence (Dirección Nacional de Inteligencia Estratégica Militar, DINIEM).[68]

The SI, situated under the presidency and the highest-ranking agency of the system, has the general role of managing the intelligence community as well as responsibility for the production of national intelligence assessments. DINIC,[69] under the Ministry of Security,[70] produces criminal intelligence; it is responsible for the functional management and coordination of the intelligence activities of the national police effort. This consists of the national police and security forces, and the twenty-three provincial police forces. DINIEM, under the Defense Ministry, in accordance with the provisions of article 15 of the National Defense Law, is tasked with the production of strategic military intelligence.

The law provides a range of safeguards to prevent the use of intelligence agencies for political purposes and operations, and it provides for the protection of human rights and civil liberties. It states that the functioning of the system must adhere strictly to the relevant provisions under the Constitution, statute, and regulatory frameworks. The law also prohibits the intelligence community agencies:

- ⊚ From obtaining information, collecting intelligence, or keeping data on individuals because of their race, religion, private actions, and political ideology, or due to their membership in partisan, social, union, community, cooperative, assistance, cultural or labor organizations, or because of legal activities performed within any field.
- ⊚ From exerting influence over the institutional, political, military, police, social, and economic situation of the country, its foreign policies, political parties, or influencing public opinion, individuals, media press, or any kind of associations whatsoever.

Arrangements for executive control and coordination of intelligence include the empowerment of the president of the nation to determine the strategic outlines and general objectives of the national intelligence policy. In addition, the law articulates procedures for secret expenditure control and the judicial authorization for the interception of communications. The law incorporates doctrinal definitions, criminal provisions, and provisions concerning personnel and training. Decree 950 of 2002 provided regulations for the provisions of the law, in short that intelligence activities must be conducted in accordance with the general provisions of the Personal Data Protection Law (Law 25,326).

The current statute also provides for legislative intelligence oversight in the form of the Congressional Joint Committee for the Oversight of Intelligence Activities and Agencies. The committee's responsibilities include the legality of intelligence activities, intelligence policy, the management and administration of the intelligence system and agencies, the system's effectiveness, personnel education plans, secret budgets and expenditures, data on requests for interceptions of communications, and public complaints about the agency or its personnel.

The National Intelligence Law did not solve debates about the relative merits of the centralizing or decentralizing approaches to the intelligence structure. The resulting formula is, therefore, a hybrid. It combines relative centralization at the top (where the SI concentrates most of the executive's control competences) and decentralized lower echelons (under some degree of ministerial control).[71]

Balance and Outcome

Using concepts derived from path dependence theory, this section discusses the outcomes of the process of intelligence democratization in Argentina. It also presents findings about the status of the current situation and its challenges in relation to effectiveness and transparency, as well as other relevant factors.

The Nature of the Process

In the case of Argentina's democratization of intelligence, it has not experienced a single "critical juncture" that has driven profound change; on the contrary, the process is best described in terms of "incremental policy change."[72] Politicians have opted instead for structural alterations and partial reforms rather than overall, comprehensive reform. The starting point was the establishment of democratic institutions. The concept of layering here offers a useful approach to understanding this incremental change. The relevant institutional layers in Argentine intelligence reform have included national intelligence, military intelligence, criminal intelligence, the congressional role, legislation, and regulatory frameworks. Each layer recognizes key actors who were the architects of change as well as specific trigger events. The clash between new and old institutions and practices can be seen in each layer. In addition, each layer is placed in its own time and has its significant events and punctuated changes. The vicissitudes and discontinuities in the development of the new internal intelligence agency, from its establishment in 1992 and through its 2001 reconstitution as a criminal intelligence agency, are typical. Another example is the delays in the effective reform of military intelligence.

The original impulse toward reform in the 1980s came from the legislature, with the executive mainly following suit. The intelligence sector remained very much in transition while the military lobbied against changes, and even still performed illegal operations. Following the enactment of the 2001 statute, the executive took a more active role in furthering reforms. Throughout, the reform process has been hindered by factors such as the complexity of intelligence reform, the remnants and practices of the authoritarian past, resistance and reluctance to change in a number of quarters, variable and often insufficient political will, and finally, persistent tendencies to politicize intelligence.[73] The most significant factor driving progress has been the willingness of decision makers to democratize intelligence—initially, this effort was led by legislators and their advisers; more recently, the momentum has included the ministerial administrators in charge of policy implementation.

In sum, two distinct but partially overlapping stages can be seen in the reform of Argentina's intelligence community. The first stage was focused on debating and passing legislation to reorganize the intelligence community and permit the exercise of executive and legislative control and oversight. And the second stage was characterized by a set of executive actions taken to enhance control over the system, as seen with military intelligence reform, declassification of archives on human rights grounds, and refurbishing criminal intelligence.

Achievements and Challenges Ahead

Since the mid-1980s the role of intelligence in Argentina's domestic politics, illegal wiretaps, the militarization of intelligence, debates on intelligence legislation, and scandals all have been topics that captured media attention. During the 2000s, at least two major national newspapers have taken a critical stance toward the intelligence sector as well as toward different administrations on issues of intelligence.[74] Until the last decade, in the absence of democratically passed intelligence legislation, reform efforts were variously weak and unsuccessful, and often opportunistic or politically driven. The ideological surveillance scandal of 1993 demonstrated that even a democratic government was capable of falling seriously short in terms of observing appropriate executive and legislative controls over domestic intelligence activities.

An important step toward intelligence democratization and the exercise of civilian control was the appointment of civilians as intelligence chiefs, a practice that still continues. Occasionally, democratic leaders have insisted on handing some domestic security tasks over to the military, but this has tended to run afoul of the legislative framework of the civil–military relations model that has been adopted by a democratic Argentina.[75] As noted above, in spite of the legal prohibition to perform domestic intelligence, military intelligence continued to conduct domestic activities until the comprehensive overhaul of 2006. Likewise, although the National Intelligence Law established new provisions for communication intercepts, illegal wiretaps continued to be a recurrent cause of public concern during the 1990s.[76] The misuse of secret funds also continued to be a significant ongoing problem. However, successful prosecutions of such malfeasance are a good indication that institutional constraints such as judicial measures can work. Critical weaknesses in Argentina's intelligence in terms of warning and emergency response were also exposed by the two international terrorist attacks during the 1990s. In Decree 815 of 2005, President Kirchner acknowledged the government's responsibility regarding the bombing of the Asociación Mutual Israelita Argentina. Significantly, regional efforts to cooperate on intelligence and counterterrorism have since been coordinated by civilian officials in collaboration with members of the intelligence agencies. This is an important step for the exercise of democratic control.

In the 2000s, the executive sponsored and implemented a second generation of reforms concerning military intelligence and airport security intelligence. The secrecy policy related to the disclosure of information and the declassification of files is a major step in terms of transparency, and the relevance of its impact for human rights must not be underestimated. However, intelligence is still a subject of controversy and sporadic scandals, and it still lacks the confidence of society. The NGOs that focus on media and human rights have exposed incidents of misconduct and blunders. The new law has not yet had quite the impact on changes in culture and practices that had been hoped for. Moreover, the legislature has been less effective than it might be in exerting congressional oversight.[77] As a legislative adviser with a prominent role in developing the intelligence bills warned, the lack of experience of both members of the intelligence community and legislators with living harmoniously under the new legal framework is perhaps the greatest obstacle to overcome in the future.[78] It has also been observed that "the main challenges for Argentina now are to ensure that intelligence remains an issue of interest to Congress, to develop further mechanisms to support intelligence control, and to ensure that priorities, resources, and capacities are congruent."[79] These challenges remain. Experts and academics concur that there is still a long way to go in the democratization of intelligence.

Conclusion

Path dependence and institutional change may prove useful in explaining the outcomes of the complex process of intelligence democratization, and in articulating the issues that arise in new democracies pursuing intelligence reform. The restoration of democracy by itself is not a sufficient condition to trigger intelligence democratization and reform. A genuine fresh start never occurs, a central question being whether the existing intelligence machinery can adapt its organization, policies, and practices to the new political environment— assuming it even *can* be adapted—and how.[80] Sooner or later, democracies and democratic leaders reach a point where, for a range of possible reasons, they have a real need to exert control of their intelligence communities. The political realization of the magnitude and significance of violations of human rights by security and intelligence agencies appears to be one such necessary condition. In this case, a significant driver of intelligence democratization initiatives is an accurate appreciation of the legal abuses and human rights violations committed by the preceding military regime. Consequently, an effective investigation of past activities by a special commission coupled with prosecution in civilian courts serve as significant drivers in the initial stages of the reform process.

The twenty-first century found Argentina's intelligence community reorganized, with a new structure, responsibilities, and accountability mechanisms under the law enacted in 2001. The main pressure for reform came from Congress, and only after 2003 did the executive take up this initiative. In the meantime, the judiciary also dealt with several key cases. As mentioned above, punctuated changes occurred in certain institutional layers, with moments of backsliding arising from problems like politicians looking to military commanders to lead the intelligence sector. Throughout the decades of democratization examined here, there has been a consistently weak political commitment to maintaining the momentum of intelligence reform over time. For all these reasons it is still premature to speak about deeply rooted intelligence reform in Argentina. Intelligence democratization remains an ongoing process characterized by periodic bursts driven by significant events, moments of crisis, and the responses of politicians.

Notes

1. For a comparative perspective on democratic civilian control and effectiveness in Argentina, Brazil, Chile, and Colombia, see Thomas C. Bruneau, "Democracy and Effectiveness: Adapting Intelligence for the Fight against Terrorism," *International Journal of Intelligence and Counterintelligence* 21, no. 3 (2008): 448–60. For a comparison of military intelligence reforms, see Gregory Weeks, "A Preference for Deference: Reforming the Military's Intelligence Role in Argentina, Chile and Peru," *Third World Quarterly* 29, no. 1 (2008): 45–61. On legislation and mechanisms for coordination and control of intelligence in Latin America, see FLACSO–Chile, *Reporte del Sector de Seguridad en América Latina y el Caribe* (Santiago: FLACSO–Chile, 2007), 115–25. For an account on legal structures, see José M. Ugarte, "América Latina, Actividad de Inteligencia y su Control: El Estado de la Cuestión," paper prepared for annual meeting of Latin American Studies Association, Toronto, October 6–9, 2010.

2. According to Carlos Maldonado, South American intelligence services confront two types of dilemmas, old ones, such as lack of legitimacy, deprofessionalization, lack of national intelligence systems, militarization, securitization, and politicization; and modern ones, such as foreign interference, remilitarization, privatization of intelligence, and failed or unfinished reforms. Carlos Maldonado, "Dilemas Antiguos y Modernos en la Inteligencia Estratégica en Sudamérica," *Security and Defense Studies Review* 9, nos. 1–2 (2009): 50–51.

3. See Thomas C. Bruneau and Florina Cristiana (Cris) Matei, "Intelligence in the Developing Democracies: The Quest for Transparency and Effectiveness," in *The Oxford Handbook of National Security Intelligence*, edited by Loch K. Johnson (Oxford: Oxford University Press, 2010), 771.

4. This chapter is based on revised excerpts from Eduardo E. Estévez, "Comparing Intelligence Democratization in Latin America: Argentina, Peru, and Ecuador Cases," paper delivered at International Political Science Association–European Consortium for Political Research Joint Conference, Universidade de São Paulo, São Paulo, February 16–19, 2011. It also draws from "Intelligence Democratization in Argentina: Achievements and Challenges," by Eduardo E. Estévez, unpublished, June 2010.

5. Erving Goffman, *Asylums: Essays on the Social Situations of Mental Patients and other Inmates* (Garden City, NY: Doubleday, 1961).

6. New institutionalism and path dependence have been applied in comparative studies of intelligence and security apparatuses. See Priscila Carlos Brandão, *Serviços Secretos e Democracia no Cone Sul: Premissas para uma Convivência Legítima, Eficiente e Profissional* (Niterói, Brazil: Editora Impetus 2010); and Lawrence P. Markowitz, "Unlootable Resources and State Security Institutions in Tajikistan and Uzbekistan," *Comparative Political Studies* 44, no. 2 (2011): 156–83. Also see Amy Zegart, *Flawed by Design: The Evolution of the CIA, JCS and NSC* (Stanford, CA: Stanford University Press, 1999).

7. E.g., institutional "lock-in," increasing returns, self-reinforcing and reactive sequences, and "mechanisms of reproduction."

8. Jürgen Beyer, "The Same or Not the Same: On the Variety of Mechanisms of Path Dependence," *International Journal of Social Sciences* 5, no. 1 (2010): 1.

9. Taylor C. Boas, "Conceptualizing Continuity and Change: The Composite-Standard Model of Path Dependence," *Journal of Theoretical Politics* 19, no. 1 (2007): 33–34; Beyer, "Same or Not the Same."

10. This typology of modes of gradual change also includes mechanisms, e.g., displacement, drift, conversion, and exhaustion. See Wolfgang Streeck and Kathleen Thelen, "Introduction: Institutional Change in Advanced Political Economies," in *Beyond Continuity. Institutional Change in Advanced Political Economies*, edited by Wolfgang Streeck and Kathleen Thelen (Oxford: Oxford University Press, 2005), 31.

11. Ibid., 23.

12. James Mahoney, "Conceptualizing and Explaining Punctuated Versus Incremental Change," paper prepared for annual meeting of the American Political Science Association, Washington, September 2–5, 2010, 9.

13. John W. Hogan and David Doyle, "The Importance of Ideas: An A Priori Critical Juncture Framework," *Canadian Journal of Political Science* 40, no. 4 (2007): 883–910.

14. Tulia G. Falleti and Julia F. Lynch, "Context and Causal Mechanisms in Political Analysis," *Comparative Political Studies* 42, no. 9 (2009): 1152–59, and table 1.

15. Jeffrey T. Checkel, "Process Tracing," in *Qualitative Methods in International Relations: A Pluralist Guide*, edited by Audie Klotz (New York: Palgrave Macmillan, 2008), 116.

16. According to Aguilar and Hite, authoritarian legacies can condition democratic transition and even be embedded in certain cultural and institutional practices of the new regime. See Paloma Aguilar and Katherine Hite, "Historical Memory and Authoritarian Legacies in Processes of Political Change: Spain and Chile in Comparative Perspective," in *Authoritarian Legacies and Good Democracies*, edited by Paola Cesarini and Katherine Hite (Notre Dame, IN: University of Notre Dame Press), 191–231.

17. Gerald Alexander, "Institutions, Path Dependence, and Democratic Consolidation," *Journal of Theoretical Politics* 13, no. 3 (2001): 255. See also Beyer, "Same or Not the Same."

18. Bruneau and Matei, "Intelligence in the Developing Democracies," 771.

19. See Peter Gill's typology of security intelligence services: Peter Gill, "Securing the Globe: Intelligence and the Post–9/11 Shift from 'Liddism' to 'Drainism,'" *Intelligence and National Security* 19, no. 3 (2004): 468–70.

20. Eduardo E. Estévez, "Argentina's Intelligence in the Twenty-First Century/After Twenty-Five Years of Democracy," paper delivered at Fifty-First International Studies Association Annual Convention, New Orleans, February 17–20, 2010.

21. Florina Cristiana Matei and Thomas Bruneau, "Intelligence Reform in New Democracies: Factors Supporting or Arresting Progress," *Democratization* 18, no. 3 (2011): 602–30. These authors consider that in intelligence democratization there are neither total successes nor total failures.

22. "Security forces" is not synonymous with "armed forces." Security forces include (1) the National Gendarmerie and (2) the Naval Coast Guard, intermediate forces that both fulfill law enforcement duties at the federal level and are prepared to perform national defense tasks, and (3) the Airport Security Police.

23. Laura Kalmanowiecki, "Origins and Applications of Political Policing in Argentina," *Latin American Perspectives* 27, no. 2 (2000): 37–40.

24. Patricia Funes, "'Ingenieros del Alma': Los Informes sobre Canción Popular, Ensayo y Ciencias Sociales de los Servicios de Inteligencia de la Dictadura Militar Argentina sobre América Latina," *Varia Historia* 23, no. 38 (2007): 423.

25. See, e.g., Decree 2,985 of 1961.

26. Ana Tereza Lemos-Nelson, "Latin American Rambos: The Post–Cold War Syndrome of Deregulation of State Use of Violence," paper presented at "Democracy and the New Millennium," Fifty-Seventh Annual Meeting of Midwest Political Science Association, Chicago, April 15–17, 1999.

27. This secret law was published on September 21, 2006, under the provisions of Law 26,134.

28. For a historical perspective of the last century, see Luis A. Romero, *A History of Argentina in the Twentieth Century* (Buenos Aires: Fondo de Cultura Económica, 2006).

29. The United Kingdom refers to these as the "Falkland Islands." The operation to recover by military means the Malvinas Islands, ordered by de facto president Lieutenant-General Leopoldo Fortunato Galtieri, took place on April 2, 1982.

30. A very detailed study of this period is by Wolfgang Heinz, "Determinants of Gross Human Rights Violations by State and State-Sponsored Actors in Argentina 1976–1983," in *Determinants of Gross Human Rights Violations by State and State-Sponsored Actors in Brazil, Uruguay, Chile, and Argentina (1960–1990)*, edited by Wolfgang S. Heinz and Hugo Frühling (The Hague: Kluwer Law International, 1999), 593–737.

31. An example is the participation of SIDE personnel in the clandestine detention center known as "Automotores Orletti," in the city of Buenos Aires; the number of victims was sixty-five. See Centro de Estudios Legales y Sociales, "Justicia por los Crímenes de la Dictadura," chapter 1 of the *Informe sobre la Situación de los Derechos Humanos en Argentina 2007* (Buenos Aires: Centro de Estudios Legales y Sociales, 2007), n37, available at www.cels.org.ar.

32. See Martin Edwin Andersen, *Dossier Secreto: El Mito de la Guerra Sucia* (Buenos Aires: Editorial Planeta, 1993), 222–26.

33. See J. Patrice McSherry, *Predatory States: Operation Condor and Covert War in Latin America* (Lanham, MD: Rowman & Littlefield, 2005). According to McSherry, Operation Condor extended to other South American countries and there were attempts to export it to Central America.

34. Enrique H. J. Cavallini, "The Malvinas/Falkland Affair: A New Look," *International Journal of Intelligence and CounterIntelligence* 2, no. 2 (1988): 209.

35. For more information, see Eduardo E. Estévez, "Executive and Legislative Oversight of Intelligence in Argentina," in *Who's Watching the Spies? Establishing Intelligence Service Accountability*, edited by Hans Born, Loch Johnson, and Ian Leigh (Washington, DC: Potomac Books, 2005), 160–79; and Priscila Carlos Brandão Antunes, "Establishing Democratic Control of Intelligence in Argentina," in *Reforming Intelligence: Obstacles to Democratic Control and Effectiveness*, edited by Thomas C. Bruneau and Steven C. Boraz (Austin: University of Texas Press, 2007), 195–218.

36. See Gerardo Young, *SIDE: La Argentina Secreta* (Buenos Aires: Editorial Planeta, 2006), 70–71.

37. J. Patrice McSherry, *Incomplete Transition: Military Power and Democracy in Argentina* (New York: St. Martin's Press, 1997), 151.

38. The taking of the military infantry regiment of La Tablada by the MTP (Movimiento Todos por la Patria) took place on January 23, 1989.

39. Decree 83 of January 25, 1989.

40. Decree 327 of March 10, 1989; and Decree 392 of February 26, 1990.

41. For more details, see J. Patrice McSherry, "National Security and Social Crisis in Argentina," *Journal of Third World Studies* 17, no. 1 (2000).

42. Young, *SIDE*, 103–4.

43. "La Inteligencia Militar," *La Nación* (Buenos Aires), July 25,1989.

44. Young, *SIDE*, 107–8.

45. Ibid., 115, 180.

46. Regulatory Decree 1,273 of 1992, article 10.

47. See "La Orden para el Espionaje Ideológico," *Clarín* (Buenos Aires), July 7, 1993.

48. See *La Nación*, July 2, 1993.

49. Held in Buenos Aires, December 1–3, 1993; Britt Snider, general counsel, US Senate Select Committee on Intelligence, and James X. Dempsey, assistant counsel, Subcommittee on Civil and Constitutional Rights of the US House Committee on the Judiciary, were the invited international speakers.

50. Argentinean government, "Report of the Argentine Republic on its Implementation of Security Council Resolution 1373 (2001)," Security Council, United Nations, S/2001/1340, December 31, 2001, 10–11, www.unhcr.org/refworld/pdfid/46d571621.pdf.

51. Sergio Moreno and Adriana Meyer, "Espías de Muy Corto Vuelo," *Página 12*, Buenos Aires, March 6, 2000.

52. "El Ejército hizo Tareas de Espionaje en Córdoba," *La Nación*, June 12, 1999.

53. Florencia Fontán Balestra, "Towards a Democratic Control of Argentina's Intelligence Community," International Center for Criminal Justice, Harvard Law School, 2000, 24–46. See also "El Servicio de Inteligencia Estatal," editorial, *Clarín*, February 8, 2000.

54. See Laura Zommer, "La Sindicatura le Apunta a Santibañes," *La Nación*, October 19, 2000.

55. Jaime Garreta, "El Diseño de un Nuevo Marco Jurídico Regulatorio para la Actividad de Inteligencia del Estado en la Argentina," *Security and Defense Studies Review* 2, no. 2

(Winter 2002–3): 270–71. See also Elsa Llenderrozas, "Del Espionaje Domestico a la Inteligencia Estratégica: Los Caminos hacia una Ley de Inteligencia," paper delivered at REDES 2001, Center for Hemispheric Defense Studies, Washington, May 22–25, 2001.

56. See Eduardo E. Estévez, "Developments of the Democratization of Intelligence in Argentina: Trends in Secrecy Policy–Implications for Comparing Transitional Settings," paper prepared for fourth European Consortium for Political Research Conference, Pisa, September 6, 2007.

57. E.g., see Gustavo Ybarra and Lucas Colonna, "Sigue en Vigor la Polémica 'Ley Espía,'" *La Nación*, May 2, 2005.

58. Halabi, Ernesto c/ P.E.N.–ley 25.873 dto. 1563/04 s/ amparo ley 16.986, Corte Suprema de Justicia de la Nación (H. 270. XLII), Fallo, Buenos Aires, February 24, 2009.

59. Alejandra Dandan, "Las Valijas salieron por un Mecanismo Aceitado," *Página 12*, Buenos Aires, February 15, 2005.

60. Decree 145 of February 22, 2005.

61. For more details, see Centro de Estudios Legales y Sociales, "Políticas de Defensa y Control Civil," chapter 2 in *Informe sobre la Situación de los Derechos Humanos en Argentina 2007*. Also see Centro de Estudios Legales y Sociales, "El Efecto, en el Plano Judicial y Político, de la Denuncia Penal por la Inteligencia Ilegal en la Base Almirante Zar de Trelew," Centro de Estudios Legales y Sociales, Buenos Aires, March 2007.

62. See Jefatura de Gabinete de Ministros, "Memoria Anual Detallada del Estado de la Nación 2008," Buenos Aires, March 1, 2009, 85–94.

63. "Prosecution for Menem and Cavallo Confirmed," Télam, National News Agency of Argentina, December 22, 2009, http://english.telam.com.ar/index.php?option=com_content&view=article&id=8229:prosecution–for–menem–and–cavallo–confirmed&catid=42:politics.

64. Young, *SIDE*, 5–8, 302.

65. See TOF no. 3 sentence of August 10, 2011, on judicial case no. 95–08 "Béliz, Gustavo Osvaldo s/inf. art. 222 del C.P.," www.cij.gov.ar/nota-7467-Difundieron-los-fundamentos-de-la-sentencia-que-absolvio-a-Gustavo-Beliz.html.

66. Daniel Santoro, "Exclusivo: La Lista de los Agentes del Batallón 601 de Inteligencia," *Clarín*, January 23, 2010.

67. E.g., see Jaime Rosemberg, "Mucho Misterio y Escasa Actividad en la Comisión que debe Controlar la SIDE," *La Nación*, August 11, 2009.

68. For a detailed description of the law and the regulatory decree, see Geneva Centre for the Democratic Control of Armed Forces, "Intelligence Legislation Model–Argentina," Toolkit–Legislating for the Security Sector Series, no. 3.5, Aidan Wills (series ed.), Geneva, 2011.

69. This is the successor to the Directorate for Internal Intelligence, created by the Internal Security Law 24,059 of 1992.

70. Due to reorganization of the executive ministries, since December 2010 the National Directorate for Criminal Intelligence has been under the jurisdiction of the recently created Ministry of Security, Decree 2,009 of December 15, 2010.

71. See Estévez, "Executive and Legislative Oversight," 171–72; and José M. Ugarte, "Nueva Ley de Inteligencia," *La Nación*, December 14, 2001.

72. In the context of civil–military relations, Brandão recognized as the critical juncture the end of the military dictatorship and the impact of the defeat in Malvinas, the period when the military lost the ability to establish rules of the political game. Brandão, *Serviços Secretos*, 78.

73. E.g., while analyzing the military intelligence reform in Argentina, Chile, and Peru, Weeks suggests considering the "civilian indifference" as an element in a rational choice analysis of such reforms under the span of civil–military relations. Weeks, "Preference for Deference," 46–47.

74. *Clarín* and *La Nación*.

75. Ernesto López, "Nuevos Desafíos a la Defensa y la Seguridad: El Impacto en las Relaciones Civiles-Militares, el Caso Argentino," paper delivered at REDES 2002, Center for Hemispheric Defense Studies, Brasília, August 7–10, 2002, 10.

76. See "Escuchas Ilegales y Cultura Política," *Clarín*, December 22, 2007.

77. See Alberto Binder, "Perversa Inteligencia sin Control," op-ed, *Clarín*, November 24, 2009.

78. Garreta, "Diseño," 281.

79. Antunes, "Establishing Democratic Control," 215.

80. Peter Gill and Mark Phythian, *Intelligence in an Insecure World* (Cambridge: Polity Press, 2006), 178.

CHAPTER 13

Sweden: Intelligence the Middle Way

Wilhelm Agrell

It's exactly when formalities have to be observed so carefully and completely, as in Sweden, that it's easiest to circumvent them and do as you please.

—From the novel *The Queen's Diadem*, by C. J. L. Almqvist, 1834

In many respects the creation, development, and nature of the Swedish national intelligence institutions is no different from that of a number of other small states in Northern Europe. The region was deeply affected by World War II and early in the Cold War became a geostrategic conflict zone and still to some extent remains one, although in a new European security context. Sweden, like its Nordic neighbors, is a stable democracy with an independent legal system, a free press, and a society built along the "middle way" protected by a long peace. So, judging from the outer appearance, not very much peculiarity should be expected, not even in such a peculiar domain as intelligence. However, the outer appearance might in this respect be misleading, as the Swedish novelist Carl Jonas Love Almqvist let one of his main characters observe in one of the closing chapters of his classical early-nineteenth-century novel—quoted above—which was based on the plot to assassinate King Gustaf III at a masked ball in 1792. Here Almqvist had, as a gifted writer, grasped one of the Swedish state's central features, which has to some extent remained intact for centuries.

The "Organizing" of Intelligence

Like most other small European states, Sweden lacked the framework for an intelligence culture until the late 1930s. There was a limited understanding of the need for intelligence, there was no specific institution for its conduct, and hence there were no clusters of specialists who could have constituted the basis for a profession. There were some forerunners in the diplomatic corps, in naval radio interception, and in the General Staff, where the first intelligence-related actions were taken against Norway during the process of that country's secession from its forced union with Sweden in 1905. In the 1930s, however, increasing international tension and the threat not only of war but also of a completely new kind of warfare affecting all society became the prime movers for defense preparations and, among them, the creation of foreign and domestic intelligence institutions.

In the typical Swedish way, intelligence was systematically "organized," institutions were created, and instructions were written. Formalities were, at least initially, closely observed, while the actual function (let alone efficiency) of the institutions was expected to result from the ongoing process of bureaucratic establishment. In 1937 a new Defense Staff was formed to handle joint interservice functions such as war planning and signals communications. The new staff organization also contained an intelligence branch of around twenty officers, with a foreign and a domestic section, the latter dealing with military counterintelligence and protection against sabotage. The means for intelligence collection were limited to the study of open sources, along with reporting from the fifteen service attachés stationed in the neighboring countries and the major powers. Most were military attachés from the army, and there were also some naval attachés and a few air force attachés, of whom the air attaché to Moscow, Captain Stig Wennerström, was to play a significant although somewhat unexpected role in Swedish postwar intelligence.

Collection was initially the weak spot, and it became even more so as the war broke out, with increasing demand for rapid and accurate information from beyond the national borders, while the listening posts provided by the attachés were either lost (as in Poland, the Baltic states, and eventually all over Europe) or hampered by wartime restrictions.[1] Also, the diplomats were important intelligence collectors, but there was a certain level of mutual mistrust between the Intelligence Department and the Foreign Ministry; the Foreign Ministry reluctantly agreed to send copies of diplomatic reports to the Intelligence Department, but it reserved the right to decide which reports and at what time.[2] The Intelligence Department, conversely, could circumvent the Foreign Ministry through the employment of personal letters (*handbrev*), sent by the service attachés with the diplomatic bag directly to the head of the Intelligence Department.

With the outbreak of World War II in 1939 and the subsequent Swedish declaration of neutrality, three new actors entered the intelligence field. The first was the G-Bureau, later renamed the C-Bureau (Centralbyrån), a unit for secret intelligence collection that was under the Defense Staff but was kept separate from the Intelligence Department. The C-Bureau established a large intelligence network that was never fully documented. However, the permanent staff of the bureau remained small, and operations were often run personally by the chief, Major Carl Petersén, who preferred to keep operational matters to himself. The staff included a number of well-educated academics, among them Gunnar Jarring, later an ambassador and international negotiator, and Thede Palm, the holder of a doctorate in the history of religion and later Petersén's successor.

The second hastily established intelligence unit dealt with signals intelligence. The Swedish navy had started the first efforts to monitor Soviet radio communications, and the Cryptographic Department of the new Defense Staff took on the overall responsibility for decrypting foreign military and diplomatic communications. This activity started in the autumn of 1939, using mainly civilian personnel either called in or serving voluntarily; among the latter was a professor of mathematics, Arne Beurling.[3] The Cryptographic Department scored considerable successes against the Soviet low-level cipher system during the Finnish–Soviet Winter War, and the results were shared with Finnish radio intelligence, a liaison arrangement that was politically uncomplicated as Sweden had not declared itself neutral in that specific conflict and supported Finland with arms and other supplies.[4]

The major breakthrough for signals intelligence was, however, provided by the Germans after the occupation of Denmark and Norway from April to June 1940. One of the Swedish concessions demanded by Germany was the right to use land lines, which were believed to be more secure than radio communications, for telecommunications with occupied Norway. The German machine-crypto was nevertheless successfully solved by Beurling, thanks to inadequate handling of the system by the German operators. The net result was that the Cryptographic Department managed to read about 150,000 German telegrams between the summer of 1940 and the summer of 1942, when the Germans realized that their cryptography system had been compromised.[5]

The decrypted German traffic had a vast intelligence potential, which the Swedish intelligence service could exploit only to a limited degree.[6] The most important aspect was without doubt that of warning, or, to be more precise, what the telegrams did *not* contain. Monitoring the build-up in the late spring of 1941 for Operation Barbarossa, the Defense Staff and the government were not only fully aware of the coming German attack against the Soviet Union, they also knew that the German plans did not presuppose an occupation of Sweden.[7] A more direct use was made of the decrypts of the Stockholm–Berlin diplomatic traffic, whereby senior officials at the Swedish Foreign Ministry could check how the German diplomats reported back on conversations and negotiations.[8] However, the Stockholm–Berlin traffic also contained material of a more problematic nature. Some of the telegrams related German conversations with senior Swedish military officers and were potentially embarrassing for the latter. Because the decrypts were distributed by the Defense Staff, a secret order was issued that telegrams containing information concerning Swedish officers with the rank of colonel or above should be withheld and not given wider circulation without prior approval. This internal censorship toward the government eventually became known by the minister of defense, Per Edvin Sköld, who promptly took action to stop it. Signals intelligence had by now grown out of the Defense Staff organization and had been constituted as an independent agency, Försvarets radioanstalt (FRA), directly under the Ministry for Defense, giving it a special position among the intelligence institutions, with far-reaching consequences.

The last of the intelligence institutions set up during World War II, the General Security Service (Allmänna säkerhetstjänsten), was by far the largest, most powerful, and least known. Having originated with an initiative from the Defense Staff in the late 1930s that stressed the need for a civilian counterpart in combating espionage and subversion, the General Security Service was instigated as a "sleeper" organization, to be put into effect in case of war or threat of war. Neither the government decision to create the service, nor its instructions, were put before Parliament. The service thus had a status based on a secret government decision that affected a large number of agencies, something that was regarded as an advantage.

Parliament, conversely, remained in the dark about the existence of the General Security Service until 1943, when the careless arrest of some prominent citizens led to an investigation by the government ombudsman, which eventually resulted in the director being fined for misconduct of duty. If there was a director with the title security chief, there had to be an organization under his command, and in this way Parliament was finally informed about the existence of a huge surveillance apparatus with unlimited authority to monitor telephone, telegraph, and mail communications on a massive scale without a court order. In January 1945 the government, eager to distance itself from politically damaging fallout of the wartime conduct of domestic surveillance, handled the issue with a traditional Swedish method, establishing a parliamentary commission in which the most outspoken critics were included. The inquiry lasted almost three years, and the commission presented its major finding on the General Security Service in 1948, by which time the organization had been dissolved and the issue had lost much of its previous public and political significance.[9]

The Three Pillars of Intelligence

Two of the wartime intelligence institutions were dismantled as peace settled, only to rise again from the ashes as the threat from the Cold War became obvious in 1947–48. The secret C-Bureau had to some extent been discredited for having cooperated with the German Abwehr, at least in the eyes of the Western powers. More devastating perhaps was the fact that the bureau, due to personal disputes among its staff, came under investigation for dubious financial transactions and inaccurate bookkeeping. Even if not very much came out of the investigation besides some missing receipts, one case of suspected private bicycle repair was duly noted, and a sour remark that Major Petersén seemed to have had a preference for meeting his agents in remote places like Istanbul, the accusations nevertheless received media attention and thus effectively "outed" the secret organization, which was gradually wound down, only to be hastily reorganized to handle intelligence collection from the Baltic ports, the former Baltic states, and Finland's eastern border.[10] Thede Palm, who succeeded Petersén, found himself in a new role, heading the semiautonomous organization, renamed the T-Office (T-Kontoret), possibly referring either to the name of the chief or the cover name Technical Department, chosen to be as nonilluminating as possible.

The General Security Service was swiftly wound down in 1945. Not waiting for the outcome of the parliamentary investigation, the government abolished the emergency legislation and dismantled the entire service, a process that was completed in 1946. The only remaining element was the Radio Surveillance Department (RKA), which had been successfully shielded from public or parliamentary scrutiny. The RKA was an organization tasked with the monitoring and tracking of illegal domestic radio transmitters and should not be confused with the FRA, although the two continued to have a mix of close cooperation and endless turf battles until the outbreak of the signals intelligence controversies at the beginning of the twenty-first century. The RKA, being mainly a counterintelligence instrument, was merged into the Sixth Department of the State Police. This, in turn, was renamed the Third Department, later the equally confusing Special Policing Department, and subsequently the more accurate Security Department and Security Police, or Säpo. The latter was initially a rather ill-sounding public acronym, to which the organization itself, however, became so accustomed that it became the official abbreviation of its name in the 1980s.[11]

The third pillar of Swedish intelligence, the FRA, was the one that had "won the war," at least in terms of intelligence output and prestige. The tremendous success achieved against German traffic had not only facilitated the FRA's organizational growth and its independent position vis-à-vis the military intelligence structure, but also had given it the role of crown jewel, surrounded by an air of secrecy and mystery.[12] Given the geopolitical position of Sweden in the Cold War, signals intelligence became even more important, both for early-warning purposes and for strategic intelligence collection.

The organizational heritage of the 1940s, which was to remain intact during the Cold War and beyond, did not until the turn of the century contain any central body for the coordination and guidance of intelligence, let alone for joint analysis and dissemination. In principle, all parts of the intelligence structure, which initially also contained independent intelligence departments of the three armed services and agencies for defense research and defense procurement, were guided by the government. But because there was no joint administrative body, and influenced by the extreme secrecy surrounding intelligence matters in a country like Sweden, things were handled directly by the minister of defense or the prime minister personally.[13] Having other things on their minds, the top politicians, at least up to the mid-1960s, normally took a very limited interest in intelligence matters. One indication of this is the fact that the head of secret intelligence, Thede Palm, recalls having been summoned by the prime minister, Tage Erlander, fewer than ten times during his nineteen years as head of the T-Office, even though the two were well acquainted and had a common academic background at Lund University in the 1930s.[14] A peculiar circumstance was the virtual nonexistence of a cabinet office; the prime minister, Erlander (in office, 1945–69), ran the government virtually on his own until he managed to recruit the young student politician Olof Palme as his political assistant in the mid-1950s, incidentally from a position at Defense Staff Intelligence.[15]

From the perspective of the prime minister and his closest associates on security matters, intelligence in the 1950s and 1960s was on the whole more of a (necessary) source of trouble than a policy asset. Time and again the prime minister was dragged into crisis management domestically and externally due to intelligence matters. For example, in 1950 the air force, obviously after information acquired by the T-Office but without government approval, conducted a daring photo-reconnaissance mission from northern Sweden toward Kandalaksya in the northwestern USSR, crossing Finnish airspace in Lappland. The prime minister was informed afterward about the flight, not by the military but by the chief of the Security Police, who in his turn had received the information in confidence from the head of military security.[16]

This lack of coordination and elementary contact also reflected an overall feature of Swedish public administration, whereby the heads of the agencies enjoyed a high degree of independence, and whereby the ministers were, and still are, forbidden by the Constitution to intervene in operational matters (*ministerstyre*). There was, especially in the field of intelligence, a gray zone, but this worked both ways, as illustrated by a comment by Thede Palm that the head of the Security Police informed the prime minister about every sensitive matter simply to keep his back clean, whereas Palm followed the opposite line and kept away from the politicians, making all decisions by himself to grant them solid deniability.[17] As a consequence, the weak structure for intelligence guidance became even weaker, with the government being only partially informed or not informed at all about what the agencies were up to. One amazing example is the Swedish participation in the US–British Venona Project dealing with the deciphering of Soviet radio communications from the 1940s. The work in Sweden began in 1962 after an initiative from the British General Command Headquarters, and on the Swedish side was carried out jointly by the FRA and the Security Police. However, not only military intelligence but also the government was kept in the dark, and it took until 1973, when the project was almost terminated, before the chief police commissioner informed the prime minister, who at that time was Olof Palme.[18]

The smooth cooperation between the FRA and the Security Police in a concrete operational matter illustrates another aspect of the "nonsystem" of Swedish intelligence: the virtually unlimited potential for informal contacts, information exchange, and mutual support. Although the intelligence structure as a whole lacked overall guidance, officials within the agencies could cooperate at an operational level, to a large extent through personal contacts and mutual trust, employing the Swedish principle of horizontal coordination (*samverkan*). This was a fundamental principle in the armed forces and in the huge institutional structure for total defense, established in parallel with the intelligence agencies during World War II and preserved during the entire Cold War. Even if intelligence was a closed domain, in some respects extremely closed, it could nevertheless facilitate joint efforts from this culture of cooperation and coordination within the "extended family" of intelligence officials in neighboring agencies. Horizontal cooperation outside the intelligence profession was far more restricted and one-sided.

One illustrative example of these informal networks and their role in an intelligence context occurred during a Soviet/Swedish diplomatic controversy in 1957, initiated by a Soviet note accusing Sweden of clandestine intelligence operations and infiltration of armed émigrés into the Baltic republics. Many details about personnel addresses and telephone numbers were subsequently published by Soviet newspapers, all pointing in the direction of the T-Office, as Swedish journalists started to discover. To end this investigative journalism, the Defense Staff gave the military representative on the Board for Psychological Defense the task of discreetly approaching the editors in chief of the most active newspapers, who also had wartime assignments on this board. After this, the papers promptly stopped their investigations.[19]

Neutral Intelligence Liaison: Apples in Exchange for Pears

Swedish intelligence foreign liaison had an early start; in some respects it preceded other forms of intelligence collection.[20] Already in the autumn of 1936, a Swedish officer from the Defense Staff concluded a liaison arrangement with the German Abwehr, concerning intelligence from the east.[21] The close contacts between the Defense Staff and Abwehr continued until 1943–44, when competing and increasingly exclusive liaison arrangements were established with the representatives of the Western Allies, first of all the American Office of Strategic Services.[22] The FRA established parallel contacts with the British signals intelligence, whereby the latter was able to conduct telemetry collection against the German missile research center at Peenemünde from a site in southern Sweden.[23] The General Security Service had upheld a close liaison with the Gestapo up to 1942 and was, along with the C-Bureau, not without reason, regarded with some suspicion by the Western intelligence services. The new geostrategic conditions created by the outcome of the war had far-reaching consequences for the intelligence field. For Sweden it was of paramount importance to monitor military forces and activities in the east.[24] This interest was to a large extent shared by the three Scandinavian countries, constituting a strong incentive for intelligence cooperation, established already during the final stages of the war and continued in an informal triangular configuration, with the somewhat odd feature of nonaligned Sweden acting as a mediator between the NATO countries Denmark and Norway.[25]

On the Swedish side, there was no single authority or committee coordinating intelligence liaison between the different institutional actors. Palm and the T-Office played an important role in establishing contacts between FRA and its Danish and Norwegian counterparts, but this was soon further developed on a bilateral basis. In a rare case of intelligence coordination, typically enough in the horizontal and informal fashion, in 1946 representatives of the Defense Staff intelligence and security departments, the FRA, and the T-Office agreed to handle future intelligence liaison with US representatives along three separate lines: intelligence, counterintelligence, and signals intelligence. The Swedish agencies in this way divided an American offer between themselves so that each would get a slice of the pie but also, independent of each other, be responsible for establishing the specific liaison arrangement.[26]

This formula was to remain valid throughout and well beyond the Cold War. Each agency established and developed individual liaison arrangements based on an exchange, information-sharing, or cooperative basis. The information sharing became especially important in the fields where the Swedish intelligence agencies were dependent on technological assistance from the outside, which in most cases meant the United States. One early example of such "technology for information-sharing" deals was the informal agreement in 1947 between US Air Force intelligence and the head of photo-reconnaissance at the Defense Staff, Captain Thorén, who incidentally was the brother of the director of the FRA, both being naval officers. The deal meant that the US Air Force would supply its Swedish counterpart with aerial cameras on loan "in return for photographic intelligence."[27] The delicate nature of the agreement was underlined by the instructions to the US military attaché in Stockholm to handle the matter directly with the Defense Staff intelligence and not through the Swedish Air Force. It was also assumed by the Americans that the transaction would create considerable goodwill: "It may prove desirable for a photo intelligence officer to accompany the shipment since the receipt of the cameras on loan may cause the Swedes at that particular moment to be willing to release a great amount of photo intelligence material to us."[28]

There is no reference to the Swedish government approving this agreement or being informed about the content, let alone the consequences. The incident with the flight toward the Kola Peninsula in 1950 was most likely a part of the subsequent program.[29] The remark by the prime minister in his diary is notable: "Now the question: Have the military idiots told the Americans about their adventures? Probably so, unfortunately."[30] This comment indicates not only a lack of government approval for the individual mission but also a lack of knowledge concerning the underlying liaison agreement, granting the US Air Force information sharing from a mission conducted with *their* cameras.

The most extensive liaison arrangement was, however, the links established by the FRA to the corresponding services in the Scandinavian countries—but first and foremost to the British signals intelligence, a role later taken over by the United States. The Scandinavian "market" was divided by 1954 so that Britain continued to deal with the FRA, while the National Security Agency entered into formal agreements with Norway and Denmark.[31] From the second half of the 1950s, American contact gradually overshadowed the British, which to a large extent was due to the advanced signals intelligence equipment that the United States could supply for very favorable prices or on loan.[32]

It was, however, neither the economy nor the crossing of lines with foreign partners that constituted the main problem in the growing web of intelligence liaison, but the potential political fallout in case of revelation. This was a part of a wider problem connected with secret Swedish contacts with the Western powers, motivated by the same geostrategic circumstances that had created the incentive for intelligence liaison. The problem in these contacts, stretching back to the closing stages of the war, when the nominally neutral Sweden adjusted its policy from concessions toward Germany to concessions toward the Western Allies, was the overarching domestic consensus on nonalignment and neutrality, or, in the words of the official definition of Swedish national security repeated throughout the Cold War: "Nonalignment in peace aiming at neutrality in war." This meant that not only binding arrangements but also such measures that would undermine the credibility of a declaration of neutrality in the event of war between east and west were ruled out. Starting in the early 1970s, the nonalignment and subsequent self-imposed limitations were jointly described as a "Policy of Neutrality" (Neutralitetspolitik).[33]

For Swedish intelligence, the result of this policy drift was a paradox. Although liaison had to be carried out with discretion in the first postwar years, it increasingly became a contradiction in terms—an officially denied activity that, if it became known, would be impossible to defend within the neutrality doctrine and thus could threaten to undermine the credibility of this doctrine externally, but perhaps first of all internally, as it was perceived by the Swedish public. However, instead of producing tight central control and a limited conduct of intelligence liaison, the effect became almost the opposite. On the military operational level, the secret Western contacts were handled by a very limited number of officials but were nevertheless regarded as so potentially devastating for the Policy of Neutrality that they were gradually phased out and the key planning documents were destroyed in the 1980s.[34]

Intelligence liaison in a similar way had to be limited to a small number of officials within the agencies, and documents received through liaison were given extremely limited circulation and a special classification, Special Intelligence (S-underrättelser), the very existence of which was secret. Liaison, in this way, developed into a closed subculture within the agencies, where it could not only continue but gradually expand. When the very existence of liaison with foreign powers finally was disclosed in 1973, the public was thoroughly unprepared, and the supreme commander, in an attempt to play down the significance, compared the practice with exchanging apples for pears. In the report of a Parliamentary Commission investigating the revelations, Swedish intelligence liaison was described as something natural and on the whole uncomplicated: The Swedish intelligence services were comparatively small and could facilitate exchange with others. The issue of neutrality was avoided by pointing out that liaison had to be conducted in a way that did not harm "a third party."[35] How this would come about was not specified; no names of countries were mentioned, and the types of information exchanged were not described, except for information concerning Swedish citizens that was not to be forwarded "except after review in the individual case."[36] The commission did, however, highlight one fundamental weakness in the conduct of liaison: Because each agency worked on its own, there was not only a lack of coordination but also a lack of overall assessment of what material was exchanged and what the country actually received in return. However, not very much changed in the liaison structure, even if a mostly symbolic oversight body was set up by the parliament, and it would take another twenty-five years until a small coordinating body was set up within the Ministry of Defense.

Behind the careful wordings of the report of the 1974 Intelligence Commission, the first of its kind ever in Sweden, lay a serious structural dilemma. As with all small states entering into nontransparent continuous intelligence cooperation with major powers, there was a problem of control and integrity. Thede Palm had experienced this when he established contact with Reinhardt Gehlen and the West German foreign intelligence service, the BND. Gehlen was eager to place a liaison staff in Stockholm, but Palm said no, knowing that the T-Office was a small organization that could be easily overwhelmed by requests and initiatives from such a liaison station, which would have degraded Palm's staff to the role of subcontractor to BND.[37]

Another aspect of this structural dilemma was that the Swedish intelligence agencies, with their limited resources and expertise, could be supplied with material containing intentionally or unintentionally tainting assessments. It has been argued that the United States and/or Britain could have been involved in the alleged submarine intrusions in Swedish waters in the early 1980s.[38] The Western powers, however, had at their disposal far more effective methods for influencing Swedish threat perceptions and strategic dispositions in the form of the close intelligence cooperation whereby Swedish intelligence during the same period was provided with alarming intelligence assessments concerning Soviet aggressive aspirations in the Far North, assessments that obviously affected the overall picture of Swedish military intelligence.[39]

Domestic Intelligence in Deep Shadows

Along with secret intelligence, the Security Police resurfaced with the advent of the Cold War and a subsequent surge in a perceived threat from spies, saboteurs, and communist subversion. By 1948 the police also saw the return of their most powerful instrument: the right to conduct secret wiretapping to investigate suspected crimes against the state security. "Suspected crimes" soon turned out to be a somewhat fluid term, and the Security Police initiated a massive intelligence collection on communists and suspected communists, filling the Central Registry with files, reaching a peak in the mid-1960s with around half a million registered names (from a population of 7.7 million).[40] The means employed were traditional surveillance and a widespread use of informers, as well as wiretapping, of which the party headquarters of the Swedish Communist Party constituted the largest single target.

Sometime in 1952 or 1953, another and separate domestic intelligence project was initiated, focusing on persons employed in sensitive positions in the armed forces and the total defense complex. The Domestic Department of the Defense Staff had been assigned the task of screening conscripts for certain sensitive assignments. This was done in cooperation with the Security Police, which checked the names against the Central Registry. But the armed forces were also dependent on civilian personnel and contractors, along with employees in the defense industry and other companies or agencies with relevance for the total defense. Although there were divisions and crossing lines of responsibility among the intelligence agencies, the main divide here was the one between the Security Police and the various actors in the defense domain. There was certainly ongoing cooperation in specific concrete matters (*samverkan*), both formalized and informal, but the organizations on each side of the divide were nevertheless very different in their professional outlook, with the police being far more legalistic in their approach than military intelligence and security. These differences, along with the existence of a gray zone of unclear responsibility, resulted in a cautious and, as it turned out, in some cases hostile relation at the top, fed by a fair amount of bureaucratic territoriality. An additional aspect complicating the matter was a distrust on behalf of the Social Democratic Party organization and labor unions against the police, which was to some extent deeply rooted in experience from political struggle and strikes but also influenced by the more recent experience of the wartime General Security Service, which was not always successful in separating social democrat sympathizers from Communists and other suspicious left-wing elements. The incentive to cooperate with the Security Police was thus limited, especially on the local level.[41]

In 1951, Lieutenant Birger Elmér was employed by the Intelligence Department and assigned the task of monitoring and analyzing Soviet propaganda broadcasts against Sweden. Elmér had studied psychology and would later write a doctoral dissertation on propaganda analysis. Two years later, in 1953, another young reserve lieutenant, Olof Palme, joined the Intelligence Department, possibly influenced by a contact with Elmér, because they knew each other and already had cooperated in intelligence-related matters. The close relationship between the two was to prove decisive for Elmér's career as well as for the rise of a new secret intelligence structure.[42] Contrary to most senior officers, Elmér was an outspoken social democrat and later also acquired party membership. Referring to these party contacts, he soon managed to make himself useful in a number of ways. With considerable entrepreneurship, he established contacts far above and beyond his formal position, including the social democrat minister of defense, Torsten Nilsson, the senior official of the central trade union (*Landsorganisationen*), and Social Democrats in Finland, Denmark, Norway, and Germany.

Through his party and labor union contacts, Elmér became aware of a possible solution to the problem concerning screening of suspected security risks without relying on the Security Police. In the struggle against the Communists for the control over local trade unions, the social democrats established in the late 1940s a nationwide network, covering about 20,000 workplaces with party representatives (*arbetsplatsombud*). Elmér's innovative idea was to tap this network of often-detailed knowledge about their adversary on the left. However, neither the police nor the military could approach this semiclandestine party structure with any hope of cooperation. This could only be accomplished by an organization staffed by well-known social democrats, hence trusted by their party comrades in the labor movement.[43] A further concern, often referred to in retrospect, was US demands on security clearance regarding Communist infiltration of industries and other facilities handling sensitive technology exported to Sweden in accordance with agreements signed in 1952 and 1958.[44]

Elmér's vision, with himself playing the key role, grew step by step. In 1958 a small unit with the designation Group B was created with Elmér as head and attached to the Domestic Department, though localized in a separate premise. In the coming years Elmér established a nationwide and international network and started the collection of information on suspected security risks, and in the beginning of the 1960s Group B moved to a new building in a Stockholm suburb under the suitable cover of the company name "Collector." At that stage friction between Elmér and Thede Palm, and also between Elmér and the Security Police, was increasing. At a meeting between Palm and the head of the Security Police, Thulin, the latter asked several times in what kind of work Elmér was engaged. Palm answered that he did not know, but that he thought Elmér did some processing on material he got from Thulin. To this Thulin answered that this probably had been the intention, but that he had declined such an arrangement. Thus neither the T-Office nor the Security Police knew what purpose Group B had.[45]

Palm's relations with Elmér had been frosty from the onset, with Elmér as a junior intelligence officer establishing his own liaison arrangements with foreign partners. Neither were Palm's relations much better with the rapidly rising star, Palme. There were differences in personality, but also in political and professional outlook. In his memoirs Palm rather bitterly comments that Elmér was allowed to "establish a security service on behalf of his political party" using government funding.[46] The close relation between Elmér and Palme proved to be more decisive than the old friendship between Palm and Erlander. In 1964, Palm began receiving signals from the government that it was time for him to withdraw. He also had growing difficulties with the head of Section II of the Defense Staff, who incidentally disliked both Palm and Elmér and wanted "those gentlemen" to be placed outside the Defense Staff and have nothing to do with it, except the duty to send over reports.[47]

Without support from either the minister of defense or the prime minister, Erlander, and with Palme entering government, the stage was set for the first—and only—major reshuffling of the postwar intelligence structure, the creation of the Information Bureau (IB). In 1965, Palm was removed and placed in internal exile at the Department of Military History of the War College. No doubt a bitter man, he nevertheless kept quiet, as he had done for twenty-five years. The T-Office and Group B, now called the B-Office, were merged into a new combined secret service (or special service, as it was sometimes called), with Elmér as its first director. With the creation of the IB began a brief inter-lude of close but at the same time extremely nontransparent government–intelligence relations, mostly handled on a person-to-person basis between Elmér and Palme. If the wartime General Security Service was little known and lacked parliamentary consent, the IB was completely detached from any constitutional or legal framework; it was an officially nonexistent entity without any outside insight or control and with a nondocumented information channel directly to Palme, first as minister of education and then, starting in 1969, as prime minister.[48]

If Palm was easy to get rid of, the same was not the case for the Security Police. Thulin's successor in 1962, P. G. Vinge, described in his memoirs the shock he experienced when he visited "AB collector" and realized that Elmér and his organization were operating as a parallel security service outside any legal framework.[49] In 1969, shortly before Erlander left office, the chief police commissioner, Carl Persson, brought the issue to a decision. At a meeting with Erlander, where his imminent successor, Palme, also was present, Persson asked the prime minister if it was the Security Police or the IB that should be entrusted with the responsibility for the country's internal security. This was a rhetorical question, and Erlander had to promise that the domestic intelligence conducted by the IB would be discontinued. Elmér, furious over the decision, was forced to comply, but without any external control of his organization, he could simply reactivate domestic intelligence after a brief interlude.[50]

All this, however, came to a sudden halt in the spring of 1973, when the Swedish left-wing magazine *Folket i Bild Kulturfront* published a feature story that effectively outed large parts of the organization. As in many similar cases, the magazine had gotten its information from an insider, an employee who had been sacked after inventing sources and pocketing their reimbursements. This was the end for the IB and Elmér as the first (and last) director. The now-not-so-secret organization was restaffed and placed back under the Defense Staff, with a role similar to that of the old T-Office. The unit changed its name several times and finally in the 1990s, under the designation Office for Special Collection, became a part of the newly formed Military Intelligence Directorate (Militära Underrättelstjänsten, MUST), as an independent part of the head-quarters. The IB was formally dissolved in 1974, but Elmér remained in the shadows as a consultant. As a nonsocialist government entered service in 1976, the first since the 1930s, the new minister of defense discovered that funding was still trickling to the nonexistent IB and demanded an immediate stop to the flow and the removal of Elmér and his old confidants from everything that had to do with defense intelligence, something that did not stop Elmér from remaining in the background at least to 1980, after which he retired to his farm in southern Sweden, incidentally growing apple trees.[51]

"The IB Affair" resulted in the setting up of the 1974 Parliamentary Intelligence Commission. Although the investigation took a broad grip over a number of key organizational and political issues, like the subsequent probes by the justice ombudsman (*Jutitieombudsman*) and the attorney general, it failed to clarify the extent and nature of the domestic intelligence activities conducted by the IB. From the very outset, the social democrat representative denied any connection between the party and the IB and explained the number of former labor union men in the IB as purely coincidental. The bubble finally burst in 1998, two months before a general election. This time it was the IB's old director, Birger Elmér, who was the perhaps unintentional source. A few years earlier, Elmér had been among a large number of former civil servants, officers, and politicians questioned by another parliamentary commission, this time investigating Swedish clandestine links with the Western powers in the period before 1969.[52] Although the commission was not supposed to investigate intelligence relations—in fact, intelligence matters had been explicitly mentioned as something they should *not* look into—the members nevertheless asked many questions regarding intelligence matters. The hearings were closed and the transcripts were classified, so very little of this became public, at least initially. However, a number of journalists and researchers, realizing the potential of the material, started the process of getting the transcripts declassified in accordance with the Swedish equivalent of the US Freedom of Information Act. Applications could be filed over and over again, and by way of attrition bits and pieces of the classified sections of the transcripts were released, among them one where Elmér bragged about his idea to use the Social Democrat Party for domestic intelligence collection. Thus ended this peculiar twenty-five-year-long intelligence disaster—or, in the words of Lars Olof Lamperts, the researcher tasked by the appointed 1999 Security Service Commission to once and for all investigate the IB, "an unprecedented example of failed political crisis management."[53]

The Post–Cold War Maze and the Return of Unfinished Business

With the perceived end of the Cold War, much of the logic of the existing intelligence system had been eroded, but the wider implications still remained unclear. In 1996, the government finally appointed a new intelligence commission, the first in two decades. This commission, however, was nonparliamentarian and was chaired by a senior jurist, staffed by experts, and assigned a limited mandate. Although tasked with investigating the impact of transforming intelligence requirements and an updated (or rather introduced) legal framework, it was not authorized to investigate or suggest any organizational changes. A new intelligence agenda thus had to be implemented within the old Cold War intelligence structure and without too much reforming of its institutions. Such a reform would have demanded a full parliamentary commission, and would inevitably have upset the relative balance of power that had been established after the turbulence in the 1960s and 1970s.

The report, issued in 1999, was a typical product of the late 1990s security agenda, stressing the need to transform intelligence from focusing on military surveillance toward a broader span of possible future national security threats, including support for peacekeeping operations; the flow of refugees (i.e., the flow that Sweden had just experienced from the Balkans); transborder organized crime; and the smuggling of components, raw materials, and the know-how associated with weapons of mass destruction. Typically for assessments shortly before the new millennium, international terrorism was just mentioned in passing but was not regarded as something crucial from an intelligence perspective.[54]

More than any other part of the Swedish intelligence structure, the FRA had enjoyed a long period of anonymity and lack of political reform efforts during the Cold War and beyond. Apart from the downing of a signals intelligence aircraft in 1952 and a prolonged struggle by the relatives of the aircraft's lost crew members in the 1980s and 1990s to clarify their fate, the FRA had remained almost totally unknown in its rural setting outside Stockholm and monitoring stations in remote parts of the country. In official documents, it was only mentioned in passing; the 1974 investigation only gave a brief description of it on a single page but did disclose that its current budget showed that signals intelligence received about 80 percent of the total share.[55]

That "health remains quiet" (*Hälsan tiger still*) is an old Swedish proverb, and it probably held true for the FRA during the late Cold War. But in the 1990s things began to change on two fronts. First, the need for military surveillance of the Baltic Sea region decreased due to the dismantling of the Soviet armed forces and the independence of the Baltic states. There were far fewer targets and activities to monitor, and far less demand from Swedish military and political intelligence customers. This increased the relative importance of worldwide communications intelligence, the traditional hallmark of the FRA ever since the Swedish victory over the Geheimschreiber. This most secret activity during the Cold War had initially been conducted through monitoring of radio transmissions, supplemented with the access to telegraphic and telex cable communications to and from foreign institutions in Sweden. This latter source had been cut off in 1945, with the termination of the wartime emergency laws, and the newly appointed foreign minister, Östen Undén, himself a professor of international law, had opposed such access on legal and ethical grounds. But in 1948, with the Cold War in full swing, access was nevertheless granted through a secret government decision.[56]

This "cable access" remained unknown throughout the Cold War but would become known after fifty years, if not renewed. The significance for intelligence collection had decreased drastically in the 1970s and 1980s with the introduction of satellite communications that could be intercepted without physical access. In the early 1990s, the 1948 government decision was altered and the access was terminated, an action probably dictated mainly by the government's fear of another intelligence scandal. From the perspective of the FRA, this terminated access did not seem to matter particularly much. Not foreseen at that time was the coming rapid development of the international network of fiber-optic cables with the huge transmission capacity needed for Internet traffic. Just a few years later, the FRA suddenly found itself in a situation where it was increasingly cut off from the large telecommunication flows then moving back from satellite links to cables. The dilemma this created was considerable. On the one hand the FRA could continue with business as usual, but then most likely it would lose important sources, and in the longer run also the cryptological competence that was its backbone. On the other hand the FRA could press the government to renew the cable access, but then risk that the whole Swedish communications intelligence enterprise would become widely known.

The first attempt to find a way out of this dilemma was a compromise. In 2003, a one-man investigation carried out by the former supreme commander, General Owe Wiktorin, suggested that the FRA—for the sake of protecting information security in vital infrastructure, but also for individual citizens— would be given access to the global telecommunications network through the operators. The stated purpose was thus not intelligence collection but protection against hackers and other forms of hostile Internet activities. Article 8 of the European Convention, which ensures citizens the right to private communications, was highlighted, not as an obstacle but as an argument for supervision to protect these rights.[57]

External events, however, generated a serious crack in the silent consensus necessary to solve the signals intelligence dilemma in a smooth and, as it was intended, discreet way. Although not directly affecting Swedish security, the September 11, 2001, terrorist attacks on the United States nevertheless increased the threat of terrorism, or rather the perceived scale of a possible attack. This inevitably reactivated an old controversy in Sweden dating from the 1930s over the dividing line between the armed forces and the police. Until then, the armed forces had been ruled out for internal police tasks, even in case of severe crimes such as terrorist attacks. But terrorists using aircraft or having at their disposal advanced weapons could not be handled by the police. This problem was transferred to an investigation (11 September-Utredningen), but the underlying latent conflict between the defense and the police proved hard to overcome, even though both sides realized that this had to be done.[58] It took five years until the tug of war was decided, mainly in favor of the police. A law passed in 2006 mandated that military resources could be employed in extreme situations, when resources not available to the police were demanded. But in these contingencies, the police would still be in charge and the military support would be under their command.[59]

Although not primarily dealing with the intelligence aspects of possible attacks by international terrorist, the conflict over the "ownership" of the terrorism threat nevertheless rapidly spilled over to the intelligence domain, and thus it fed underlying structural conflicts within the defense intelligence agencies and between defense intelligence as such and the Security Police, which since the mid-1990s had been supplemented by Criminal Police Intelligence. This latter conflict rapidly escalated to the political level, where it caused growing friction between the Ministry of Defense and the Ministry of Justice.

All this occurred behind the scenes and remained almost completely invisible to those not directly concerned until the autumn of 2007. There were two interlinked territorial conflicts. The first concerned the secret intelligence department, the Office for Special Collection. This was basically the only producer of raw intelligence within MUST, besides the service attachés controlled by the directorate itself. Otherwise, MUST was dependent on other intelligence producers, first of all the FRA and the Ministry of Foreign Affairs. The FRA had, shortly after World War II, suggested reorganizing to a centralized collection agency whereby the FRA would take over photo-intelligence (at that time run by the brother of the FRA director) and the unwanted baby, the C-Bureau. The High Command had at that time stopped all such plans, but in the late 1990s they resurfaced, now against the background of a transforming and widening role for national intelligence, whereby the efforts of the collecting agencies had to become more closely coordinated—or so it was argued. A less altruistic reason could have been that *all* the intelligence agencies now had problems remaining relevant from a customer's perspective.

The second territorial aspect of this silently prepared reshuffling was the transformation of secret intelligence, from the traditional Cold War foreign intelligence collection focused on the East, to a more general intelligence collection agency, with the capacity to run sources and collect information concerning the whole span of transborder threats. But there were two caveats. The first one was a bill passed in 2000, the first ever regulating defense intelligence, which—as it soon turned out, rather unfortunately—explicitly limited the scope of defense intelligence to the surveying of external *military* threats against the nation, thereby excluding almost all the new transborder threats, leaving them to the police, customs, and other civilian agencies. The second obstacle, once again far more difficult to overcome, was the Security Police.

In 2007, after several years of in-house processing in the Ministry of Defense and Ministry of Justice, the government was finally prepared to propose a package solution, containing three interlinked new or rewritten laws.[60] The first was new wording in the Law of Defense Intelligence that replaced "external military threats" with "external threats," a seemingly minor change, but as it emerged one with wide-ranging implications. The second part of the package was a brand-new Law of Signals Intelligence, the first one ever in Sweden. The law's text, which was very brief and did not even mention the FRA, nevertheless contained the important clarification that signals intelligence also could be collected in all types of transmission, including in cables crossing the national border. Permission nevertheless had to be given by a new board, but signals intelligence collection did not like the well-established police wiretapping court order, because it was a part of Defense Intelligence (as now defined) and not law enforcement. Finally, the package's third part was an addendum to a law on electronic communication, containing an obligation for telecommunications operators to make their cross-border traffic available at certain tapping points, an instruction not entirely unlike the 1939 emergency legislation making the diplomatic cable traffic available to the Defense Staff's Cryptographic Department. The main reasons behind this proposed package of laws were presented as legalistic ones because Sweden, like the United Kingdom and Germany, had to comply with the European Convention, which stipulated that the rights of citizens in accordance with Article 8 had to be supported in law. Although important for its legal rationale, the regained cable access was nevertheless the crucial issue from an intelligence perspective.

In the summer of 2008, the government was finally prepared to present the bill to Parliament. The tug-of-war had by then burst into the open, with the chief police commissioner, echoing Carl Persson in 1969, firmly opposing the bill as a threat to individual integrity and a reopened door to domestic military intelligence with a resemblance to the IB. On June 18, with the summer holiday only days away, the Swedish parliament was supposed to pass the bill without undue delay and lengthy debates. However, what from the beginning had been presented as a minor technical and legal matter had by now transformed into a major public controversy, fed by widespread fear of massive eavesdropping and the reestablishment of the Cold War surveillance system, now in the name of protection against terrorism. Facing a possible defeat, to persuade rebels on the government benches to vote in favor, the government had to add a long list of concessions that proved very difficult to include in a new, modified bill on tightened procedures for approval, improved control, and limited access to signals intelligence as a source. One of the concessions was the promise to deprive the Security Police of the right to file requests for signals intelligence, a decision that was heavily questioned after the narrowly misfired suicide bomber attack in central Stockholm on December 11, 2010.[61]

In July 2008, in the midst of the public and political turmoil over the "Cable Law," a group of US antiterrorist officials visited Sweden on a rather delicate mission. The terrorist-screening information-negotiating team was to negotiate the terms for Swedish adherence to the US Enhanced Visa Waiver Program, which in practice meant concluding a formal agreement on the exchange of information on terrorist suspects. Through at that time an unforeseen form of communication intelligence, the report containing a summary of the meetings was made public in the giant WikiLeaks release of US State Department cables in the autumn of 2010. According to the US summary, which, of course, reflects the perspective of the negotiating team, the Swedish representatives from the Ministry of Foreign Affairs and Ministry of Justice were positive about antiterrorist intelligence cooperation but very reluctant to sign any formal agreement on the matter. The Swedes expressed "a strong degree of satisfaction with current informal information sharing agreements" with the United States covering "a wide range of law enforcement and antiterrorism cooperation." However, in light of the newly passed surveillance law, the Swedish representatives explained, it would be impossible for the Ministry of Justice to avoid presenting a formal data-sharing agreement for Parliament. According to the Swedish representatives, as a result the existing informal cooperative arrangement would be more intensely scrutinized by Parliament and thus jeopardized. US ambassador Michael Wood summarized his view of the Swedish attitude to the conduct of intelligence in the following words: "The Ministry of Justice's notion of a one-sided, informal data exchange arrangement reflects Swedish constitutional restrictions on the use of intelligence, combined with a willingness to continue feeding information to the US through existing informal channels."[62]

Echoing the words in Almqvist's famous novel, this rare insight into the management of a bilateral liaison arrangement also illustrates the enhanced importance of intelligence in foreign relations, not only as a tool but also as an arena. This is even more visible in the European context, where the symbolic role of intelligence cooperation and participation in emerging multilateral structures has become an essential element in the conduct of intelligence.[63] Cooperation is not only conducted to acquire information, but intelligence is also conducted to facilitate participation in cooperation on a bilateral or multilateral basis.

Conclusion: The Practice of Muddling Through in a Noncommunity

From the outset, a permanent weakness of the Swedish intelligence culture was the lack of a concept of a system; this lack mirrored both the overall structure of public administration and the low priority given to intelligence matters in the formation of national policy, with the Palme–Elmér relationship in the 1960s and early 1970s as a brief and not too encouraging interlude. To keep the "gentlemen" at arm's length remained a valid prescription for politicians against trouble, as both the IB Affair and the Cable Law controversy were to confirm. The alternative line, the establishment of a political and public consensus on intelligence, would have presupposed both the political will and a solid potential for public acceptance, neither of which seemed at hand in the period after World War II when no imminent security threat had profoundly altered the underlying premises.

However, being Sweden, there were nearly always ways of muddling through, also in the face of political confusion, agency rivalry, and more or less widespread mistrust among the public. Even at the height of the conflict between the IB and the Security Police, the former continued to send its reports from domestic surveillance to the latter, where they were duly filed in the Central Registry under the source cover name Erik. Two of Elmér's key subordinates also regularly had lunch at an officers' club in Stockholm with an inspector from the Security Police, where they informally exchanged information and mutual requests.[64]

The outcome of the parliamentary clash over the Cable Law in 2008 was a typical political compromise where both sides had to make concessions in order to gain something. From an intelligence perspective, however, the outcome was disastrously dysfunctional, because it deprived the Security Police of the right to request (although not receive) signals intelligence material from the FRA. During the Cold War this would have been of limited importance, given that the Security Police then relied most on other sources and anyway had their own Radio Control Department to monitor radio communications associated with foreign intelligence activities. In the new security environment, however, the worldwide monitoring of telephone and Internet traffic was an essential tool, and the lack of this would threaten to virtually blind first of all counterterrorism efforts.

In 2009, shortly after the Cable Law controversy, a permanent National Center for Threat Assessments that was focused on terrorism was established at the Security Police with representatives from the FRA and MUST. This was the first attempt ever not only to institutionalize the informal links across agency boundaries but also to jointly assess and grade threats against Sweden and Swedish interests. But the National Center for Threat Assessments also meant that analysts for the first time not only met but worked together. Although not officially admitted, the effort thereby quietly solved the signals intelligence dilemma. Although the Security Police had been removed from the customer list, the Intelligence Directorate had remained. With the new definition of defense intelligence, the directorate was tasked with the monitoring of external threats, including terrorism on the international scene, with a subsequent need for signals intelligence coverage that was in principle identical to that of the Security Police. The overlapping tasks that had so infuriated the chief police commissioner in 2007 thus, as events unfolded, offered a smooth, informal way out of the unwanted cul-de-sac of the rewritten Cable Law.

Epigraph

Quotation from the English translation of the novel by Yvonne L. Sandstroem (Columbia: Camden House, 1992), 217.

Notes

1. Probably the most valuable intelligence channel was the Swedish Berlin legation, where the naval attaché, Captain Forshell, had very close contacts with senior officers in the German Naval Command. Wilhelm Carlgren, *Svensk underrättelsetjänst 1939–1954* (Stockholm: Liber, 1985), 26.

2. Ibid., 13–16.

3. On Beurling, see Bengt Beckman, *Svenska kryptobedrifter* (Stockholm: Bonniers, 1996).

4. For the development and result of the signals intelligence, see C. G. McKay and Bengt Beckman, *Swedish Signals Intelligence 1900–1945* (London: Frank Cass, 2003).

5. For the circumstances around the German discovery and countermeasures, see McKay and Beckman, *Swedish Signals Intelligence*, 219–22.

6. On the content of the German traffic, see Klaus-Richard Böhme, *Kryposektion IV: Försvarsstaben läser hemliga tyska telegram 1941–42* (Stockholm: Ersatz, 2006). Carlgren, *Svensk underrättelsetjänst*, 71, observes that no initiative was taken for a joint Defense Staff–Foreign Ministry evaluation and that the material, as other types of raw intelligence, was assumed to speak for itself.

7. Carlgren, *Svensk underrättelsetjänst*, 71–80.

8. McKay and Beckman, *Swedish Signals Intelligence*, 163–64, quoting the memoirs of the undersecretary of state Eric Boheman, relating a case where Boheman could use the decrypts to check how the German minister had "improved" the outcome of a diplomatic demarche.

9. The Parliamentary Investigative Commission on refugee matters and Security Service (the Sandler Commission) produced three reports, on refugee matters (Statens Offentliga Utredningar, or Official Reports of the Swedish Government; hereafter SOU 1946:36), on information provided Germany on refugees (SOU 1946:93) and finally on the Security Service itself (1948:7). Strangely enough there is not a single scholarly work devoted to the history and operations of the General Security Service, the only overview being a chapter in a dissertation in criminology on the conduct of the Swedish legal system under emergency conditions, based mainly on the Sandler Commission. Janne Flyghed, *Rättsstat i Kris* (Stockholm: Federativ, 1992), 265–338.

10. On the reestablishment of secret intelligence, see the memoirs of Thede Palm, *Några studier till T-kontorets historia* (Stockholm: Kungl.Samfundet för utgivande av handskrifter rörande Skandinaviens historia, 1999).

11. The hazards of being too invisible was illustrated in the Wennerstöm case, where the eventually decisive information from the colonel's observant cleaning lady was considerably delayed due to the lack of a "Säpo" entry in the Stockholm telephone directory.

12. It was not until the 1980s that the full extent of the cryptologic achievements against the German traffic became public. The first summary of the material was given by Carlgren, *Svensk underrättelsetjänst*, and a more comprehensive and technical account was given by Beckman, *Svenska kryptobedrifter*.

13. Niklas Wikström, *Den svenska militära underrättelsetjänsten 1948–1956* (Stockholm: Swedish National Defense College, 2006), 127–31. In his review of the military intelligence

in the first decade of the Cold War, Wikström concludes that the leading members of the government neither appear to have been particularly informed nor interested in intelligence matters and formed their opinion independently of intelligence assessments.

14. Palm, *Några studier*, 97. There are even fewer references in Erlander's diaries, so far published up to 1961.

15. On Palme and his early career, see Kjell Östberg, *I takt med tiden: Olof Palme 1927–1969* (Stockholm: Leopard, 2008). For early intelligence contacts as a student politician, see Karen Paget, "From Stockholm to Leiden: The CIA's Role in the Formation of the International Student Conference," *Intelligence and National Security* 10, no. 2 (2003): 134–67.

16. Prime Minister Erlander commented on the matter in his private diary. Tage Erlander, *Dagböcker 1950–1951*, entry 757 (Hedemora: Gidlunds, 2001).

17. Palm, *Några studier*, 97. As an example, he refers to the decision to invite Reinhard Gehlen to Sweden on a clandestine visit to establish liaison between the T-Office and BND, a case where it was better for the government to be kept in the dark.

18. Wilhelm Agrell, *Venona: Spåren från ett underrättelsekrig* (Lund: Historiska Media, 2003). A shorter version will become available in English.

19. The incident is described in the diary of the chief of the Defense Staff, Major General Richard Åkerman, September 3, 1957, Richard Åkerman's personal archive, War Archive, Stockholm.

20. For a more detailed account of the foreign liaison, see Wilhelm Agrell, "Sweden and the Dilemmas of Neutral Intelligence Liaison," and Magnus Petersson, "The Scandinavian Triangle: Danish–Norwegian–Swedish Military Intelligence Cooperation and Swedish Security Policy during the First Part of the Cold War," both in *Journal of Strategic Studies* 29, no. 4 (2006): 607–51.

21. Carlgren, *Svensk underrättelsetjänst*, 15.

22. On the Office of Strategic Services in Scandinavia, see Tore Pryser, *USAs hemmelige agenter: Den amerikanske etterretningstjenesten i Norden under andre verdenskrig* (Oslo: Universitetsforlaget, 2010).

23. Wilhelm Agrell, *Den stora lögnen* (Stockholm: Ordfront, 1991), 126. The arrangement was established on British initiative and approved by the Swedish undersecretary of state. The Defense Staff, however, when informing the regional military command, did not mention intelligence collection but described the operation as an experiment carried out by the air force on a radar station with the support of some British technical experts.

24. For a detailed account on the collection of maritime intelligence in the first postwar years, see Sam Nilsson, *Stalin's Baltic Fleet and Palm's T-Office: Two Sides in the Emerging Cold War 1946–1947* (Stockholm: Swedish National Defense College, 2006).

25. Petersson, "Scandinavian Triangle," 612–14.

26. Notes from meeting September 25, 1946, signed by Colonel Juhlin-Dannfelt, head of Section II at the Defense Staff. Former top secret documents of the head of the section, Royal War Archives (Krigsarkivet), Stockholm.

27. Letter from Major General George C. McDonald, US Air Force, Director of Intelligence to Military Attaché, Stockholm, November 20, 1947, RG 341, entry 214, box 39, US National Archives (NA), College Park, MD.

28. Memorandum for Record, Lieutenant Colonel Fuller, September 11, 1947, RG 341, entry 214, box 39, NA, College Park, MD.

29. For the early Swedish aerial reconnaissance missions, see Lennart Andersson and Leif Hellström, *Bortom horisonten: Svensk flygspaning mot Sovjetunionen 1946–1952* (Stockholm: Freddy Stenboms förlag, 2002).

30. Erlander, Dagböcker.

31. Matthew Aid, "In the Right Place at the Right Time: US Signals Intelligence Relations with Scandinavia 1945–1960," Journal of Strategic Studies 29, no. 4 (2006): 594–95. On the US–Norwegian formal agreement, see Olav Riste, The Norwegian Intelligence Service: 1945–1970 (London: Frank Cass, 1999).

32. See Wikström, Den svenska militära, 89–90. Also see Agrell, Den stora lögnen, 129–30; and Aid, "In the Right Place," 601.

33. See Sverker Åström, Sweden's Policy of Neutrality (Stockholm: Svenska Institutet 1977). Åström was undersecretary of state, and the semiofficial character of the booklet was underlined by the fact that it was published in English and not translated to Swedish until 1983.

34. See Robert Dalsjö, Life-Line Lost: The Rise and Fall of "Neutral" Sweden's Secret Reserve Option of Wartime Help from the West (Stockholm: Santérus, 2006), 258–59. It is not entirely clear to what extent this dismantling actually affected the actual prepared liaison arrangements, now embedded in the planning by regional and even local commanders, as for instance the detailed and continued coordination of Danish and Swedish preparations to close the Sound between Zealand and Southern Sweden in case of war. See Mikael Holmström, Den dolda alliansen: Sveriges hemliga NATO-förbindelser (Stockholm: Atlantis, 2011).

35. Den militära underrättelsetjänsten, Betänkande av 1974 års underrättelseutredning, SOU 1976:19 (Stockholm: Fritzes, 1976), 112–13.

36. SOU 1976:19, 113. It is worth underlining that this concerned only military intelligence and neither the Security Police nor FRA.

37. Palm, Några studier, 89–91.

38. See Ola Tunander, The Secret War against Sweden: US and British Submarine Deception in the 1980s (Portland: Frank Cass, 2004). Tunander's interpretations and handling of sources have been heavily criticized by, among others, General Bengt Gustafsson (supreme commander, 1986–94), in Sanningen om ubåtsfråga: Ett försök till analys (Stockholm: Santérus, 2010), 117–31.

39. This dissemination of US Naval Intelligence reports to Sweden and their impact on Swedish military threat-perceptions are described in the official investigation by ambassador Rolf Ekéus, Fred och säkerhet: Svensk säkerhetspolitik 1969–89, SOU 2002:108.

40. Rikets säkerhet och den personliga integriteten: De svenska säkerhetstjänsternas författningsskyddande verksamhet sedan år 1945, SOU 2002:87 (Stockholm: Fritzes, 2002).

41. SOU 2002:87, 507–12.

42. On Elmér and Olof Palme, see Lars Olof Lampers, Det grå brödraskapet: En berättelse om IB, SOU 2002:92 (Stockholm: Fritzes, 2002), 490–99; and Kjell Östeberg, I takt med tiden: Olof Palme 1927–1969 (Stockholm: Leopard Förlag, 2008), 167–75.

43. This description mainly rests on two accounts given by Elmér in the 1990s, but to some extent substantiated by other accounts. No contemporary documentation has ever been found and possibly never existed. SOU 2002:87, 504–14.

44. SOU 2002:92, 130–33.

45. SOU 2002:92, 139, quoting Palm's diary, October 9, 1958. The diary is deposited among his private papers at the War Archives but remains closed until 2015. Using extraordinary legal authority, the Security Service Commission, which was appointed in 1999 to investigate military and police surveillance, demanded access to the closed diary, a decision fiercely resisted by the archive.

46. Palm, Några studier, 52. According to Palm's memoirs, both Elmér and Palme on some occasion signaled that they wanted to join his organization but were turned down because Palm never employed someone who had volunteered and only handpicked people.

47. Transcript of statement by General Bo Westin to the Commission on Neutrality Policy (Neutralitetspolitikkommissionen) 1993.

48. SOU 2002:92. It turned out to be impossible for the Security Service Commission to reconstruct the frequency of contacts between Elmér and Palme, since none of them had left any documentation. According to a foreign intelligence officer working under Elmér at the IB, Elmér and Palme had informal meetings on a weekly basis.

49. P. G. Vinge, *Säpochef 1962–1970* (Stockholm: Wahlström och Widstrand, 1988).

50. SOU 2002:87, 531–35.

51. SOU 2002:87, 541.

52. *Om Kriget kommit . . . Förberedelser för mottagande av militärt bistånd 1949–1969: Betänkande av Neutralitetspolitikkommissionen,* SOU 1994:11 (Stockholm: Fritzes, 1994).

53. SOU 2002:92, 510.

54. *Underrättelsetjänsten: En översyn—Betänkande av 1996 års underrättelsekommitté,* SOU 1999:37 (Stockholm: Fritzes, 1999).

55. SOU 1976:19, 77. The total intelligence budget for 1974–75 was SEK 101 million, which was a little more than 1 percent of the total defense allowances. The budget of the Security Police was not included in this figure.

56. *Protokoll över kommunikationsärende, hållet inför Hans Kungl: Höghet Kronprinsen-Regenten i statsrådet å Stockholms slott den 23 april 1948,* Ministry of Communications, secret archive, National Archives, Stockholm.

57. *Försvarets radioanstalt: En översyn—betänkande av utredningen om översyn av Försvarets radioanstalt,* SOU 2003:30 (Stockholm: Fritzes, 2003).

58. *Vår beredskap efter den 11 september, betänkande av 11 september-utredningen,* SOU 2003:32 (Stockholm: Fritzes, 2003).

59. *Lag om försvarsmaktens stöd till polisen vid terrorismbekämpning,* SFS 2006:343 (Stockholm: Riksdagen, 2006).

60. *Regeringens proposition 2006/07:63* (Stockholm: Försvarsdepartementet, 2007).

61. As it turned out, the suicide bomber had not been a total bolt out of the blue, but had exchanged calls to and from a mobile telephone in Iraq on the day he carried out his attack.

62. *Secret section 01 of 02 Stockholm 000748 sipdis Sate,* November 7, 2008.

63. For inter-European intelligence cooperation, see Björn Fägersten, *Sharing Secrets: Explaining International Intelligence Cooperation* (Lund: Lund Political Studies, 2010).

64. Lampers, *Det grå brödraskapet,* 415–23.

CHAPTER 14

Intelligence Culture, Economic Espionage, and the Finnish Security Intelligence Service

Lauri Holmström

In the domain of international intelligence, Finland offers a perspective into a developing intelligence culture with the potential to facilitate change in how intelligence is perceived and practiced by a small nation. Finland has no civilian domestic or foreign intelligence service. The national intelligence machinery is divided between the Finnish Defense Forces and the Police of Finland. The Finnish Security Intelligence Service, previously known in English as the Finnish Security Police (Suojelupoliisi, Supo) is the operational security authority that has performed the tasks of counterespionage, counterterrorism, and security work in Finland since 1949.[1] The service is a part of the Finnish Police. The Finnish Military Intelligence Center (FINMIC, Puolustusvoimien tiedustelukeskus) is a unit of the Defense Command of Finland and its Intelligence Division. FINMIC analyzes Finland's security environment as well as the operating environment of the Defense Forces. The Finnish Intelligence Research Establishment (Viestikoelaitos) is the signals intelligence unit of the Finnish Defense Forces, which functions under the Finnish Air Force. Finland is a nonaligned country that participates in the NATO Partnership for Peace program.

This chapter examines Finnish intelligence and how it is represented by Supo in the post–Cold War era. The focus is especially on how Supo's intelligence culture is reflected in counterespionage efforts against high-technology economic espionage.[2] The strategic objective of protecting the nation's economic life from illegal economic intelligence has been a priority for Supo since the agency's founding. Its organizational culture still leans heavily on the Cold War experiences and on the historical legacy of the service as a security police force. However, Supo's intelligence culture is currently in transition. In recent years modest steps have been taken toward a service that is more oriented toward security intelligence, wherein elements of the old culture have been merged with new administrative practices. This has led to a more international form of Finnish security intelligence, wherein elements of the larger Finnish grand strategy are also present. This chapter starts with a historical overview of Supo and its recent organizational changes. This is followed by an exploration of the operative environment of the service with regard to economic espionage and high technology. The chapter then develops the ideas brought forward by Stephen Welch on intelligence culture and applies them to the Finnish case of Supo. Finally, the conclusion offers a synthesis on Supo intelligence culture in the contemporary world as well as pathways into future research on the subject matter.

Historical Overview and Recent Organizational Developments

Supo was preceded by the Detective Central Police (Etsivä keskuspoliisi) from 1919 to 1937 and by the State Police (Valtiollinen poliisi, Valpo) between 1937 and 1949. During the years 1945–49 Valpo was dominated by Communists and known as "Red Valpo." A new organization called the Security Police was established in 1949 to replace the dissolved Valpo. Headquartered in Helsinki, Supo today employs about 220 persons and in 2010 had a budget of €17 million. The fundamental task of Supo is the protection of parliamentary democracy and security interests of Finnish society. The principal values of the service are legality, reliability, and quality.[3] Supo is tasked with preventing undertakings and crimes that may endanger the governmental and political system and internal or external security, and with investigating such crimes. Supo also maintains and develops the overall preparedness for preventing activities endangering national security. The matters investigated by the agency are determined by the National Police Board.[4] The Finnish National Bureau of Investigation (NBI, Keskusrikospoliisi) is the national center for intelligence activities focused on serious and organized crime. NBI also serves as the national center of international criminal police cooperation. In intelligence matters Supo is responsible for gathering and analyzing intelligence and the NBI for criminal investigation. Supo changed its English name from the Finnish Security Police to the Finnish

Security Intelligence Service in 2010 to signify its continuing evolution from the realm of police responsibilities and toward a more security intelligence-oriented service.

To date, the history of Supo has been recounted in three authorized volumes, the latest and most comprehensive being the official history titled *Ratakatu 12: Suojelupoliisi 1949–2009*, which commemorates the sixtieth anniversary of the service.[5] According to the leading Finnish intelligence historian Kimmo Rentola, there was no room for complete neutrality in the field of intelligence during the Cold War. Where Finland could find common interests with opposing sides in areas such as cultural or economic relations, in the world of intelligence and counterintelligence these fundamental questions were rendered into operational measures by the main threat to Finnish national security, the Soviet Union, which by its aggressive and systematic actions defined the answers. The relationship between Supo and the Western intelligence community during the Cold War was built on the idea that Supo saw the adversary of the opposing side as an ally. This idea was reciprocated by the West in both actions and exchanges of information that were helpful to Supo. Even if Finnish aims were not served by undertakings such as intelligence operations conducted against the Soviet Union from Finland, Supo cooperated with Western services in operational matters from its inception. Despite having deeper relations with the West than almost any other branch of the Finnish government during the Cold War, the service was never a full member of the Western intelligence community; Supo's most important communal cooperation took place between the Nordic intelligence services.[6]

Even when the Russians possessed much knowledge and information on Supo during the Cold War, they still had difficulties understanding the nature and position of the agency in Finnish society. Supo was often compared with major Western intelligence services or to the USSR's mighty KGB (Committee for State Security, Komityet gosudarstvennoy bezopasnosti) itself. As for the relationship between the KGB and Supo, Rentola concluded that a distinct model of operation was created, which on the Finnish side adapted to the realities of Cold War foreign policy and the official position of the Finnish state, while reserving the potential to respond and keep an eye on the Soviet intelligence machinery operating in the country. However, the model never achieved a mutually recognized stable form. On the Soviet side it was characterized by persistent pressure and a search to find any weak spots. This was countered on the Finnish side by evasive maneuvers and delaying tactics. Throughout its existence, the KGB considered Supo to be its enemy.[7]

Matti Simola has studied the organizational history of Supo and observed that it has gone through four different designs in the last twenty years. In 1992 a structure was established whereby the main focus areas of the agency were placed directly under its director in three units: Counterespionage, Security, and Development and Support Functions. When Eero Kekomäki retired as director in 1996, Seppo Nevala was appointed as his successor. During Nevala's tenure a new organizational structure was implemented in 1998. The central idea in this transformation was the division of work between operational matters and development projects. Nevala also introduced a second reorganization of Supo in 2004, in which the focus was placed especially on developing research and analysis functions as well as reporting. In addition, the Operational, Preventive, and Strategic lines were built on the notion that operational matters were to be separated from strategic and preventive security work. In Nevala's view Supo was "taking a few practical steps toward a security service." Simola has noted that under Nevala, Supo also became more international.[8]

Ilkka Salmi became the director of Supo in 2007. In 2008 the service got its first communications manager.[9] The current organization of the service was introduced in 2009. With the restructuring process, the line organization was discarded. Today Supo has four operational units: the Counterespionage Unit, the Counterterrorism Unit, the Security and Regional Unit (including security clearances and vetting), and the Field Surveillance Unit. The service is divided into an Operational Branch and a Strategic Branch. The Operational Branch is led by the operational deputy director and is composed of the four operational units introduced above. The Strategic Branch contains the Situational Awareness Unit, the International Relations Unit, and the Internal Services Unit. It acts under the command of the strategic deputy director, who is also responsible for the agency's legal matters. The director of Supo oversees both branches and is in direct contact with the Communications Office. Approximately 55 percent of Supo's staff members are police personnel, of which 30 percent are commanding officers, 40 percent are senior officers, and 30 percent are officers. About half of the rest of the staff members work as specialists or senior specialists, and the other half carry out clerical, support, and occupational tasks. One in three employees has an academic degree, and their average age is a little under forty-four years.[10]

The institutional position of Supo within the Finnish government is under the Ministry of the Interior. This is somewhat of an anomaly in the Nordic intelligence realm, where the Swedish Security Police (Säkerhetspolisen, SÄPO), the Norwegian Police Security Service (Politiets sikkerhetstjeneste), and the Danish Security and Intelligence Service (Politiets Efterretningstjeneste) all operate under the Ministry of Justice in their respective countries.[11] Finland is also set apart from the other Nordic countries with regard to foreign intelligence. In contrast with Finland, for example, in Denmark the Defense Intelligence Service (Forsvarets Efterretningstjeneste), situated under the Ministry of Defense, acts as both the foreign and military intelligence agency and also handles human intelligence duties abroad.[12] This dimension of intelligence is absent from the Finnish national intelligence machinery. Furthermore, it is also important to note that Finland has no specific law on intelligence. In comparison with large Western intelligence agencies, Supo comes closest to the United Kingdom's Security Service (MI-5) in operational terms. In the Nordic countries, contrary to other European nations, the security services have traditionally been police organizations. It is also of note that the Estonian Security Police (Kaitsepolitsei) is similarly a police organization and is administered by the Estonian Ministry of Internal Affairs.[13]

Economic Espionage and High Technology in Finland

Economic espionage has been on the rise since the end of the Cold War.[14] Both nations and corporations face a growing threat from entities using illegitimate methods that attempt to acquire new technologies, innovations, and information in a wide variety of disciplines. Throughout its existence, Supo has worked to ensure the economic security of the Finnish state and counter illegal and covert intelligence efforts aimed at the nation's economic life.[15] In the Finnish case, the interest of the state to confront economic espionage can be seen as encompassing three separate elements. First, the government has created a public education system that provides the companies operating in the country with academically trained recruits. Second, for the economy to function properly, the state must be able to provide a safe and favorable environment for business. And third, economic espionage can compromise questions of national security when it targets, for example, dual-use technology that contributes to the security of the state.

Recent economic intelligence cases have clearly demonstrated that companies, research facilities, and other communities risk the most damaging information losses via their staff. The storage and systematization of large amounts of information by technological means has made it easier to engage in practices such as insider crime. This is why, even when information security issues are becoming more important, intelligence organizations still strive to recruit human sources. The recruitment of an agent is a slow and deliberate process, and it includes assessing factors such as the target's access to information, motivation, and reliability.[16] One of the most informative examples of recent high-technology economic espionage in Northern Europe has been the 2002 Ericsson espionage case, where three employees of the company stole corporate secrets and tried to sell them to Russian diplomats working in Sweden. It has been called the first real economic espionage case in the country and the first economic espionage case that has led to a sentence for serious espionage.[17]

The globalization of trade and research has also advanced the opportunities for economic espionage by increasing international cooperation, which in turn has facilitated new options for recruiting and using people for the purposes of illegally gathering economic intelligence and also sharing and selling classified information. This has left the national intelligence agencies that deal with economic espionage with the difficult challenge of separating normal working relationships from those that have a potential to turn into a security risk.[18] In the case of high technology, research that is based on international collaboration can make it very hard to determine what specific information should be protected in projects that stretch over a long period and may involve a number of people from different organizations. Changes in the post–Cold War global economy have shifted intelligence priorities toward high-technology industries and research institutes.[19] In Finland this has been significant because of the large investments in research and development in high technology.

After the Cold War the level of foreign intelligence in Finland increased from the second half of the 1990s to the early years of the 2000s. In 2006, the number of foreign intelligence officers grew a little but did not affect the number of aggressive recruitment cases.[20] During recent years both the quantity and quality of foreign intelligence officers operating in Finland have stayed the same. The main foreign intelligence offensive in Finland is aimed at key areas of high-technology research and development and the political system. Lately, issues such as the international energy questions, which encompass both political and technological questions, have also been targets of foreign intelligence. Scientific and technological intelligence efforts in Finland are characterized by a very wide gathering of open-source intelligence, with targets ranging from universities to small companies. Because of the extreme care taken in the selection of both the desired technology and the key persons connected to it, recruitment efforts have been relatively rare; but a few cases surface each year. In 2010, Supo conducted an investigation into a few intelligence operations abroad that had targeted Finnish official representatives, civil servants, and businesspeople more aggressively than what had been previously observed.[21]

Foreign intelligence has been particularly interested in high-technology sectors that have dual-use capabilities, such as telecommunications and information technology. Other important targets of economic espionage include nuclear technology, biotechnology, medical science and pharmacy, new materials, nanotechnology, and positioning technology. Constant targets for foreign military intelligence involve technological purchases that can be considered interesting from the military perspective as well as assessing Finland's military capability, defense policy, and international military cooperation. The foreign intelligence services operating in Finland prioritized confidential conversations, situational estimates nearing completion, and plans on which work was still being done. In addition, foreign intelligence officers have targeted the cooperation between business and research that seeks to produce practical, marketable applications. The constant level of foreign intelligence in Finland shows that gathering secret and confidential information through human sources has not lost its meaning in the modern world. At the same time, organized crime and intelligence attacks against information systems pose a new and growing threat. In 2007, about 10 percent of the Finnish companies interviewed by Supo said that they had been a target of illegal intelligence activity during the last two years. Similar numbers were reported in a survey conducted by the Central Chamber of Commerce of Finland and the Helsinki Region Chamber of Commerce in 2008.[22]

The Finnish economy relies increasingly on technological innovations. In the view of Supo, protecting research, innovations, and other relevant information related to the field will become even more significant in the future than it is today.[23] Innovative companies are the main drivers of Finland's economy, and technology has become the most important industry in Finland. It constitutes 60 percent of Finnish exports, and 80 percent of research-and-development investments are directed toward technology.[24] Remarkable technological advances of intellectual property in Finland have been achieved through close cooperation between the state, the research centers, and the companies. This has been made possible by the continued emphasis placed on higher education and by the creation and development of a national innovation system.[25] Innovation has been integral in the restructuring of the Finnish economy. During the past twenty years the research-and-development intensity of Finland has grown to the second-highest level within the European Union, and the share of high-technology products in total Finnish exports is among the highest in the industrial world.[26]

The international competitiveness of Finland is linked to the rise of high-technology companies and the emergence of a knowledge-based economy. A modern technology policy that has been a priority for the political leadership is responsible for advancing economic growth through technological development. Economic espionage corrodes the national investment and innovation frameworks supported by the state and causes financial and intellectual losses to companies and research centers. Economic espionage can also act as a deterrent to innovation and may in the long run even cause losses to consumers around the world.[27] Both national and international companies look for a stable and secure environment in which to base their operations. Security can, in this regard, be viewed as one of the building blocks of Finland's competitiveness in the global economy.

The counterespionage and preventive security work of Supo related to the problem of economic espionage has its starting point in the idea that the entire national innovation system is protected. The basis for this work is laid out in threat analyses. The agency builds on this through the consultation and vetting services that place Supo in cooperation with businesses on a daily basis. In addition to these means, the operational security work of Supo's Counterespionage Unit is focused on the intelligence threats aimed at the Finnish economy.

The service also works closely with international security and intelligence services and security authorities.[28] The challenge for Supo is twofold. First, it needs to continue to effectively and openly inform and serve companies and other communities targeted by economic espionage and other security challenges such as proliferation issues. Second, it needs to secure its own operations against illegal economic intelligence efforts while performing its overt functions related to economic security. It is important to note here that Supo does not investigate instances of corporate espionage where both parties are privately owned companies. The matter becomes an interest of the agency only when a foreign state is connected to the case. Countering economic espionage has also been publicly recognized by Supo's leadership as one of its main priorities.[29] During the years 2003–8, the prevention of illegal intelligence was awarded the most resources in Supo's budget. In 2010, a total of 39 percent of the resources allocated to the agency were assigned to the prevention of illegal intelligence efforts.[30]

An Intelligence Culture in Transition

Henrikki Heikka has researched Finnish strategic culture from a historical perspective. Traditionally, Finnish post–Cold War foreign policy has been approached as a shift from cautious neutrality to rapid integration within the core of Europe. Heikka has argued that instead of studying Finland's post–Cold War grand strategy as evidence of a change, it should be thought of as a sign of continuity. Finland's strategic culture has historically been based on a republican understanding of the country's role in defending an antihegemonic security order in Europe. In the post–Cold War era, Finland's strategy can, in Heikka's words, be said to be composed of three main elements: full integration of Finland with the rest of Europe in order to achieve an active role in the making of Europe's grand strategy; connecting Russia more closely with the rest of international society, especially through the European Union; and maintaining a credible national defense and developing Finnish interoperability with NATO.[31]

The element of continuity in Finland's strategic thought is largely based on the experience of its being a neighbor of Russia, where republican ideals have never been accepted and Europe's antihegemonic constitutions have not been respected. Heikka has described the Soviet era from the point of view of Finnish strategic culture as "essentially a long war of defending republicanism against a revolutionist empire next door."[32] How, then, is this experience reflected in Finnish intelligence culture as practiced by Supo? From an institutional perspective, it is clear that the Finnish national intelligence actors have always been and currently are all either military or police entities. This fact supports the picture of Finland as a nation that seeks continuity also in the domain of intelligence and security through its operational security authorities. Supo's intelligence culture can therefore also be viewed as a product of Finland's grand strategy. This is perhaps most clearly visible in the role that preventive security work has in the day-to-day workings of the agency. Active engagement with Finnish society and especially the private sector can be seen as an effort to continue the practices of the Cold War era into the twenty-first century. They also represent a part of the larger national security culture of Finland, where the police and armed forces have the monopoly on intelligence matters and have historically been involved with all segments of society in the name of national security. An example of this larger engagement from the perspective of the Finnish Defense Forces is the institution of the National Defense Courses, where high-ranking military officials and public leaders are invited to a series of courses at the National Defense University (Maanpuolustuskorkea-koulu) that focus on Finland's current and emerging security challenges. The courses comprise Finnish foreign, security, and defense policies as well as the capabilities of the Finnish Defense Forces to meet the requirements recognized by the political leadership. Finland's integration into Europe since the 1990s has been largely political and economic. Supo's role in countering economic espionage can be seen to connect to that objective in three ways. First, the work of the agency seeks to secure the competitiveness of the companies deemed important to Finland. Second, a functioning and secure business life makes it easier for the government to be a credible political player in the European Union. And third, Supo's leadership has ensured that this element of continuity is present in the agency's strategy.

In chapter 2, Stephen Welch contrasts the theories of Gabriel Almond and Robert Tucker that put forward the following ideas about political culture and its research. In Almond's view, political culture is at least partly an independent variable that correlates with democratic stability. To be further used in research, political culture must be "operationalized," for example, in the form of an attitude survey, which is a quantifiable mode of measurement. Through operationalization it is possible to separate the concept of political culture from "the general culture."[33] Conversely, Tucker understands the concept of political culture to be important for helping researchers formulate meaningful questions, focus on relevant issues, work with data, and approach the study of society and its political life in general without explaining anything itself.[34] Welch also notes that political culture should not be understood to be the same as public opinion. Whereas political culture can be used to explain larger issues, such as the continued support for democracy as the means of governance, public opinion functions inside the political culture of a nation-state, where it has an effect on, for example, who is elected to power.[35] However, as Philip Davies has noted in his research on intelligence culture and intelligence failure, theories of culture are complicated to operationalize and test with any real degree of diligence.[36]

Welch sees political culture as an applied concept of culture, which means that consequences and results in a specific social domain can be accounted to that culture.[37] In the field of intelligence, this means that intelligence culture is projected in the outcomes of the intelligence system it represents. However, as Welch duly points out, intelligence culture represents a limited and clearly defined field of activity to which the concept of culture can be applied. From this Welch finds an incentive to look into the study of intelligence organizations to support the research on intelligence culture. But the benefits are also limited here, because organizational culture is as challenging to study as political culture. Welch divides his study of behavior in an organization into two main categories: the practices, methods, and customs of behavior; and the different ways in which these are constituted, explained, or accounted for. When studying cultural difference and continuity, it is important to be aware that what we do and what we say about what we do are two separate things. For example, a survey on the behavior of the personnel of an intelligence organization will not uncover the motives behind their behavior but only the existing modes of explaining their behavior in the relevant environment.

Why is the organizational culture of a company, a group, or, in this case, an intelligence community important? Should not the study of the structure and functions of a secretive organization provide us with enough information to conduct well-rounded research on its inner workings that would leave little or no room for guesswork? The answer, in Edgar Schein's words, is that organizational culture solves the basic problems of survival and adaptation that an agency faces in its external operational environment. The experience of the post–Cold War Supo has precisely been about adaptation to new political and operational realities as well as survival and continuity on an institutional level. Finland's membership in the European Union since 1995 and the inclusion of Supo in the Club de Berne since 1993 and in the Counter Terrorist Group since 2001 have been important milestones in the internationalization of Finnish security intelligence. The fall of the Soviet Union, the rise of global Islamic terrorism, and the continued threat of economic espionage, along with the media spotlight on some of Supo's cases, have all been tests of persistence for Supo. Organizational culture is also responsible for the integration of a group's internal processes that safeguard its ability to continue to adapt and survive.[38]

According to Schein, leadership is a fundamental process that creates and shapes organizational culture. In researching a given organizational culture, it is important to acknowledge the influence of the national culture where the organization in question operates. Organizational culture can be approached through the study of the observed behavioral regularities, the norms and values embraced by an organization, the philosophy and rules of an organization, and, finally, the atmosphere that is perceived both in and outside the organization. Culture, in this respect, should be seen as the property of an independently stable social unit. To study organizational culture one must recognize the special features of the subject of interest. These features can best be observed through the past accounts, actions, and personal histories of important figures in the organization. The study of organizational culture must therefore be viewed as historical in its nature.[39]

The idea of leadership as the most intrinsic part of organizational culture is one of the core themes in Schein's thinking. In Schein's view it is important to understand how the individual intentions of an organization's founders and leaders have become a shared and consensually validated set of definitions that are adopted by the organization and passed on to its new members.[40] The role of leadership in Supo is naturally strong because of its modest size. The effects of decisions made at the top level are felt quickly, and the director can put his personal touch on the way most things are run. Supo's leadership is responsible for recognizing, upholding, and developing its intelligence culture, which encompasses both past and present as well as future ideas of what the service does and how it achieves its goals. This strategic vision is then manifested at Supo's operational levels, which can be further acknowledged as embodying the Finnish conception of security intelligence at work.

However, because behavioral regularities alone cannot inform us if we are investigating a cultural artifact, it is only by the discovery of deeper cultural levels that underlie all human interaction that we can begin to distinguish between what is and what is not an artifact of the culture in question.[41] To solve this problem, here the choice has been made to examine the intelligence culture of Supo through the dependent variable of security intelligence as it is understood by the service. Supo defines security intelligence as the "identification of internal and external security threats, the related operational information gathering and analysis, and the timely reporting of resulting intelligence information to support decision making."[42] Davies has studied intelligence culture and compared intelligence failure in Britain and the United States. He has observed that, in comparing national ideas of intelligence, in the American view information is an element of intelligence, whereas the British understanding is that intelligence is a specific type of information. This is not just a semantic difference, as Davies points out, for it has extensive institutional implications. The contrast between these two definitions is an example of how the idea of what we define as intelligence is reflected in the way an intelligence organization based on that interpretation of the concept is formed and functions.[43] In this regard Supo's definition of security intelligence is closer to the British than the American concept. In Davies's view, the British definition of intelligence points toward an integrative intelligence culture that is prone to groupthink. The opposite American definition of intelligence would lead toward a disintegrative culture that is characterized by turf wars.[44] However,

Supo's definition also takes into consideration the process that produces actionable intelligence for the decision maker. It is therefore more of a description of the agency's mode of operation, in which intelligence information plays a role more than a specific definition of intelligence itself.

Defining security intelligence as the mode of operation can deliver two changes for Supo. It can be argued that the definition and its implementation into Supo's processes can increase the service's self-understanding, which in turn can be helpful in achieving its leadership's strategic goals. The other possible transformation is related to how the agency is perceived in the international field of operations by fellow security and intelligence services. This will almost certainly also have an effect on how Supo will see itself as a part of the international intelligence community in the future.[45]

One of the main arguments presented by Welch in chapter 2 is that the research of any applied culture, such as intelligence culture, does not require an understanding of the larger culture in which the intelligence culture is based. Even when one examines a closed organization or a group such as the intelligence agency of a particular nation, one is still in essence trying to bring into focus the characteristics of an evolving social unit that is attached to a larger host culture. In a limited analysis such as this chapter's, it is not meaningful or even possible to dig deeply into Finnish strategic culture and examine its manifestations of norms, values, and practices in public administration in the past or the present. Welch has further noted that this would likely not be fruitful anyway, because in many cases the cultural values of a nation are expressed in situations where, for example, the people of a given agency are being tasked with comparing their organizational practices with those of other agencies. He further asserts that the study of intelligence culture can be advanced somewhat separately from the larger debate on scholarly cultural analysis and need not wait for its resolution. This can be done by focusing on things such as the organizational designs, mandates, and customs that all form a part of the intelligence culture of an agency. Welch also highlights special "points of friction" between different practices and ways of accounting for them inside an intelligence organization as the most fruitful place to begin research on intelligence culture. By examining these friction points, "national," "intelligence," "agency," or some other characteristics of behavior will rise to the fore, depending on the nature of the possible dissent as described by the friction point.

With regard to Supo, the relationship between its cautious openness and its security of operational activities and international relations is perhaps the most visible point of entry for the researcher. Its new and cautiously open policy has made Supo a visible participant in Finnish public discussions that are related to its areas of expertise. This change has been felt especially in media inquiries related to terrorism. The risk is that the media can get lost in the details, take them out of their original context, and use them to create journalistic products that can have a negative effect on the public—with Supo left to weather the possible fallout. The reverse side of this phenomenon is the situation where media pressures can possibly hamper Supo's operational activities and attempt to steer the course of its work.[46] As Schein has noted, organizational culture can also be addressed through the atmosphere that is perceived outside Supo. According to a recent survey (2011), 78 percent of Finns think that Supo has performed its duties either very well or somewhat well. In addition, 85 percent of those interviewed said that their confidence in Supo was either high or rather high.[47] This would put the service in a good position to deal with outside pressures from a cultural point of view.

As was noted above, defining the concept of security intelligence can facilitate changes in how Supo reflects on itself and how it is perceived by others. However, if one tries to impose these ideas on a possible but ultimately hypothetical projection of the future, no tangible results can be expected. In the case of Supo it can be argued that it has been useful to adopt an actionable term that in some way illustrates the change in its model of operations from a security police force to a security service. It is nonetheless an entirely different idea to attempt to measure the possible effect of a theoretical concept in Supo's day-to-day workings. In a bureaucratic organization it will always take time before new ideas and customs are fully absorbed and adopted.[48] The culture of Supo affects essentially all its functions and has a direct impact on the results it achieves. One friction point in the evolution of Supo's intelligence culture can be thought to be the gradual replacement of the old, unified, and strong organizational culture by something new in the future. There are two main reasons for this development: the change in the weight and importance of Supo's operational units, and the strategic move made by its leadership toward more of a security service operational model. One of the special features of Supo's culture is the strong traditions of a police organization, which the service still very much follows. In the international field of operations, Supo is still thought of as an internal security police force, and this is also reflected in its culture and customs. Thus, the discrepancy between how Supo views itself and how it is seen by other services will also influence the development of its intelligence culture—especially on the level of international relations. From the point of view of organizational culture, Supo's intelligence culture can thus be understood as the organization's self-conception as an actor in both the national and international spheres of operations.[49]

Conclusion

What, then, is the essence of Finnish intelligence culture as represented by Supo, and how does it relate to the problem of economic espionage in Finland?

If we take as our starting point the notion that an intelligence culture is projected in the outcomes of the intelligence system it represents, we can answer
this question in a way that is supported by factual evidence and does not require
an extensive theoretical framework to function. Supo's work on preventing illegal economic intelligence is based on the concept that the entire national
innovation system is protected. This strategic objective has been on the agenda
of the agency throughout its existence in different forms. The consultation and
vetting services represent a part of the culture of the service that seeks to engage
with the society it serves. The operational security work constitutes another
dimension of the culture of the agency, but recent activities in this area can
only be researched through the perspective of intelligence theory or specific
case studies based on publicly available material.[50]

The role of leadership and the form and functions of organizational design
also influence Supo's intelligence culture. Historically, the fact that much
emphasis has been placed on countering economic espionage must be understood to be a product of the continuity in Supo's work and culture. The legacy
of the Cold War naturally carries a lot of weight for the organizational culture
in Finnish intelligence, but it can be argued that Supo's management in the
post–Cold War period has fused together elements of the old culture with new
administrative practices and a modern mode of operation that have created a
more international machinery for Finnish security intelligence. It can be further asserted that Supo's intelligence culture, as well as its actions, also reflect
deeper Finnish cultural values and the traditions of Finnish grand strategy. The
future will show how durable the concept of security intelligence will be for
Supo, and how the concept itself will evolve in relation to the agency's
organization.

It can be argued that both Supo and its intelligence culture are currently in
a period of transition. To a large extent the agency is still acting as it did during
the Cold War. This also applies to Supo's actions with regard to countering
economic espionage. The position and functions of the service in Finnish society, the durability of the old security police force's philosophy in the workings
of the agency, and the strong role of preventive security work are all proof of
this reasoning. However, the advent of a new culture that is oriented toward
security intelligence, as instigated by the leadership of the service, has placed
the old culture on a collision course with the new culture. How this issue is
resolved will not only be decided inside Supo; it will probably also have an
impact and in turn be influenced by the major trends in Finnish grand strategy
and especially how Finland approaches questions of intelligence and security in
the near future.

It is also entirely feasible that the emergence of a new Supo intelligence
culture will not achieve a lasting impact on the way the agency acts or perceives
itself among international security and intelligence services. In that situation,

the nascent Supo intelligence culture would also have no influence on the evolution of other Finnish intelligence institutions. However, an enduring change in the development of the Finnish intelligence culture could facilitate broader transformations in how intelligence is understood and used by the Finnish government to support decision making, how the Finnish national intelligence actors identify themselves and their tasks, and how the Finnish national intelligence organizations continue to progress as institutions in the future. This development would also support the Finnish grand strategy. After the Cold War Finland quickly exchanged its policy of neutrality for rapid political and economical integration with Europe. The chosen means were different, but the historical goal of defending republicanism stayed the same. In much the same way it is possible that in the future new practices and instruments could be used to drive Finnish strategic aims with regard to intelligence and security.

When setting requirements and priorities for the intelligence process, the first priority is the definition of intelligence.[51] Supo has now taken this step with its description of security intelligence. The need for efficient intelligence machinery in Finland will grow in the future. If this challenge is to be met in a decisive manner, a functioning, specific law on intelligence must be enacted. It can be argued that one of the roles of an emergent intelligence culture is to assist the organization it serves to better understand how it can reach its strategic goals in operational terms now and in the future. Without a working culture of intelligence, a state's security apparatus is in danger of falling into a situation of constrained existence while becoming disconnected from the society it is tasked to protect. Anssi Kullberg has identified this issue in his research on Finland and terrorism. On the state of intelligence in Finland, he writes: "The two basic levels of intelligence, gathering and analysis of information, must not be overwhelmed by burgeoning bureaucratic processes and coordinating efforts. Intelligence should not be regarded as spying or as criminal investigation but rather as a natural part of sophisticated activities carried out by the authorities of an independent country. Without such intelligence, decision making is based on vague assumptions, panic reactions, and outside impulses, which all may lead to miscalculations and, in the worst case, to miscarriages of justice."[52]

Although Supo's intelligence culture does not necessarily explain anything by itself, one can use it as a tool for gaining a deeper understanding of specific intelligence issues by studying the history, organization, and operations of the agency on a clearly defined field or through a case study on a subject such as the prevention of economic espionage against high-technology targets.[53] For more relevance and usefulness, this kind of research should also be comparative. As noted above, the most logical context for this would be the intelligence agencies of the other Nordic countries or other European nations with the same type of security intelligence system as Finland. In addition, if Finnish strategic culture is thought of as a variation of Nordic strategic cultures, this might also prompt broader questions, such as what is currently meant by Nordic political and strategic culture in general and with regard to security and intelligence in particular.[54] The results would not only be beneficial for academic research on intelligence but would also deepen each service's self-understanding, which is a crucial component of the continued evolution and success of any organization.

Notes

1. In Finnish, the service still uses its old name, Suojelupoliisi. In English, the acronym Supo is also in use, despite the new official name of the agency, which has been in use since August 27, 2010. In this chapter Supo is used in both past and current contexts as instructed by the service.

2. The author is grateful for the kind and generous cooperation of Supo with regard to this chapter. The views conveyed here are the author's own and do not represent the official position of Supo. The official documents and reports of Supo and the Swedish Security Police (Säkerhetspolisen, SÄPO) have been made available on the web pages of the respective services. However, they have also been published as printed sources. The decision has been made to refer to them as documents authored by the agency in question and by simply using the title of the source.

3. Finnish Security Intelligence Service, 2011; *Finnish Security Intelligence Service Annual Report 2010*; Finnish Security Police 2008–10; Finnish Security Intelligence Service, 2011. All available at www.suojelupoliisi.fi.

4. Act on Police Administration, section 10. The updated Finnish version of the law is found on Finlex, 2011, www.finlex.fi/fi/laki/ajantasa/1992/19920110.

5. Kimmo Rentola, "Suojelupoliisi kylmässä sodassa 1949–1991," in *Ratakatu 12: Suojelupoliisi 1949–2009* (The Security Police in the Cold War 1949–1991, in Ratakatu 12: The Security Police 1949–2009), edited by Matti Simola (Hämeenlinna: WSOY, Kariston Kirjapaino Oy, 2009). The two earlier volumes on the history of Supo are Matti Simola and Jukka Salovaara, eds., *Turvallisuuspoliisi 75 vuotta* (Security Police 75 Years) (Helsinki: Painatuskeskus Oy, 1994); and Matti Simola and Tuulia Sirvio, eds., *Isänmaan puolesta: Suojelupoliisi 50 vuotta* (For the Fatherland: The Security Police 50 Years) (Jyväskylä: Gummerus Kirjapaino Oy, 1999). At the moment there are no major historical sources in English that deal with Supo.

6. Rentola, "Suojelupoliisi kylmässä sodassa," 159.

7. Ibid., 153–58; Kimmo Rentola, "Cooperation between Enemies: The Finnish Security Police and the KGB," draft of article presented at Norcencowar Workshop, Seili, Turku Archipelago, June 28–30, 2010.

8. Matti Simola, "Suojelupoliisin organisaatio 1992–2009" (The Organization of the Security Police 1992–2009), in *Ratakatu 12*, ed. Simola. For accounts of earlier organizational history of Finnish security intelligence, see Matti Simola, "Toimitiloista ja viimeisten vuosikymmenien organisaatioista" (On the Facilities and Organizations of the Last Decades), in *Turvallisuuspoliisi 75 vuotta*, ed. Simola and Salovaara, 189–95; and Matti Simola, "Suojelupoliisin organisaatio ja johto" (The Organization and Leadership of the Security Police), in *Isänmaan puolesta*, ed. Simola and Sirvio, 213–21.

9. Simola, "Suojelupoliisin organisaatio," 263; Finnish Security Intelligence Service Annual Report 2010, 3. Ilkka Salmi is on a four-year leave of absence as the director of the EU Situation Centre (SitCen) since February 2011. Antti Pelttari was appointed as the new

director of Supo on March 17, 2011. The Finnish government appoints the director of Supo. Before his appointment to the post of director of Supo, Ilkka Salmi worked as a special aide to the interior minister, Anne Holmlund (National Coalition Party, in office April 19, 2007–June 22, 2011. Salmi's successor, Antti Pelttari, also worked previously under Minister Holmlund as state secretary.

10. Finnish Security Police 2008–10 (2009), 41–45; Simola, "Suojelupoliisin organisaatio," 264–65, 268. The Regional Unit was fused with the Security Unit in October 2011.

11. Swedish Security Police, 2011, www.sakerhetspolisen.se. Norwegian Police Security Service, 2011, www.pst.politiet.no. Danish Security and Intelligence Service, 2011, www.pet.dk. In Iceland the National Commissioner's National Security Unit (Greiningardeild Ríkislögreglustjóra) is responsible for intelligence matters. National Commissioner of the Icelandic Police, 2011, www.logreglan.is. For an analysis of the evolution of Swedish intelligence institutions, see chapter 13 in the present volume, by Wilhelm Agrell.

12. Danish Defense Intelligence Service, 2011, http://fe-ddis.dk.

13. Simola, "Suojelupoliisin organisaatio," 266; Estonian Security Police, 2011, www.kapo.ee.

14. Samuel Porteous defines economic espionage as "the use of, or facilitation of, illegal, clandestine, coercive or deceptive means by a foreign government or its surrogates to acquire economic intelligence. The acquisition of an actual piece of technology, such as physical examples of technological information or documents, is assumed to be included in this definition." He further explains industrial espionage to be "the use of, or facilitation of, illegal, clandestine, coercive or deceptive means by a private sector entity or its surrogates to acquire economic intelligence." Where business intelligence explores information that is openly available, industrial espionage is inherently about stealing corporate secrets. Samuel Porteous, *Economic Espionage (II)* (Canadian Security Intelligence Service, Commentary 46, 1994). For the discussion related to concepts of economic espionage see, e.g., Hedieh Nasheri, *Economic Espionage and Industrial Spying* (Cambridge: Cambridge University Press, 2005); Phillip C. Wright and Géraldine Roy, "Industrial Espionage and Competitive Intelligence: One You Do; One You Do Not," *Journal of Workplace Learning* 11, no. 2 (1999): 53–59, at 53–55; Ben Rothke, "Corporate Espionage and What Can Be Done to Prevent It," *Information Systems Security* 2 (November–December 2001); Coskun A. Samli and Laurence Jacobs, "Counteracting Global Industrial Espionage: A Damage Control Strategy," *Business and Society Review* 108, no. 1 (2003): 95–113, at 96–97; Omid Nodoushani and Patricia A. Nodoushani, "Industrial Espionage: The Dark Side of the 'Digital Age,'" *Competitiveness Review* 12, no. 2 (2002): 96–101, 96; and Mark McCourt, "Keeping Up with New Threats," *Security* 45, no. 3 (March 2008): 16–18, 16.

15. Finnish Security Intelligence Service (2011), 21; Finnish Security Police 2008–10 (2009), 17. Matti Remes, "Supo huolestui PK-yritysten tietoturvasta," *Prima* 5 (2009): 30–34, 32–34.

16. Michael Herman, *Intelligence Power in Peace and War*, Royal Institute of International Affairs, 5th ed. (Cambridge: Cambridge University Press, 1996), 53–56; Forrester Consulting, "The Value of Corporate Secrets: How Compliance and Collaboration Affect Enterprise Perceptions of Risk," paper commissioned by Microsoft and RSA, Security Division of EMC, March 2010; Swedish Security Police, *Annual Report 2003*, 2004, 25–27.

17. Stockholms Tingsrätt, Rotel 1301, Avd 13, Dom, Mål nr B 7025–02 (Judgment of the Stockholm District Court in the Ericsson Espionage Case). For more information and analysis of the Ericsson case, see Lauri Holmström, *Industrial Espionage and Corporate Security:*

The Ericsson Case, Reports of the Police College of Finland 87/2010 (Tampere: Tampereen yliopistopaino–Juvenes Print Oy, 2010).

18. Lisa A. Kramer and Richards J. Heuer Jr., "America's Increased Vulnerability to Insider Espionage," International Journal of Intelligence and Counter Intelligence 20, no. 1 (2007): 51–52.

19. Julie Anderson, "The HUMINT Offensive from Putin's Chekist State," International Journal of Intelligence and Counter Intelligence 20, no. 2 (2007): 258–316, at 269; Holmström, Industrial Espionage, 17–20.

20. Finland held the presidency of the Council of the European Union from July to December in 2006, and it is possible that this might have had some effect on the level of foreign intelligence activities with regard to the Finnish state.

21. Finnish Security Intelligence Service, Annual Report 2010, 2011, 7–8; Finnish Security Police 2008–10 (2009), 14; "Suojelupoliisi: Suojelupoliisin vuosikertomus 2006" (Finnish Security Police, Annual Report 2006) (2007); "Yrityksiin kohdistuvan ja niitä hyödyntävän rikollisuuden tilannekuva syksy 2007" (Situational Picture of Crime That Uses and Targets Companies, Fall 2007), 11; "Suojelupoliisi: Suojelupoliisin vuosikertomus 2007" (Finnish Security Police, Annual Report 2007) (2008), 6.

22. Finnish Security Intelligence Service, Annual Report 2010, 7–8; "Suojelupoliisi: Suojelupoliisin vuosikertomus 2006"; "Yrityksiin kohdistuvan ja niitä hyödyntävän rikollisuuden tilannekuva syksy 2007," 11; "Suojelupoliisi: Suojelupoliisin vuosikertomus 2007" (2008), 6; "Yritysten rikosturvallisuus 2008: Riskit ja niiden hallinta—Keskuskauppakamari ja Helsingin seudun kauppakamari" (The Security of Companies with Regard to Crime: Risks and Risk Control), 22–30; "Yrityksiin kohdistuvan rikollisuuden tilannekuva: Tietoturvallisuus ja maksuteknologia; Keskusrikospoliisi, teematilannekuva 3.4.2009, RTP 164/213/09" (Situational Picture of Crime That Targets Companies: Information Security and Payment Technology) (2009), 4; "Yrityksiin kohdistuvan ja niitä hyödyntävän rikollisuuden tilannekuva syksy 2009: Keskusrikospoliisi/rikostietopalvelu 7.10.2009, Arkistoviite KRP (Keskusrikospoliisi) /RTP 5230/213/09" (Situational Picture of Crime That Uses and Targets Companies, Fall 2009) (2009), 17–18; "Yrityksiin kohdistuvan ja niitä hyödyntävän rikollisuuden tilannekuva syksy 2010, 5.11.2010: Keskusrikospoliisi, arkistoviite KRP/RTP 5969/213/10" (Situational Picture of Crime That Uses and Targets Companies, Fall 2010) (2010), 6, 11–12; "Yritysten rikosturvallisuus 2010: Taloustaantuman vaikutukset yritysten kilpailukykyyn vaikuttavaan rikollisuuteen—Helsingin seudun kauppakamari" (The Security of Companies with Regard to Crime: The Effects of the Economic Downturn on Crime That Affects the Competitiveness of Companies) (2010), 23–26.

23. Finnish Security Intelligence Service; "Finnish Security Police 2008–10" (2009), 17.

24. Teknologiateollisuus ry (Federation of Finnish Technology Industries), 2011, www.techind.fi.

25. For a discussion of the Finnish national innovation system, see Osmo Kivinen and Jukka Varelius, "The Emerging Field of Biotechnology: The Case of Finland," Science, Technology & Human Values 28, no. 1 (2003): 141–61. For more on Finnish innovation, see Ministry of Employment and Economy, "Finland's National Innovation Strategy" (2008); Evaluation of the Finnish National Innovation System: Full Report, Taloustieto Oy (on behalf of the Ministry of Education and the Ministry of Employment and the Economy), Helsinki University Print (2009), www.evaluation.fi; HighTech Finland, 2011, www.hightechfinland.fi; Finnish innovation system, 2011, www.research.fi/en/innovationsystem. In the past, the term "innovation" has been used mainly to signify original scientific discoveries,

but in the current technology policy discourse it has expanded to include inventions that have possible marketable applications. An innovation system is organized action that strives to create, develop, and exploit innovations. Within the framework of the national innovation system and technology policy, the private and public sectors and universities are expected to work together transcending institutional boundaries. Knowledge is now considered intellectual property as well as a potential product that can be exploited in the market. This reconceptualization can be seen as the industrialization of the production of scientific knowledge. Timo Räikkönen and Veikko Rouhiainen, *Riskienhallinnan muutosvoimat: Kirjallisuuskatsaus, VTT Tiedotteita—Research Notes 2208* (Forces of Change in Risk Control. Literature Review), VTT Technical Research Centre of Finland (Espoo: Otamedia Oy 2003), 31–32; McCourt, "Keeping Up with New Threats," 16.

26. Thomas R. Leinbach and Stanley D. Brunn, "National Innovation Systems, Firm Strategy, and Enabling Mobile Communications: The Case of Nokia," *Tijdschrift voor Economische en Sociale Geografie* 93, no. 5 (2002): 489–508, at 491–93; Francesco Daveri and Olmo Silva, "Not Only Nokia: What Finland Tells Us about New Economy Growth," *Economic Policy*, April 2004, 117–63, at 129; Kivinen and Varelius, "Emerging Field," 144.

27. Merril E. Whitey and James D. Gaisford, "Economic Espionage as Strategic Trade Policy," *Canadian Journal of Economics / Revue canadienne d'Economique* 29, special issue: part 2 (April 1996): 627–32, at 632. For more on the discussion on post–Cold War challenges to economic security and the connections between security, technology, and the economy, see, e.g., Chris Clough, "Quid Pro Quo: The Challenges of International Strategic Intelligence Cooperation," *International Journal of Intelligence and Counter Intelligence* 17, no. 4 (2004): 607–8; and Ernest R. May, "Intelligence: Backing into the Future," *Foreign Affairs* 71, no. 3 (Summer 1992): 64.

28. Finnish Security Intelligence Service, *Annual Report 2010*, 4, 21–24; Finnish Security Police, "Finnish Security Police 2008–10," 17.

29. Remes, "Supo huolestui PK-yritysten tietoturvasta," 32–33.

30. Simola, "Suojelupoliisin organisaatio," 269; Finnish Security Police, "Finnish Security Police 2008–10," 45; Finnish Security Intelligence Service, *Annual Report 2010*, 6.

31. Henrikki Heikka, "Republican Realism: Finnish Strategic Culture in Historical Perspective," *Cooperation and Conflict* 40, no. 1 (2005): 91–119, at 93. For more on the politics of postneutrality in Europe, see Christine Agius, "Transformed beyond Recognition? The Politics of Post-Neutrality," *Cooperation and Conflict* 46, no. 3 (2011): 370–95.

32. Heikka, "Republican Realism," 92, 103.

33. Gabriel A. Almond and Sidney Verba, *The Civic Culture: Political Attitudes and Democracy in Five Nations*, abridged ed. (London: Sage, 1989). See chapter 2 in the present volume, by Stephen Welch.

34. Robert C. Tucker, "Culture, Political Culture, and Communist Society," *Political Science Quarterly* 88, no. 2 (June 1973): 173–90, at 179; chapter 2 by Welch.

35. See chapter 2 by Welch.

36. Philip H. J. Davies, "Intelligence Culture and Intelligence Failure in Britain and the United States," *Cambridge Review of International Affairs* 17, no. 3 (October 2004): 495–520, at 496.

37. Paul Egon Rohrlich, "Economic Culture and Foreign Policy: The Cognitive Analysis of Economic Policy Making," *International Organization* 41, no. 1 (Winter 1987): 61–92; Jeremy Richardson, *Policy Styles in Western Europe* (London: George Allen & Unwin, 1982); Alan Macmillan and Ken Booth, "Appendix: Strategic Culture: A Framework for Analysis,"

in *Strategic Cultures in the Asia-Pacific Region*, edited by Ken Booth and Russell Trood (London: Macmillan, 1999), 363–72.

38. Edgar H. Schein, *Organizational Culture and Leadership, A Dynamic View* (San Francisco: Jossey-Bass, 1987), 50.

39. Ibid., ix, 2, 6–8.

40. Ibid., 51.

41. Ibid., 9.

42. Finnish Security Intelligence Service, *Annual Report 2010*, 6.

434. Davies, "Intelligence Culture and Intelligence Failure in Britain and the United States," 500–501.

44. Ibid., 508; Isabelle Duyvesteyn, "Intelligence and Strategic Culture: Some Observations," *Intelligence and National Security* 26, no. 4 (August 2011): 521–39, at 526–27.

45. Confidential interview, 2011.

46. Ibid.

47. A survey concerning the views of Finnish citizens on Supo's activity is carried out yearly at the request of the agency. The latest published survey was conducted in February 2011 with a total of 1,000 interviews. The respondents were between fifteen and seventy-nine years. The confidence interval of the results is plus or minus percentage points. Finnish Security Intelligence Service, *Annual Report 2010*, 11.

48. Confidential interview, 2011.

49. Ibid.

50. For more on the challenges of studying economic espionage in practice, see Holmström, *Industrial Espionage*, 12–16.

51. Duyvesteyn, "Intelligence," 525.

52. Anssi Kullberg, "Radikalismi Suomen muslimiyhteisöissä: Ulkomaisten konfliktien ja kansainvälisen islamismin vaikutus," in *Suomi, terrorismi, Supo: Koira joka ei haukkunut—Miksi ja miten Suomi on välttynyt terroristisen toiminnan leviämiseltä?* (Radicalism in Finland's Muslim Communities: The Effect of Foreign Conflicts and International Islamism in Finland, Terrorism, Supo—The Dog That Did Not Bark: Why and How Finland Has Avoided the Expansion of Terrorist Activity?) edited by Anssi Kullberg (Helsinki: WSOY, 2011), 295. The translation of the quotation from Finnish is by the author.

53. Isabelle Duyvesteyn has observed that there is empirical evidence that proves how the perception of geopolitical conditions informs priorities and definitions of intelligence, which further influence collection mechanisms, assessments, and dissemination in the political domain. Duyvesteyn, "Intelligence," 529.

54. Heikka, "Republican Realism," 109.

PART IV

Conclusion

CHAPTER 15

Legacies, Identities, Improvisation, and Innovations of Intelligence

Philip H. J. Davies and Kristian C. Gustafson

Tradition is a guide and not a gaoler.

—W. SOMERSET MAUGHAM

Like so many other institutions in human social and political affairs, intelligence is a field characterized by the presence of culture as a medium through which people both understand and act. As Talcott Parsons observed, culture may articulate both ends and means, but human action is "voluntaristic"—that is, individuals act of their own accord but use culture rather than being directed by it.[1] Culture tells us less what people will do than how they will go about doing it. Beliefs, concepts, values, and norms are, in the last analysis, toolkits to help human beings navigate this life individually and collectively. In this sense those who would try and set cultural explanations against "materialist," "realist," or "structural" accounts have fundamentally misunderstood not only the explanatory role and value of cultural approaches but also the actual processes whereby "realist," "structural," and "materialist" factors play into institutions, decisions, and actions.

Therefore, those who reduce all human affairs to culture and ideology— concluding thereby that because something is socially constructed it is *nothing but* social construction—are as mistaken as biological reductivists who would reduce human affairs to environmental natural selection and evolutionary strategy at the genetic level. In this sense there is an important parallel with physics. Uncertainty has been as axiomatic in social science as it has been in physics for far longer but in ways that have been less coherently articulated. Mayo and the Chicago team who first described the Hawthorne Effect demonstrated, in effect, that the human observing a system directed the humans being observed.[2] It took modern physics two centuries to mine down far enough into the observable effects of matter and energy to reach the doubt-ridden realms of the Planck scale. By contrast, in the study of humanity by humanity, the magnitude of the observing system has always been the same as the magnitude of the system being observed, with all that this implies. Frankly, however, the hard sciences have proven rather better at managing uncertainty than the social sciences, where there has been far too much willingness to equate the uncertain with the unknowable and then to take that as a license to opt for tendentious, partisan, pleasing tales that cast the world in the light of preferred political preconceptions. In the process analysis is conflated with advocacy, and conviction substitutes for caveated estimation because, after all, the human mind does not manage uncertainty well or comfortably.

And yet here is the rub: Intelligence, broadly or narrowly understood, is ultimately about managing uncertainty where one must and mitigating it when one can. At a certain level it matters little whether that management of uncertainty serves regimes that are benign or malign, actors that are state or substate, or governments or corporations—the process of knowing remains the same. It should be no surprise not only that both Indian and Chinese thinkers on intelligence should concern themselves with validating as well as collecting information but also that they should both do so through strikingly similar rules of threes. Thus Kautilya asserts that when information received from "three different sources it shall be held reliable" but "if they [the three sources] frequently differ, the spies concerned shall be either punished in secret or dismissed."[3] As Sawyer notes in his seminal *The Tao of Spycraft*, the Chinese rule of three varies only in their tradition of trying to apply some epistemological reasoning to why it worked.[4] Although the tale of the defeat of the king of the Sung Dynasty (who executed the first and second spy to bring bad news, convincing the third to lie) is used to illustrate the soundness of the rule of three and the idea of validation via multiple sources, other sources understood that "words act in such a way that their credibility stems from greater numbers. Something untrue, if reported by ten men, is still doubted; by a hundred is taken to be so; and if by a thousand becomes irrefutable." Accordingly, the *Lü-shih Ch'un-ch'iu* observed that "the way words are obtained must be analysed. . . . If one learns something and analyses it, it will be fortunate; if not, it would be better not to have learned it."[5] Credibility, doubt, and interpretation of perceptual evidence were all things that classical Chinese philosophers of government (and intelligence) mused over, if not in a systematized way. Presaging Donald Rumsfeld by many centuries, the same *Lü-shih Ch'un-ch'iu* pointed out: "Knowing that one does not know is best. The misfortune of those who are mistaken is not knowing but thinking that they know. Many things seem to be of the same category but are not, thus they lose their state and destroy their people."[6]

In no small way this bridge between cultures and across centuries serves nicely to demonstrate the argument made in the introduction to this book about the cross-cultural commensurability of intelligence as a core state function. Intelligence reporting is never self-explanatory and is very rarely completely trustworthy. It arises from conditions of acute uncertainty, which typically result from the active denial and deception efforts of those about whom the intelligence practitioner and their masters would know. And so where the cognitive task is similar, the resulting formulas resemble each other. On the operational side, the roles of spies in war in Kautilya, Sun Tze, and other Chinese political philosophers are largely similar—they classify spies in a similar way, for instance, and share ideas like the rule of three—but ultimately they have different intellectual roots. More significantly, there are major institutional differences between "classical" Chinese and Indian society. Though both were highly stratified between the very top of the social hierarchy and the bottom, India never displayed the relatively meritocratic social mobility that China's secular state machinery offered, and the Chinese never had to navigate the same rigid divisions created by Hinduism's caste system. Consequently, in covert collection it was necessary for Kautilya to posit two different classes of mendicant female spies, one to deal with Kshatriya and Brahmin women and the other to reach the women of the Sudras and lower castes below them. Conversely, far less use, effect, and diversity of religious cover were available to the increasingly secular and religiously pluralistic polity of imperial China than in India, where the basic political, military, and economic institutions framed their authority in terms of religious legitimacy.

Laminated Legacies

Much of what this volume has examined is best understood in terms of the notion and impact of *legacy* on communities and institutions. This legacy may be ancient, profoundly pervasive, and deep; or it may be a shallower and more recent one to which the members of that community subscribe less comprehensively or completely. And so Sun Tze and his successors have been formative to the strategic thought not only of the Chinese but also the Japanese, but other influences have overlaid that deep legacy. Japan, of course, evolved its own discourse of strategic thought grounded in the inaccurately termed "feudalism" of the *yamabushi*, the Samurai, with indigenous classics such as the *Hagakure* and, better known to Westerners,[7] swordsman Miyamoto Musashi's *Gorinosho* ("Book of Five Rings"[8]), which provided an intermediate stratum of ideas and approaches that the modernized, industrialized, and increasingly globalized *Nihonjin* can mine down into and extract insights from that can be alloyed with newer, more recent influences.

A more striking laminated forging is shared by two other states examined in this volume, Pakistan and Indonesia. Each of these has its deepest intellectual roots embedded in the Sanskrit tradition, subsequently overlaid by Islam, followed by colonial subordination to the British and Dutch empires, respectively. In Indonesia the state locates itself consciously in the precedent of the Indianized empires of Srivijaya (based in Palembang, Sumatra) and Majapahit (chiefly in Surabaya, Java), which survives even today in the Hindu-Buddhist principalities of Bali. Indeed, as one translator of the Malay epic of Hang Tuah has recently noted, even texts like the *Hikayat Hang Tuah* that date to the Muslim era frame their accounts and the legitimacy of the local sultanates in terms of divine and semidivine origins and rights that owe more to a Hindu cosmology than the Islamic notion of a khalifate and its *darul Islam*, realm of Islam.[9] Islam reinforced the Javanese kingdoms in some ways, adding a new religious discourse of authority while transforming society by, for example, doing away with the strictures of the Hindu caste system—and yet the Indonesian word for "warrior" today remains *kesatria*.

Under the Dutch came a new but external authoritarian rule, little more or less severe and uncompromising than the traditional princes and their courts, better organized and more formidably armed, but bounded by rational-level constraints that never occurred to Javanese absolutism. And having been displaced briefly by the Japanese, they eventually gave way to Sukarno's nationalist revolutionaries. Judging from their conduct, however, the intelligence institutions of postcolonial Indonesia seem to have drawn chiefly on the regime protection, disruption, and provocation so essential to Kautilya's "institutes of espionage." This deep legacy appears to have fused with the additional regime protection interests and sanguinary methods that John Dziak has argued are endemic to the security apparatuses of many revolutionary regimes and their resulting "counterintelligence states."[10]

Pakistan, by comparison, had a very different experience of colonial administration—and, indeed, of Islamization. After the decline of the Chandraguptas, the diverse and struggling principalities of India would not experience anything close to unification until the eighth-century arrival of the Persian Moghuls. But their reach was always contested, with Hindu resistance a recurrent challenge, and much of the stratification of Pakistani society by informal notions of caste has proven more resilient in Pakistan than in Indonesia, despite the Islamic notion of equality before God and the otherwise strict adherence to Islamic doctrine that pervades so much of Pakistani society. It is worth keeping in mind that Inter-Services Intelligence (ISI) evolved from the British-designed Joint Intelligence Bureau, yet another case in support of Philip Murphy's observations about the British habit of exporting and field-testing experimental intelligence arrangements among Commonwealth governments before implementing them at home.[11] And yet, despite the attempt to establish a UK-model professional military, the notion of a comparably professional and apolitical joint intelligence component did not take, and the ISI became something very different. Indeed, to look at the ISI's action orientation, it is impossible not to see in its use of the Mujahideen in the 1980s, the Taliban in the 1990s, and the Kashmiri Islamic militants almost continuously since Partition a modern reflection of the "firebrand" (*tikshna*) and poisoner (*rasada*) so significant among Kautilya's "institutes of espionage." Although the administration of the ISI is that of a modern, albeit militarized, intelligence agency, the sense of communal identity that guides its priorities and binds the loyalties of its membership and their masters is steeped in self-perception as part of a global *ummah*. It is this latter ideational stratum that has so often effectively enslaved the deep and shallow legacies of the Sanskritic kingdoms and the British Empire, respectively, to the cause of Jihadism.

Beyond the West and Westphalia

One of the most striking features shared across the non-Western, or perhaps more accurately non-Westphalian, approaches to intelligence is the degree to which they are principally about the role of espionage. Also common to these traditions is the degree to which the role and status of espionage are relatively undifferentiated from both covert action on one side and diplomacy on the other. In the contemporary West there exists a keen and long-running debate about the suitability of intelligence agencies as information agencies or as vehicles of political and paramilitary special activities.[12] By contrast, to Sun Tze, Kautilya, the Byzantine emperors, and Arab potentates, espionage, sabotage, disruption, and assassination were all variations on a common enterprise. To a very real degree their traditions are discourses not of intelligence but of the nature and role of covert capability in statecraft. Indeed, there are moments when even the use of the word "spy" seems a mistranslation. What is really in question is the role, variety, direction, and significance of clandestine operators. Intelligence as information is almost a by-product of a concept of government and governance that assumes and frequently relies upon a supporting clandestine infrastructure. And, as noted above, we have evidence only of the Chinese thinkers dwelling on the deeper problems of knowledge and analytic judgment that lie beyond validating and collating those sources.

By the same token, if we were to ask a student of world politics what to him or her constituted the normal vector for the conduct of relations between states, we might get the answer "diplomacy"—what one scholar has called "the essential institution for the conduct of interstate relations."[13] This word on its own is often used as shorthand for foreign policy, when using the term "diplomat" is equal to "statesman," which can be evidenced by the discussions of such elder statesmen as Henry Kissinger, the late Richard Holbrooke, and Christopher Meyer.[14] In different times and places, the duties of the diplomat have included those actions that might today be called covert action. The Byzantine diplomat, for instance, was a general agent of the state. In his efforts to avoid costly and dangerous war, he employed bribery, trickery, covert subsidy, extraordinary rendition, and even assassination to achieve what his state needed.[15] Likewise, among the primary tasks of Kautilya's ambassadors was the establishment of espionage and potential sabotage networks within their host country and the monitoring and penetration of the host government's clandestine efforts against the ambassador's own government. On the Arabian Peninsula one sees less evidence of formally constituted diplomatic missions, but that goes hand in glove with a great reliance on covert surveillance and intervention. One also sees in these precedents a similarly weak differentiation between state representatives of a nation and private citizens of that nation resident in a foreign land. Leading members of the expatriate community, who were abroad for personal or commercial reasons, were often also tasked to represent their government to the local political leadership as well as economic and status elites.

Today, however, the Western and Westphalian definition of diplomacy tends to eschew any act that moves toward violence. One scholar has offered that the "juxtaposition of diplomacy and war as polar opposites appears as a peculiarly Western notion not necessarily found in other traditions."[16] It is within this globalized Western tradition that we may therefore use the definition of diplomacy offered by the Portuguese diplomat José Calvet de Magalhães, where diplomacy is "an instrument of foreign policy for the establishment and development of peaceful contacts between different states, through the use of intermediaries recognized by the respective parties."[17] Although it may not always be the case into the future, at the moment it would be hard to deviate from de Magalhães's definition. What one can draw from these discussions about diplomacy is that it is the baseline function of interstate relations—that it is about "getting our way," with peaceful means, inside mutual and consensual mechanisms.[18] At the international level, this is normal political interaction, frozen in place as the norm through the construction of the United Nations and the rest of the Westphalian framework of global politics. Most Western states thus may use diplomatic cover for intelligence operations; but they draw a fairly firm line between intelligence-gathering "spies" (intelligence officers) and diplomats. It is a construct particular to those states whose histories and political traditions encompass the Thirty Years' War and its settlement, and perhaps those that underwent the process of the Reformation and the Enlightenment. But the argument evident here is that the hard line between the diplomat and the intelligence officer may be predominantly a Western construct, and other political traditions—Russo-Byzantine, Subcontinental, Chinese, and Islamic— may not see such a divide as evident or necessary. And such an approach may not be purely an archaic approach but also formative of contemporary practice.

Reflections at an Angle

The literature of cultural study takes it as axiomatic that the understanding of consciousness, individual or collective, is a reflexive undertaking. Ordinarily, one would take this to mean that one reflects inwardly, being aware of being aware, as it were, the Kantian notion of a transcendental awareness. In so doing, one becomes self-aware of the process of understanding, ideally as much to serve in helping oneself to understand others—the conceptual (often reified) Others—as much as oneself. One points a cognitive mirror at oneself and then, obliquely, at oneself regarding the Other. But in this collection we have something of an opportunity to perceive something of ourselves in the image one would not ordinarily detect.

Less of an axiom than simply a common assumption is that there is some sort of nominally homogenous "Western" episteme and approach to government and governance, which has been shaped across the inheritors of the European tradition by a common experience of the Enlightenment and modernization. But two chapters in this collection suggest a more complex narrative, in which there are two very distinct Western traditions of governance and therefore of intelligence. It is also a common practice to speak of an "Anglo-American" tradition that binds the United States and the English-speaking parliamentary democracies that belong to the Commonwealth. The late, pioneering H. Bradford Westerfield was echoing more than just Winston Churchill's notion of historically united "English-speaking peoples" when he wrote in 1997 of an Anglo-American intelligence tradition.[19] And, indeed, there can be little doubt that there are profound, even fundamental differences between the political and therefore intelligence values, norms, and conduct within the "Anglosphere" liberal tradition and the Continental European notions of governance rooted in feudal and especially Bourbon Absolutism. It was not mere jingoistic idiosyncrasy that led the 1923 Secret Service Committee to shudder at the prospects of a "Continental system of domestic espionage" when it shut down the overzealous Basil Thompson's Directorate of Intelligence.[20] Micrometer political surveillance and "informing" on one's neighbors to "the authorities" continue to have a legitimacy in many nominally democratic European states— many of which have no history of stable democracy predating World War II— that they never have had in the "Anglosphere." Even France's successive republics have been relatively authoritarian in political and administrative culture.

Again, however, two chapters in this collection should serve at least as a reminder, actually as a wake-up call, to the fact that there is a Continental European body of states and a tradition of liberal values, norms, government, and governance that owes nothing to the post-1945 or post-1989 mentoring of the Anglophone democracies. Thus chapters 13 and 14 on Sweden and Finland, respectively, bring home the fact that Scandinavia has a constitutional tradition that, though it has often been allied with the Anglosphere, has not owed its existence (but perhaps its survival on occasion) to the Anglosphere. Indeed, there are interpretations of the history of Anglo-American liberal democracy vis-à-vis Anglo-Saxon, Jute, and Danish influences and legacies. And consultative if not representative bodies appear in Scandinavia quite early in the modern era—and, as if often overlooked, Swedish freedom of information legislation dates as far back as the late eighteenth century, long predating even the United States' statutory avant-garde of the 1970s. Indeed, the "principle of public access" predates the establishment of American democracy itself by a decade.[21] And, of course, from the stories of Britain and Sweden allying themselves in the Thirty Years' War to Norway's role in World War II and NATO, there is a narrative of nonhostility and frequent alliance between the Anglo-Saxon and Scandinavian worlds that is well established and almost as rooted in common values and interests as that within the Anglosphere. And so, perhaps those working from within the Anglo tradition need to reflect on and redefine our own identities, not as branches of an Anglo-Saxon or Anglo-American tradition but as an Anglo-Scandinavian tradition—a tradition broader, deeper, richer, and much older than that which we have previously taken for granted.

The Syncretic Spy

The convergence of cognitive requirements and challenges and diverse histories and contexts, and the ongoing hammering and forging of layers of cultural and institutional legacy, are mediated throughout by the human capacity for both improvisation and innovation. In improvisation one riffs and recombines on preexisting themes and forms while innovation builds anew, albeit always building on a foundation of the old. Innovation made routine folds back into history and becomes a part of the foundation and improvisation that create the new cycle of innovation. There is a degree of commonality between the notion developed here of laminated legacies and the role of legacy in path dependency theory discussed in chapter 12 of this volume. But where path dependency tends to emphasize how culture and legacy delimit thought and action, it is just as important to understand how they enable action as well, providing the raw materials of invention in a manner reminiscent of Claude Levi-Strauss's notion of "bricolage." The *bricoleur* interprets and deals with the world by drawing on, combining, chopping, and changing useful fragments of legacies; in Levi-Strauss's words, he or she "builds up structures by fitting together events or the remains of events" in contrast with science, which "simply by virtue of coming into being, creates its means and results in the form of events, thanks to the structures which it is constantly elaborating and which are its hypotheses and theories."[22] Significantly, Levi-Strauss omits the most significant and formative "events" in science, which are those experimental tests that allow its practitioners to choose between alternative competing theories and hypotheses. The cumulative consequences of experimentation and falsification, of course, completely undermine the kind of epistemological equivalence between scientific knowledge and manipulating "the remains of events" that Levi-Strauss would like to assert.[23] But the idea of "fitting together . . . the remains of events" is a compelling way of visualizing how almost any form of social construction takes place. After all, what are cultural artifacts like traditions and conventions but the remains of events? What Levi-Strauss articulates so well—what other thinkers in what the Germans call the *giesteswissenschaften*, the spiritual or cultural studies ("sciences" might be the literal translation, but it is a misleading term for what the activity entails), underestimate—is this: People innovate with tradition. They fabricate ideas, approaches, understandings, and methods that are both chronologically and substantively new from intellectual matter that is old and even ancient. In its way, the United Kingdom's Joint Intelligence Committee was as new and innovative in the practice of intelligence as the first reconnaissance satellite, but assembled from conventions and practices rooted in attitudes and conventions that dated back decades or more rather than shiny, freshly manufactured, technologically ground-breaking component parts.

In the last analysis, intelligence is about understanding. It feeds into understanding and supports understanding without subsuming all that understanding should entail. The mythopoetic understanding that underpins the idea of bricolage assumes and exploits a shared knowledge of the symbols, signs, and codes that are the "remains of events." Such artifacts are comprehensible in the linguistic sense, because they rest on communicative competence that can be acquired, and this comprehension can be articulated, translated, and conveyed with varying degrees of fidelity to others who might not share these fragments of legacy. So, in part, the intelligence practitioner seeks to comprehend actions and institutions that are themselves the consequence of bricolage. In another part, intelligence institutions and the states where they are located are themselves the products of bricolage, and likewise are comprehensible. In the last analysis what the contributors to this volume have sought to do is achieve, and convey, just such an understanding of how intelligence has been assembled and given shape and meaning through very different symbols, signs, codes, and other remnants from those so often taken for granted in the thought and pronouncements of the English-speaking world.

Notes

1. This is the essential message of his seminal book; see Talcott Parsons, *The Structure of Social Action* (New York: Basic Books, 1969; orig. pub. 1937).

2. Elton Mayo, *Hawthorne and the Western Electric Company: The Social Problems of an Industrial Civilisation* (London: Routledge, 1949).

3. Kautilya, *Arthashastra*, 21.

4. Ralph Sawyer, *The Tao of Spycraft: Intelligence, Theory and Practice in Traditional China* (Boulder, CO: Westview Press, 2004), 297.

5. Ibid., 298.

6. Ibid., 308.

7. Yamamoto Tsunetomo, *Hagakure: The Book of the Samurai*, translated by William Scott Wilson (London: Kodansha Europe, 2000).

8. Miyamoto Musashi, *The Book of Five Rings*, translated by William Scott Wilson (London: Kodansha Europe, 2002).

9. Muhammad Haji Salleh, "Translating *Hikayat Hang Tuah*," in *The Epic of Hang Tuah*, translated by Muhammad Haji Salleh and edited by Rosemary Robson (Kuala Lumpur: Institut Terjemahan Negara Malaysia, 2011), xlii–xliii.

10. John J. Dziak, *Chekisty: A History of the KGB* (Lexington, MA: Lexington Books, 1985), 1–5 passim.

11. For a general discussion of the idea of what might be called prototyping in the empire, see Philip Murphy, "Creating a Commonwealth Intelligence Culture: The View from Central Africa 1945–1960," *Intelligence and National Security* 17, no. 3 (Summer 2002).

12. See, inter alia, Charles Beitz, "Covert Action as a Moral Problem," *Ethics and International Affairs* 3, no. 1 (1989): 45–60; William E. Colby, "Public Policy, Secret Action," *Ethics and International Affairs* 3, no. 1 (1989): 61–71; Loch K. Johnson, "On Drawing a Bright Line for Covert Operations," *American Journal of International Law* 86 (April 1992): 284–309; and David P. Forsythe, "Democracy, War, and Covert Action," *Journal of Peace Research* 29, no. 4 (November 1992): 385–95.

13. Christer Jönsson, "Diplomacy, Bargaining and Negotiation," in *Handbook of International Relations*, edited by Beth A. Simmons, Walter Carlsnaes, and Thomas Risse (London: Sage, 2002), 212.

14. Keith Hamilton and Richard Langhorne, *The Practice of Diplomacy: Its Evolution, Theory, and Administration* (New York: Routledge, 1995), 1.

15. Ibid., 14–20.

16. Raymond Cohen, "Reflections on the New Global Diplomacy: Statecraft 2500 BC to 2000 AD," in *Innovation in Diplomatic Practice*, edited by Jan Melissen (New York: Palgrave, 1999), 4.

17. José Calvet de Magalhães, *The Pure Concept of Diplomacy* (Westport, CT: Greenwood Press, 1988), 59.

18. Christopher Meyer, *Getting Our Way: The Inside Story of British Diplomacy* (London: Weidenfeld & Nicolson, 2009).

19. H. Bradford Westerfield, "American Exceptionalism and American Intelligence," *Freedom Review* 28, no. 2 (Summer 1997).

20. See, e.g., Christopher Andrew, *Secret Service: The Making of the British Intelligence Community* (London: Sceptre, 1986), 405.

21. For a comparative analysis of Swedish open government practice with those of the United Kingdom and the United States, see K. G. Robertson, *Public Secrets* (London: Macmillan, 1984).

22. Claude Levi-Strauss, *The Savage Mind* (Chicago: University of Chicago Press), 22.

23. Ibid., 15.

CONTRIBUTORS

Wilhelm Agrell has a twin academic background in history, in which he defended his PhD thesis in 1985 and of which he became an associate professor in 1987, as well as in peace and conflict research, of which he became an associate professor in 2003. Since 2006 he has been professor of intelligence analysis at Lund University, the first in the subject in Sweden. He has written extensively on military research and development, security policy, regional conflicts, and the role and transformation of intelligence. He is a member of the Royal Swedish Academy of War Sciences and of the external advisory board to the Swedish Security Service.

Emmanuel Kwesi Aning has taught in several universities around the world, including in Denmark, South Africa, the United Kingdom, the United States, Nigeria, Austria, and Ghana. He presently serves as dean and director of the Faculty of Research and Academic Affairs at the Kofi Annan International Peacekeeping Training Centre in Accra. Until 2007 he served as the African Union's first expert on counterterrorism, peace, and security. He has extensive publications to his credit and serves on several editorial boards. He was recently appointed to the World Economic Forum's Council on Conflict Prevention. He received his PhD from the University of Copenhagen.

Abdulaziz A. Al-Asmari is a Saudi Arabian diplomat. While posted to the United Kingdom, he joined the Brunel University Centre for Intelligence and Security Studies, where he worked on "Paramilitary Groups as Intelligence Actors." After he completed his master's in philosophy, he researched the history and development of the Islamic theory of intelligence at Brunel University's Department of Politics and History, where he received his PhD. He received his undergraduate degree from the State University of New York.

Emma Birikorang is a research fellow and program head for the Regional Partnerships for the Peace and Security Programme at the Kofi Annan International

Peacekeeping Training Centre. She is currently undertaking research on African Peace and Security Mechanisms and the Economic Community of West African States–African Union regional peacekeeping frameworks. She also facilitates training modules on security-sector reform and conflict prevention. She received a BA in languages (English and French) from the Kwame Nkrumah University of Science and Technology and an MA in international politics and security studies from the University of Bradford. She is currently a doctoral candidate at the School of Oriental and African Studies of the University of London.

Philip H. J. Davies is the director of the Brunel University Centre for Intelligence and Security Studies and originator of Brunel's highly innovative MA program in intelligence and security studies. He recently completed a substantial comparative study of national intelligence in the United Kingdom and the United States, *Intelligence and Government in Britain and the United States: A Comparative Approach* (Praeger Security International, 2012), and he has published extensively on the management and organization of intelligence institutions and on the concept of national intelligence cultures. He was a contributor to the current UK Joint Intelligence Doctrine.

Eduardo E. Estévez is president of Fundación de Estudios Económicos y Políticas Públicas in Argentina. With a background in defense and civil–military relations, he has specialized in two fields, security—including police reforms and citizen security—and intelligence. His most recent government assignment was as general director of crime prevention policy at the Ministry of Security of the Province of Buenos Aires. He has served as coordinator-director and adviser at Argentina's National Directorate for Crime Prevention Coordination and Analysis of the Interior Security Secretariat. He has written widely on intelligence democratization and public security.

Peter Gill is an honorary senior research fellow at the University of Liverpool. Previously, he was a research professor in intelligence studies at the University of Salford. He is the author of *Policing Politics* (Frank Cass, 1994) and *Rounding Up the Usual Suspects?* (Ashgate, 2000) and coauthor of *Intelligence in an Insecure World* (2nd ed., Polity, 2006). He is coeditor of the two-volume *PSI Handbook of Global Security and Intelligence: National Approaches* (Praeger, 2008) and *Intelligence Theory: Key Questions and Debates* (Routledge, 2009). His current research, which is supported by a Leverhulme Emeritus Fellowship that he was awarded in 2010, is on the democratization of intelligence in former authoritarian regimes, and includes his contribution to the present volume.

Kristian C. Gustafson is deputy director of the Brunel University Centre for Intelligence and Security Studies and director of its very successful MA program in intelligence and security studies. He was formerly an officer of both the Canadian and British armies, and he has been part of operations in the Balkans and Afghanistan. He completed his PhD at the University of Cambridge and taught at the Royal Military Academy Sandhurst before moving to Brunel. He has written on covert action (especially on the case of US intervention in Chile, in his book *Hostile Intent*) and on horizon scanning. He contributed to the new UK Joint Intelligence Doctrine.

Lauri Holmström is a PhD candidate at the University of Helsinki. He received his master's degree in political history from the University of Helsinki and completed the intelligence and security studies MA at Brunel University. He previously researched Finland's role in American intelligence during World War II as well as issues of economic espionage and corporate security in the modern world. He has held a range of posts in the Finnish government.

Robert Johnson is the deputy director of the Oxford Changing Character of War Programme and a lecturer on the history of war at the University of Oxford. His primary research interests are conflicts in the Middle East, Afghanistan, and Pakistan, including the interactions between intelligence and conventional operations, war by proxy, insurgency and counterinsurgency, and strategy. He has published a number of books and articles, and he is the author of *The Iran-Iraq War* (Palgrave, 2010) and *The Afghan Way of War: How and Why They Fight* (Hurst and Oxford University Press, 2011).

Ken Kotani is a senior fellow of the National Institute for Defense Studies at the Ministry of Defense in Tokyo. He received his MA in war studies from King's College London and his PhD in international history from Kyoto University. He was a visiting fellow of the Royal United Services Institute in London in 2008–9 and is now a visiting lecturer of the National Defense Academy of Japan. His major field of study is the intelligence history of Japan and the United Kingdom. He is an author of *Japanese Intelligence in World War II* (Osprey, 2009) and is the coauthor of *the Pacific War Companion* (Osprey, 2005).

Ernest Ansah Lartey is the head of the Conflict and Security Programme in the Research Department of the Kofi Annan International Peacekeeping Training Centre. His research interests include security-sector reform, postconflict peace building, and elections security. He has published a number of papers covering these specific interests. He also provides teaching support to training programs at the Kofi Annan Centre.

Ralph D. Sawyer is an independent scholar who studied at the Massachusetts Institute of Technology and Harvard University, and who specializes in Chinese military and intelligence issues, with a particular focus on the revitalization of traditional concepts in current military doctrine. His analytical works include *Ancient Chinese Warfare* (Basic Books, 2011), *The Tao of Spycraft* (Basic Books, 2004), and *The Tao of Deception* (Basic Books, 2007). His translations, all of which feature extensive historical introductions, range from the *Seven Military Classics of Ancient China* (Westview Press, 1993) to Sun-tzu's *Art of War* (Westview Press, 1994), Sun Pin's *Military Methods* (Westview Press, 1995), and the *Hundred Unorthodox Strategies* (Westview Press, 1996). Along with serving as a consultant to conglomerates and defense agencies, he is a fellow of the Centre for Military and Strategic Studies and senior research fellow with the Warring States Project.

Carl Anthony Wege is a tenured professor at the College of Coastal Georgia. He has published numerous articles on Hezbollah and associated topics. He has traveled to China, Argentina, South Africa, Zimbabwe, and Israel in various academic capacities and has taught courses on terrorism for many years.

Stephen Welch is lecturer in politics in the School of Government and International Affairs at the University of Durham. He is the author of *The Concept of Political Culture* (St. Martin's Press, 1993) and of several articles on political culture, and his forthcoming book is *The Theory of Political Culture* (Oxford University Press).

Lee Wilson is a research associate in the School of Political Science and International Studies at the University of Queensland. He is the author of a forthcoming monograph on Indonesian martial arts, *Pencak Silat: The Constitution of a National Martial Art in Indonesia* (KITLV Press). He coedited the recent volume *Southeast Asian Perspectives on Power* (Routledge, 2012). His current research focuses on citizen militia groups in newly democratizing Indonesia.

INDEX

Abbas, Mahmoud, 155n1
Al-Abbas, Abu Al-Fadhl, 100
Abbi Waqas, Saad bin, 111n57
Abe, Shinzo, 192
Abi Talib, Ali bin, 99, 101, 111n55
Abi Waqqas, Saad bin, 101
Abu Bakr, Abdullah, 99–100
Abu Bakr, Asma bint, 99–100
Abu Sufyan, 100–103, 106–7, 111n59
Afak, Abu, 105
Afghanistan
  Iran and, 148
  the ISI and conflict in, 121–27
  US–Pakistani relations and, 115–17
agents provocateurs, 54
Aguilar, Paloma, 233n16
Ahmadinejad, Mamoud, 147
Ahmed, Mahmood, 130
Ahmed, Mahmud, 139n57
Alexius I (emperor of Byzantine Empire), 73–74
Alfonsín, Raul, 223–24
Alhaja, Ali, 154n33
Al Jarmi, 75
Almond, Gabriel, 14–15, 141, 273
Almondian paradigm, 14–18
Almqvist, Carl Jonas Love, 239, 258
Anderson, John, 83
Andrew, Christopher, 3

al-Ansi, Al-Aswad, 105–6
Anzorreguy, Hugo, 224
Arab and Islamic intelligence culture
  Arabic intelligence terminology, 90–94
  espionage, early Arab records of, 94–97
  impact of Muslim intelligence activities, 108–9
  pre-Islamic origins of, 89–90
  the Prophet Muhammad and, 99–108
  religious texts and, 97–98
Argentina
  authoritarianism to democracy, intelligence and, 219–20, 232
  democratization, main events in, 223–27
  the Dirty War in, 222
  legal framework of intelligence sector, 228–29
  origins, legacies, and challenges of the intelligence sector, 221–23
  outcomes of intelligence democratization, 229–31
Arisue, Seizo, 195
Armitage, Richard, 130, 194
arms-smuggling networks, Iranian, 145
Arthashastra (Kautilya), 50–52, 55–56, 62–63. *See also* Kautilya
Art of War (Sunzi), 30–35, 38–39
al-Asbahani, Abu Faraj, 95–96

Asgari, Ali, 150
Ashiq, Haroon, 119
Ashoka the Great (emperor of Maurya
    Empire), 51–52
assassination, 38–39, 62, 104–6, 143
Åström, Sverker, 262n33
Atmar, Hanif, 117
Aum Shinrikyo, 185
Al-Awsi, Omeir bin Wahab, 105
Al-Awwam, Al-Zubair bin, 101, 111n56

Bagbin, Alban, 217n29
Baluchistan, 148
al-Bashir, Omar Hassan, 144
Basil II (emperor of Byzantine Empire),
    73–74
Beeston, A. F., 95
Belenko, Victor Ivanovich, 186
Béliz, Gustavo, 227
Berlin, Isaiah, 26n23
Betts, Richard, 192
Beurling, Arne, 241
Bhakari, S. K., 64n14
Bhutto, Benazir, 117, 122, 134, 138n44
Bhutto, Zulifiqar Ali, 123–24
bin Laden, Osama, 116–17, 119, 130, 132
blowback, 145–46
Boateng, Asamoah, 213
Boheman, Eric, 260n8
Booth, Ken, 26n23
Bo Pi, 42–43
Boraz, Steven, 158
Bréhier, Louis, 75
bribery, 44–45
bricolage, 295
Bruneau, Thomas C., 158–59
Bulgaria, 84
Burke, Jason, 137n24
Bury, J. M., 74
Bush, George W., 129

Byzantine Empire
    culture of intelligence and security in,
        71–79
    diplomat, role of, 292
    Manathira/Lakhmid states, relations
        with emerging, 94
    postal system of, 72–73
    Russian intelligence culture, impact on,
        67–69, 79–84
    Russian political culture and, 69–71

Cadogan, Sir Alexander, 3
caeseropapism, 69, 73
Cañón, Carlos, 224
Carlgren, Wilhelm, 260n6
Cavallo, Domingo, 227
Central Intelligence Agency (CIA)
    Afghan Mujahideen, support for, 125
    Indonesia, actions regarding, 160–62
    Iran's SAVAK and, 142
    Khan, protection of, 129
    Sukarno, efforts to overthrow, 175n13
Chabal, Patrick, 18–20
Chandragupta (emperor of Maurya
    Empire), 51
Chen Ping, 47n46
China
    assassination and subversive programs,
        38–43
    bribery, use of, 44–45
    ecological warfare, 43–44
    intelligence activity, tradition of,
        29–30
    knowing your opponent, necessity of,
        30–33
    rule of threes in, 288
    the Spring and Autumn Period, 30–33
    spycraft, treatises on, 34–38
China, People's Republic of, 29–30
Church Committee report, 11n5

Churchill, Winston, 293
civil-military relations (CMR) model, 158–59, 174n3
clandestine activities. *See* espionage
Comnena, Anna, 74, 81
comparative analysis
  intelligence as a subject of, 7–8
  isolation, protection against examining cases in, 4–5
  strengths of, 5–6
Constantine V (emperor of the Byzantine Empire), 81
Constantine VII (emperor of the Byzantine Empire), 77, 87n64
counterintelligence state, 71, 73, 79–80
Cui Hao, 35
culture
  Anglo-American and Scandinavian, relationship of, 293–94
  concept of, 13
  duality of, 23
  explanatory role of, 287–88
  intelligence (*see* intelligence culture)
  as laminated legacy, 289–91
  organizational, 21–22, 274–75
  political (*see* political culture)

Daloz, Jean-Pascal, 18–20
Davies, Philip, 189, 273, 275
Day, Tony, 161
de Magalhães, José Calvet de, 292
democratic intelligence, 158
democratization, path dependency theory and, 220–21, 231–32
De Santibānes, Fernando, 226
Al-Dhamiri, Amru bin Ummaya, 106
Dianatr, Akbar, 156n64
Dikshitar, V. R. Ramachandra, 64n14
Dilks, David, 3
diplomacy, 60–62, 291–93

Duaji, Susno, 173, 179n94
Duncan, Ron, 165
Du You, 35–36
Duyvesteyn, Isabelle, 284n53
Dziak, John, 8, 70–73, 79–80, 290

ecological warfare, 43–44
economic espionage, 269–72, 281n14
Egypt, Islamist influence in, 146
Eisenhower, Dwight, 175n13
Elkner, Julie, 82
Elmér, Birger, 250–53, 259
embezzlement, 58
Erlander, Tage, 244, 251–52
espionage
  Byzantine sources on, 78–79
  Chinese sources on, 34–43
  clandestine activities, impact on Islam of, 98–101
  in diplomacy and war, 60–62
  early Arab records of, 94–97
  economic, 269–72, 281n14
  Kautilya on special operations, 54–55
  Kautilya's "institutes [or categories] of," 50, 52–55, 290–91
  non-Western government and, 291
  in routine government, Kautilya on, 55–60
  See also spies
ethnocentrism, 4

Fardust, Hussein, 142
Finland
  economic espionage, 269–72, 277–78
  foreign intelligence activities of (*see* Finnish Security Intelligence Service [Supo])
  intelligence activities, organizational structure for, 265
  Russia and, 272
  security/strategic culture of, 272–73

Finnish Security Intelligence Service
(Supo)
adaptation to new political and operational realities, 274
economic espionage, 271–72
history and recent organizational developments, 266–69
intelligence culture of, 277–80
intelligence role and culture of, 265–66
public opinion regarding, 277
security intelligence and the intelligence culture of, 272–77
Franco, Francisco, 157
Fraser, Peter, 62
fraud and theft by the ruler, 59–60
Funes, Patricia, 222
Furaihah, Amir bin, 99

Gabriel, Richard, 90, 99, 111n66
Geertz, Clifford, 17–20, 25n19
Geertzian paradigm, 17–20
Gehlen, Reinhardt, 182, 249, 261n17
Germany, 143, 153n25
Ghana
democratic development and intelligence culture, 199–201, 208–9, 215
evolution of intelligence culture, 201–6
judicial oversight, 212–14
the media and the intelligence services, 214–15
parliamentary oversight, 210–11
political history and regime types, 204–5
predemocratic era policies, 206–8
Gilani, Daood, 137n24
Gilani, Yusuf Raza, 115
Giustozzi, Antonio, 139n66
Glubb, John, 94
Godson, Roy, 81, 108, 112n82
government
espionage and, Kautilya on, 50, 55–60

regime and state security, 56–57
revenue, commerce, and law enforcement, 57–60
Greece, 84
Griffith, Samuel B., 63n1
Guan Zhong, 31–32, 46n11
Gul, Hamid, 126, 130, 134, 137n31
Gustafson, Bengt, 262n38

Habibie, Jusuf, 168
Hadith, 97–98
Hajar, Aws bin, 92, 96
Haldon, John, 72
Hamzah, Chandra M., 179n94
al-Hanafi, Thumamah bin Athal, 100–101
Handel, Michael, 45n5
Han Feizi, 33
Han Xin, 35
Haq, Ehsanul, 130
Haqqani, Jalaluddin, 130–31
Haqqani, Sirajuddin, 121–22, 131
Haqqani network, the, 115–17, 131–33
Heikka, Henrikki, 272
Hekmatyar, Gulbuddin, 126
Hendropriyono, A. M., 168
Herder, Johann Gottfried von, 18
Hite, Katherine, 233n16
Hitti, Philip K., 95
Hofstede, Geert, 21
Holbrooke, Richard, 292
Hussein, Javed, 120

India
Asian balance of power, role in, 50
Kautilya and espionage in, 49–51, 62–63 (see also Kautilya)
Mumbai attacks, 119, 122, 128
Pakistan and, 116, 118–19, 121–22

Pakistan and the insurgency in
Kashmir, 127–28
Indonesia
civil society, intelligence reform and,
167
context for security-sector reform
(SSR), 162–63
decentralization in, 166
democratic control of intelligence,
establishing, 169–71
economic society, intelligence reform
and, 164–65
financial independence of the military
from the government, 178n82
independence to New Order in, 159–62
intelligence democratization in, 157–58
laminated forging in, 290
oversight of intelligence, establishing,
172
political society, intelligence reform
and, 165–67
postauthoritarian intelligence reform,
limitations of models for describing,
172–74
the rule of law, intelligence reform and,
163–64
security and intelligence apparatus
since 1999, 167–69
Inglehart, Ronald, 15
intelligence
commensurability and, 7–8, 289
core functions of, 7–8
definition of, 158
democratic reform of, models of,
158–59, 174n3
diplomacy and, 291–93
Kautilya's *Arthashastra*, legacy of,
49–50
scholarly approaches to study of, 3–4
uncertainty and, 288–89
as understanding, 295–96

intelligence culture
Arab and Islamic (*see* Arab and Islamic
intelligence culture)
bottom-up approach to, 21–23
of the Byzantine Empire, 71–79
friction between practices and
accounting for practices, focus on, 24
of the ISI, 120–23 (*see also* Inter-
Services Intelligence)
political culture and, 13–14, 16, 24, 274
(*see also* political culture)
Russian (*see* Russia)
intelligence democratization, 157–59
International Security Assistance Force
(ISAF), 132
Inter-Services Intelligence (ISI)
the Afghan conflicts and, 123–27
assessments of, 134–35
culture of, 118–19, 291
insurgency and the ends of, 131–33
Islamists in post–9/11, 129–31
Islamization of, 123–26
Kashmir operations, 127–28
nuclear proliferation and, 128–29, 148
organization, strategy, and culture of,
120–23
reputation of, 117
the US and the Haqqani, relations
with, 115–17
Western concerns regarding, 117–18
Iran
Afghanistan and, 148
center/periphery divide in, 147
Germany, Israel, and, 153n25
Germany and, 143
intelligence culture, limitations
imposed by, 151
Iraq and, 142, 148–49
Islamist revolutionary state, the 1979
Revolution leading to, 141

Iran (*continued*)
  nuclear capabilities of, Pakistan and,
    128, 148
  Pakistan and, 148
  Russia and, 142
  security architecture of, 141–46
  security establishment, assessing,
    149–52
  "shatterbelt" of access points for
    enemies of, 146–49
  Sudan and, 144–45
Iraq, 142, 148–49
ISI. *See* Inter-Services Intelligence
Islam, Arab intelligence culture and. *See*
    Arab and Islamic intelligence culture
Israel
  Germany, Iran, and, 153n25
  Iran and, 145–46
  Mossad intelligence agency (*see*
    Mossad)

Al-Jahiz, 89
Jamal, Syed, 126
Al-Jamhi, Omeir bin Wahab, 107
Jamiat-e-Ulema Islam, 132
Japan
  Cabinet Intelligence and Research
    Office, 183
  Defense Intelligence Headquarters of
    the Ministry of Defense, 184
  discourse of strategic thought in,
    289–90
  history of intelligence from World War
    II to the Cold War, 182–83
  intelligence culture, limitations
    imposed by, 151, 182, 195–97
  intelligence development in, 181–82
  intelligence organizations of, 183–86
  intelligence reform in, 186–97
  Ministry of Foreign Affairs, 183–84
  National Police Agency, 185–86
  Public Security Intelligence Agency,
    184
Jarring, Gunnar, 241
Jenkins, Romilly, 77
Jia Chong, 35
Jie Xuan, 37–38, 46n22, 47n30
Jihadists, the ISI and, 115–22
Jing Ke, 39
Jones, Seth, 139n66
Juan Zhu, 38
Justinian (emperor of the Byzantine
    Empire), 81

Kamal, Majid, 154n33
Karikari, Kwame, 217n39–40
Karzai, Hamid, 116
Kashmir, 118–19, 127–28
Kautilya
  context for work of, 51–52
  espionage in diplomacy and war,
    60–62, 292
  espionage in routine government,
    55–60
  information, rule of three sources
    applied to, 288
  "institutes [or categories] of espionage,"
    50, 52–55, 290–91
  intelligence theory and practice, impact
    on, 49–51, 62–63
  Sunzi, contrast with, 50, 55, 60–61
Kayani, Ashfaq Parvez, 116
Kekaumenos, 74
Kekomäki, Eero, 268
Kennan, George, 82
Khabeeb bin Uday, 106
Khadeejah, 99
Khaled Sheikh Mohammed, 132
Khamenei, Ayatollah Ali, 142, 147
Khan, Abdul Qadeer, 128–29

Khan, Aziz, 130
Khar, Hina Rabbani, 120
Khatami, Mohammed, 144
Al-Khattab, Umar bin, 98, 107
Al-Khazraji, Abu Amie, 107
Khomeini, Ayatollah Ruhollah, 141, 147, 151
Khwaja, Khalid, 131
Kirchner, Cristina Fernández de, 227
Kirchner, Nestor, 226–27, 231
Kissinger, Henry, 292
Knight, Amy, 68, 80
Koizumi, Junichiro, 186
Konoe, Fumimaro, 192
Kuhn, Thomas, 15
Kullberg, Anssi, 279
Kurdistan, 149
Kwadjo, Johnny, 203, 206

Lamperts, Lars Olof, 253
Lashkar-e Toiba, 137n24
law enforcement, 57–59
Lecapenus, Romanus, 87n64
Leeser, Anita, 129
legacy, 289–91
Lemos-Nelson, Ana, 222
Leontiev, Konstantin, 70
Leo the Deacon, 79
Levchenko, Stanislaw, 193
Levi-Strauss, Claude, 294–95
Li Jing, 32
Limann, Hilla, 207
Li Mu, 44
Lindsey, Tim, 161
Linz, Juan, 163
Li Quan, 32, 37, 41–42
Li Si, 35, 45
Litvinenko, Alexander, 81
Liudprand (Bishop of Cremono), 75
Lotman, I. M., 70

Lucas, Edward, 68
Luttwak, Edward, 77, 79

Ma'bad Al-Khuzai, 103–4
Macmillan, Alan, 26n23
Maddrell, Paul, 188
Makaarim, Mufti A., 167
Maldonaldo, Carlos, 232n2
Malik, Rehman, 115
Manshawi, Ali, 154n33
Maqdah, Muir, 154–55n41
Markov, Georgi, 81
Marshall, Alan, 62
Martínez, Carlos Alberto, 224
Marwan, Asma' bint, 104–5
Matei, Florina Cristiana, 159
Maugham, W. Somerset, 84, 287
Maurice, 77
Mayo, Elton, 288
Mbai, Ansyaad, 169
McLeod, Ross, 165
Mehsud, Beitullah, 121, 134
Menem, Carlos, 224, 227
Mensah, Herbert, 213–14
methodology
    comparative (*see* comparative analysis)
    political culture and, 15 (*see also* political culture)
    surveys, 23
    variables, nature of social science, 6
Meyer, Christopher, 292
Mill, John Stuart, 5
Mills, John, 217n35
Misbahi, Abu al-Kassam, 143
Mohlrabi, Gholam, 156n64
Morsi, Mohammed, 146
Mossad
    Iran's SAVAK and, 142
    Kurdistan, presence in, 149
Mousavi, Mir-Hossein, 147

Mufateh, Hojatolislam Mohammed, 142
Mugniyah, Imad, 145, 154n32
Muhammad, the Prophet, 90, 97–108,
    109n4
Mullen, Mike, 115, 120
Mumbai attacks, 119, 122, 128
Al-Munthir, Al-Naman bin, 95
Murai, Jun, 182–83
Murphy, Philip, 291
Musashi, Miyamoto, 290
Musharraf, Pervez, 121, 128–31, 133–34
Muslim Brothers, 146

Nakasone, Yasuhiro, 193
Nasir, Javed, 127
Nawaz, Shuja, 125, 129
Nevala, Seppo, 268
Newton, Isaac, 18
Nikephoros Phokas, 78
Nilsson, Torsten, 250
Nkrumah, Kwame, 201–3, 207
nuclear proliferation, 128–29, 148

Obolensky, Dimitri, 67–70
Ogata, Taketora, 182
Omori, Yoshio, 189
organizational culture, 21–22, 274–75
Oros, Andrew, 183
Ostrogorsky, George, 69
oversight, 169

Pakistan
    India and, 116, 118–19, 121–22
    intelligence activities in (see Inter-
        Services Intelligence)
    Iran and, 148
    Kashmir, insurgency in, 127–28
    Kautilya's legacy and the sponsorship of
        jihadists, 63
    laminated forging in, 290–91

    the United States, the ISI and relations
        with, 115–17, 120–21, 129–31
Palm, Thede, 241, 243–46, 249, 251–52
Palme, Olof, 244–45, 250–51
Parsons, Talcott, 6, 25n19, 287
Pasha, Ahmed Shuja, 116
path dependence theory, 220–21, 231–32,
    294
Pelttari, Antti, 280–81n9
Pena, Robert, 223
Peoples Mujahidin Organization, 153n18
Perón, Juan Domingo, 222
Persson, Carl, 252, 257
Petersén, Carl, 241, 243
political culture
    the Almondian positivist paradigm,
        14–18, 273
    dialectic of, moving beyond the, 21–23
    dialectic of approaches to, 20–21
    the Geertzian interpretive paradigm,
        17–20
    intelligence culture and, 13–14, 16, 24,
        273–74
    Russian, Byzantine influence on, 69–71,
        79–80 (see also Russia)
Popplewell, Richard, 52, 63
Porch, Douglas, 63
Porteous, Samuel, 281n14
postal system, intelligence functions and,
    72–73
Procopius, 72, 76
Psellus, Michael, 73
Purwopranjono, Muchdi, 164
Putin, Vladimir, 68, 70, 82–83
Pye, Lucian W., 17, 20

al-Qaeda, 116–17, 119
Quantson, Kofi, 202–3
Quran, the, 97–98

Rafsanjani, Akbar Hashemi, 144
Rahman, Akhtar Abdur, 124–25
Rashid, Ahmed, 135
Rashid, Sheikh, 138n44
rational choice theory, 16
Rawlings, Jerry, 208
Rayshahr, Mohammed, 143
religion
    espionage in India and, 53–54
    resurgence in Russia, 82–83
Rentola, Kimmo, 267
revenue, espionage and the collection of, 58–60
Rezaii, Mohsen, 142
Rianto, Bibit Samad, 179n94
Rigi, Abdol Malek, 155n52
Roman Empire, 71
Romania, 84
Roosevelt, Archie, 152
Rúa, Fernando de la, 226
Russia
    Byzantine influences on the intelligence culture of, 67–69, 79–84
    Finland and, 272
    Iran and, 142
    political culture, Byzantine mark on, 69–71
    resurgence of religion in, 82–83
Ryter, Loren, 179n93

Sábato, Ernesto, 223
sabotage, 62
Saddam Hussein, 142, 148
Safavi, Rahim, 154n33
Safi-Id-a-Din, Abdallah, 145–46
Salmi, Ilkka, 268, 280–81n9
Sawyer, Ralph, 288
Scandinavia, constitutional tradition of, 294
Schein, Edgar, 274–75, 277

secrecy, 11n5
security-sector reform (SSR) model, 158–59, 174n3
Serbia, 84
Shah, Ijaz, 134
Shah, K. J., 63
Shahzad, Syed Saleem, 119
Shakai Agreement, 116, 121
Shamasastry, Rudrapatnam, 50–52, 58, 62, 64n6, 64n14, 65n33
Sharif, Nawaz, 138n44
Shi Zimei, 29, 32, 36–37, 46n14
Shul'ts, Vladimir, 82
Shultz, Richard, 81
Sima Shang, 44
Sima Tan, 35
Simola, Matti, 267–68
Six Secret Teachings (Liutao), 39–41
Sköld, Per Edvin, 242
Sorege, Richard, 193
Sorokin, Piotr, 25n19
sovereign statehood, 176n25
Soviet Union. See Union of Soviet Socialist Republics
special operations. See espionage
spies
    categories of, Kautilya on, 50, 52–55
        (see also Kautilya)
    terminology in Arabic for, 91–94
    types of, Sunzi on, 34–35 (see also Sunzi)
    See also espionage
spycraft. See espionage
Stalin, Joseph, 80–82
Stepan, Alfred, 163
Suárez, Facundo, 223
Subianto, Prabowo, 163
Subrandio, 160–61
Sudan, Iran and, 144–45
Suharto, 160–65, 167–68

Sukarno, 160–61, 175n13, 290
Sukarnoputri, Megawati, 168
Sun Bin, 33
Sunnah, 97–98
Sun Tze. *See* Sunzi
Sunzi
    Art of War, 30–36, 38, 45, 45n3, 45n5
    Japanese, impact on, 289
    Kautilya, contrast with, 50, 55, 60–61
Supo. *See* Finnish Security Intelligence
    Service
Su Qin, 44
Sweden, 239
    domestic intelligence in the shadows,
        249–53
    foreign intelligence in the post-Cold
        War era, 253–58
    intelligence via informal muddling
        through, 258–59
    neutral intelligence liaisons, 246–49
    "organizing" of intelligence in, 240–42
    police *vs.* armed forces, terrorism and
        the dividing line between, 255–56
    the three pillars of intelligence in,
        243–45

Tabari, Muhammed ibn, 96–97
Taeb, Hossein, 147
Taha, Ali Othman, 154n33
Tai Gong, 35, 39
Taimiya, Ibn, 111n67
Taliban, the, 116–17, 121–22, 126,
    129–35, 138n39
Tankel, Stephen, 137n24
"Techniques for Secret Plots" (Li Quan),
    41–42
Thalib, Munir Said, 164
Theophanes, 75–76, 81
Thompson, Basil, 293
Thulin, 251–52

Toynbee, Arnold J., 70
Trocki, Carl A., 173
Trotsky, Leon, 81
Tsafrir, Eliezer, 155n57
Tucker, Robert, 17, 273
Tunander, Ola, 262n38
al-Turabi, Hassan, 144, 153–54n32
Turner, Michael, 5

uncertainty, 288–89
Undén, Östen, 254
Union of Soviet Socialist Republics
    (USSR), 70, 76, 267. *See also* Russia
United Kingdom
    Foreign Office and Secret Intelligence
        Service, separation of, 80
    Ghana, colonial administration in, 202
    Indonesia, confrontation with, 161
    Joint Intelligence Committee as inno-
        vation through tradition, 295
    secrecy and intelligence, 11n5
United States
    Central Intelligence Agency (*see*
        Central Intelligence Agency)
    distinctive intelligence culture of,
        Turner's model of, 5
    nuclear proliferation, actions regarding,
        129
    Pakistan and the ISI, relations with,
        115–17, 120–21, 129–31
    secrecy and intelligence, 11n5
    terrorist watch list, Pakistan and, 127
Ushakov, A. I., 80
Uspensky, B. A., 70

Vaca, Eduardo, 225
Verba, Sidney, 14–15, 17
Vinge, P. G., 252

Wahid, Abdurrahman, 168
Wahidi, Ahmad, 156n64

Waldman, Matt, 133
Walsingham, Sir Francis, 74
Wang Jian, 44–45
war
  the Byzantines and, 71–72
  espionage and, 60–62
Al-Ward, Urwa bin, 92
Wei Liaozi, 45
Welch, Stephen, 273–74, 276
Wennerström, Stig, 240
Wen Zhong, 43
Westerfield, H. Bradford, 293
Wikström, Niklas, 260–61n13
Wiktorin, Owe, 255
Williams, Raymond, 16
Wittgenstein, Ludwig, 22
Wood, Michael, 258
Wu Zixu, 43

Xi Shi, 43
Xun Huo, 35

Yahnus, Wabrah bin, 106
Yao Li, 39
Yi Yin, 35
Yofre, Juan Bautista "Tata," 224
Yoshida, Shigeru, 182
Yousaf, Mohammad, 125, 137n33
Yudhoyono, Susilo Bambang, 169
Yue Yi, 47n46
Yu Rang, 38–39

Al-Zabeedi, Muhammad Murtadha, 91
Zhang Zhao, 35–36
Zheng Dan, 43
Zia ul Haq, 121, 124–25, 127, 137n26